REBECCA J. SCOTT

Slave Emancipation in Cuba

The Transition to Free Labor, 1860-1899

University of Pittsburgh Press

FOR C.G.

Published by the University of Pittsburgh Press, Pittsburgh, Pa. 15261
Copyright © 1985 by Princeton University Press
Afterword copyright © 2000 by the University of Pittsburgh Press
Manufactured in the United States of America
Printed on acid-free paper

10 9 8 7 6 5 4 3 2

ISBN 0-8229-5735-3

SLAVE EMANCIPATION IN CUBA

Contents

Illustrations

Tables

TABLES

Preface

On the night of February 12, 1882, in the midst of the sugar harvest, thirty-five "apprentices" of the Mapos estate in central Cuba fled their owners. They proceeded to the nearby town of Sancti Spíritus, where they presented appeals to the local Junta de Patronato, one of the boards established to administer an 1880 Spanish law that had nominally freed all Cuban slaves but also placed them under the "patronage" of their former masters and obliged them to labor for token wages. Twenty-two of the Mapos apprentices, or *patrocinados*, returned to the estate on February 13, and the other thirteen returned the following day. Later in the week some were briefly called back to the junta, and a *síndico* (legal protector of slaves) visited the estate. The majority of the apprentices apparently resumed work, while two, Lucas Cambaca and Filomena Conga, remained at the junta by order of a local judge.

The full legal effects of the group's appeals did not emerge in the estate records until almost a year later. In January 1883, the daybook noted a sudden drop in the number of apprentices on the estate; the junta had declared some 64 of the 265 Mapos apprentices exempt from the *patronato*. Some were freed through self-purchase, some because they were ruled to be over the age of sixty and thus free in virtue of an 1870 law providing freedom for children and the elderly. In subsequent months the estate saw a steady stream of departures as *patrocinados* paid for their freedom, fled, sought aid from the junta, or negotiated for the freedom of their children. By the harvest of 1883-1884, the plantation was operating with only about 160 apprentices, and was hiring additional free workers in an effort to maintain adequate labor.[1]

The events on this one estate highlight the complexities of the

[1] See Libro que contiene documentos del estado general de la finca Mapos, Archivo Provincial de Sancti Spíritus, Cuba, Fondo Valle-Iznaga (hereinafter APSS, Valle-Iznaga), leg. 24.

relationship between slaves and masters, and between each and the power of the state. The *patrocinados* on Mapos showed their willingness to challenge their master by appealing to the junta. Nevertheless they returned to, and remained on, his plantation while the legal process they had initiated marched slowly forward. The colonial government, even while enacting a law intended to maintain masters' authority, had provided mechanisms with which *patrocinados* could seek to escape that authority. But the juntas through which they had to appeal were constituted by members of the white elite, including former slaveholders, and *patrocinados'* access to resources was limited. Some *patrocinados* had enough money, often from the sale of crops from provision grounds, to purchase their freedom; but even money was not necessarily enough, for masters could, for example, attempt to maintain control over children nominally freed by the 1870 law, and thus block the departure of parents. While masters often attempted to stall the acquisition of freedom by their apprentices, they were also adapting to the decline in the number of their bound laborers, taking on new free workers, and altering the organization of production. Thus although most masters opposed abolition up until almost the last minute, they did not adopt a stance so intransigent as to provoke a break with the legal authority of the state.

Emancipation in Cuba was prolonged, ambiguous, and complex, unfolding over an eighteen-year period through a series of legal, social, and economic transformations. Because of the extended and halting nature of the process, the history of abolition provides an unparalleled opportunity to examine the disintegration of chattel bondage in a plantation society. The designers of "gradual emancipation" sought to minimize certain kinds of social change. But the intentions of planters and of government policy makers could not entirely determine the course of change: slaves and, later, *patrocinados* had their own ideas about freedom, and through their actions they altered and accelerated the transition. Different kinds of initiatives became important at different points in the process. In the late 1860s and early 1870s slaves joined in an anticolonial insurgency that forced the issue of slavery; in the 1880s challenges within a new legal framework reshaped relationships; in the end, even individual self-purchase hastened the elimination of slavery. As the planter monopoly of power within the plantation was undermined, slaves found weak points where they might press their claims.

The course of abolition also affords insight into the structure of Cuban slavery itself, for the institution was dismantled piece by piece: young children and the elderly were legally freed and the use of the whip banned in 1870; meager wages for *patrocinados* were introduced in 1880; stocks and chains were outlawed in 1883. By examining the effects of such changes, one can illuminate the ways in which the social relations of slavery had depended upon various elements of the legal system of slaveholding.

A study of the gradual shift to free labor in Cuba also provides evidence for evaluating various explanations for the decline of slavery. The pattern of decline varied across regions of the island, and these regions differed in their social and economic characteristics. Correlations between the rates of decline and the organization of production, the degree of mechanization, and the surrounding social and political environment may thus suggest which forces hastened and which stalled emancipation.

The transition rested upon a variety of intermediate forms of labor organization, and therefore provides a basis for comparing "racial" slavery with other voluntary and involuntary labor systems. Cuban planters employed slaves, Yucatecan and Chinese contract laborers, convicts, rented slaves, free day laborers, salaried employees, workers paid by the task, and sharecroppers. The coexistence of these forms of labor, sometimes on a single plantation, provides a striking example of flexibility within an economy still based primarily on slave labor. At the same time, the problems that arose when diverse forms of labor were combined illustrate some of the inflexibilities of slave-based structures.

Emancipation involved not only a reordering of individual lives but also a reordering of production itself. Cuba was in one sense a postemancipation success story, for sugar output increased after abolition. The gradual and constrained legal shift had made it possible to avoid certain kinds of confrontation or collapse. Little drama or anticipation was associated with the day of final abolition itself, for the vast majority of slaves had already become free, and neither former masters nor former slaves were unfamiliar with wage labor. New mills and old could draw upon a free work force of former slaves, smallholders, and new immigrants. Even so, the aftermath of emancipation was in many ways problematic, as former slaves found many of their aspirations blocked and numerous former masters lost control over sugar production to newly formed central mills.

While gradualism muted some expectations, the process of emancipation raised others. Former slaves who had joined in the 1868-1878 insurrection, had challenged their masters in the courts, had fought for control over their children, had fled the plantations, or had raised crops to purchase their freedom were not prepared simply to accept whatever was offered them. Moreover, the transformation of social relations in the countryside, particularly the rise of cane farming and the opening up of the closed world of the plantation, made certain sorts of political mobilization more feasible. The story that begins with a legal process of abolition undertaken in response to an anticolonial rebellion thus ends with the incorporation of former slaves into another rebellion, one that would conclude with Spain's loss of her last major colony in the New World.

Acknowledgments

A historian's first debt is to the institutions that have preserved and made available the documents essential to historical research. I would like to thank in particular the staffs of the Archivo Histórico Nacional and the Biblioteca Nacional in Madrid, the Archivo General de Indias in Seville, the Biblioteca Nacional José Martí and the Archivo Nacional de Cuba in Havana, the Archivo Provincial of Sancti Spíritus, Cuba, and the U.S. National Archives in Washington. I am also very grateful to the staff of the Casa de Velázquez in Madrid, and to its former director, François Chevalier, for their kind hospitality during my stay there in 1977-1978.

A further debt is to those who made such research possible through financial assistance. Here thanks are due to the Latin American Studies Program of Princeton University, the International Doctoral Research Fellowships program of the Social Science Research Council and the American Council of Learned Societies, the Fulbright-Hays program, the Woodrow Wilson International Center for Scholars, and the Michigan Society of Fellows. The final preparation of this volume for publication was carried out during my tenure as a Fellow at the Center for Advanced Study in the Behavioral Sciences. I am grateful for financial support for that fellowship provided by the National Endowment for the Humanities (Grant FC-20029) and by the Andrew Mellon Foundation. For computing facilities and data processing, I am indebted to Princeton University, the University of Michigan, and the Centro de Computación del Poder Popular de la Ciudad de La Habana.

I am grateful to Cambridge University Press for permission to incorporate material that appeared in a somewhat different form in my essay, "Explaining Abolition: Contradiction, Adaptation and Challenge in Cuban Slave Society, 1860-1886," *Comparative Studies in Society and History* 26 (January 1984), to Duke University Press for material from my "Gradual Abolition and the Dynamics of Slave

Emancipation in Cuba, 1868-1886," *Hispanic American Historical Review* 63 (August 1983) and to the Center for Latin American Studies, University of Pittsburgh, for material from my "Class Relations in Sugar and Political Mobilization in Cuba, 1868-1899," *Cuban Studies/Estudios Cubanos* 15 (Winter 1985). The data in Table 2 are taken from David R. Murray, *Odious Commerce: Britain, Spain and the Abolition of the Cuban Slave Trade* (Cambridge, England: Cambridge University Press, 1980), and are reprinted by permission. Those in Table 7 are from Duvon C. Corbitt, *A Study of the Chinese in Cuba, 1847-1947* (Wilmore, Ky.: Asbury College, 1971), and are also used by permission.

Special acknowledgment is due to Oscar Lorenzo and Sara Millán, who helped me find my way around during my research visits to Cuba in 1977, 1978, and 1979, and to Julio Vargas, who brought me endless bundles of documents on endless hot afternoons. Many Cuban scholars were very generous with their time and with references to sources, and I would like to thank in particular Olga Cabrera, Pedro Deschamps Chapeaux, Tomás Fernández Robaina, Araceli García Carranza, Gloria García, Zoila Lapique, María Lastayo, Julio LeRiverend, José Luciano Franco, Fe Iglesias, Rogelio Martínez-Furé, Manuel Moreno Fraginals, Raul Rodríguez la O, and Carlos Venegas. Paul Estrade and María Poumier-Taquechel, both French scholars of Cuba, were also kind and helpful.

Many other people have helped me develop this work through their comments on papers or portions of the manuscript. Although they are too numerous to mention here, I am very grateful to them all. The members of my doctoral committee—Stanley Stein, Linda Lewin, Franklin Knight, and James McPherson—deserve special thanks. Ira Berlin, David Brion Davis, Peter Eisenberg, Stanley Engerman, Eugene Genovese, Charles Gibson, Thomas Holt, and Sidney Mintz also provided helpful advice on various recent drafts of the manuscript.

In the pages of this book I will have occasion to disagree on several major points of interpretation with Manuel Moreno Fraginals. So it is perhaps appropriate to say at the outset that I have benefited greatly from his help and encouragement while I was conducting research in Cuba, from his recent critical reading of this manuscript, and, most important, from his own extraordinary study of Cuban society, *El ingenio*.

Still more difficult to describe are the debts owed to one's family. To say that I thank Anne Firor Scott for reading drafts of the first ten chapters, Andrew Scott for giving advice at several stages, and Peter Railton for reading every page and tirelessly discussing historical interpretation, is to express a small portion of my gratitude.

Finally, I dedicate this study, with great affection, to Charles Gibson. He does not work on Cuba, on slavery, or on emancipation. But throughout this project he has been a model and an inspiration. He tells me—and his own work shows—that writing history can be like building a house: if one does the carpentry well, it will stand the storms. I do not know whether I have met that standard; I will always be grateful to him for having set it.

Abbreviations Used in the Notes

AGI	Archivo General de Indias, Seville
Diversos	Sección de Diversos
AHN	Archivo Histórico Nacional, Madrid
Ultramar	Sección de Ultramar
ANC	Archivo Nacional de Cuba, Havana
CA	Fondo Consejo de Administración
GG	Fondo Gobierno General
ME	Fondo Miscelánea de Expedientes
ML	Fondo Miscelánea de Libros
APSS	Archivo Provincial de Sancti Spíritus, Sancti Spíritus, Cuba
Ayuntamiento	Fondo Ayuntamiento
Valle-Iznaga	Fondo Valle-Iznaga
BNC	Biblioteca Nacional José Martí, Havana
CC	Colección Cubana
BNE	Biblioteca Nacional, Madrid
Manuscritos	Sección de Manuscritos
MAE-Paris	Ministère des Affaires Étrangères, Paris
CC	Correspondance Commerciale
MAE-Madrid	Ministerio de Asuntos Exteriores, Madrid
Ultramar	Sección de Ultramar
PRO	Public Record Office, London
FO	Foreign Office Papers
RAH	Biblioteca de la Real Academia de Historia, Madrid
FD	Colección Fernández Duro
CR	Colección Caballero de Rodas
USNA	U.S. National Archives
RG 76	Record Group 76, Spanish Treaty Claims
leg.	*legajo* (bundle)
exp.	*expediente* (file)

Introduction

I

Sugar and Slavery

Notwithstanding all we hear and know of the enervating
influence of the climate, the white man, if not laborious
himself, is the cause that labor is in others. With all its
social and political discouragements . . . this island is
still very productive and very rich.
—*Richard Henry Dana, 1859*[1]

Chattel slavery, the holding of property in men and women, formed
the basis of a sophisticated and productive sugar industry in Cuba
well into the final third of the nineteenth century. In 1868 the island
produced 720,250 metric tons of sugar, more than 40 percent of the
cane sugar reaching the world market in that year. But just as Cuba
reached this level of production, the abolition of slavery began. Slavery had been maintained in Cuba while it was being abolished elsewhere, and emancipation, when it came, required almost two decades to complete. Like Brazil, Cuba was a holdout, finally
terminating slavery only in the 1880s. Subsequently, Cuban sugar
production grew still further, reaching the one-million-ton mark just
six years after final abolition.[2] This congruence of events raises questions about the relationship between slavery and the development
of sugar production in Cuba, and about why emancipation came
when and as it did.

There are several approaches to the problem of explaining the
ending of slavery in Cuba. One is to analyze abolition as a political
process, largely carried out by Spain in response to the domestic and
international pressures that arose from slavery's persistence in Cuba

[1] Richard Henry Dana, Jr., *To Cuba and Back: A Vacation Voyage* (Boston: Houghton Mifflin, 1859; reprint ed., Carbondale, Illinois: Southern Illinois University Press,
1966), p. 81.
[2] Manuel Moreno Fraginals, *El ingenio: Complejo económico social cubano del
azúcar*, 3 vols. (Havana: Editorial de Ciencias Sociales, 1978) 3: 37, 38, provides
production figures.

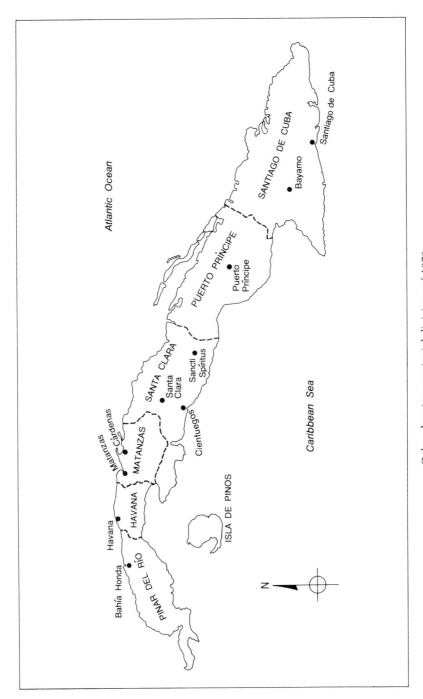

Atlantic Ocean

SANTIAGO DE CUBA

Santiago de Cuba

Bayamo

PUERTO PRÍNCIPE

Puerto
Príncipe

SANTA CLARA

Santa
Clara

Sancti
Spíritus

Cienfuegos

Matanzas

Cárdenas

MATANZAS

Bahía Honda

Havana

HAVANA

PINAR DEL RÍO

ISLA DE PINOS

Caribbean Sea

N

Cuba, showing provincial divisions of 1878

long after its extinction in most of the New World.[3] Another approach is to view the ending of slavery primarily as an attempt to resolve difficulties within the sugar economy, including, some scholars have argued, a growing internal contradiction between the rigidity of slave labor and the need for technological advancement.[4] A complementary interpretation sees the shift to free labor as largely an economic question, and portrays enlightened planters as either taking the initiative or posing little objection.[5] One might also combine these approaches, portraying a politically expedient colonial policy as serving the higher interests of the local elite, though this would raise the further question of why abolition in fact took so very long to accomplish.

Rather than choose among, or attempt to synthesize, these approaches, I shall embark on a somewhat different tack. In addition to evaluating the pressures exerted on the Spanish government, I shall examine the behavior of a wider range of actors—including slaves, freedmen, and insurgents. While exploring the problems that planters perceived and the ways they sought to resolve them, I shall question the accuracy of the historical claim that they faced "internal contradictions" that could be resolved only through abolition.

---

[3] The analysis by Arthur F. Corwin best exemplifies this approach: *Spain and the Abolition of Slavery in Cuba, 1817-1886* (Austin: University of Texas Press, 1967).

[4] The thesis of the incompatibility of slave labor and technology is argued in Moreno's *El ingenio* 1: 220-21 and expressed succinctly in several articles by the same author, including "El esclavo y la mecanización de los ingenios," *Bohemia*, June 13, 1969, pp. 98-99, and "Desgarramiento azucarero e integración nacional," *Casa de las Américas* 11 (September-October 1970): 6-22. More recently Moreno has cited the importance of a variety of factors in determining the course of abolition, but he continues to emphasize the key role of a structural "crisis" "provoked by the steadily decreasing profitability of slave-based labor and by the difficulties resulting from the adoption of new technologies." See his essay "Plantaciones en el Caribe: El caso Cuba—Puerto Rico—Santo Domingo (1860-1940)," in his *La historia como arma y otros estudios sobre esclavos, ingenios y plantaciones* (Barcelona: Editorial Crítica, 1983), p. 75. Franklin W. Knight argues that "slave labor was woefully incompetent to deal with the scientific advances of the industry," and refers to slavery in Cuba as "partly the victim of the steam engine," though he does not see mechanization itself as inclining planters toward abolitionism. See Franklin W. Knight, *Slave Society in Cuba during the Nineteenth Century* (Madison: University of Wisconsin Press, 1970), pp. 182, 178.

[5] Eugene D. Genovese ascribes a leading role in Cuban abolition to "some of the island's wealthiest planters" who, along with other reformists of the 1860s, are said to have "understood the importance of general economic renovation and the extent to which slavery inhibited it." He argues that in Cuba "the sugar planters had a purely economic stake in slavery and . . . when that stake waned, they could move into a wage-labor system." *The World the Slaveholders Made: Two Essays in Interpretation* (New York: Random House, Pantheon Books, 1969), pp. 69-70.

My emphasis throughout will be on the *links* among the different kinds of pressures—social, economic, political, military—and on the interactions among masters, slaves, rebels, and administrators. The goal, then, is not simply to discover a series of factors that brought about abolition, but rather to understand the dynamics of the process of emancipation and the transition to free labor.

This analysis must begin with Cuban society itself. The composition of the population shaped both social relations and the labor market. Regional differences in the island's economic and social development helped to determine the geographical pattern of the transition to free labor. Specific characteristics of plantation slavery in Cuba—such as provision-ground cultivation and seasonal work patterns in sugar—influenced the evolution of labor relations. Finally, slaveholders' perceptions of their relationship to their workers and to the Spanish government conditioned their responses to the prospect of abolition.

Cuba stood out among the Caribbean sugar islands for its large and growing white population. When the government carried out a census of the island's inhabitants in 1861-1862, it became clear that the balance of the population had shifted markedly since 1846, the date of the previous census. Whites, who had been a minority, were now a majority, their numbers having multiplied through immigration and natural growth from about 426,000 to about 730,000. Within the population of color, slaves still predominated, outnumbering the free persons of color by a ratio of about 1.7 to 1, though this represented a decline from the ratio of about 2 to 1 that had prevailed in 1846. The number of free persons of color had grown rapidly, but they had merely maintained their share of the total population (16 percent) in the face of the even more rapid increase in the white population. The 34,000 Asians (Chinese indentured laborers) and 740 Yucatecans (brought under contract from Mexico) represented a tiny fraction of the total (see Table 1).[6]

[6] The 1846 census data are from Cuba, Comisión de Estadística, *Cuadro estadístico de la siempre fiel Isla de Cuba, correspondiente al año de 1846* (Havana: Imprenta del Gobierno y Capitanía General, 1847). Censuses were taken in Cuba in 1841 and 1846. Both were controversial, and there have been suspicions that the second undercounted slaves. It nonetheless seems appropriate to use that of 1846, both because it was more recent and because it probably reflected a real decrease in the slave population as a result of the high mortality and decline in importation in the mid-1840s. The census that I refer to as that of 1862 was taken between June 1861 and June 1862, and its tables vary both in the dates to which the counts are attributed

SUGAR AND SLAVERY

TABLE 1
Population of Cuba, 1846 and 1862

	1846		1862		Increase
White	425,767	(47.4%)	729,957	(53.7%)	71.4%
Free colored	149,226	(16.6%)	221,417	(16.3%)	48.4%
Emancipado[a]			4,521	(.3%)	
Slave	323,759	(36.0%)	368,550	(27.1%)	13.8%
Asian			34,050	(2.5%)	
Yucatecan			743	(.1%)	
Total	898,752	(100.0%)	1,359,238	(100.0%)	51.2%

SOURCE: 1846 figures are from Cuba, *Cuadro estadístico de la siempre fiel Isla de Cuba, correspondiente al año de 1846* (Havana: Imprenta del Gobierno, 1847); and 1862 figures are from Cuba, Centro de Estadística, *Noticias estadísticas de la Isla de Cuba en 1862* (Havana: Imprenta del Gobierno, 1864), "Censo de población de la Isla de Cuba en el año que terminó en 1º de Junio de 1862."

[a] *Emancipados* were Africans found on captured slave ships, legally freed, and contracted out under government authority.

The white population was overwhelmingly Creole (that is, born in the New World), though with a substantial and disproportionately powerful minority of Spaniards (that is, those born in Spain), many of them merchants, shopkeepers, or government employees. There was frequent tension between Spaniards and Creoles over issues of politics and commerce, and occasionally open separatism on the part of Cubans. The Creole elite had developed in large measure during the course of the sugar revolution of the nineteenth century, leaving many eighteenth-century patriarchal traditions behind. Spanish merchants had also profited from the island's economic growth, both in their role as providers of slaves and credit and in their role as sellers in the protected Cuban market. Though planters were frequently indebted to, and resentful of, Spanish merchants, the two groups generally closed ranks on the issue of the maintenance of slavery. The sugar elite, both Spanish and Creole, also cultivated and benefited from a close relationship with a long series of colonial administrators, helping to block the implementation of unfavorable metropolitan rulings.[7]

and in the total population enumerated. For Table 1 I have used the figures listed in the census as "Censo de población de la Isla de Cuba en el año que terminó en 1.º de Junio de 1862," in which the Chinese and Yucatecans are counted separately. Elsewhere in this work I use the figures from later tables in the census that group Chinese, Yucatecans, and whites together and divide the population into finer categories of residence. See Cuba, Centro de Estadística, *Noticias estadísticas de la Isla de Cuba en 1862* (Havana: Imprenta del Gobierno, 1864).

[7] On the composition of the white population, see Fe Iglesias, "Características de

Sugar planters, however, constituted only a tiny minority within white society, and a substantial part of the population was not directly part of the sugar economy. Almost 236,000 whites lived on *sitios de labor* and *estancias*, small farms predominantly devoted to the raising of food crops, with another 75,000 on tobacco farms and 52,000 on *potreros*, stock-raising farms. Some 311,000 whites lived in the cities and towns of the island, and fewer than 42,000 on the sugar estates.[8] While sugar planters' adherence to Spain had helped maintain the island's loyalty in the decades since Spain's mainland colonies had broken free, they alone could not indefinitely insure the security of the Cuban countryside, given the large number of small farmers, tenants, and laborers.

The island's free population of color included descendants of slaves liberated generations earlier as well as those recently manumitted. The large proportion of women among those who obtained freedom contributed to the group's relatively high rate of growth. Most free persons of color lived in towns and cities, where they usually worked as day laborers, artisans, and domestics, though some attained professional and semiprofessional positions. The rural free population of color was concentrated in the eastern part of the island. Some 23,700 of the 84,500 free persons of color in the eastern districts lived on *estancias*, while another 15,500 lived on tobacco farms and 7,400 on ranches and stock-raising farms. The eastern department's free population of color thus had a distinctly rural character, while that of the western department was 65 percent urban.[9]

Though legally allowed to own property (even slaves), free blacks and mulattos suffered from widespread social discrimination, including limited access to public gatherings and prohibitions on in-

la población cubana en 1862," *Revista de la Biblioteca Nacional José Martí*, 3rd series, 22 (September-December 1980): 93. For a picture of Havana and its Spanish merchants at mid-century, see Antonio de las Barras y Prado, *La Habana a mediados del siglo xix* (Madrid: Imprenta de la Ciudad Lineal, 1925). On the development and composition of the planter class, see Knight, *Slave Society*, pp. 21-22 and chap. 5, and Moreno, *El ingenio*, vol. 1. For a discussion of the influence of the sugar elite on the formulation of government policy concerning the slave trade, see David R. Murray, *Odious Commerce: Britain, Spain and the Abolition of the Cuban Slave Trade* (Cambridge, England: Cambridge University Press, 1980).

[8] Cuba, Centro de Estadística, *Noticias estadísticas*, "Distribución de la población en los pueblos y fincas de la isla." In this context, the category "whites" includes Chinese contract laborers.

[9] On occupations, see Pedro Deschamps Chapeaux, *El negro en la economía habanera del siglo xix* (Havana: Unión de Escritores y Artistas de Cuba, 1971). For statistics, see Cuba, Centro de Estadística, *Noticias estadísticas*, "Distribución."

terracial marriage. Despite a generally more flexible system of ethnic classification than that prevailing in the U.S. South, the concept of an African "stain" continued to stigmatize the Cuban descendants of slaves.[10] One Spanish resident of Havana in the 1860s explained candidly that all blacks were obliged to show respect to whites in order for whites to maintain the "moral force" necessary to keep the "black race" in submission, since it would be difficult to do so on the basis of material force alone.[11]

Free persons of color constituted an uncertain element in the colonial equation. The Spanish administration had long sought to use them as a counterweight to the slave population, even to the extent of arming batallions of free mulattos and blacks.[12] In the 1840s, however, authorities suspected free persons of color of collaboration in a rumored general slave uprising and arrested, tortured, and executed members of Cuba's precarious free colored middle sector. The colored small-scale farmers, tenants, and squatters in the east, where in most districts they outnumbered slaves, were a similar unknown in the balance of power.[13] As in virtually all slave societies, mulatto free persons had often sought to distance themselves from blacks in an effort both to avoid the "stain" of shared slave ancestry and to assert the importance of differences in social status and gradations of skin color. At the same time, however, slaves and free persons of color had often been joined by ties of kinship and shared membership in the *cabildos de nación*, particularly in the towns. To the extent that there was a continuous process of manumission, absolute caste-like barriers were unlikely to develop.[14]

The island's slaves were both recognized by the white elite as the

[10] See Verena Martínez-Alier, *Marriage, Class and Colour in Nineteenth-Century Cuba* (Cambridge, England: Cambridge University Press, 1974).

[11] Barras y Prado, *La Habana*, pp. 111-12.

[12] Deschamps Chapeaux, *El negro en la economía*, pp. 57-86.

[13] On the 1844 uprising and its repression, see Murray, *Odious Commerce*, chap. 9, and references cited therein; and Robert Louis Paquette, "The Conspiracy of La Escalera: Colonial Society and Politics in Cuba in the Age of Revolution." Ph.D. thesis, University of Rochester, 1982. For population figures by district, see Cuba, Centro de Estadística, *Noticias estadísticas*, "Censo."

[14] See Martínez-Alier, *Marriage*, especially pp. 96-99. On the U.S. South, see Ira Berlin, *Slaves Without Masters* (New York: Random House, 1974). For a discussion of *cabildos*, see Chap. XI, below, and Fernando Ortiz, "Los cabildos afro-cubanos," *Revista Bimestre Cubana* 16 (Jan.-Feb., 1921): 5-39. On the free persons of color, see Deschamps, *El negro*, and Paquette, "Conspiracy."

TABLE 2
Slaves Imported into Cuba, 1840-1867[a]

Year	Number	Year	Number	Year	Number
1840	14,470	1850	3,100	1860	24,895
1841	9,776	1851	5,000	1861	23,964
1842	3,000	1852	7,924	1862	11,254
1843	8,000	1853	12,500	1863	7,507
1844	10,000	1854	11,400	1864	6,807
1845	1,300	1855	6,408	1865	145
1846	1,500	1856	7,304	1866	1,443
1847	1,000	1857	10,436	1867	—
1848	1,500	1858	16,992		
1849	8,700	1859	30,473	Total	246,798

SOURCE: David R. Murray, *Odious Commerce: Britain, Spain and the Abolition of the Cuban Slave Trade* (Cambridge, England: Cambridge University Press, 1980), p. 244.

[a] These totals are the estimates published by the British Foreign Office and are based on reports of the British commissioners in Havana. (In 1841 no figure was published, and the figure here is taken from the commissioner's reports.)

basis of Cuba's prosperity and perceived as a potential threat to its security. The decade of the 1850s saw an upsurge in the contraband transatlantic slave trade, partially offsetting the decline that would otherwise have resulted from deaths and manumissions in a population that did not have a positive natural rate of increase (see Table 2). By the end of the decade, however, the absolute number of slaves appears to have begun to decline. Slave registration figures, though distinctly unreliable, showed a total of around 373,000 in 1855-1857.[15] By 1861-1862 the census counted just 368,550, and the 1867 slave registration showed 363,288.[16]

The experience of slavery itself varied widely within Cuba, from the cities and towns, where slaves filled a broad range of occupations, to the rural settings, each with different characteristics and work rhythms. Though slaves in towns were highly visible to travelers—and are in some ways more visible to historians—most Cuban slaves in the 1860s lived in the countryside, and the largest group (47 percent) lived on sugar estates. Indeed the proportion of the slave labor force employed in sugar was even greater than 47 percent

[15] Knight cites the figures from the 1855, 1856, and 1857 "capitations" in *Slave Society*, p. 63.
[16] Cuba, Centro de Estadística, *Noticias estadísticas*, "Censo," and AHN, Ultramar, leg. 4884, tomo 8, exp. 160.

10

because of the relatively small numbers of slave children on sugar plantations, compared to the cities.[17]

Rural slaves who were not employed in sugar labored on various kinds of plantations, farms, and ranches (see Table 3). The slaves on *sitios de labor* and *estancias*, both small food-producing farms, numbered almost 32,000 and of necessity had closer relations with their owners and performed a wider range of tasks than most plantation slaves. Over 31,000 slaves lived on intensive stock-raising farms, *potreros*, that were sometimes independent and sometimes tied to *ingenios*, on occasion sharing their work force with a nearby estate. About 26,000 slaves lived on the island's coffee plantations, where conditions were traditionally viewed as less oppressive than those on *ingenios*.[18] Cattle ranchers owned few slaves each, most of them men. With greater open space, the ranches may have offered relatively independent working conditions, but the sex ratio must have made family life very difficult. Tobacco farms also held few slaves per farm, with *vegas* in the district of Pinar del Río averaging four or five slaves each, and those in the Eastern Department averaging less than one slave each. In the western Pinar del Río and San Cristóbal districts, most of the residents of tobacco farms were whites, while in the eastern Santiago de Cuba district, most were free persons of color.[19]

The diversity of situations in which Cuban slaves lived and the range of their activities suggest that one should exercise considerable caution in attributing a general "character" to Cuban slavery. While some earlier scholars saw Cuba as an instance of a mild New World slavery, strongly influenced by the Catholic Church, recent research has shown that the Church could not determine practices within the plantation once large-scale capitalistic agriculture had developed. Thus the image of a paternalistic slavery characterized by concern for the soul of the slave is out of keeping with the regime

[17] Cuba, Centro de Estadística, *Noticias estadísticas*, "Distribución." It is thus somewhat misleading to emphasize the urban experience, as Herbert S. Klein does, and portray Cuba just prior to emancipation as a "rich world of economic opportunity" for the slave, one that had provided him with a "rich industrial heritage." See *Slavery in the Americas* (Chicago: The University of Chicago Press, 1967), pp. 162-63.

[18] On the reputation of the coffee estates, see Knight, *Slave Society*, pp. 65-67.

[19] All of the figures in this discussion are from Cuba, Centro de Estadística, *Noticias estadísticas*, "Distribución," and "Registro general de fincas rústicas."

TABLE 3
Distribution of Slave Population by Place of Residence, 1862

Residence (Census category)	Males	Females	Total	Percentage of Slaves in Island	Slaves as Percentage of Residents	Male Slaves per 100 Female Slaves
Ingenios (Sugar plantations)	109,709	62,962	172,671	47%	79%	174
Poblados (Towns)	37,014	38,963	75,977	21%	15%	95
Potreros (Stock-raising farms)	20,414	11,100	31,514	9%	35%	184
Cafetales (Coffee plantations)	14,344	11,598	25,942	7%	77%	124
Sitios de labor (Small farms)	14,253	10,597	24,850	7%	11%	135
Vegas (Tobacco farms)	11,622	6,053	17,675	5%	15%	192
Estancias (Small farms)	4,220	2,698	6,918	2%	8%	156
Haciendas (Ranches)	4,311	1,909	6,220	2%	18%	226
Other establishments	2,675	1,500	4,175	1%	19%	178
Other farms	1,655	769	2,424	1%	20%	215
Total (calculated from table)[a]	220,217	148,149	368,366			149

SOURCE: Cuba, Centro de Estadística, *Noticias estadísticas*, "Distribución de la Población en los Pueblos y Fincas de la Isla."
[a] Because of apparent omissions in the original, these totals do not equal those cited elsewhere in the census.

of the developed *ingenio*.[20] Verena Martínez-Alier, studying the position of the Church on the delicate issue of intermarriage, has also shown the reluctance of many Church leaders and parish priests to press for the recognition of the spiritual equality of all men. As Martínez-Alier has argued, the authorities were well aware of the precepts of Catholic morality, but did not feel bound by them: "On the contrary, they manipulate these values in accordance with the circumstances and as a rule subordinate them to the interests of the State."[21]

One institution often cited as distinguishing the status of the Cuban slave from that of slaves elsewhere was *coartación*, or gradual self-purchase. Under Spanish law, a slave who made a substantial down payment on his or her purchase price—thus becoming *coartado*—gained certain privileges. He or she could not be sold for a price greater than the appraised value at the time of the *coartación* and was entitled to a portion of the rental if hired out. In theory, *coartación* provided an avenue for self-emancipation and created an intermediate status between slave and free.[22] As slave prices rose, however, the possibility that a slave would be able to accumulate the purchase price receded. Herbert Klein cites the example of *coartación* through a down payment of 50 pesos, one-quarter of a purchase price of 200 pesos.[23] But by the 1860s slave prices were from three to six times that much, putting self-purchase far beyond the reach of almost all slaves.[24] The total number of freedom papers

[20] The earlier thesis was associated particularly with Frank Tannenbaum and Herbert Klein. See Frank Tannenbaum, *Slave and Citizen: The Negro in the Americas* (New York: Random House, 1946), and Klein, *Slavery*. Major challenges to it are contained in Knight, *Slave Society*, and Moreno, *El ingenio*. Cuba, particularly in the eighteenth century, showed a greater diversity of economic activity, a smaller proportion of slaves in the population, and a larger free population of color than many other Caribbean sugar islands. These features did help to give Cuban slavery a special character and created a heritage that would influence society in the nineteenth century. But it does not follow that all aspects of this character persisted until abolition, for the intervening decades saw a dramatic concentration of resources in sugar production, massive importations of slaves, and a weakening of countervailing forces that might offset the hegemony of the planter class.

[21] Martínez-Alier, *Marriage*, p. 47.

[22] Klein, *Slavery*, pp. 196-99. See also Hubert H. S. Aimes, "Coartación: A Spanish Institution for the Advancement of Slaves into Freedmen," *The Yale Review* 17 (Feb. 1909): 412-31.

[23] Klein, *Slavery*, p. 197.

[24] For estimates of slave prices in the 1860s see Hubert H. S. Aimes, *A History of Slavery in Cuba, 1511 to 1868* (New York: G. P. Putnam's Sons, 1907; reprint ed., New York: Octagon Books, 1967), pp. 267-68. For the valuations of slaves on specific estates, see Manuel Moreno Fraginals, Herbert S. Klein, and Stanley L. Engerman,

issued between 1858 and 1862 averaged about 1,900 per year, and this figure included manumissions as well as self-purchase by *coartados*.[25] While in any given year there could be more slaves becoming *coartados* than achieving full freedom, other evidence suggests that the number actually in the status of *coartado* at any one time was small. When the slave population was counted in 1871, it included only 890 male *coartados* and 1,247 female *coartadas*, less than one percent of the total. Over 40 percent of the *coartados* lived in the urban *jurisdicción* of Havana, while the sugar areas had very few.[26]

The significance of these figures goes beyond their relevance to the debate on the relative "severity" of Cuban slavery—a discussion grown somewhat barren. More important, in conjunction with other findings, they cast doubt on the notion that the nature of the integration of former slaves into Cuban society after abolition was determined by extensive prior social mobility and by Church-inspired "mores and attitudes that permitted the Negro to be treated as a coequal human being."[27] *Coartación*, combined with a generally more positive attitude toward manumission than was found, for example, in the United States, was clearly important in developing Cuba's large free population of color. But on the eve of final emancipation *coartación* affected only a tiny fraction of Cuba's slaves. Understanding the integration of the majority of freed men and women into Cuban society requires both a closer examination of Cuban sugar plantations and a direct look at the process of emancipation itself and its aftermath.

It is clear that the exigencies of technology and profitability tended to turn the semimechanized, capitalistic, export-oriented sugar plantation of the mid-nineteenth century into a prison, the slaves into mere factors of production.[28] On the other hand, to focus solely on

---

"The Level and Structure of Slave Prices on Cuban Plantations in the Mid-Nineteenth Century: Some Comparative Perspectives," *American Historical Review* 88 (Dec. 1983): 1201-18. See also note 83, below.

[25] Cuba, Centro de Estadística, *Noticias estadísticas*, "Cartas de libertad expedidas a esclavos en la isla en el quinquenio de 1858 a 1862." The estimate of 6.2% of slaves being freed through *coartación* each year, cited by Klein, is based on a miscalculation by Aimes. Klein, *Slavery*, p. 199.

[26] Resumen general de los esclavos existentes en esta Provincia formado por Jurisdicciones con arreglo al censo de Enero de 1871, Havana, November 15, 1872, AHN, Ultramar, leg. 4882, tomo 3, exp. 39.

[27] Klein, *Slavery*, p. 105. See also Tannenbaum, *Slave and Citizen*, p. 100.

[28] The most emphatic and well-documented statement of this view is in Moreno, *El ingenio*.

these characteristics may lead to new errors—to characterizations that too rigidly reflect an ideal type. By concentrating on the logic of the enterprise, one may overlook aspects of its reality.

Manuel Moreno Fraginals, for example, has written that plantation slaves "did not know economic, personal, or family responsibility because they lacked an economy of their own."[29] Because of radical "deculturation" under slavery, he argues, abolition was "traumatic" for many of them.[30] "Deculturation" and the denial of a personal economy to the slaves may indeed have been the aims of planters, and may have conformed to the logic of capitalistic slave plantations. But this does not mean that they were everywhere actually achieved. That the experiences of enslavement, transportation to the New World, and forced labor were devastating, no one can doubt. But that they left most slaves incapable of recreating a cultural life is unlikely.[31] In the Cuban case, patterns of provision ground cultivation, lodging, and family life created experiences and expectations that would later help to provide the basis for an active involvement by many slaves in the process of emancipation.

Though slaveholders in Cuba and elsewhere in the Caribbean had traditionally granted provision grounds or *conucos* to their slaves, on which the slaves were to grow their own food, the economics of the sugar boom made it profitable for masters to put land into cane and to import food to feed the slaves.[32] Nonetheless, *conucos* were apparently revived and encouraged even on large estates in the mid-nineteenth century by advocates of "better treatment" as a means of tying slaves to the plantation, improving their health and longevity, and discouraging sabotage by fire.[33] The key to such changes was not simply whether religion or custom granted a limited right of private property to the slave, or even whether imported food was cheaper than home-produced, but whether, all things considered, it was convenient for the plantation to have a portion of its food produced relatively independently by slaves. "All things considered"

[29] Ibid., 2: 45.
[30] Manuel Moreno Fraginals, "Aportes culturales y deculturación," in Manuel Moreno Fraginals, ed. *África en América Latina* (Paris: UNESCO, and Mexico: Siglo Veintiuno Editores, 1977), p. 22.
[31] See Sidney W. Mintz and Richard Price, *An Anthropological Approach to the Afro-American Past: A Caribbean Perspective* (Philadelphia: Institute for the Study of Human Issues, 1976).
[32] Knight, *Slave Society*, p. 68.
[33] Moreno, *El ingenio* 2: 89.

would include the reactions of planters to the behavior of slaves—their skills, their work habits under different situations, their resistance—as well as slaves' responses to planters' behavior. The analysis thus shifts away from the "rights" granted under Catholic slavery and toward the circumstances under which, despite a rigorous plantation regime, slaves did obtain access to land and were able to produce crops.

Records of purchases of animals and produce from slaves are common in surviving plantation account books of the second half of the nineteenth century. Goods sold included maize, yucca, *malanga*, *boniato*, plantains, and pigs.[34] Contemporary observers also suggested that the cultivation of provision grounds was a very general phenomenon.[35] To be sure, the slaves' actual experience of selling goods to the plantation was often a travesty of the free market for the bargaining power of the two sides was hardly equal. James O'Kelly witnessed one such sale in the 1870s and noted that "the use of the word 'buy' in the transaction should be seen as a euphemism."

One of the superintendents of the estate called out a woman's name. Almost immediately a wretched-looking creature advanced to where the superintendent was standing, and, taking up a position of absolute subservience, with head bowed and eyes cast down, awaited in silence the further wishes of the superior being before whom in spirit she was prostrated. She had not long to wait. A pig was wanted; she had one ready to be killed; it was to be delivered up, and, in return, she would receive two dollars. The poor creature curtsied awkwardly, mumbled an assent, and the "purchase" was completed.[36]

O'Kelly, an abolitionist, minimized the autonomy allowed to the slave. But his moral point about the humiliation of the woman involved does not contradict an economic and social interpretation of the significance of production for sale. Cultivation of provision

[34] See the purchases recorded in the Libro Mayor del ingenio Nueva Teresa (Años 1872-86), ANC, ML, 11245; in the Libro que contiene documentos del estado general de la Finca Mapos y del ingenio de elaborar azúcar, Desde 1881-1884, APSS, Valle-Iznaga, leg. 24; and in the Libro Diario del Ingenio Delicias, 1872-82, ANC, ML, 10802.

[35] See, for example, Francisco Acosta y Albear, *Memoria sobre el estado actual de Cuba* (Havana: A. Pegó, 1874), p. 14, and Jacobo de la Pezuela, *Diccionario geográfico, estadístico, histórico de la Isla de Cuba* (Madrid: Mellado, 1863) 1: 214.

[36] James O'Kelly, *The Mambi-Land or, Adventures of a Herald Correspondent in Cuba* (Philadelphia: J. B. Lippincott, 1874), p. 59.

grounds represented opportunity for initiative, relatively unsuper-
vised labor, and a source of funds—a limited "personal economy."[37]

The point is made not to suggest special generosity on the part of
the master, but rather to emphasize that such exchanges required
masters to deal with slaves in terms of money rather than strictly
in terms of forced labor. The slave who grew vegetables for sale, or
who was given a piglet to raise on halves with the plantation, learned
something of the market economy, however miserably he or she
was compensated for the effort. And what slaves thus learned could
affect the way they would behave during and after emancipation.

A somewhat similar point could be made about the family. Moreno correctly points out the vulnerability of any marriage among
slaves, the sexual imbalance in the slave population, and the prison-
like regimen of the plantation. But he goes on to argue that, because
of these, "a family unit within the *ingenio* was a foreign body, naturally rejected," basing his argument on the objective conditions of
life for slaves and on his claim that slaves knew no economic, personal, or family responsibility.[38] However, one should not confuse
the absence of legal marriage with an absence of perceived family
responsibility, nor assume that hostile conditions made the formation of families impossible. Evidence from other societies challenges both of these views.[39] Moreover, there is direct evidence of
slave family ties, even on Cuban sugar estates.

A predominant symbol of the Cuban slave plantation at its height
was the *barracón*, a prison-like barracks, often described as segre-
gating males and females. Such an institution, quite obviously,
would strongly discourage family formation. But *barracones*, large
and expensive to construct, were principally confined to the developed mills of Havana and Matanzas. They were rarer in Santa Clara,
and absent in Santiago de Cuba and Puerto Príncipe. Even in the
advanced zone of Cárdenas in Matanzas, of the 221 *ingenios* existing
in 1850, a slight majority retained the old *bohío* or hut system.[40]

[37] For a more general discussion of the importance of provision grounds, see Sidney
W. Mintz, *Caribbean Transformations* (Chicago: Aldine Publishing, 1974), chap. 7.
[38] Moreno, *El ingenio* 2: 45.
[39] See, for example, Herbert Gutman, *The Black Family in Slavery and Freedom,
1750-1925* (New York: Pantheon Books, 1976), and B. W. Higman, *Slave Population
and Economy in Jamaica, 1807-1834* (Cambridge, England: Cambridge University
Press, 1976).
[40] See Juan Pérez de la Riva, *El barracón y otros ensayos* (Havana: Editorial de
Ciencias Sociales, 1975), particularly "El barracón de ingenio en la época esclavista,"

A slaveholder in 1840 portrayed one such group of *bohíos*. His account was biased by an obvious self-interest in the matter and by his romanticism. The details he invokes in his description of the two-room huts that the slaves built for themselves are nonetheless significant.

Where they live is in the parlor. There the blacks do almost everything, there they have a fire burning constantly, there they cook, there they eat, there they talk. The bedroom serves only to hold the clothes chest, to hang straw baskets with God knows how many things inside, to put away the baskets in which they rock their small children, and for the godchildren and relatives to sleep in, because the masters of the hut stay in the parlor.[41]

In such circumstances, the institution of the family was clearly not a "foreign body naturally rejected." Indeed, this description portrays relations of kinship and godparenthood beyond the units of parents and children. None of these had to be legally sanctioned to be recognized and valued by slaves, through in fact baptismal records of slave children do sometimes list godparents.[42]

Even within *barracones*, slaves found ways to make their cells less prison-like, and the sexes were not invariably separated. They were still frightful places to live—squalid, smoky, confining. But contemporary descriptions of them reflect the existence of both family relations and a private economy. Álvaro Reynoso, in 1861, noted that "in these rooms the blacks establish divisions and subdivisions, they construct lofts or granaries to store their harvests."[43] Another

pp. 15-74. Pérez de la Riva points out the ambiguities in the usage of the words *barracón* and *bohío*; in this discussion I have restricted the term *barracón* to barracks and *bohío* to huts, and used only evidence in which the reference of the observer is clear. On the geographical distribution of *barracones* see Moreno, *El ingenio* 2: 74-75.

[41] "Bohíos" (1840), in BNC, CC, C.M. Suárez R., tomo 6, no. 3.

[42] For instances of the presence of *padrinos* and grandparents at slave baptisms, see Libro 16 de Bautismos de Pardos y Morenos, Archivo Parroquial de la Iglesia Mayor del Espíritu Santo, Sancti Spíritus, Cuba. In many cases the father was listed as "no conocido"; in others he was named and the child was legitimate. For a listing of slaves' children from the *ingenio* Angelita along with their godparents, see Libro Diario del ingenio "Angelita" de la propiedad de Sr. J. A. Argudín, fol. 199, ANC, ML, 11536. Sixteen children baptized on June 13, 1870, are listed. All of the mothers who are identifiable from other records were Creole; all were between ages twenty and forty. Most *padrinos* and *madrinos* were also Creole, but a substantial number (ten out of thirty-two) were African (Lucumí or Gangá). One set of godparents was white, the man listed as French. It is not entirely clear what the status of the mother was in that instance.

[43] These observations by Reynoso are quoted by Francisco Pérez de la Riva in *La habitación rural en Cuba* (Havana: Editorial Lex, 1952), p. 69.

observer in 1875, horrified by the dampness and filth of these barracks, wrote, "In each of these pestiferous dungeons, a whole family lived in a condition more foul and degraded than any beasts of the field."[44]

It should by now be clear that the questions of mistreatment, private economy, and family are in some ways separable. Slaves could be cheated, yet participate in a money economy. They could be ill-housed, yet struggle to maintain families. They could be treated worse than beasts, yet not become like beasts.

These arguments are not meant to substitute a romantic image of cozy families in thatch-roofed huts for the devastating picture of deracinated individuals in squalid barracks. They are instead intended to convey a sense of the range of slave adaptations to even the worst circumstances. While a conscious policy of "good treatment" might ameliorate some of these circumstances, such intentions of planters were by no means a necessary precondition for initiatives by slaves, though some measures, such as balancing the sex ratio on an estate, would make family formation more likely.

By focusing on the dehumanizing conditions in the largest mills, one may capture the essence of capitalist, slave-based sugar production. If one portrays these conditions only in their starkest terms, however, it is not possible to understand fully the initiatives taken by slaves, their collective efforts, their creative use of small concessions. If one insists that family life was impossible within the *ingenio*, it is difficult to make sense of the efforts of slaves to purchase the freedom of their spouses and children. If one insists that plantation slaves lacked all economic responsibility and experience of private economic activity, it is difficult to see how they gathered the funds to make these purchases.

One should not fall into the error of making the exception seem ordinary, or exaggerating the "space," the room for initiative, the autonomy of slaves. The sex ratio was often unbalanced and families were under continual threat of disruption; *conuco* production was limited and vulnerable; acquiring capital was never easy; harsh phys-

---

[44] Frederick Trench Townshend, *Wild Life in Florida, with a Visit to Cuba* (London: Hurst and Blackett, 1875), p. 195. Fredrika Bremer, a Swedish visitor to Cuba in 1851, also referred to the *barracón* of the *ingenio* Ariadna as having "one room for each family." Fredrika Bremer, *Cartas desde Cuba* (Havana: Editorial Arte y Literatura, 1980), p. 79.

19

ical punishment damaged slaves as it damages all human beings. There is no way to know whether a numerical majority of rural slaves had provision grounds, or whether a majority established some kinds of family ties. Even if these were minority patterns, however, they were part of the cultural background that slaves drew upon in gaining freedom and took into freedom. They provided goals to be sought, even if such goals were not always achieved.

Despite the diverse situations in which slaves found themselves, the character of labor in sugar shaped the lives of Cuban slaves more than any other single factor. Even for urban slaves, knowledge of conditions on sugar estates to which they might be sent served as a form of discipline.[45] There was a kind of symmetry to the process whereby such infamous working conditions arose: the particular labor needs of sugar cultivation and processing were thought to require slave labor, and then the presence of slave labor on the estates reinforced the coercion to which all sugar workers were subject.

SUGAR. The process of sugar production varied widely in Cuba, from huge enterprises employing hundreds of slaves and producing thousands of tons of sugar per season to tiny mills with a few slaves each, producing less than one hundred tons. In 1860 Cuban sugar plantations (using the term to apply to the combination of land and mill) included some 1,382 *ingenios* as well as several hundred very small *trapiches*, the latter generally producing for local consumption. Manuel Moreno Fraginals has categorized the *ingenios* of 1860 in three major groups: animal-powered, with an average production capacity of 113 tons of sugar per grinding season, of which there were 359 (excluding the very small ones); semimechanized, using steam engines, with an average production capacity of 411 tons, of which there were 889; and mechanized, using steam power and more advanced processing technology (including vacuum pans), with an average production capacity of 1,176 tons, of which there were 64. Despite their enormous capacity, the mechanized mills were still responsible for only about 15 percent of total production in the island in 1860. The animal-powered mills produced only 8 percent. It was

[45] Juan Francisco Manzano, an urban slave of the early nineteenth century, vividly depicted in his autobiography the practice of punishing urban slaves by sending them to an *ingenio*, and the terror this inspired. See Edward J. Mullen, ed., *The Life and Poems of a Cuban Slave: Juan Francisco Manzano, 1797-1854* (Hamden, Connecticut: Archon Books, 1981), p. 93.

the semimechanized mills that yielded 77 percent of the marketed sugar crop.[46]

The two departments of Cuba, the Eastern and the Western, differed radically in the level of development of their sugar plantations. The most reliable compilation of data on Cuban sugar in 1860, that of Carlos Rebello, vividly reflects this division. He listed 1,065 *ingenios* located in the Western Department, of which 78 percent were operated by steam power, and 300 in the Eastern Department, of which only 40 percent were steam powered. The average product per mill in the east was 158 tons, reflecting the predominance of small, animal-powered mills. The average product in the west was 459 tons per mill, reflecting the predominance of semimechanized mills, and the presence of some mechanized mills.[47]

The regional differences in sugar production can be seen even more clearly if one divides the island into smaller units. The six provinces of Cuba—Pinar del Río, Havana, Matanzas, Santa Clara, Puerto Príncipe, and Santiago de Cuba—were not formed until 1878. In the 1860s, the island was divided instead into some twenty-nine *jurisdicciones*. For the purposes of analysis, it is possible to regroup these *jurisdicciones* into the later provinces. Tables 4 and 5 show several of the key characteristics of the sugar industry in each of these artificially formed "provinces."[48]

Matanzas, with the highest number of steam-powered mills and

[46] Moreno, *El ingenio* 1: 170-73, tables 1 and 3. The tons are metric tons.

[47] Carlos Rebello, *Estados relativos a la producción azucarera de la isla de Cuba* (Havana, 1860). For a careful examination of this work and its origins, see Moreno, *El ingenio* 1: 170n and 3: 252-53. Rebello includes the later province of Puerto Príncipe in the Eastern Department, while the 1862 census does not.

[48] The major adjustment that needs to be made in order to group the jurisdictions into provinces is the division of the jurisdiction of Güines into two parts, since it was divided in 1878 between the provinces of Havana and Matanzas. (For the 1878 boundaries, see U.S. War Department, *Report on the Census of Cuba. 1899* [Washington, D.C.: Government Printing Office, 1900], pp. 700-702.) This can be approximated by separating the population of the *partido* of Alacranes and adding it to Matanzas, while including the rest of Güines in Havana. Although figures for the slave population of Alacranes are recorded in the 1862 census, those living on *ingenios* are not enumerated separately. The census lists 8,853 slaves in the *partido*, or 35 percent of the slave population of the jurisdiction of Güines. However, Alacranes contained 41 *ingenios*, or 46 percent of the *ingenios* of Güines, so its proportion of the plantation slave population would be expected to be higher than its proportion of the total slave population. If one uses the figure of 46 as the likely percentage of the slaves on *ingenios* in Güines who were located in the district of Alacranes, one arrives at an estimate of 6,751 such slaves in Alacranes. This, then, is the number I have omitted from Havana and included in Matanzas to derive the 1862 provincial estimates of slaves on *ingenios*.

21

TABLE 4
Cuban Sugar Production, 1860 Harvest

Province	Total Product (metric tons)[a]	Caballerías in Cane[b]	No. of Ingenios	Average Product		No. of Steam-Powered Mills	Percent of Mills Steam-Powered	Average No. of Cabs. per Mill	No. of Mills with Vacuum Apparatus
				Per Mill	Per Cab.				
Matanzas	265,644	9,661	442	601	27.5	409	93%	21.9	44
Santa Clara	145,163	5,068	395	368	28.6	235	59%	12.8	10
Havana	38,999	2,537	126	310	15.4	97	77%	20.1	4
Pinar del Río	38,644	1,986	102	379	19.5	88	86%	19.5	7
Santiago de Cuba	31,953	1,093	198	161	29.2	84	42%	5.5	0
Puerto Príncipe	15,434	414	102	151	37.3	36	35%	4.1	1
Total, Cuba	535,857	20,759	1,365	393	25.8	949	70%	15.2	66

SOURCE: Compiled from Carlos Rebello, *Estados relativos a la producción azucarera de la Isla de Cuba. . . .* (Havana: n.p., 1860).
[a] Rebello's figures have been converted at a rate of one metric ton equals 2,204.6 lbs.
[b] One *caballería* equals 33.3 acres.

TABLE 5
Plantation Income and Slaveholdings by Province, 1862

Province	No. of Ingenios[a]	Total Income (thousands of pesos)	Average Income (thousands of pesos)	Slaves on Ingenios	Average No. of Slaves per Ingenio
Matanzas	456	9,632	21	72,689	159
Santa Clara	492	6,384	13	44,106	90
Havana	130	2,120	16	19,404	149
Pinar del Río	97	1,925	20	16,830	174
Santiago de Cuba	239	1,689	7	14,181	59
Puerto Príncipe	117	453	4	5,461	47
Total, Cuba	1,531	22,203	15	172,671	113

SOURCE: Calculated from Cuba, Centro de Estadística, *Noticias estadísticas*, "Registro general de fincas rústicas," and "Distribución." See note 48 for the method of compiling provincial totals from figures for *jurisdicciones*.
[a] At least part of the difference in the number of *ingenios* recorded in 1860 (Table 4) and 1862 is due to a different method of counting, which made small mills more likely to be included in 1862.

the largest number of mills with vacuum apparatus, had the largest total output, the largest average output by far at 601 metric tons per mill, the greatest area planted in cane, and the largest total number of slaves on sugar plantations. Santa Clara was next in total output and in number of mills in 1860, but its substantial number of animal-powered mills lowered both the average output and the average income of its mills. Santa Clara did have the second largest number of slaves on sugar plantations, the second largest area planted in cane, and the second highest total income from sugar.

Turning to the far-western province of Pinar del Río, one finds a sharp drop in total output, number of mills, area planted in cane, and number of slaves in sugar. Pinar del Río was in large measure a tobacco region, and sugar did not command as high a portion of its land or slaves. Those mills that were in Pinar del Río, however, tended to be large—they had an average of 174 slaves each and a substantial average output. Havana shows a similar picture: sugar did not loom so large in its economy (only 23 percent of the province's slaves lived on plantations), nor was the total output anywhere near as large as that of Santa Clara or Matanzas.[49]

Moving east to the provinces of Santiago de Cuba and Puerto Príncipe, one encounters an abrupt decline in average output per mill, reflecting the predominance of smaller, animal-powered mills. The number of slaves per mill was small, fifty-nine in Santiago de Cuba and just forty-seven in Puerto Príncipe, as was the average area planted in cane. The rich soil of the east could produce more cane per unit of land, but the backwardness of the grinding apparatus in eastern mills lowered overall productivity.[50]

The distribution of the island's fully mechanized mills also shows a distinct regional pattern. Matanzas had forty-four, followed by Santa Clara with ten, Pinar del Río with seven, and Havana with four. Just one mechanized mill, located in Puerto Príncipe, operated in the eastern part of the island.[51]

There was thus more than an east-west division of the sugar in-

[49] For the proportion of the province's slaves who lived on *ingenios*, see Cuba, Centro de Estadística, *Noticias estadísticas*, "Distribución."

[50] On the fertility of the soil in the east, see Ramón de la Sagra, *Cuba: 1860. Selección de artículos sobre agricultura cubana* (n.p., 1860; reprint ed., Havana: Comisión Nacional de la UNESCO, 1963), p. 139.

[51] Rebello, *Estados*. My count of mechanized mills differs slightly from that of Moreno, probably as a result of ambiguities in Rebello's text.

dustry in Cuba. Differentiations existed within the two regions as well: the core province of Matanzas with big, steam-powered mills, including the great majority of the mechanized mills on the island; the less evenly developed province of Santa Clara, with a mixture of types of plantation, from animal-powered *trapiches* to fully mechanized mills; the provinces of Havana and Pinar del Río, with far fewer mills but considerable average output due to the small proportion of animal-powered mills and the presence of a few mechanized mills. In the east, such semimechanized production as there was tended to be heavily concentrated in the area around the city of Santiago de Cuba, with most of the region dominated either by estates using animal-powered *trapiches* or by other forms of agriculture.[52]

Virtually all Cuban mills at mid-century were integrated units, combining the growing of cane and the manufacture of sugar from its juice. Work on a sugar plantation involved elements of both field and factory but differed from other forms of agricultural and industrial work. The botanical characteristics of cane and the level of technology employed in the mill largely determined the pace of work. Cane had to be cut when the proportion of sucrose in the juice was highest, and, above all, the juice had to be extracted within 24 to 48 hours to prevent spoilage. Thus planters needed to mobilize large amounts of labor for a specific period of time—the *zafra*—and to coordinate harvesting with the processing of cane. Interruptions in the flow of labor available to cut and haul cane and to provide fuel, or bottlenecks in processing caused by equipment failure, would affect both the total amount of cane that could be cut and the percentage of sucrose extracted. The harvest on Cuban plantations lasted for several months during the winter and early spring and was the period of peak labor demand. During the rest of the year the laborers worked in planting, weeding, cultivation of foodstuffs, and care of animals, as well as tasks of maintenance and construction.[53]

Given this organization of production, planters required a secure supply of labor during the harvest, and needed to maintain and enforce an extraordinarily intense pace of labor in the fields and mills

[52] Ibid., and Cuba, Centro de Estadística, *Noticias estadísticas.*
[53] The best description of both labor and technology in nineteenth-century Cuban mills is in Moreno, *El ingenio*, vols. 1 and 2.

simultaneously. Slavery facilitated meeting these requirements. By tying workers to the workplace, slavery protected planters from the potential competition for labor, wage demands, or even strikes that might result from intense dependence on workers during the harvest. By permitting physical coercion slavery further enabled masters to force workers to perform the demanding tasks required, even at the cost of exhaustion and injury. The intensity of that labor, and the pain it caused, are captured by the words of an elderly slave on the plantation of Anselmo Suárez Romero:

... sleep overcame them, that sleeping they loaded cane, that sleeping they skimmed the cane juice in the evaporators, that sleeping they stopped the cooking of the juice in the pan, that sleeping they beat the sugar in the cooling troughs, that sleeping they carried the molds to the draining table, that sleeping they spread out the bagasse in the mill yard.[54]

The seasonality of sugar production, however, brought planters other problems. Slaves represented an investment of capital and had to be maintained year-round. For reasons of security, they also had to be kept at some kind of work. Any innovation that increased the amount of cane that could be processed per day in the mill, and thus increased the number of cane cutters and loaders needed during the grinding, potentially presented the problem of how to maintain those slaves for the rest of the year. Economically, the addition of free laborers would have offered the advantage that they could be fired after the harvest, assuming that they could somehow provide for their own maintenance during the dead season. But in the 1860s few free laborers willingly worked in cane or submitted to the demands of a slave plantation during the *zafra*.[55] Plantations did rent additional slaves during the harvest which provided a measure of flexibility while leaving the task of maintaining them to their owners.[56]

[54] "Costumbres de Campo," BNC, CC, C.M. Suárez R., tomo 6, no. 3.

[55] Arthur Corwin confidently asserts, as evidence of the growing importance of free laborers in the sugar harvest, that "41,661 whites, most of them peasant Creoles, were employed as cane workers" (Corwin, *Spain and the Abolition of Slavery*, p. 136). This claim, however, is based on a serious misreading of the evidence of the 1862 census. The figure 41,661 is the total number of whites—men, women, and children—*resident* on estates classified in the census as *ingenios*. Included among them were tens of thousands of Chinese contract laborers (classified by the census as white), as well as planters, administrators, artisans, bookkeepers, doctors, technicians, tenants and their familes, and some wage workers. The figure thus in no way represents the number of free wage laborers engaged in cutting cane. See Cuba, Centro de Estadística, *Noticias estadísticas*, "Distribución."

[56] In his description of the *ingenio* San Martín, Ramón de la Sagra mentions that

A number of nineteenth-century writers, as well as several modern scholars, have argued that slavery was incompatible with a further characteristic of Cuban sugar production: the need to adopt more advanced technology in the face of competition from beet sugar.[57] In its simplest form, the argument held that slaves were incapable of dealing with complex machinery. The original expression of this belief was distinctly tinged with racism; its modern counterpart is based on the notion that only free labor is compatible with mechanization. Either this is taken as an a priori principle or it is justified in terms of the low level of education, training, and motivation of individuals held in bondage. The argument obviously has a certain logic. Slaves might be expected to labor with indifference, or even engage in sabotage, thus impeding advances in productivity.

The argument nonetheless has several weaknesses. There is abundant evidence from other slave societies that slaves could work in mills, factories, and mines, as well as fields, in both pre-industrial and industrial settings. The possibility that slaves might sabotage the means of production did not prevent masters from employing them with expensive equipment. Indeed, one North American railroad promoter singled out as an advantage of slave labor the fact that it was "not liable to strikes & riots & the consequent of tearing up rail & burning depots & bridges." In the Tredegar Iron Works in Richmond, Virginia, slaves were employed along with expensive technicians "in order to increase competitiveness." The initial point is not whether slaves were better or worse suited for such labor than free workers; the point is that they were not, simply by virtue of being slaves, strictly incompatible with it.[58]

The division of labor within sugar plantations also challenges the rigid association of slave labor with unskilled labor. In early colonial Brazil, slaves were used in preference to free Indian workers in the skilled aspects of sugar working; they were permanent workers

---

the *dotación* consisted of 435 slaves, 127 "blacks rented during the harvest," and 348 Chinese. See his *Cuba: 1860*, p. 117.

[57] A strong exponent of this view was Ramón de la Sagra. See his *Cuba: 1860*. The argument was echoed by Francisco de Armas y Céspedes in his *De la esclavitud en Cuba* (Madrid: Establecimiento tipográfico de T. Fortanet, 1866). Its most notable modern proponent is Manuel Moreno Fraginals (see note 4 above). See also Knight, *Slave Society*, p. 182.

[58] Robert S. Starobin, *Industrial Slavery in the Old South* (New York: Oxford University Press, 1970), pp. 177-78. See also David Brion Davis, *Slavery and Human Progress* (New York: Oxford University Press, 1984), pp. 31-32, 326-27.

whose training was a worthwhile investment.[59] In Puerto Rico after emancipation, former slaves apparently worked in the boiling-houses and took the skilled job of ditching for irrigation, because they had been trained to these under slavery.[60] In Louisiana, as in Cuba, vacuum pans for sugar processing were introduced under slavery. One planter reported himself highly pleased with the Rillieux double vacuum pan, noting that "the apparatus is very easily managed" and that "my negroes became acquainted with it in a short time." By the 1861 grinding season, seventy Louisiana plantations were using vacuum pans.[61]

There are, in effect, two doubtful elements to the claim of a "contradiction" between slavery and technology. One is the notion that slaves could not or would not acquire the skills necessary to handle machinery. This is challenged by the evidence. The second is the idea that all mechanization requires an overall increase in the skill level of the work force, something thought possible only with a free work force. This is neither theoretically convincing nor empirically correct. Indeed, one development economist, Albert Hirschman, though not directly addressing the question of slavery, has argued persuasively that certain "process-centered" industries, which are often capital-intensive, are particularly suited to a labor force lacking in prior industrial experience. In such industries many of the operations are machine-paced, thereby reducing variation in productivity, despite variations in experience and motivation. He cites sugar as an example.[62] Keith Aufhauser has also argued that it is a mistake to assume that technological advance necessarily requires

[59] See Stuart B. Schwartz, "Indian Labor and New World Plantations: European Demands and Indian Responses in Northeastern Brazil," *American Historical Review*, 83 (Feb. 1978): 43-79.

[60] A British consular official in Puerto Rico in 1875 also observed that "in the process of sugar-making, the more skilled 'liberto' (i.e., freed slave) is generally employed within the boiling-house, while the free labourer does the regular tasks of cutting and carrying the cane." Quoted by Sidney Mintz in Julian H. Steward et al., *The People of Puerto Rico* (Urbana: University of Illinois Press, 1956), p. 344. On *libertos* as ditchers, see Mintz, *Caribbean Transformations*, p. 114. The relative skill requirements of ditching and cane cutting depended in part on the presence or absence of complex drainage and irrigation systems, far more common in Puerto Rico. See also Andrés A. Ramos Mattei, ed., *Azúcar y esclavitud* (San Juan: Universidad de Puerto Rico, 1982).

[61] J. Carlyle Sitterson, *Sugar Country: The Cane Sugar Industry in the South, 1753-1950* (Lexington: University of Kentucky Press, 1953), pp. 149, 154.

[62] Albert O. Hirschman, *The Strategy of Economic Development* (New Haven: Yale University Press, 1958), chap. 8.

that workers be legally free or that the work force on balance be more highly skilled. Under capitalist industrialization, the division of labor may take the form of a separation of work processes into simple, coordinated tasks.[63] Thus like the iron manufacturer who combined a small number of free artisans with a large number of slaves to reduce costs, a sugar planter could employ a few specialists and many less-skilled workers, slave or free.

This was, in part, the pattern in the mechanized Cuban mills. Fully free workers were a tiny fraction of the total labor force in sugar, even on the most developed plantations, and were generally isolated from the rest of the *dotación*. The presence of salaried mechanics and technicians, along with the traditional administrators and bookkeepers, hardly affected the overall demand for labor and did not significantly undermine the slave plantation regime. It is thus difficult to see how, in an industry such as sugar, the juxtaposition of advanced technology and a subjugated work force can be seen as, in itself, contradictory and bound to lead to crisis, though one might argue that slavery's effects on the larger society would block economic development in a wider sense.[64]

Acknowledging that free white sugar workers were scarce, even on the most advanced plantations, several authors suggest that the key to mechanization lay instead in the Chinese, legally free men brought to Cuba under contract. Arguing that "the highly mechanized plantations were filled with Chinese," Manuel Moreno Fraginals asserts that the Chinese worker "permitted the initiation of the process of industrialization in sugar."[65]

[63] See R. Keith Aufhauser, "Slavery and Technological Change," *The Journal of Economic History* 34 (March 1974): 34-50, and the comment by Heywood Fleisig in the same issue, pp. 79-83.

[64] There are numerous ways, both Marxist and non-Marxist, to construe the argument concerning "internal contradictions." Eugene Genovese and Keith Hart have suggested, in personal communications, directions in which one might develop alternate forms of an internal contradiction argument. Genovese points to problems of entrepreneurship, capital accumulation, and market development under slavery; Hart points to the effects of slavery on the rate of circulation of capital. While I am not convinced that either of these formulations can save the internal contradiction thesis, I will not attempt specifically to refute them, since they have not yet been worked out in sufficient detail with reference to the Cuban case. Moreover, what is at issue here is not whether one can show an incompatibility between slavery and certain forms of capitalist economic development, but whether one can establish the existence of mechanisms by which such an incompatibility actually produces a thrust toward the abolition of slavery in a particular society.

[65] Moreno, *El ingenio* 1: 308-309. On this point, Moreno echoes the nineteenth-century observer Ramón de la Sagra.

TABLE 6
Chinese Workers' Contracts Sold in the Port of Havana, 1848-1874

Year	Number	Year	Number	Year	Number
1848	571	1860	6,193	1868	7,368
1853	4,307	1861	6,973	1869	5,660
1854	1,711	1862	344	1870	1,227
1855	2,985	1863	952	1871	1,448
1856	4,968	1864	2,153	1872	8,160
1857	8,547	1865	6,400	1873	5,093
1858	13,385	1866	12,391	1874	2,490
1859	7,204	1867	14,263		
				Total	124,813[a]

SOURCE: J. Pérez de la Riva, *El barracón y otros ensayos* (Havana: Editorial de Ciencias Sociales, 1975), p. 471.

[a] This is the total given in the Pérez de la Riva volume. It may reflect a minor typographical error; the total of the annual figures given is actually 124,793.

The importance of Chinese labor in the survival and development of the Cuban sugar industry is undeniable, but the reasons for its significance are complex. Some 125,000 Chinese workers were brought to Cuba between 1847 and 1874, delaying the crisis in labor supply that would otherwise have accompanied the attenuation of the slave trade (see Table 6). Many were indentured by force or deceit and shipped to an unanticipated fate in Cuba. Once landed, they were offered for sale as though they were slaves, although technically it was their contracts that were sold. The majority were taken to sugar plantations where they were housed in huts or barracks, fed on maize, plantains, and dried beef or fish, organized into gangs, and sent to work under armed drivers in the fields and mills. Despite an 1854 prohibition of corporal punishment, the Chinese were whipped. Although their contracts were for eight years, they were at times obliged to recontract upon expiration or leave the country at their own expense.[66]

[66] See Juan Pérez de la Riva, "Demografía de los culíes chinos en Cuba (1853-1874)," and "La situación legal del culí en Cuba," in his *El barracón y otros ensayos*, pp. 469-507, 209-45. For information on treatment of the Chinese, see the remarkable volume, China, Tsung li ko kuo shih wu ya mên, *Report of the Commission Sent by China to Ascertain the Condition of Chinese Coolies in Cuba* (Shanghai: Imperial Maritime Customs Press, 1876; reprint ed., Taipei: C'eng Wen Publishing Company, 1970). A major recent study of the Chinese in Cuba is Denise Helly, *Idéologie et ethnicité. Les Chinois Macao à Cuba: 1847-1886* (Montreal: Les Presses de l'Université de Montréal, 1979). The text of the 1849 regulations, which permitted whipping, and that of the 1854 ruling, which did not, may be found in Juan Jiménez

29

Held under guard and treated as *cimarrones* if they fled, the Chinese can hardly be said to have been voluntarily selling their labor power, even when they received the stipulated wage. In their "contracts" they formally relinquished the right to bargain or to protest their wages, acknowledged to be far lower than those of free workers or rented slaves. They were allowed to own property and to work on it on their own time, but were not to leave the master's land without written permission. The 1854 regulations permitted them to purchase back the remainder of their contract at any time— though only if they also compensated the master for the original purchase price, for any value added since purchase, for all lost time, and for his inconvenience in finding a replacement. Furthermore, no such redemption could be made during the time of the harvest.[67] The limited civil rights of the Chinese were thus compromised by their obligation to labor on the estate. They were debt peons of a sort, but debt peons always at risk of being reduced to the status of those alongside whom they worked: slaves.

From the point of view of the plantation, such indentured workers were similar to slaves in another respect as well: the purchase of long-term contracts for several hundred pesos made their labor to a large extent a form of fixed capital, not variable capital. The employer paid much of the cost of their work before that work was performed. Indentured workers could not be laid off in dead season; they had to be fed whether they worked or not; the investment in their contracts had to be amortized over a number of years.

One former importer of indentured Chinese, transformed into a promoter of free Chinese immigration when the trade came under attack, calculated in 1874 the costs of different forms of Chinese labor. Although his totals may have been faulty, the proportions of different expenditures for an indentured worker are striking (see Table 7). Only a small part of the cost of Chinese contract labor was taken up in money wages. It was an odd form of "wage labor" indeed in which the worker had almost the same effective legal status as a slave, and in which twice as much was spent on the purchase of

---

Pastrana, *Los chinos en las luchas por la liberación cubana (1847-1930)* (Havana: Instituto de Historia, 1963), pp. 127-40.

[67] See the 1854 rulings in Jiménez Pastrana, *Los chinos*, pp. 130-40, and Pérez de la Riva, "La situación legal." Pérez del la Riva sees the situation of the coolies as virtually equivalent to that of slaves.

TABLE 7
Estimated Costs of Indentured and Free Chinese Labor, 1874

INDENTURE	
Cost of one "coolie" under contract for 8 years	$ 400
Interest on capital invested for 8 years at 12%	384
Wages for 8 years at $4 per month	384
Maintenance for 8 years at $15 per month	1,440
Total	$2,608
FREE LABOR	
Wages for 8 years at 35 cents per day	$1,008
Maintenance for 8 years at $15 per month	1,440
Total	$2,448

SOURCE: Duvon C. Corbitt, *A Study of the Chinese in Cuba, 1847-1947* (Wilmore, Ky.: Asbury College, 1971), p. 23.

his contract and on foregone interest on that investment as was paid in wages.[68] Of course, maintenance and foregone interest were part of the real wage cost. The point here is that, like slavery, the employment of Chinese indentured laborers involved fixed investment and fixed maintenance costs.

Under the circumstances, it is difficult to see in what way the economic motivations of planter and Chinese contract laborer, in their work relations, would have been substantially different from those of master and slave. If they were not substantially different, this casts additional doubt on the idea that juridically "free" workers—in this case the Chinese—were essential to mechanization. Indeed, many of the Chinese were not employed with machinery at all but were used as agricultural workers, performing precisely the same tasks as slaves. The text of an 1868 letter from the agent of an importer to a prospective buyer is revealing. The agent reported the arrival of a "superior" group of Asians: "young, and above all purely agricultural, which is precisely what is needed in the island, to be able to dedicate them immediately to the common labor of the *ingenios*."[69]

This is not to deny that indentured laborers stood, to some extent, in an intermediate position in the labor hierarchy and were on oc-

[68] Francisco Abellá, *Proyecto de emigración libre china dirigido a los Sres Hacendados de la Isla de Cuba.* Quoted in Duvon C. Corbitt, *A Study of the Chinese in Cuba, 1847-1947* (Wilmore, Kentucky: Asbury College, 1971), p. 23.
[69] ANC, Fondo Valle, Esclavos, tomo II (tomo 2-J), leg. 1, doc. 18a.

31

casion perceived as especially suited for work with machinery. Once this perception existed—whether owing to racism or to belief that they really were "free workers"—then masters might take steps to change the circumstances of the Chinese in ways that made them likely to behave differently. Some provided them with better food, and then employed them in selected tasks.[70] A few saw it as in their interest to treat indentured Chinese as an entirely separate category of workers. Juan Bautista Fernández, who had taken over the Candelaria plantation when it had only a few slaves and free black workers, decided to introduce entirely Chinese labor and arranged to contract forty-seven coolies. By the time the plantation was visited by Ramón de la Sagra in 1857, it was operating without a white overseer or white sugar master. La Sagra was impressed by the ability of the Chinese laborers who worked in the fields and in the *batey* (mill yard), and also did the masonry, carpentry, locksmithing, repairing of the mill, building of the wagons, etc. According to La Sagra, the master used no physical punishment, paid the Chinese more than was stipulated in their contracts, and behaved toward them with "strict justice." He also, however, took great pains to prevent their communication with people outside the plantation, in order not to undermine "discipline." Though the example encouraged Sagra's enthusiasm about Chinese labor, it can hardly be considered representative. Candelaria was a relatively small mill, producing just seventy *bocoyes* of sugar, and was obviously run by an unusual and experimental master.[71] The slaveholding owners of huge, mechanized mills, like Julián Zulueta and Tomás Terry, showed no inclination to operate this way.[72]

In theory, planters could have treated the Chinese as free wage workers operating under long-term contracts. Instead, most treated them as virtual slaves. Nor was it only the most backward planters

[70] Juan Pérez de la Riva, "Duvergier de Hauranne: un joven francés visita el ingenio Las Cañas en 1865," *Revista de la Biblioteca Nacional José Martí* 56 (Oct.-Dec. 1965): 85-114.

[71] Ramón de la Sagra, *Historia física, económico-política, intelectual y moral de la isla de Cuba* (Paris: Hachette, 1861), pp. 149-50.

[72] When Tomás Terry had difficulties with runaway Chinese, his innovative response was to photograph them all for easier identification and capture. See *El Sagua* (June 9, 1872). Zulueta was involved both in the slave trade and in the importation of coolies. Their plantations, as late as 1877, contained primarily slave laborers. See Chapter IV, below.

who made this choice.[73] When, in 1873, a Commission of Enquiry was sent by China to determine the condition of the Chinese in Cuba, it investigated, among others, some of the most technologically advanced mills in Cuba: Las Cañas, España, Flor de Cuba. The resulting report painted an unrelenting portrait of whippings, suicides, labor in chains, withheld stipends, unpaid labor on public works, and forced recontracting. Though the investigators had been obliged to gather testimony under the eyes of overseers and administrators, they catalogued endless abuses. The picture was one of forced labor, not free.[74]

An examination of the *treatment* of Chinese contract laborers by planters, however, does not tell the whole story of their situation. Equally striking as the reports of abuses are the accounts of protests and complaints by the Chinese workers themselves. It is clear from the commission report that these indentured laborers were aware of a distinction between slave labor and free, one which they felt was not being observed. Many believed that they were being treated as slaves by an incomparably barbarous group of foreigners who refused to recognize them as free men. Incredulous and indignant, some indentured Chinese took violent actions to try to end their mistreatment:

We stabbed to death the administrator, on account of his cruelty. We, 24 in all, proceeded to the jail and surrendered ourselves. Our master, by an outlay of $680, induced the officials to order 12 of our number to return to the plantation, and on our refusal, an officer of low rank discharged fire-arms, wounding nine and killing two. There are 22 still in jail, and we consider it preferable to the plantation.[75]

Others persistently appealed for their own rights under law:

My master owed me $108, and when I complained to the official I was brought back and again forced to labor for five months, still receiving no money. As he stated that, as a punishment for my bringing a charge against him, he would sell me to a sugar plantation, I and two others proceeded to Havana in order to renew the complaint, and were there placed in confinement in the depot, where I have now worked without wages during seven

---

[73] Moreno argues that in the advanced mills the Chinese were effectively wage workers and implies that only on estates still using the Jamaica train were they treated as slaves. *El ingenio* 1: 308-309.
[74] China, *Report of the Commission.*
[75] Ibid., p. 58.

or eight years. My master has never been called upon to reply to my accusation.[76]

First-hand accounts of the Chinese as plantation workers reveal a complex process whereby angry, hungry, mistreated immigrants were cowed into relative submission through physical violence and forms of cultural violence such as the cutting of their queues.[77] One contemporary observer, on whose plantation Chinese contract laborers were employed in the 1860s, wrote of them:

They were orderly and cleanly; the poorest, lowest, coolie carried his contract on his person, and never hesitated to assert his rights, but sometimes had to be reminded that the planter also had rights; and it generally happened that each new lot arriving on a plantation had to be interviewed by the captain of the *partido* two or three times, to reduce them to a proper regard for the discipline of a well-managed estate.[78]

She described one such "interview," which followed an uprising of the Chinese on her estate. The captain preceded his public reading of their contracts with blows from his sword and followed it by ordering his soldiers to cut off all the queues of the Chinese. "How quickly they wilted! How cowed they looked!"[79]

Once the relations of power were established, some of the Chinese did become precise and methodical workers, thus gaining a reputation for ability with machinery. Ramón de la Sagra, a great enthusiast of Chinese labor, referred to the "identification of the intelligent labor of the Chinese with the constant regularity of the industrial operations submitted to the incessant stroke of the piston," and waxed lyrical about the sight of double lines of Chinese workers at La Ponina, "rapid in their movements as a transmission belt, operating the filling of the molds with the mathematical regularity of a pendulum."[80] This behavior, however, seems to have had as much to do with the cultural background of the Chinese and their self-conception as with the fact that they were to be paid a four-peso-a-month wage. That some of the Chinese became efficient

[76] Ibid., p. 24.
[77] See ibid., and Eliza McHatton Ripley, *From Flag to Flag: A Woman's Adventures and Experiences in the South during the War, in Mexico, and in Cuba* (New York: D. Appleton and Co., 1889). Eliza Ripley was the wife of a Louisiana planter who moved to Cuba after the fall of the Confederacy. They bought and operated the plantation Desengaño in Matanzas.
[78] Ripley, *From Flag to Flag*, p. 177.
[79] Ibid., pp. 174-75.
[80] Sagra, *Cuba: 1860*, p. 34.

workers is testimony to their own sense of order and hope for full freedom, combined with the effects of coercion; it was not inherent in their fictitious intermediate legal status, which often allowed them to be systematically reduced to virtual slavery. It would thus be misleading to place great weight on their formal status as wage laborers in an explanation of how they could help plantations mechanize.

It can be argued that slave labor was incompatible with technological development for reasons other than the motivational structure and behavior of slaves. Slavery required substantial fixed investment in labor, tying up resources that could otherwise have been used to purchase necessary machinery and the land on which to grow the cane to supply the new machinery. Thus, so the argument would go, development was inhibited, competitiveness reduced, and profitability decreased. Some support for this argument can be found in evidence of the indebtedness of many planters. The issue, however, is a complex one. Certain forms of indebtedness might be expected to rise during a period of expansion, without necessarily signaling the unprofitability of the enterprises involved. Indeed, investment in slaves, while tying up capital, also created the basis on which one could obtain credit for further investment.[81] However large the mortgages of individual planters, total production did increase from about 428,800 tons in 1860 to 718,700 tons by 1869.[82] (See Table 8.) Clearly capital was being invested to increase output, despite the high cost of slaves. In fact, the high cost of slaves in itself suggests that there was still money to be made in slave-based sugar production, for demand for slaves might be expected to fall, depressing prices, if there were not.[83]

[81] On planters' debts, see Knight, *Slave Society*, pp. 119-20. Moreno cites a figure of 95 percent of all sugar plantations mortgaged in 1863, but adds that many of these debts were paid off during and after the Ten Years' War. See Moreno, "Plantaciones en el Caribe," pp. 75-76. The issue of mortgages is a difficult one, since some involved short-term credit arrangements and should not be seen as evidence of unprofitability.

[82] Moreno, *El ingenio* 3: 37.

[83] Government estimates of the average cost of slaves in 1860, 1861, and 1862 yielded figures ranging from $510 to $836. The average for the 9,495 slaves whose prices in voluntary sales were recorded over the period was $555; that of the 204 slaves sold at auction was $736. The compilers considered the second figure more reliable. See Estado que demuestra el número de esclavos vendidos, May 8, 1863, AHN, Ultramar, leg. 3547. The estimates of slave prices given by Hubert Aimes vary widely—he cites figures for newly imported slaves of $1,000 in 1861, $600 in 1862, and $700-$750 in 1864, and $1,000 for acculturated slaves in 1864. Aimes, *History of Slavery*, p. 268. Roland Ely records average figures of $700 and $1,000 per slave

TABLE 8
Cuban Sugar Production, 1840-1870

Year	Metric Tons	Year	Metric Tons	Year	Metric Tons
1840	161,248	1850	294,952	1861	533,800
1841	169,886	1851	365,843	1862	454,758
1842	192,769	1852	329,905	1863	445,693
1843	182,081	1853	391,247	1864	525,372
1844	208,506	1854	397,713	1865	547,364
1845	98,437	1855	462,968	1866	535,641
1846	205,608	1856	416,141	1867	585,814[a]
1847	267,474	1857	436,030	1868	720,250
1848	260,463	1858	426,274	1869	718,745
1849	239,128	1859	469,263	1870	702,974
		1860	428,769		

SOURCE: Manuel Moreno Fraginals, *El ingenio: complejo económico social cubano del azúcar*, 3 vols. (Havana: Editorial de Ciencias Sociales, 1978), 3: 36, 37.
[a] Typographical error in source corrected.

The question of the actual level of profitability of Cuban estates is an exceptionally complex one. Surviving documents rarely permit the direct calculation of rates of return. Furthermore, the notion of an "average" profitability of Cuban estates is deceptive. The wide range in size, output, and degree of capital investment carried with it a similar range of profitability. Juan Poey, himself a modernizing planter, estimated that 1200 of Cuba's 1500 plantations yielded around 4 percent on their capital, including only the proceeds from dry sugar, and excluding molasses and other byproducts. The remaining 300 yielded a return of 6 to 8.5 percent on capital, though about half of those were so indebted and mortgaged that much of the benefit went elsewhere. Those with the largest amount of capital, he believed, were getting the highest rate of return.[84] Poey's precise figures may well have been underestimates, since he was lobbying for changes in Spain's tariff policy to favor Cuban planters. They nonetheless reflect the great gap between the economic situation of the larger estates and that of the small.

paid by Tomás Terry in 1859, and $1,200 in 1868. Roland T. Ely, *Comerciantes cubanos del siglo xix* (Bogotá: Aedita Editores, 1961), pp. 121-22, n. 322. Moreno, Klein, and Engerman find prices for prime-age Creole males rising sharply between 1856 and 1859, from 668 pesos to 1,271. Prices then drop somewhat to 914 pesos in 1863, a level still well above that of 1856. See Moreno, Klein, and Engerman, "The Level and Structure of Slave Prices," p. 1207.

[84] Poey is cited by A. Gallenga in *The Pearl of the Antilles* (London: Chapman and Hall, 1873), p. 125.

It is not possible on the basis of Cuban evidence to make a direct empirical comparison between the profitability of slave labor and free. Some free smallholders and tenants cultivated cane and sold it to *ingenios* for grinding; some Chinese worked in sugar-houses on estates where slaves cut cane; but exclusively free labor was not used on the island in the 1860s for the entire process of sugar production, except in a few instances in the eastern region on such a small scale as to be incomparable with the major slave plantations of the western districts. The field was thus open to totally opposed claims. Ramón de la Sagra insisted that free labor would in the end yield greater profits; the reformist Francisco de Armas agreed in theory but opposed any substantive steps toward prompt abolition; the planter Julián Zulueta argued for heavy mechanization using both slave and Chinese labor; while the Conde de Pozos Dulces argued for concentration on the agricultural sector.[85]

Whatever the theoretical economic advantages and disadvantages of slave labor for the planter, as a practical matter it had long seemed the only option and had allowed for substantial growth.[86] That this growth was unbalanced and dependent goes almost without saying. Like many other plantation societies, Cuba was providing an agricultural export commodity, largely for processing elsewhere. United States tariff legislation aggravated this tendency by penalizing the sugar with the highest sucrose content, which was ready for direct consumption, and giving preference to that with the lowest, which needed further refining in North American refineries.[87] Determining the role of slavery as such in this "backwardness," however, remains problematic. And planters actually willing to contemplate abolition as an alternative were few and far between.

As the decade of the 1860s advanced, however, internal and external events posed direct challenges to the continued coexistence in Cuba of sugar, slavery, and colonialism. The transatlantic slave trade came under increasingly effective attack as Union policy dur-

[85] Sagra, *Cuba: 1860;* Francisco de Armas y Céspedes, *De la esclavitud en Cuba;* Zulueta's approach is described in Gallenga, *Pearl,* pp. 97-98; on the Conde de Pozos Dulces see Moreno, *El ingenio* 2:201-204 and 3: 216-17.

[86] The general trend of production is upward throughout the sixties and early seventies. See Moreno, *El ingenio* 3: 37. (The one apparent exception in Moreno's table—a total of 285,814 tons in 1867—appears to be a typographical error. The figure should be 585,814 tons.)

[87] Ibid., 2: 194-95.

ing the Civil War challenged the use of U.S. ships in the trade and Britain adopted a more aggressive strategy of suppression by blockading areas of supply on the West African coast and stepping up patrols around Cuba. Though tens of thousands of slaves were imported each year in the late 1850s and in the early years of the 1860s, the numbers rapidly fell in 1863 and 1864, and reached zero by 1867[88] (See Table 2).

The abolition of slavery in the United States affected not only the slave trade to Cuba but also the long-range prospects of the institution within the island. Cuba's main trading partner had now abolished slavery, eliminating the lingering hope of some planters that Cuba might be annexed to the United States as a slave state. Furthermore, both slaveholders and officials feared—with some justification—that the example of the United States might lead to a disruption of the internal order of Cuban slavery. The refrain of a song reported to have been sung in the fields of Cuba went:

> Avanza, Lincoln, avanza.
> Tú eres nuestra esperanza.[89]
>
> Advance, Lincoln, advance.
> You are our hope.

The captain general in 1866 expressed apprehension that the outcome of the American Civil War could contribute to a "slackening of the links of obedience and respect which the coloured race should entertain for the white and on which the tranquillity of this territory largely depends."[90]

One short-term response to these difficulties was to tighten discipline. Verena Martínez-Alier has documented the imposition of an increasingly segregationist policy in the mid-1860s, including the denial of permissions for interracial marriage between 1864 and the mid-1870s.[91] Such repression of free persons of color might help to avoid social disruption that could threaten slavery, but the only possible long-run solution was to find additional sources of labor and alternative forms of organization.

The issue of the future of slavery had long been inextricably tied

[88] Murray, *Odious Commerce*, chap. 14 and figures on p. 244.
[89] I would like to thank Rogelio Martínez-Furé for this reference, from his forthcoming collection of Afro-Cuban music.
[90] Quoted in Martínez-Alier, *Marriage*, p. 31.
[91] Ibid., p. 32.

to the question of the maintenance of Spanish power. For decades the fear of loss of planter support and thus of domination over Cuba had made Spain unwilling even to take steps against the slave trade. But now some Cuban reformists were themselves looking to free labor as the long-run hope of the island. This position was part, however, of a broader criticism of Cuba's economic relationship with Spain, and particularly of high duties and taxes. Such reformists were generally committed to economic progress, primarily through white immigration, but they were circumspect on the question of slavery. Some agreed with Ramón de la Sagra on the virtues of free labor; some also viewed the abolition of slavery as linked to the question of political reform, believing that "while slavery exists there will be no government established here in which they can have a voice; that the island will continue to be governed by a repressive, censorious system, under pretext of preserving order."[92]

When in 1866 the Spanish government called together a meeting, including delegates from the colonies, to discuss colonial political and social reforms, the debate on slavery was moved into the open. The delegation from Puerto Rico, where slaves were considerably less numerous than in Cuba, forced the question onto the agenda by calling for abolition in their province as a precondition for other reforms. The response of the Cuban delegates revealed the ambiguities of their reformism.[93] In theory, they believed in the eventual extinction of slavery, and in theory they also believed in the superiority of free labor. But they insisted that, for the moment, slavery had to be sustained in order to prevent the collapse of the sugar industry. Cuban reformers did support—as Spain now did—repression of the slave trade, for the contraband trade appeared to them as a weapon of Spanish merchants against Cuban planters, and the influx of Africans seemed a threat to the racial balance of the island. (Ironically, though, some of these same reformers continued to purchase contraband slaves at the same time they called for an end to

[92] For a discussion of reformist ideology, see Raúl Cepero Bonilla, *Azúcar y abolición* (Havana: Editorial Cenit, 1948, reprint ed., Barcelona: Editorial Crítica, 1976), chap. 7. The quotation cited is from "a Cuban gentleman of conservative opinions," describing the views of "the more intelligent of the Cubans, including a small number of slaveholders." It appears in Hall to Seward, Matanzas, November 18, 1868, in U.S. Department of State, *Correspondence between the Department of State and the United States Minister at Madrid. . . .* (Washington, D.C.: Government Printing Office, 1870), p. 71.

[93] See Corwin, *Spain and the Abolition of Slavery*, pp. 140-42.

the traffic.)[94] On slavery itself, the furthest they could go was to support a very "gradual" emancipation.

In pursuit of formulas for gradual abolition, delegates to the reform commission made suggestions that would later turn up in Spanish legislation: the freeing of all children born to slaves, the freeing of slaves over age sixty, lotteries for the purchase of freedom, tutelage for those freed, and so on.[95] All were efforts to move slowly and symbolically toward the extinction of slavery without disrupting the social order of the plantation or the supply of labor.

The concept of "gradual abolition" had special connotations. It was seen not as an alternative to the indefinite preservation of the by now beleaguered institution, but rather as a means of *avoiding* immediate emancipation. Adherence to gradual abolition thus reflected both a strategic acceptance of an eventual transition to free labor and a tactic to delay that transition. Like elimination of the slave trade, it was a step intended to show that Cubans were "not opposed to gradual extinction" of slavery, for "in this way we will calm the execration and hate of the abolitionist centers of Europe."[96]

But even such modest proposals for the ending of slavery were not to be accepted. Once the commission meetings were over, it became apparent that there was extensive opposition within Cuba to any steps toward emancipation. The majority of Cuban planters shied away from drastic changes in the labor system and took a position quite consistent with their immediate self-interest: the maintenance of slavery and the social structure supporting it, continued protection of their "property" by Spain, and avoidance of the "cuestión social." Most preferred not to see the issue raised at all.[97]

The Spanish government was reluctant to risk alienating such planters, did not wish to face the loss of revenues from Cuba that might result from disruption of the sugar industry, and could not

[94] There is no way to explain the ethnic composition of the slave population on Tomás Terry's plantation Caracas other than to assume that he acquired contraband slaves in the 1850s, 1860s, and possibly 1870s. See Chap. IV, below.

[95] See Corwin, *Spain and the Abolition of Slavery*, chap. 11.

[96] Angulo de Heredia, speaking in 1866 on the suppression of the slave trade, quoted in Corwin, ibid., pp. 196-97. For a more generous interpretation of reformist views on slavery, see Elías José Entralgo, *La liberación étnica cubana* (Havana: Universidad de la Habana, 1953).

[97] See Knight, *Slave Society*, chap. 7; Corwin, *Spain and the Abolition of Slavery*, chap. 8; and Cepero Bonilla, *Azúcar y abolición*, chaps. 7, 10, and 13, for further discussion of planter attitudes.

afford any scheme of compensation for slave property. The commission proposals on slavery remained a dead letter.

The apparent failure of the Cuban delegates to the reform commission to secure major reforms in the political and economic spheres was even more resounding. The commission report had asked for extensive tax and administrative reform, elimination of customs duties on imports, representation in the Cortes, and application of the rights of the Spanish Constitution to the residents of Cuba and Puerto Rico. None of these was granted. While lifting some customs and tax burdens placed on Cuba by colonial legislation, the Spanish government imposed a new direct tax on income in the Antilles.[98]

The new taxes combined with long-standing feelings of nationalism to strengthen overt opposition to Spanish rule among certain landholders, small-scale planters, and professionals in the eastern part of the island. Though the continued maintenance of slavery was not the major grievance of most of those opposing Spain, the issue would soon become entangled with the struggle against colonialism in the insurrection known as the Ten Years' War.

[98] See Corwin, *Spain and the Abolition of Slavery*, chap. 11, and Knight, *Slave Society*, chap. 8. Ramiro Guerra argues that the changes in taxation were on balance favorable to Cuban producers, and he thus sees the charge of utter failure on the part of the reformists as unwarranted. In his view, major blame for increasing tensions rested on Spanish intransigence and on the financial crisis of 1867. See Ramiro Guerra y Sánchez, *Manual de Historia de Cuba.* 2nd edition (Havana: Consejo Nacional de Cultura, 1962), pp. 658-61.

PART ONE

Conflict, Adaptation, and Challenge, 1868-1879

II

Insurrection and Slavery

In reply to your letter of the 12th of this month we
must tell you that we believe you have misinterpreted
this Assembly's circular concerning the freedom of the
slaves, which you so erroneously characterized as null
and void. What this decree says is that all those citizens
who are slaves now cease to be such; that those fit for
armed service shall increase our ranks, and that those
who are not shall remain on the estates serving the
fatherland with planting, harvesting, and other labors.

—*From the rebel Representative Assembly to Antonio Rodríguez,*
Commander of the rebel 6th Battalion. April 18, 1869.[1]

On October 10, 1868, on the *ingenio* Demajagua in Manzanillo in
eastern Cuba, Carlos Manuel de Céspedes and a group of conspirators
declared themselves in revolt against Spanish rule. Their rebellion
drew upon accumulated grievances against the economic and political policies of the mother country, which were felt by different
sectors in different ways. Creole planters in the eastern region, operating with limited capital resources, had been losing ground as the
sugar industry grew in the western end of the island. The new taxes
imposed by Spain in the 1860s, which may have been particularly
offensive because they were direct rather than indirect, weighed
heavily on small-scale sugar planters, farmers, and shopkeepers.
Eastern intellectuals and professionals had long been developing a
Creole identity, and some had been involved in earlier conspiracies.
Céspedes himself had been exposed to various kinds of liberalism
in Europe and resented the repression of liberties under Spanish
political domination. Black, white, and mulatto *campesinos* also
joined the struggle for reasons that are now difficult to reconstruct,

---

[1] Papeles de Antonio Rodríguez, Colección Fernández Duro, Biblioteca de la Real
Academia de Historia, Madrid (this collection is referred to hereinafter as RAH, FD),
leg. 3.

but that undoubtedly included hostility to Spanish privileges and taxation.[2]

Shared opposition to Spanish colonialism, however, by no means meant unanimity on the aims of the revolt. Some of the insurrectionists favored annexation to the United States, others sought full independence. Many were hostile to the institution of slavery, in part because of their resentment of large-scale western slaveholding planters, in part because aid in the maintenance of slavery was a component of Spain's hold over the island. The leaders of the insurgency, however, initially drew back from full abolition. They wished to avoid alienating potential supporters among slaveholders and to obtain revenues and goods for the war effort from continued agricultural production. At the same time, they sought to take a stand on slavery that would promote the insurrection and increase its popular and international appeal. The rebels thus took partial steps toward formal abolition, while attempting to avoid disruption of the social relations of slavery.

At the beginning of the rebellion, Céspedes called for gradual and indemnified emancipation. His act of freeing his own slaves to fight in the rebellion, though important symbolically, legally represented nothing more radical than the exercise of the right of a master to manumit his slaves. Though the major leaders of the revolt had less of a direct economic investment in slavery than the planters of the west, they nonetheless respected the basic principle of slaveholding, and in November 1868 Céspedes decreed the death penalty for anyone inciting slaves to rebellion. In December, the rebel leadership spelled out their policy: abolition would *follow* the triumph of the revolution. Slaves of planters who had joined the rebellion would not be accepted into the army without their owners' permission. This position was consistent with the old reformist aim of the eventual elimination of slavery, and with the eastern insurgents' desire to court certain western slaveholders.[3]

[2] The pioneering works on the Ten Years' War are Cepero Bonilla, *Azúcar y abolición*, and Ramiro Guerra y Sánchez, *La guerra de los diez años, 1868-1878*, 2 vols. (Havana: Cultural, 1950-1952; reprint ed., Havana: Editorial de Ciencias Sociales, 1972). See also Jorge Ibarra, *Ideología Mambisa* (Havana: Instituto Cubano del Libro, 1972); Knight, *Slave Society*; Hugh Thomas, *Cuba: The Pursuit of Freedom* (New York: Harper and Row, 1971), chaps. 20, 21; Benito Besada Ramos, "Antecedentes económicos de la Guerra de los Diez Años," *Economía y Desarrollo* 13 (Sept.-Oct. 1972): 155-62; and Guerra, *Manual de historia de Cuba*, 2nd ed., chap. 22.

[3] Cepero Bonilla, *Azúcar y abolición*, chap. 11.

As the rebellion spread, this hesitation on the issue of abolition could not be maintained. The rebels of Camagüey (Puerto Príncipe), a cattle-raising area with only a small number of slaves, insisted on stronger steps. In February 1869, the Revolutionary Assembly of the Central Department, rejecting Céspedes's leadership, called for the abolition of slavery, promising future indemnification.[4] Insurgent leaders were becoming increasingly aware of the need for North American support, which, following the ratification of the Thirteenth Amendment and the election of Ulysses S. Grant to the presidency, seemed to be contingent upon an abolitionist stance. When the different rebel groups joined at the Assembly of Guáimaro in April 1869, they drew up a declaration proclaiming that "all inhabitants of the Republic are entirely free." Henceforth all slaves were to be considered *libertos*, freed men and women.[5]

Although the decree was categorical, the subsequent Reglamento de Libertos (regulations relating to freedmen) established the tutelage of *patronos* over their former slaves and thus mitigated its impact. The Reglamento made labor obligatory for *libertos*, who were to be remunerated with a nominal wage of three pesos per month. If *libertos* left their masters, they had to report to a government office that would then allocate them to a new master, whose estate they could not leave without permission. Hours of work were fixed, except in domestic labor. *Patronos* were to give *libertos* land in usufruct to cultivate, on which *libertos* could build *cabañas* for themselves and their families in a location set by the master. Masters were allowed to discipline *libertos*, if necessary, by denying them their days of rest.[6]

This set of regulations stopped far short of converting *libertos* into wage workers or free citizens. They were still under direct government authority and were to be treated quite differently from other inhabitants of the Republic. Céspedes, however, saw even this much freedom as excessive. In May 1869 he approved the provisions of the Reglamento, but wrote: "As long as the war of independence

[4] I have based my discussion of insurgent policy and practice primarily on documents captured by the Spaniards and preserved in the Colección Fernández Duro. The abolition decree from Camagüey can be found in RAH, FD, leg. 6, doc. 79.

[5] See Guerra, *Guerra* 1: 109.

[6] The Reglamento can be found in RAH, FD, leg. 5, doc. 49. It is also reproduced in Hortensia Pichardo, ed., *Documentos para la historia de Cuba*, 2 vols. (Havana: Editorial de Ciencias Sociales, 1977, 1976) 1: 380-82.

continues, there should be no change in the situation of the *libertos*."
He noted that the previous policy had been to enroll some *libertos*
as soldiers, and employ the rest in agriculture, and he argued that
this was still the best policy. It was not yet time, he wrote, for
libertos to hire out their services to new masters, for this would
hurt production. He also doubted that the government could find
employment for all those *libertos* who might abandon, or be abandoned by, their masters. He advised that the Reglamento be passed,
but not applied immediately.[7] The rebel government formally promulgated the Reglamento two months later, in July 1869, though it
is doubtful that it was systematically enforced. It remained in effect
until the end of December 1870, when it was revoked in favor of
full freedom. Thus, as Raúl Cepero Bonilla argued thirty years ago,
the revolution can be said to have been unequivocally abolitionist
only from 1871 onward.[8]

The ambivalence of insurgent leaders was deeply rooted in their
background and their situation. Though abolition was one of the
most stirring battle cries of the insurrection, and full use was eventually made of the issue in rebel propaganda, it was easier to fight
a war if freed slaves were simply distributed to the army and to the
plantations to do their appointed share, without reference to their
own wishes.[9] Upper- and middle-class whites raised in a slaveholding
society, when put in positions of authority, also had a strong tendency to view blacks as manpower rather than as individuals. Groups
of *libertos*, still referred to as *la negrada*, were sent back and forth,
allocated to agriculture or manufacturing, concentrated or dispersed
according to the desires of the leaders of the rebellion.[10] Wartime
exigency and class and cultural prejudices caused insurgent leaders
to view *libertos* as useful but potentially dangerous, and to restrict
their freedom accordingly. Further, the rebel system of provisioning
officers by providing them with *ayudantes*, generally former slaves,

[7] Céspedes to the Cámara de Representantes, May 21, 1869, RAH, FD, leg. 5, doc.
49.

[8] Cepero Bonilla, *Azúcar y abolición*, chap. 12. For a skeptical view on the enforcement of the Reglamento, see Guerra, *Guerra* 1: 109-10.

[9] For examples of rebel propaganda on the theme of abolition, see the handbills "A
Nuestros Hermanos Ausiliares del Gobierno Español," RAH, FD, leg. 6, doc. 23, and
"A los Esclavos del Tirano," in RAH, FD, leg. 6, doc. 18.

[10] The evidence that *libertos* were treated as labor gangs rather than as free individuals is abundant. See for example Quesada to C. Mayor General, Río Seco, June
13, 1869, RAH, FD, leg. 3.

to collect their food and serve them, tended to replicate within the military the old social relationship of master and slave.[11]

Insurgent leaders fell easily into habits of personal command—particularly toward female former slaves—which virtually eliminated any freedom of action a *liberto* might have hoped to acquire. Black women were often perceived as unpaid domestic servants and treated accordingly.[12] General policy was ambiguous about this informal exploitation of female labor. In July 1869 M. Quesada ordered *libertas* to be dispersed among honorable families who would use them in domestic service or "in labors proper to their sex in service of the Republic."[13] The insurgent civil government of Camagüey in November of the same year ordered that all *libertas* should be sent to the civil government rather than being dealt with directly by subprefects, though it did not specify what would be done with them there.[14]

Women posed a further problem, for some of them wished to accompany their husbands, sons, and brothers into military service, while the authorities preferred them to remain where they were. In one case, a freedwoman and her mother insisted on following the troops rather than returning to the plantation. The local official wrote in exasperation that the women alleged "that the decree has declared them free and they resist in virtue of their independence returning to that estate." The logic of the women's position was as apparent as the frustration of the administrator. He advised the estate's owner to appeal to the military court in order to recover the recalcitrant *libertas*.[15]

By 1870 a general policy was spelled out: "All women who have previously worked in agriculture will occupy themselves in agricultural tasks without delay."[16] This ruling did not single out *libertas*, but was clearly intended to apply to them. They were not

---

[11] For a description of *ayudantes*, see O'Kelly, *The Mambi-Land*, p. 261.

[12] One subprefect explained that he needed the services of the *liberta* Pilar because the other *liberta* he had did not know how to wash and iron. J. Agustín Bora to C. Prefecto del partido Porcayo, November 25, 1869, RAH, FD, leg. 2, carpeta 11, doc. 484.

[13] Circular from M. Quesada, RAH, FD, leg. 3, carta no. 890.

[14] Circular from Gob. Civil del Camagüey, November, 1869, RAH, FD, leg. 2, carpeta 11, doc. 462.

[15] ". . . las morenas alegan que el decreto las ha declarado libre y se resisten en virtud de su Independencia a volver a esa finca." Libertos, March 12, 1868, RAH, FD, leg. 2, carpeta 11, doc. 376.

[16] Circular number 567, March 1, 1870, RAH, FD, leg. 6, doc. 46.

to be allowed any choice; they were to serve the revolution by remaining in field work.

Former slaves, however, had ideas of their own on how best to serve the revolution. While it is clear that many rebel officers intended to keep treating *libertos* like slaves, it is equally clear that many *libertos* had no intention of continuing to behave like slaves. Some ended up in the hills, where they formed small communities. James O'Kelly, a journalist who visited Cuba Libre in 1871, described one settlement composed almost entirely of blacks, predominantly women. Life in these communities involved both artisanal activities and cultivation: women spun thread, made hammocks, shoes, sandals, and hats, while men and children hunted and harvested sugar cane and sweet potatoes. O'Kelly was surprised to find that property within the settlement was held privately: "each one is the absolute master of what he gathers, and distributes as seems good to him the result of his labor." The journalist had not expected former slaves to have any concept of ownership, but given the tradition of *conuco* cultivation and the raising of animals, it seems quite explicable.[17] These settlements, though officially administered by rebel prefects, seem to have had a good deal in common with maroon communities, societies of runaway slaves that had long existed in the hills of eastern Cuba.[18]

Insurgent officials were sometimes unsure whether communities of *libertos* should be viewed as necessary support for rebels in the field or as dangerously independent groups of ex-slaves. As early as 1869 insurgent officers had expressed concern about the existence of "encampments of freedwomen" which served as a "focus of desertion for the troops." Quesada ordered commanders to disperse these groups and assign the women to families in the area.[19] As O'Kelly's testimony shows, however, some such settlements survived.

This uncertainty of rebel leaders went beyond a fear of semi-autonomous groups of *libertos* and became a generalized double

[17] O'Kelly, *The Mambi-Land*, p. 184 and chap. 12. These activities may also have owed something to African traditions.

[18] On Cuban *palenques*, see José Luciano Franco, *Los palenques de los negros cimarrones* (Havana: Departamento de Orientación Revolucionaria del Comité Central del Partido Comunista de Cuba, 1973), chap. 4.

[19] M. Quesada al Com^te Militar de ____ (apparently a circular letter), July 31, 1869, RAH, FD, leg. 3, carta no. 890.

standard. An order issued in July 1869 allocated the men of a particular unit: "send the whites to arms and the *libertos* with rare exceptions to agriculture; and as a general rule all the ex-servant citizens should dedicate themselves to this service." They were to be made "to work with industriousness" in the sown fields.[20]

When carried to an extreme, this invidious treatment of former slaves could lead to difficulties. The Assembly, for example, felt called upon to rebuke one officer in the field for provoking complaints by referring to the abolition decree as "null and void" and simply distributing the former slaves as he saw fit.[21] There were also certain drawbacks to moving *libertos* around on the basis of demand for their labor, as Rafael Morales emphasized in a circular issued in March 1870. He noted that many who owned land were hoping to be granted *libertos* to cultivate it. They would have to be told, he explained, that this was not always possible, in part because many *libertos* were in the army, and in part because the only area in Republican territory where they were abundant was Las Villas (Santa Clara). It was inconvenient, impolitic, and unfair, he wrote, to uproot those people from their homes except out of extreme necessity.[22] *Libertos* who were transferred against their will to estates and workshops might be expected to flee if the opportunity arose, as in some cases they did. The administrator of a rebel tannery wrote wearily in January 1870 of the flight of *libertos* and an Asian from his shop. He also expressed concern that the presence in the area of seven *libertos* recently arrived from an *ingenio* would further disrupt his operations.[23]

Insurrectionist policy had been intended to avoid disruption, but in fact it created a series of problems. If *libertos* were legally free, even within the restrictions of the Reglamento de Libertos, they might try to exercise their rights as free people. That is what the free women who wished to accompany their families did; it is what those who fled the estates and workshops did. Furthermore, the effort to effect nominal abolition without any "change in the situ-

[20] Order dated Sta. Catalina, July 12, 1869, RAH, FD, leg. 4, no document number.
[21] Asamblea de Representantes to Antonio Rodríguez, April 18, 1869, Papeles de Antonio Rodríguez, RAH, FD, leg. 3.
[22] Circular de Rafael Morales, Secretario de Estado, Departamento del Interior, al Gobernador de Estado, March 1, 1870, RAH, FD, leg. 6, doc. 46.
[23] Fuga de negros in RAH, FD, leg. 2, carpeta 11, no document number.

ation of the *libertos*" quickly created new conflicts that the authorities were obliged to mediate.

Some *libertos* chose to view revolutionary prefects as their potential defenders and, when they were mistreated, appealed to the prefects for justice. In doing so, they brought conflict with their masters into the open. The prefect might be unsympathetic, but raising the issue could be disruptive all the same. The action called masters before a third party to answer for their behavior toward *libertos*, something no former slaveowner was likely to view with equanimity.

The case of the *liberta* Rosa illustrates the dynamics of the situation. She fled her master, Francisco Socarrás, and appealed to the prefect and to the military court for protection. Her master protested to the president of the Republic, who replied that if the master was neither cruel nor corrupt then the *liberta* had no right to separate herself from him. An investigation was ordered, and in the ensuing inquiry Rosa testified that the master's son-in-law had whipped her belly when she was pregnant, then sent her to the fields and provoked a miscarriage. She claimed that, when the master was told by another *liberta* that Rosa was miscarrying, he replied that that was what he wanted. Furthermore, she claimed that on the day she fled, Socarrás had tried to "seduce her almost by force." When asked whether Socarrás had ever told the slaves on his plantation that they were free, she replied that he had not. The slaves knew of abolition only because they had overheard conversations in the house.[24]

Socarrás recounted a different version of events. He agreed that Rosa had miscarried but denied knowing why. He admitted that he had never read the decree of abolition to his slaves but denied mistreating them or attempting to seduce Rosa. He said that he had failed to read the decree because he had not received it and claimed that in any case he had told his male slaves that when the rains came he would give them a *potrero* (livestock-raising area) to work on halves, and that he had offered Rosa calves to raise as her own.[25]

While it is not possible from surviving records to resolve this case, the conflict does reveal certain aspects of the effect of the insurrection on master-slave relationships. First, Rosa viewed the prefect as

[24] See the case of Rosa vs. Francisco Socarrás in Sumarios, RAH, FD, leg. 3, doc. 1.

[25] Ibid.

someone to whom she could bring her complaints, while the master viewed the president of the Republic as someone who would uphold his claim to his former slaves. Conflict between master and slave thus became a problem for the insurgents themselves. Second, even though the decree of abolition was not read to all slaves, it could be communicated to them through the slaves' own network of communication. Third, although one cannot tell whether Socarrás had actually made the offer to raise livestock on halves with his slaves, it is interesting that he chose such an offer as a plausible one to claim to have made. Shares rather than wages appeared to him the logical form of free labor under his circumstances, a way of ensuring continuity on his estate without acknowledging the *libertos'* full freedom.

If the revolution created ambivalence for insurgent leaders, it also made for uncertainty on the part of *libertos*. They were abruptly shown new alternatives but at the same time told not to act on them. The role of the insurrectionist prefects must have been particularly puzzling to former slaves, for the prefect's office seemed both a potential refuge and a potential source of punishment. In 1869, for example, the *liberta* Felipa was interrogated about her flight from her master's home. She had initially been on the *ingenio* Santa Rosa and had been moved to the *potrero* Candelaria, under orders to serve there until the war ended. During the move, she noticed the small house in which the subprefect lived, though she refused to say how she knew who he was. She made an initial attempt to flee Candelaria, but repented part way down the road and returned. Then, according to her testimony, she had a confrontation with her mistress, who sent her away telling her that she deserved to be shot. That night Felipa put her clothes together in a bundle, took her daughter in her arms, and set out for the house she had seen by the side of the road two months earlier. Though she denied it, witnesses claimed that she had arranged to meet another *liberto* on the way. Two witnesses who were themselves *libertos* said they had tried to discourage her departure.[26]

Libertos had to calculate the risks associated with flight under these new circumstances, and masters tried to ensure that the risks would remain greater than the benefits. One man wrote to the As-

[26] Various documents relating to this case are grouped in RAH, FD, leg. 3, doc. 7.

sembly to complain that a *liberto* named Dionisio had fled his estate, after committing "excesses" and propounding to the other *libertos* the idea that any crime would be forgiven if they went into the army. The estate was raising food for the rebel troops, and the man wrote that he could in fact do without Dionisio but that he wished to have him returned for eight to ten days, in order to make an impression on the other *libertos*, who were awaiting the outcome of the case.[27] At stake here was the authority of the estate administrator and the conflict between the need for soldiers and the need for provisions, as well as the question of the autonomy of *libertos*.

The increased possibility of flight could make situations that had long been humiliating now seem unbearable. The *liberta* Angelina Sánchez was a nursemaid in the house of Clara Mola. By her own account she was well-fed and clothed. One day she left one of the children in order to get her own daughter. Señora Mola angrily warned Angelina not to take her daughter from the room she was in. The *liberta* in turn "made some observations" that caused the mistress to reprimand her, to which the *liberta* answered that black children should not be left in a room alone. That night when the family had gone to bed, Angelina Sánchez, like Felipa, left with her belongings on her head and her child in her arms. She, too, had seen the house by the side of the road while she was being transferred from the *ingenio* Santa Rosa, and another "citizen of color," Virginia, had told her that the subprefect was there. In her case, as in that of Felipa, there was a suggestion that other *libertos* from the *potrero* Candelaria had helped to arrange the flight.[28]

Domestic servants like Felipa and Angelina were in a particularly ambiguous situation, still under the direct personal authority of masters but with claims to some new rights. For other *libertos*, the amount of freedom they gained depended to a large extent on where they were located with respect to the economy and the war effort. Those on estates were particularly likely to be obliged to remain at work.

The eastern end of the island, where the insurrection broke out and then took hold, had not been a primary sugar-producing area, though there were enclaves in Santiago de Cuba and Guantánamo with substantial mills. The insurgents, however, wished to maintain

[27] Petition dated March 23, 1869, RAH, FD, leg. 5, doc. 12.
[28] RAH, FD, leg. 3, doc. 7.

estate production, both of sugar and of foodstuffs, and expected to continue to employ those who had always worked on the estates. In their attempts to keep the plantations in production despite changes in the legal status of the slaves, managers of these estates adopted a mixture of coercion and paternalism. One administrator, for example, reported that he usually allowed the *libertos* to engage in *atabales* (drumming) the nights before fiestas, but that on a recent occasion he had ordered them to stop at 8:00 P.M. because he and his wife were ill. Half an hour after issuing the order he heard the sound of drumming coming from the *estancia* of Joaquín Betancourt, a man of color, and he sent his son with an armed escort to bring the *libertos* back. The *libertos* were then made to spend the night sleeping under armed guard.[29] The case illustrates the alternation between tolerance and repression on the part of the administrator and the continued assumption that the lives of *libertos* should be organized to suit the convenience of their superiors.

The disrupted conditions of the countryside and the changes in expectations brought about by the insurrection often led to a break-down of the old mechanisms of control within plantations. Some administrators responded by adapting to the desires of the *libertos* and running estates on terms more acceptable to them. The description by an African *liberto* of conditions on the *ingenio* Fernandina certainly implied a reduction in compulsion since the days of slavery. Asked whether the estate was guarded at night to avoid "disorders," he replied that there was no vigilance of any kind and that he and the others went to bed at whatever time they pleased to rest from the toil of the day. Another *liberto* confirmed the lack of supervision.[30]

There was a limit to the adaptation that would be undertaken, however. One commander observed of a specific group of *libertos*: "It is not appropriate that they should work on the *ingenio* Sabanilla dividing profits with the owner." There were, he noted, many estates on which they could instead work "for the exclusive profit of the *patria*."[31] The *libertos*, it seems, found sharecropping a more ap-

---

[29] Deserción de libertos; tratamiento de estos, RAH, FD, leg. 2, carpeta 11, no document number.
[30] Sobre averiguar el autor o autores del incendio en una casa del Ingenio "La Fernandina" de José Miguel Montejo, RAH, FD, leg. 1, doc. 18.
[31] Com^te Mil^tr de Sibanicú, July 25, 1869, RAH, FD, leg. 4, doc. 496.

pealing arrangement than working for the "exclusive profit of the patria"; the commandant did not.

Plantations outside insurrectionist control but near enough to insurgent lines to make flight to the rebels possible were also affected. Insurgent propaganda by late 1869 asserted that the Spaniards were fighting to keep blacks enslaved and openly called on slaves to burn their masters' fields and flee to the *monte*, where blacks and whites would fight side by side as equals.[32] Fear of turning slaves into open enemies seems to have restrained some overseers. Others converted their estates into virtual armed camps, drawing on the Spanish military forces for added security.[33]

Perhaps the greatest transformation in social relations in the eastern and central areas came from the presence and character of the insurgent army itself. O'Kelly remarked on what he perceived as a preponderance of blacks and mulattos in the fighting force and claimed that "the most perfect equality exists between the white and colored races, the officers taking precedence by rank, and although the majority of the officers are white, a very large proportion are colored."[34] O'Kelly's perception of "perfect equality" was exaggerated, but this was nonetheless a remarkable fighting force to have emerged from a slaveholding society.

The rebellion drew much of its strength from the white and free colored nonplantation sector, both urban and rural. These were the sharecroppers, squatters, tenants, farmers, ranchers, and artisans who gave the region its distinctive character.[35] The overall population of the Eastern Department in 1862 was 47 percent white, 33 percent free colored, and only 20 percent slave. The census of 1862 counted thousands of free persons of color living on *estancias*, to-

---

[32] See document from La Junta Libertadora de Color, Havana, October 1, 1869, RAH, FD, leg. 6, doc. 79. The text reads, in part, "Los negros son los mismos que los blancos/. . . Los negros que tienen vergüenza deben ir a pelear juntos con los cubanos./ Los españoles quieren matar a los cubanos para que los negros nunca sean libres/ . . . Cuando los cubanos que están peleando pasan por donde están los negros, entonces los negros van con ellos para ser libres / Cuando los cubanos que están peleando, están lejos de los negros; entonces los negros se huyen y se van con los cubanos; pero antes queman los ingenios/ Si en los ingenios no hubiera esclavos y se les diera a los negros *su dinero* por su trabajo, los ingenios serían buenos porque darían de comer a la gente pobre."

[33] O'Kelly, *The Mambi-Land*, pp. 63-64.

[34] Ibid., pp. 26, 221.

[35] Ramiro Guerra describes the majority of black and mulatto campesinos as "aparceros y precaristas"—sharecroppers and squatters. Guerra, *Guerra* 1: 2.

bacco farms, and *sitios de labor* in the east.[36] O'Kelly estimated that, within the army, one-third of the fighting men were white, "and the majority of the other two thirds are of color other than black, all shades of brown predominating." Thomas Jordan, a former Confederate officer who became chief of staff of the rebels, was unhappy about the composition of the troops, reporting that he was surprised to find "much more than half of them negroes (including many Africans) and Chinese."[37]

The question of the precise social and ethnic composition of the insurgency remains open, for we have neither a comprehensive record of participants nor a clear idea of the rates of participation of different groups. North American observers like O'Kelly and Jordan may have defined color categories somewhat differently from Cubans and thus overestimated the proportion of blacks and mulattos. Other sources, however, clearly underestimate this proportion. One modern scholar has argued that the revolutionary forces were not in fact composed principally of Afro-Cubans and Chinese, basing his assertion on the Spanish records of trials, executions, and exiles of rebels. But according to a Spanish soldier interviewed by O'Kelly, ". . . we do not take many black prisoners; they are generally killed if found with arms; but if they present themselves, they are sent back to their masters." This suggests that a disproportionate number of black insurgents would never be brought to formal trial, executed, or exiled.[38] Whatever the exact proportions of different groups within it, however, the multiethnic insurgent force was a remarkable legacy of the complex society of eastern Cuba, a testimony to the increasingly broad appeal of anticolonial struggle, and a source of impetus for more egalitarian policies.

Those Chinese workers who joined the insurrection presumably came primarily from the central districts, since there were very few in the east. One insurgent officer in 1869 was delighted to enlist a group of fifty-four Asians, one of whom had led a labor gang and would, he predicted, make an excellent sergeant.[39] Officially, the

[36] Cuba, Centro de Estadística, *Noticias estadísticas,* "Distribución." The 1862 census does not include Puerto Príncipe in the Eastern Department.

[37] O'Kelly, *The Mambi-Land,* p. 221; Thomas Jordan to Eduardo Agramonte, December 16, 1869 (original in English), RAH, FD, leg. 1.

[38] The argument about the proportion of Afro-Cubans is made in Knight, *Slave Society,* p. 168. The quotation is in O'Kelly, *The Mambi-Land,* p. 79.

[39] Al C. Comandante Antº Rodríguez, July 7, 1869, RAH, FD, leg. 3, carta no. 294.

Chinese in Cuba had a special status and might be expected to be more loyal to Spain than were slaves. Furthermore, tensions between Asians and slaves on plantations were common, recognized, and in some instances encouraged in order to prevent alliance against their masters. Under the circumstances of war, however, status and ethnic differences could apparently be overcome to an extent by shared grievances. The English consul in the late 1870s attributed the presence of Asians in the insurrection to the colonial government's policy of requiring them to recontract at the end of their terms or leave the country. "Neither the exigencies of war nor the want of labour can justify so gross a breach of faith; no one will more regret it than those who are the best friends of the Spanish government, for it is probably the chief, if not the only cause, why Chinese are found in the rebel ranks."[40] While this was an oversimplification, one can argue more generally that the tendency to reduce indentured Chinese to a status akin to slavery, thwarting expectations founded upon a contractual relationship, encouraged their alliance with anti-Spanish forces.

An unknown percentage of the insurgents were former slaves, drawn into the insurrection either by deserting their owners, being captured during raids, or being freed by rebel masters. Spanish officers privately estimated former slaves to be "numerous" among the insurgents by the end of the war.[41] These confidential estimates are more revealing than public statements, since the Spanish publicly emphasized the number of blacks and runaway slaves among the rebels as part of an attempt to portray the rebellion as a racial rather than a political struggle and thus dissuade whites from joining.

Slaves incorporated into the rebel army could not, however, count on full equality with white and free colored troops. *Libertos* in the army were commonly not armed, but were consigned instead to support roles. O'Kelly attributed this to the insurgent belief that "the most ignorant of the slaves" were "so broken in spirit by the flogging system that they have no self-respect, and are therefore very unreliable as fighting material," though he himself conceded that

[40] Great Britain. Parliament. *Parliamentary Papers* (Commons), 1878, vol. 67 (Slave Trade No. 1), "Report on the Labour Question in Cuba."

[41] Telegram from the Comandante General, Villas, to the Captain general, Santa Clara, October 2, 1877, AHN, Ultramar, leg. 4883, tomo 6.

there were "a great many exceptions" to this rule.[42] Racial prejudice as well as objective considerations influenced military policy. Thomas Jordan was opposed on principle to a predominantly Afro-Cuban army and advised systematic substitution of men of color for whites in noncombat posts.[43] Other officials followed a similar policy, with little regard for the abilities of the individuals involved, as in the order previously cited, which allocated the men of a particular unit on the basis of their status, the whites to arms and the *libertos* "with rare exceptions" to agriculture.[44]

Within the category of *libertos*, a further distinction was sometimes made between Creoles and Africans. O'Kelly noted that most of the ex-slaves who achieved high rank were Creoles.[45] Rebel officials generally viewed Africans as a special group, fit primarily for agriculture and service as *ayudantes*. In March 1870 the insurgent Department of the Interior issued a circular calling for those former field slaves, "especially the natives of Africa," who were in the army but who were superfluous or had not proved their valor and intelligence to be sent to agriculture.[46] The cultural gaps between whites, Creole free persons of color, and Africans exacerbated this stereotyping. When during a celebration in a rebel camp, for example, the Africans danced by themselves, mulatto soldiers hastened to describe them to a foreign visitor as "bárbaros."[47]

These ethnic and cultural differentiations were related to a larger distinction, generally not made explicit, concerning who was to be considered truly Cuban. White leaders within the rebellion often did not see Africans as Cubans, and some did not even see Creole blacks as Cubans. Though most rebel propagandists prided themselves on the interracial unity manifested within the fighting force, they portrayed this as an alliance of Cubans and blacks, not simply an alliance of different groups of Cubans. The line must have been difficult to draw, since the families of many eastern blacks and mulattos had lived in Cuba for generations, and many of the small farmers and urban free persons of color came from families that had

---

[42] O'Kelly, *The Mambi-Land*, p. 261.

[43] Thomas Jordan to Eduardo Agramonte, December 16, 1869, RAH, FD, leg. 1.

[44] Sta. Catalina, July 12, 1869, RAH, FD, leg. 4, no document number.

[45] O'Kelly, *The Mambi-Land*, p. 261.

[46] Circular, Secretaría de Estado, Departamento del Interior, No. 567, RAH, FD, leg. 6, doc. 46.

[47] O'Kelly, *The Mambi-Land*, p. 223.

been free since the eighteenth century and earlier. Such divisions nonetheless contributed to the weakening of rebel forces, as Spaniards outside and conservatives inside the insurgency accused leaders like Antonio Maceo of aiming at a "black republic" rather than at Cuban independence.[48]

However he came to be in the army, and however he was treated, the *liberto* soldier became a potentially disruptive element to established society. He could represent freedom and a degree of autonomy, a walking challenge to the old social relations of slavery. Take, for example, the case of the *liberto* Florentino Zaldivar. He asked to be freed in order to fight, and his master willingly turned him over to the regional commandant, adding that he never wanted to see him again. When, some time later, Florentino wished to take a week's leave and return to work on the plantation, the master told him that he had no work to offer, and furthermore that if he did he would not offer it to him, and ordered him off the plantation. The *liberto*, however, returned once again to see his *compañeros*, provoking a confrontation with the master.[49]

The nature of the confrontation suggests the ways in which the new mobility and the increased self-confidence of *libertos* who joined the army introduced tensions into society. Florentino (he is referred to by his first name in the records of the case) had stopped by his former master's estate on a mission to collect *viandas* at another plantation. He went straight to the kitchen, speaking to none of the white people on the estate. There, according to his former master's wife, he created a clamor among the other servants. When the master returned to the house from the fields and was told that Florentino was on the premises, he went to the kitchen and told him to be on his way. The master later reported that the *liberto* had come "bragging of a misunderstood liberty" to "entice" the rest of his servants in his absence. Florentino was indignant at the dismissal and asked the master what reason he had for sending him away. According to the master's account, he replied that he was not obliged to give any explanation at all and that if Florentino continued with

---

[48] See the text cited in note 32, above. For prejudice against Maceo, see Guerra, *Guerra* 2: 247, and the text of the letter from Maceo reproduced in Thomas, *Cuba*, p. 265.

[49] This discussion of the case of Florentino is based on evidence from RAH, FD, leg. 1, doc. 5, which contains a summary of the testimony.

his insolent words and insulting manner he would be thrown off in another way. According to the *liberto*'s account, the master replied that he should get out and that he "didn't want a black who had been his to serve anyone except him." The master claimed, and Florentino denied, that Florentino reached for his knife, whereupon the master hit him on the side of the head with the butt of his machete.

In their accounts, the master and the *liberto* portrayed the incident differently. The master described the *liberto* as contentious and insolent. The *liberto* denied that he had been told to stay off the plantation (pointing out that on his previous visit the master had given him lunch) and claimed that he had stopped merely to have some water and to see his *compañeros*. All witnesses agreed, however, that the visit created a tense encounter between the two men.

The case reflects both the master's desire to keep the *liberto* from visiting his *compañeros* who were still servants and the dramatic effect of Florentino's appearance in the kitchen of his old plantation. The master had been willing to free the troublesome slave and contribute him to the rebel cause, but he had no intention of allowing him to come back to the plantation to exercise his rights as a free man. That Florentino would nonetheless insist upon returning and visiting old friends reflected his own changed conception of his rights and in turn contributed to the further breakdown of the master's authority over his former slaves. The master reported plaintively to the authorities that the servants of his house were not very attached to him since Florentino had persuaded them that *he* was their protector.

Despite the limited intentions of the insurgent leaders with respect to slavery, the first years of the war had transformed social relations in areas under insurrectionist control. Nominal abolition encouraged those now called *libertos* to resist mistreatment and press for further rights. Pressure from blacks, mulattos, and antislavery whites within the rebel army pushed insurgent policy toward more freedom for *libertos*. The war made it easier for slaves near the fighting to escape direct control by their masters and for *libertos* to flee conditions they found intolerable. *Libertos* who actually joined the army acquired a new conception of themselves and of their relation to those who had been their masters and social superiors. Though the leaders might debate the precise extent of the freedom to be granted, maintenance of the coercion on which slavery rested became increasingly difficult as the war in various forms penetrated families and estates.

The insurrection did not, however, reach deeply into the rich western sugar areas. The insurgents themselves were divided on tactics, and western planters sympathetic to the insurrection were unwilling to call for slave uprisings.[50] In most of the western part of the island, the coercive discipline of a slave plantation regime combined with Spanish military force to create an environment inhospitable to effective insurgency. When the Cuban Junta in New York called for the *dotaciones* of sugar plantations to burn cane fields during the Christmas holidays of 1869, according to the French consul, the only districts reporting fires were Cienfuegos, Trinidad, Sancti Spíritus, and Villaclara.[51] The harvest of that year was one of the largest ever.[52] The destruction of mills in the insurrection had been confined largely to the less developed regions, and the major western mills held their slaves and continued grinding. But although the war did not directly touch the majority of Cuba's slaves, the insurrection eventually affected them as it became increasingly clear to Spain that pacification of the island would require coming to terms with the general issue of slavery. The insurrection had raised the issue and given it life through the freeing of slaves and the incorporation of *libertos* into the army. To undermine the insurgent appeal, Spain would have to find some way to respond.

[50] See Cepero Bonilla, *Azúcar y abolición*, and Guerra, *Guerra*.
[51] Report of January 7, 1870, Ministère des Affaires Etrangères, Paris, Correspondance Commerciale (hereinafter MAE-Paris, CC), La Havane, 1861-1871, tome 20.
[52] Moreno, *El ingenio* 3: 37.

III

Spain Responds:
The Moret Law

"What could cause us real troubles would be to fail to carry [to Cuba] the word 'liberty,' a word pronounced by the Cuban insurgents, and woe to us if we do not repeat it!"
—*Sr. Gallego Díaz in the Spanish Cortes, June 10, 1870*[1]

Despite the ambiguity of the initial insurgent commitment to emancipation, the reality of war had put Spain on the defensive with regard to slavery. As long as the rebellion represented abolition, however nominal and compromised, those slaves who could do so had reason to flee their masters to the insurrectionist lines, free blacks had reason to prefer the rebels to the Spaniards, and the United States government—if it should choose to invoke antislavery principles—had a rationale for recognizing or even aiding the rebels. The pressures on Madrid were contradictory. On the one hand, Spain needed to reduce the appeal of the insurrection to blacks and to those whites who favored the elimination of slavery. On the other hand, the government had no desire to damage sugar production and diminish its own revenues from Cuba, or to alienate still-loyal planters.

Calculations of the most prudent colonial policy were made more complex by the growing influence of antislavery sentiment in Spain. The Spanish Abolitionist Society, founded in 1865, had developed a considerable network of support within the Peninsula. Begun outside the political parties, appealing to young people, to free-traders, and to individual politicians, the Society achieved a striking degree of success in linking antislavery with developing liberal principles. An effective association of the two had long been lacking in Spanish political thought, largely because the issue of slavery was so closely

[1] Spain, Cortes, 1869-1871, *Diario de Sesiones de las Cortes Constituyentes* 13 (Madrid: J. A. García, 1870): 8765.

tied to the maintenance of the colonial status of Cuba. The shift in the late 1860s doubtless owed a great deal to the outcome of the U.S. Civil War, as well as to the ideological campaign waged by abolitionists. When, in 1868, a liberal revolution triumphed in Spain, the abolition of slavery was one of its stated principles.[2]

Many Spaniards were prepared to forget this commitment once they were faced with the threat and the apparent "ingratitude" embodied in the Cuban insurrection. Furthermore, there was also a vigorous opposition to abolition within Spain, particularly from Catalan merchants who saw the issue as closely tied to the maintenance of their protected markets in Cuba.[3] But strategic and international considerations required the new government to take some steps toward a repudiation of slavery, however partial. The solution that emerged was that of a "preparatory bill for the gradual abolition of slavery," introduced into the Cortes by Segismundo Moret, the minister of Ultramar and himself an abolitionist, on May 28, 1870, and amended during debate in June. All children born of slaves since September 1868 were to be free, as were all slaves upon reaching the age of sixty. A proposal for indemnified emancipation of the remaining slaves was to be submitted once Cuban delegates were seated in the Cortes—something to be expected only with the end of the war. The bill outlawed the use of the whip and provided that any slave proven the victim of "excessive cruelty" was to be freed. "Juntas Protectoras" were established to oversee enforcement.[4]

The debates in the Cortes reflected both the formal liberalism of the new regime and the defensiveness of those with threatened interests in Cuba or a strongly "integralist" vision of the island's relation to Spain. Most of the delegates agreed in one form or another

[2] On Spanish liberals and the issue of Cuban slavery see Gabriel Rodríguez, "La idea y el movimiento antiesclavista en España durante el siglo xix," in Centro de Investigaciones Históricas, Instituto de Cultura Puertorriqueña, El proceso abolicionista en Puerto Rico: Documentos para su estudio 1 (San Juan, 1974): 455-73; Murray, Odious Commerce, especially chaps. 10 and 14; and Corwin, Spain and the Abolition of Slavery in Cuba.

[3] On Catalan interests, trade with Cuba, Spanish colonial policy, and antiabolitionism in Spain, see Miguel Izard, Manufactureros, industriales, y revolucionarios (Barcelona: Editorial Crítica, 1979), pp. 151-78; Jordi Maluquer de Motes, "La burgesia catalana i l'esclavitud colonial: modes de producció i pràctica política," Recerques, Història, Economía, Cultura 3 (Barcelona, 1979): 83-136; and Raymond Carr, Spain, 1808-1939 (Oxford: Oxford University Press, 1966), chaps. 8, 9.

[4] For the final text of the Moret Law, see Fernando Ortiz, Los negros esclavos (Havana: Revista Bimestre Cubana, 1916; reprint ed., Havana: Editorial de Ciencias Sociales, 1975), pp. 452-55.

that slavery was an institution "rejected by public sentiment," but they were concerned to end slavery in such a way as to avoid "disturbances," preserve the colonial tie, and protect production. Even Romero Robledo, the most intransigent opponent of abolition, included in his discourse a ritual condemnation of slavery, though he followed it with conventional proslavery arguments and warnings of race war and "Africanization" if abolition were actually undertaken. Emilio Castelar, a strong abolitionist, criticized the Moret proposal from the other side, calling it too timid and introducing a resolution in favor of immediate emancipation.[5]

Segismundo Moret's replies to his opponents were an effective blend of rhetoric about justice and highly pragmatic appeals to national self-interest. He emphasized the importance of denying to the insurgent Cubans the propaganda advantage of portraying their fight as one of abolitionism against proslavery Spanish domination. He spoke respectfully of the interests of proprietors and defended his own cautious strategy as a necessary yet principled deference to those interests. Finally, he projected an extraordinarily romantic picture of a postemancipation society in which grateful, prayerful former slaves in modest cabins exchanged warm greetings with the generous planters who had been their masters. The proposed law, he argued, was based on faith in an "understanding" between master and slave, which he felt to be appropriate, given the present "humanitarian" character of slavery in Cuba. On July 4, 1870, the Cortes voted to pass the law.[6]

The Moret Law was in a sense an effort by Spain to capture the apparent moral high ground from the insurgents and to win gratitude from freed slaves and free people of color, while stalling abolition itself. From the first weeks of the rebellion, Spanish authorities had recognized that the threat of the insurrection was more than military. On the 24th of October, 1868, the captain general wrote to the minister of war that, although the uprising was in itself of little importance, the announcement by the rebels of abolition and general suffrage "has already made the people of color somewhat arrogant."[7]

[5] See the speech of Romero Robledo on June 9, 1870, in Spain, Cortes, *Diario* 13: 8728-32, and that of Castelar on June 20, 1870, in ibid. 14: 8981-92.
[6] See the speech of Moret on June 10, 1870, ibid., 13: 8768-73, and that of June 20, ibid. 14: 8992-99.
[7] Captain general to the minister of war, Oct. 24, 1868, AHN, Ultramar, leg. 4881.

That "arrogance"—which consisted of an appreciation of the potential for obtaining civil rights—threatened Spanish colonial interests as well as the Cuban social order.

While the main purpose was to meet the strategic needs of the moment, part of the attraction of gradual abolition had to do with long-run cultural and political considerations. It was the fond hope of the proponents of the Moret Law that a period of "tutelage" during which free-born children would remain under the authority of their former masters would enable them to "assimilate themselves to the culture and civilization of Spain."[8] This was not mere paternalism; it also reflected a basic concern of Spanish administrators. "Spanish culture" and "civilization" were more than euphemisms for proper behavior; they were values in themselves, in opposition to the concept of *Cuban* nationality. The Moret Law was conceived of both as a nondisruptive form of very gradual abolition, and as a charitable act that would place Spain—instead of the insurgents—in the position of benefactor of Afro-Cubans.

Once tentative steps had been taken toward regarding slaves as potential citizens, the issue of their loyalty increased in importance, and throughout the 1870s a struggle took place for the cultural and political allegiance of former slaves and free persons of color. Spanish colonial officials acted as patrons to black and mulatto voluntary associations and supported loyal Afro-Cuban leaders in an attempt to capture that allegiance. The struggle sometimes became a complex, three-sided one, for the alternatives included not only seeing oneself as Spanish or Cuban but also identifying oneself as African. The proportion of Cuban slaves who were African-born remained high, and the *cabildos de nación*, mutual societies organized around African ethnic groups, remained a source of identity. African languages continued to be spoken. Indeed, some freed slaves retained their African ethnonym as a surname, rather than adopting a Spanish one, and took their Creole children to activities of the African *cabildos*.[9]

While seeking to win a measure of Afro-Cuban loyalty with the

[8] Cited by Corwin, *Spain and the Abolition of Slavery*, p. 258.

[9] On the *cabildos* and societies of free persons of color, see Chap. XI, below. On African languages, see Ibarra, *Ideología*, pp. 18-20. For an example of a former slave using his African ethnonym as a surname, see Juan Lucumí al Exmo Sor Gobernador General, October 20, 1879, in AHN, Ultramar, leg. 4181.

Moret Law, Spanish officials also portrayed it as a law that even slaveowners could accept. Moret noted in debate that he had copied one article directly from a proposal submitted by Cuban slaveholders.[10] In practice, however, Cuban planters criticized the law and attempted to block its enforcement.

In 1870, in the areas under Spanish control, most proprietors viewed abolition with suspicion or outright hostility. Slavery remained crucial to their economic activities and to their way of life. True, they had feared worse than Moret's bill and had some reason to be relieved at its conservatism. But when they gathered together with the governor in the summer of 1870, Cuba's leading planters were divided on the best way to resolve the "cuestión social." Some objected even to the "free womb," or liberation of children at birth, suggesting that moral instruction, the expansion of provision grounds, and the encouragement of coartación would be the best way to end slavery. Others favored a long apprenticeship and indemnification. José Suárez Argudín, owner of ingenios in Cienfuegos and Bahía Honda, saw the issue of slavery as one of "life or death" for Cuba, both because it was a weapon used by the enemies of Spain, and because he anticipated a collapse of Cuban sugar production after abolition. Julián Zulueta, one of Cuba's major slaveholders, added that abolition should be linked with immigration and with an approach to the organization of labor that would maintain the basis of Cuba's prosperity—presumably strict regulation. There was consensus, however, that any change should be slow.[11]

Once the Moret Law had passed, planters in Cuba, with the cooperation of colonial officials, managed to stall its publication for several months. They then turned to the task of designing regulations for enforcement that would minimize its effects. The governor was blunt about the considerations involved in drawing up the reg-

[10] See the speech by Moret in the Cortes on June 17, 1870, in Spain, Cortes, Diario 14: 8920, and the Proyecto de ley, presentado por el Sr. Ministro de Ultramar, sobre abolición de la esclavitud, ibid., vol. 14, appendix to the session of May 28, 1870.

[11] A telegram of June 11, 1870, from Manuel Calvo to Julián Zulueta is revealing: "Proyecto vientre. Nada mas. Estar tranquilos." The prospect of a bill declaring "free womb" (i.e. the emancipation of newborns) and little more was obviously cause for relief. Copias de telegramas particulares de C. Manuel Calvo y de D. Zulueta. AHN, Ultramar, leg. 4815. For meetings of proprietors see Acta de la Junta de hacendados, propietarios y comerciantes para tratar de la cuestión social, June 17, 1870, AHN, Ultramar, leg. 4881, tomo 1. For a further discussion of these meetings and of the behavior of the governor, see Corwin, Spain and the Abolition of Slavery, chap. 14.

ulations. He had taken care to avoid any radical change in the order and established customs of the country, particularly in rural estates, he wrote, because to do otherwise would risk "imminent disturbance of agricultural labor."[12] Planters obtained substantially what they wanted, including retention of some forms of corporal punishment, but even so postponed publication of the Reglamento until November 1872. The Juntas Protectoras thus got a late start, and by the terms of the regulations half their members were slaveholders. Zulueta was appointed vice-president of the Junta Central.[13]

As a result of this opposition, the Moret Law turned out to be both less and more than it seemed. Less in that the freedom it afforded was limited, compromised, and in many cases quite illusory. More in that in practice its provisions led to institutional and attitudinal changes that—to a limited extent—disrupted the social order of slavery.

Because the Moret Law freed the newborn and the elderly, its author proclaimed, incorrectly but dramatically: "De hoy más . . . no nacerán ni morirán esclavos en España." (From now on . . . there will neither be born nor die any slaves in Spain.)[14] Although the freeing of all children born since 1868 meant that ultimately slavery would be extinguished, it had no immediate consequences for those children who were to have benefited from it. The epithet attached to their names in slave lists changed from *párvulo* to *liberto*, but there is no indication that any alteration in their treatment followed. They continued to be raised with their slave parents; they drew rations and in return owed unpaid labor until age 18; they were subject to the master's authority.

Nominal freedom for infants, however insubstantial, may nonetheless have changed certain expectations of the natural order of things. One visitor sympathetic to planters claimed that the birth rate on estates had increased since the Moret Law, as a result of slave mothers' perception of their children as free. "The mere word 'liberty,' it is true, has already acted as a talisman among the blacks. I have seen the *Cria*, or negro nursery, in many of the estates, and it is touching to see with what pride the slave mother lifts up in

[12] AHN, Ultramar, leg. 4883, tomo 5.
[13] See *Gaceta de la Habana*, Jan. 29, 1873, and Corwin, *Spain and the Abolition of Slavery*, chap. 15.
[14] Proyecto de ley . . . sobre abolición de la esclavitud, Spain, Cortes, *Diario*, vol. 14.

her arms the little naked *picanniny* who is some day to become a free man." But when a parent achieved his or her freedom and wished to take a child from the plantation, he or she discovered that there were debts incurred that had to be paid for the upbringing of the child. In essence, the freedom of the child had to be purchased like the freedom of the parent.[15]

For older slaves, there were other obstacles to the achievement of the promised freedom at the age of sixty. First, many slaves had no proof of age other than the records kept by masters. If a master filed fraudulent records, the slave had little recourse. Technically, he or she could appeal to the Junta Protectora, but this was a laborious and potentially corrupt procedure requiring estimates of age by a doctor. Some masters did not even bother to falsify ages—one slave list from 1875 contains slaves with ages sixty, sixty-one, sixty-three, and sixty-five, with no apparent acknowledgment that such individuals were legally free.[16] A former U.S. consul wrote, "Though the law declares that every slave who has attained the age of sixty is free, and every child born is free, there is no plantation-master who would not smile at your suggestion that he did not own every 'hand' on his place."[17]

Older slaves who actually obtained legal freedom might find their lives very little changed. On the *ingenio* Angelita in 1877, a census of the *dotación* listed—in addition to 247 slaves—twenty men and seventeen women over the age of sixty. But the daybook for the same period contains no indication that these individuals were receiving regular wages or salaries, and indeed the law, while obliging the master to maintain them if they remained on the plantation, ruled such wages "optional." The ages given for the workers also suggest that there was considerable improvisation in the record keeping, and that the occasion of drawing up the list may itself have been the first time that some of them were acknowledged as being "free."[18]

[15] The quotation is from Gallenga, *Pearl*, p. 123. See also the discussion of parental efforts to free children and masters' efforts to block them in Chaps. VII and VIII, below.
[16] Capitanía Pedánea de Santa Isabel de las Lajas, Núm° 3, Padrón general de esclavos, 1875, ANC, ME, leg. 3748, núm. B.
[17] James W. Steele, *Cuban Sketches* (New York: G. P. Putnam's Sons, 1881), p. 93.
[18] Ten men were listed as being exactly sixty years old, one as sixty-five, one as sixty-nine. The rest of the men, and the majority of the older women, were in their

The Moret Law also provided that all those held as slaves but not registered in the slave census were to be considered free. As part of the effort to suppress the slave trade by reducing the incentive to purchase contraband slaves, the Spanish government had already in 1866 called for a census of slaves and declared that henceforth all those not included in the census would be free. The census was drawn up in 1867 but was hardly complete. Some masters, to evade taxes, apparently did not register their slaves, confident that there would be no intrusion into the plantations to verify the lists. With the passage of the Moret Law, another census was ordered, actually compounding the problem by further delaying the freeing of the unregistered. Citing inaccuracies in the various counts of slaves, and protesting the injustice of freeing legally acquired slaves simply because of errors in the lists, planters stalled application of the law.[19] Throughout the 1870s individual slaveowners appealed for the inclusion of unregistered slaves in the lists, and as the decade drew to a close the rules about censuses and registers were still being refined and reiterated.[20]

Another group affected by the Moret Law were *emancipados*, those Africans who had been found on captured slave ships and "emancipated." They had remained a special category, their labor contracted out by the government. Because employers had so little interest in their long-term well-being, *emancipados* were in some cases treated worse than slaves. The Moret Law freed these ten thousand or so men and women a second time. An English observer wrote in 1873 that the "meaning of the so-called 'liberation' is neither more nor less than that the government gets rid of them." He believed that shifting responsibility for the *emancipados* to the Juntas Protectoras de Libertos meant "some chance of correction of the many abuses to which this very unfortunate class has been subjected." But, he added, "I doubt it very much indeed."[21]

seventies, eighties, or nineties. Libro diario del Ingenio Angelita Argudín, 1877, ANC, ML, 10789.

[19] On the failure to register slaves, see Sociedad Abolicionista Española, Madrid, *La violación de las leyes en Cuba* (Madrid: A. J. Alaria, 1882). For a detailed discussion of masters' stalling tactics, see Corwin, *Spain and the Abolition of Slavery*, chap. 14.

[20] For appeals for the inclusion of slaves in the registers, see ANC, ME, legs. 3814-3820, and AHN, Ultramar, leg. 4759.

[21] Acting Commissary-Judge Crawford to Earl Granville, Havana, May 28, 1873, in Great Britain, Parliament, *Parliamentary Papers* (Lords) 1875, vol. 23 (Slave Trade

The governor reported in 1870 that he had freed *emancipados* captured from slaving expeditions of 1853 and 1854 and those laboring on the public works of the Canal de Vento who merited this prize. He noted that they were recontracting with their former masters or others for periods of two to six years "under mutually advantageous conditions." This he saw as a precedent for the way that a transition to freedom could be made without disturbing the supply of labor.[22] The practice of contracting and recontracting was already familiar to Cuban employers, less as a form of free labor than as one of legal coercion. Contracts had been used with the Chinese and with the *emancipados*, and were usually characterized by restrictions on behavior, wages below competitive levels, and long terms of service. In the case of the *emancipados*, the result had been a condition little different from slavery. Now that the *emancipados* had additional legal rights, new terms appeared in their contracts, specifically the retention of their certificates of freedom by the employer. This coercive measure was later revoked on order from Madrid, but it showed the intent of both the Havana government and employers to limit mobility and strengthen control over *emancipados*.[23]

Because the Moret Law shifted many individuals—children, the elderly, *emancipados*—from one category to another, its effects seemed considerable on paper. Between 1870 and 1877, 61,766 children of slaves became or were born legally free by virtue of the provision of the law freeing those born after 1868. Over 32,000 slaves were technically free under other provisions of the law. The government's calculations—which were distinctly flawed—recorded a decline in the slave population of about 52,000 between 1871 and 1877. Recalculating these figures to reduce the effect of double-counting, one finds that the major sources of recorded decline were the freeing of the elderly (45 percent), the freeing of unregistered slaves (21 percent), deaths (19 percent), and "causes outside the law" (12 percent)[24] (see Table 9).

No. 2), "Correspondence Respecting Slavery in Cuba and Puerto Rico, and the State of the Slave Population and Chinese Coolies in those Islands."

[22] Revista política, Aug. 30, 1870, RAH, FD, leg. 7, doc. 24.

[23] See the correspondence between the minister of Ultramar and the government of Cuba, October 1870, in RAH, FD, doc. 39.

[24] Expediente promovido por haber solicitado el Ministerio de Ultramar un estado general y resumen de los esclavos existentes, de los que han adquirido la libertad por

TABLE 9
Sources of Decline in the Slave Population, 1870-1877,
Government Estimates

1. Slaves listed in the census of January 15, 1871	287,653
2. Freed for serving the Spanish flag	658
3. Freed because over the age of sixty	21,032
4. Freed because owned by the state	1,046
5. Freed because unregistered[a]	9,611
6. Freed for reasons outside the law[b]	5,423
7. Slave deaths	8,917
8. *Liberto* deaths[c]	5,256
9. Slaves calculated as remaining in 1877[d]	235,710
10. Slaves actually on tax registers, 1878[e]	184,030

SOURCE: ANC, ME, leg. 3816, exp. Af. Expediente promovido . . . , March 1878.

[a] This appears to refer to slaves not in the index to the 1871 census. It may therefore be misleading to subtract category 5 from category 1 as the junta officials preparing this report did.

[b] This presumably included some recorded self-purchase and manumission.

[c] This inclusion of *liberto* deaths also suggests double-counting.

[d] Since some of those in 3, 5, and 8 should not have been in the 1871 census, this total is unreliable.

[e] Includes only slaves over the age of eleven.

When the Junta Central Protectora in 1878 calculated the number who had been freed or died since 1870, and subtracted that from the census totals of 1871, they arrived at a figure of 235,710 still in bondage at the end of 1877. The census of that year, however, recorded only 199,094, and the tax records 184,030. The junta's mathematics were clearly faulty, and they had evidently lost track of many people (see notes to Table 9). The problem was partly due to the late start of the juntas. They had only begun operation in 1873, and thus their records did not include deaths and cases of freedom from causes beyond the law between 1870 and 1873. Furthermore, the war in the eastern end of the island made government statistics for that region unreliable. Many slaves had died or been freed in the insurrection, or were freed during pacification, without being recorded.[25]

virtud de la Ley de 4 de Julio de 70 y del número total de libertos, March 1878, ANC, ME, leg. 3816, exp. Af. In calculating the percentages, I have subtracted *liberto* deaths from the total, since *liberto* children were not included in the 1871 census and *liberto* adults were already calculated as a decline when they were freed. This leaves a total decline of 46,687.

[25] For a discussion of the problems the juntas had in trying to keep track of statistics, see the letter to the governor general from the vice president of the Junta Central Protectora de Libertos, March 11, 1878, in ibid. For somewhat different figures, see

Despite conflicting statistics, a central point remains clear: for the greater part of the decade during which it was in force, the Moret Law reduced the total number of slaves but freed relatively few slaves of working age. Although the slave population fell dramatically—from over 300,000 to under 200,000—most of those freed were children and the elderly, some of the decline was due to deaths, and fewer lives were changed as a direct result of the law than the number of legal freeings would suggest.

To emphasize the ineffectiveness of the Moret Law in ending slavery directly, however, would be to interpret its significance too narrowly. While those freed were primarily the very young and the very old, the operation of the law tended to accelerate the process of overall emancipation. As a formal measure, it was deliberately very limited, but its indirect consequences were considerable and often unforeseen. It provided a lever—a weak, fragile, awkward lever—that enabled some slaves to exert influence on their condition or that of their relatives. It made certain underlying conflicts of interest more apparent and changed the ways in which they were resolved.

Slaveholders had sensed this potential in the Moret Law from the very beginning. In June 1870, when the law was being discussed, Francisco Ibáñez, a leading planter, expressed his support in principle of the idea of "free womb" and freedom for the elderly. But he recommended that the law avoid "the intervention of Agents of Authority" to carry it out, for this could cause "abuses" and particularly could "discredit" (desprestigiar) masters on their estates.[26] The Moret Law did not directly threaten the immediate economic interests of slaveholders, since the very young and the very old could be a burden to the plantation, and changing their legal status caused no loss of labor in the short run. But for slaveholders to accept their slaves' freedom on order from the government was indirectly threatening, because it implied that on each plantation there existed an authority greater than the master's, an external authority to whom the slave might appeal.

The dangers perceived by slaveholders were similar to those which had disturbed them during the mid-nineteenth-century debates over

Estado demostrativo de los esclavos . . . , Havana, March 15, 1878, AHN, Ultramar, leg. 4882.
[26] Acta de la Junta, AHN, Ultramar, leg. 4881, tomo 1.

the proper role of ecclesiastics in a slave society. While granting in part the wisdom of evangelization among slaves, masters were often hostile to the actual presence of priests on the plantation. With the support of the government in Havana, planters had successfully argued that such outsiders undermined the essential authority of master over slave.[27]

In the 1870s, planters criticized local officials on the same grounds. The government in Havana again sided with the planters, rebuking officials who entered plantations "on the pretext of enquiring of the slaves some purely administrative fact or other, which they could and should request from the masters or the administrators." Invoking the necessity for prudence to avoid "disturbances" of the slaves, the government in 1872 called on the *capitanes de partido* to respect the inviolability of the plantation and assist masters in maintaining the "subordination and discipline" that were "so necessary for labor and for the development of agriculture." Authorities should enter the plantations only in cases of criminality or on occasions specified by the Reglamento.[28]

This defensiveness arose from multiple sources. One was simple unease at the "intervention of agents of authority," which could be disruptive of the plantation even if their tasks were bureaucratic and their motives unsubversive. Another was the fear that a slave rebellion might be sparked by insurrectionist propaganda or agitation. A third was the pressure of increasing initiatives by slaves. The environment of the 1870s, with the legal provision for the eventual end of slavery and the outbreak of rebellion in the east, encouraged some slaves to press for whatever concessions they could obtain. In doing so they made use of old techniques as well as new.

Several provisions in Cuban law had long recognized certain limited slave rights, particularly the right to *coartación*, or gradual self-purchase. There were 2,137 *esclavos coartados* in 1871, heavily concentrated in Havana, where the practice of hiring-out meant that slaves were more likely to accumulate money, and where officials to oversee the process were more accessible.[29] *Coartación* was gen-

---

[27] See Gwendolyn Midlo Hall, *Social Control in Slave Plantation Societies: A Comparison of St. Domingue and Cuba* (Baltimore: The Johns Hopkins University Press, 1971), pp. 43-51.

[28] Bienvenido Cano y Federico Zalba, *El libro de los Síndicos de Ayuntamiento y de las Juntas Protectoras de Libertos* (Havana: Imprenta del Gobierno, 1875), p. 244.

[29] See the discussion of *coartación* in Chap. I, above, and Resumen general de los

erally supervised by the *síndico*, a local functionary appointed to represent slaves in legal proceedings, later made an ex officio member of the Juntas Protectoras. Before 1870 such legal provisions did little to mitigate the situation of most slaves. But as the climate in which slavery existed changed, they took on greater significance.

By the 1870s some of the *síndicos*, who tended to be Cuban rather than Spanish, were apparently interpreting their obligations fairly broadly, a tendency that alarmed both slaveholders and the government. In 1872 the government in Havana called them to order. It had reached the government's attention, the new ruling stated, that some *síndicos* outside of Havana were taking it upon themselves to resolve issues concerning slaves, exceeding their function of mediation and conciliation with masters and representation of slaves in court. Since according to law these *síndicos* were nothing more than parties charged "honorifically" with the defense of slaves, they should in the future abstain from exceeding their authority.[30] However, at the same time that the colonial government in Havana was cautioning the *síndicos* not to overstep their mandate, the metropolitan government in Madrid called on them to protect faithfully the rights of slaves in order to prevent complaints, citing the large number of complaints that were reaching Madrid.[31] The government in Havana seems to have been concerned primarily with control, the government in Madrid with placating Spanish abolitionists through an appearance of fairness.

The actual behavior of *síndicos* varied, and they provided nothing like an absolute guarantee of slave rights. *Síndicos* were, however, a resource of sorts. When slaves or their relatives managed to acquire some money, or were willing to risk greater assertiveness, they could under certain circumstances turn to the *sindicatura* in hope of obtaining partial concessions.

A few examples illustrate the point. Juan Lucumí was a thirty-four-year-old free African-born field worker. His wife, Gonzala Lucumí, was a slave on the *ingenio* Felicia. In June 1874 Juan deposited

---

esclavos existentes . . . , AHN, Ultramar, leg. 4882, tomo 3, exp. 39. For an early discussion of self-purchase by slaves in the United States, see the essay "Buying Freedom," in Herbert Aptheker, *To be Free: Studies in American Negro History* (New York: International Publishers, 1948; second edition, 1968), pp. 31-40.

[30] Cano y Zalba, *El libro*, p. 67.

[31] Ibid., p. 71. Spanish abolitionists were instrumental in bringing complaints to the attention of the authorities in Madrid.

five hundred pesos in bills with the *síndico* of Santa María del Rosario to obtain Gonzala's freedom. Four months later, having heard nothing, he appealed to the governor general. It turned out that the case was stalled while the wife's price was being estimated. The existence of the *síndico* did not make it easy for Juan Lucumí to free his wife, but it provided a first step toward that end.[32]

Sheer persistence was often the only weapon available to a slave faced with an ineffective *síndico*. María de la Merced Montalvo, born in Africa, considered herself free by virtue of age, since she had a baptismal record showing that she had been twenty years old in 1830. She obtained a letter of support and appealed to the *síndico*. While the case was pending, the *síndico* wrote to his superiors asking for a resolution because this woman "never ceased coming to the *sindicatura*" to remind him that she had been appealing for her freedom for over a year.[33]

In 1878 one authority remarked on the enormous sums of money that were being taken in by the *sindicaturas* and described this as reflecting "the effort of the slave to improve his condition." Between 1873 and 1877 the *sindicaturas* accepted 3,359 requests for *coartación*, 1,068 requests for reduction in price, and 5,697 requests for permission to change masters, as well as giving 2,127 grants of freedom. The total number of *coartados* grew accordingly. In 1871 there had been approximately 2,137; in 1877 there were some 3,531, an increase of about 65 percent in a period when the slave population itself had fallen by about 25 percent. Much of this activity, of course, continued to be concentrated in cities. Forty-two percent of the new *coartaciones* were granted in the four districts of the city of Havana, though that area had contained only about 8 percent of Cuba's slaves in 1871.[34] The greater mobility and resources of slaves in urban areas were undoubtedly the major determinants of this pattern, but the attitudes of masters may also have been significant. Hubert Aimes suggests that, in the last years of slavery, some masters were in-

[32] Juan Lucumí al Exmo. Sor. Gobernador General, AHN, Ultramar, leg. 4181.

[33] Expediente promovido por la morena Merced Montalvo, esclava de Da. Magdalena Caravino, ANC, ME, leg. 3814, exp. Ak.

[34] Expediente promovido por este Gobᵒ Gral para conocer las operaciones practicadas en todas las Sindicaturas de la Isla durante el quinquenio de 1873 a 1877, ANC, ME, leg. 3814, exp. A. For the 1871 slave population see Resumen general de los esclavos existentes . . . , AHN, Ultramar, leg. 4882, tomo 3, exp. 39. For 1877 figures see Fe Iglesias García, "El censo cubano de 1877 y sus diferentes versiones," *Santiago* 34 (Santiago de Cuba, June 1979): 167-214.

creasingly interested in the steady income *coartación* could provide
from slaves who worked on their own account and remitted a portion
of their wages.[35] This was likely to characterize urban rather than
rural masters, since the latter tended to be more fearful of the consequences of increased slave autonomy.

The Juntas Protectoras de Libertos, specifically charged with enforcing the Moret Law, represented a similar limited commitment
to the "protection" of slaves and *libertos*. They bore little resem-
blance to parallel institutions such as the Freedmen's Bureau in the
United States or the Stipendiary Magistrates in the British West
Indies. Such institutions characteristically had the double mission
of guarding ex-slaves' interests and insuring a smooth transition by
minimizing disruption in labor. They were therefore ill-equipped to
deal with outright conflicts, and often compromised the interests
of freedmen while at the same time infuriating masters.[36] For the
Juntas Protectoras the second goal so clearly took priority that there
was no real possibility that they would serve as the champions of
slaves. They ruled in favor of individual slaves in some cases involving nonregistration or claims to freedom based on age. But their
aim was not to end the institution of slavery, and they were reluctant
even to undermine it. In contrast to the Freedmen's Bureau or the
Stipendiary Magistrates, half of the *vocales* appointed to the Cuban
juntas were to be slaveholders. The original vice-president of the
Junta Central was Julián Zulueta, owner of hundreds of slaves and
several major plantations; his successor in 1874 was Francisco Ibá-

---

[35] Aimes, "Coartación," p. 423.

[36] On the Freedmen's Bureau, see William S. McFeely, *Yankee Stepfather. General
O. O. Howard and the Freedmen* (New York: W. W. Norton and Co., 1968); James
M. McPherson, *The Struggle for Equality. Abolitionists and the Negro in the Civil
War and Reconstruction* (Princeton: Princeton University Press, 1964), chap. 8; Louis
S. Gerteis, *From Contraband to Freedman: Federal Policy toward Southern Blacks,
1861-1865* (Westport, Connecticut: Greenwood Press, 1973); and Donald Nieman, *To
Set the Law in Motion: The Freedmen's Bureau and the Legal Rights of Blacks, 1865-
1868* (Millwood, N.Y.: KTO Press, 1979), as well as numerous articles cited in Nie-
man's bibliography. For my own analysis of some ambiguities of the role of U.S.
Freedmen's Bureau, see Rebecca J. Scott, "The Battle over the Child: Child Appren-
ticeship and the Freedmen's Bureau in North Carolina," *Prologue: The Journal of the
National Archives* 10 (Summer 1978): 100-13. On the British West Indies, see William
A. Green, *British Slave Emancipation. The Sugar Colonies and the Great Experiment,
1830-1865* (Oxford: The Clarendon Press, 1976); William Law Mathieson, *British
Slave Emancipation, 1838-1849* (London: Longmans, Green and Co., 1932; reprint
ed., New York: Octagon Books, 1967); and Thomas Holt, "The Problem of Freedom:
The Political Economy of Jamaica after Slavery," unpublished.

ñez, the same planter who had expressed concern about the potentially disruptive effects of the Moret Law.[37]

Even so, to some slaves the very existence of the juntas suggested that they might, on their own initiative, raise complaints against their masters. A representative case suggests both aspects of the situation. An urban slave named Luisa appealed for her freedom on the grounds that she was not properly registered. The junta agreed, but her master intervened to stall the case, and meanwhile sent her to the countryside, presumably to punish her and to block her access to outsiders. Her brother, the literate slave of another master, forwarded an appeal to Madrid on her behalf and won the case. Only with access to someone literate, urban, and probably quite daring, was Luisa able to counter her master's obstructionism.[38]

The case also illustrates the way in which the existence of a hierarchy of colonial officials sometimes made it possible for a slave to challenge an unfavorable junta ruling by addressing an appeal directly to the ministry of Ultramar. When such appeals did reach Madrid, the standard procedure was for the minister to query the governor in Cuba about the particulars of the case. A similar procedure was followed when a case attained notoriety in the press and thus came to the attention of the minister through a protest in the Cortes. This could provoke an inquiry that might reverse a manifestly unfair decision or end a series of delays. Since stalling and noncompliance on the part of masters were major obstacles faced by those declared free by provisions of the Moret Law, such an inquiry from above could resolve the issue and produce the long-sought *carta de libertad*.[39] The strategy of appealing to higher levels had its limits, of course, since in the final analysis the ministry's decision would depend on the information presented by officials in Cuba. Thus a complaint of mistreatment could reach Madrid, be referred back to Havana, be sent to the local junta for clarification, in the end to be simply ruled "groundless" by the junta. Moreover, on issues connected in a secondary way with freedom, such as the payment of back wages in cases where freedom had been illegally

[37] See *Gaceta de la Habana* (January 29, 1873), for the composition of the Junta Central and November 28, 1872, for the composition of the Juntas Jurisdiccionales. Cano y Zalba, *El libro*, p. 142, refers to Ibáñez.

[38] El pardo Faustino, esclavo de Dn. Pedro Prado, solicita la libertad de su hermana Luisa, esclava de D. Elías Núñez, AHN, Ultramar, leg. 4759, exp. 74.

[39] For cases of appeals by slaves that reached Madrid, see AHN, Ultramar, leg. 4759.

withheld, the petitioner would likely be told to take his or her case to the regular courts, for it was a judicial matter.[40]

The dynamic of raised and frustrated expectations emerges in a different form in the case of Lázaro, an African slave working on the *potrero* San José in Havana province. He appealed for his freedom in the early 1870s on the grounds that he was sixty-six years old. However, he appeared in the register of 1871 as only forty-six years of age. Since he was African and had no baptismal record, his age remained in dispute. The appeal and queries went back and forth between Madrid and Havana from 1874 to 1880. Meanwhile, in 1875, Lázaro simply fled from the household of his owner and was never heard from again.[41]

The changes of the 1870s encouraged some slaves to pursue old cases. José León appealed for freedom because he had been in Spain with his master back in 1850, and by law any slave who entered Spain was free. For his efforts he was kept in the *depósito judicial de esclavos* for seven years while his case was discussed. A woman named Catalina Antolines cited a visit to Málaga in 1844. She was freed, money for her *coartación* was returned to her, and her masters were indemnified. Many of those making such appeals were in a sense an elite among slaves, either because they were domestic servants or because their own histories had been exceptional. The most extreme case may be that of D. Adolfo Pérez Ferrer. He had been a slave in Cuba, fled to Mexico, studied medicine there, sent his savings back to his mother, and now wished to return to Cuba as a free man to care for her during the insurrection. His remarkable request was granted on order from Madrid.[42]

The establishment of some juntas in rural areas did increase slightly the chances that field slaves would be able to gain access to these new means for obtaining freedom. In addressing the juntas, however, slaves would find themselves in front of a group of local notables, approximately half of whom were slaveholders.[43] It is dif-

---

[40] Morena esclava Felipa Galuzo. Pide su libertad y abono de jornales, AHN, Ultramar, leg. 4759, exp. 71.

[41] Lázaro, Congo, esclavo en solicitud de carta de libertad, AHN, Ultramar, leg. 4759, exp. 98.

[42] All three cases were forwarded to Madrid and are in AHN, Ultramar, leg. 4759. See Libertad del moreno José León por haber estado en España, exp. 97; Sobre libertad de la morena Catalina Antolines, exp. 86; and D. Adolfo Pérez Ferrer, esclavo, solicita un documento para regresar a la isla como libre, exp. 99.

[43] The juntas were chaired by local colonial officials and included the *síndico* as an ex officio member, as well as the *vocales*, half of whom were slaveholders.

ficult to generalize about the behavior of the juntas because most surviving records are of cases appealed from them to Madrid or Havana. Since these represent the efforts of the dissatisfied party— slave or master—to obtain a reversal, they reflect less the incidence of different kinds of treatment than the resources of the different kinds of losers. It seems generally true, however, that while slaves who brought complaints before local juntas did on occasion obtain favorable rulings in cases of exceptionally arbitrary or unfair treatment, they were unlikely to be able to extend their rights beyond a very literal reading of the law. Yet the very experience of making a complaint might embolden a slave to take further action, including an appeal to Havana.[44]

The Consejo de Administración, an advisory body composed of merchants, planters, and professionals, heard such appeals. Its approach tended to be legalistic, and appellants often became entangled in regulations and procedures. When the consejo did come to a conclusion about a particular case, it usually applied existing rules cautiously, minimizing demands on masters while defending certain narrow rights of slaves. For example, the consejo in 1876 heard the case of a slave child named Plácida. The child's mother, who lived in Güines, had obtained her own freedom, and was now requesting that her daughter not be sold to a new master in Guanabacoa. She based her case on the article of the Moret Law that forbade the selling of slave children younger than age fourteen separately from their mothers. The consejo, however, ruled that the law applied to the slave children of *slave* mothers, and that since the mother had obtained her freedom it did not apply. The child could be sold.[45] Families attempting to obtain freedom with such limited means thus often faced insurmountable obstacles, but the fact that they made the attempt reflected the changing situation.

Conflict involving the Spanish government, officials in Cuba, and slaves themselves also arose from the issue of slave registration. A new set of registers, drawn up when owners already knew of the

[44] These generalizations about the role of the junta are based on an examination of cases that reached Havana or Madrid. Examples are to be found in AHN, Ultramar, leg. 4759, and, in greater numbers, scattered through the Miscelánea de Expedientes in the ANC. In the latter, see in particular legs. 3813, 3814, 3817, 3818, and 3819.

[45] Informe del expediente instruido a consulta del Caballero Síndico 3° de esta Capital relativa a que si los esclavos menores de 14 años hijos de madres libres pueden venderse separados de ellas, ANC, CA, leg. 44, exp. 4927.

law freeing slaves over the age of sixty and thus had reason to falsify ages, was put together in 1871. It vitiated the aim of the original registration law to deter the acquisition of contraband slaves, which would have required that only slaves who had been registered in 1866-1867, at the time of the passage of the law, be recognized as legitimately held. But the 1871 registers for a time supplanted the earlier lists, much to the satisfaction of owners, who petitioned for the inclusion of still more slaves.[46]

In January 1876, however, a royal order ruled that only those slaves inscribed in *both* the 1867 and the 1871 registers were legally enslaved and that the rest should be freed. A subsequent order required that lists be drawn up and displayed publicly, showing which slaves were in both registers and which were not. Proprietors complained that this was unfair and disruptive. The lieutenant governor of Pinar del Río argued that slaveowners were vulnerable to extortion by those in a position to "arrange" the registers. Though the legal issue was clear, and officials were ordered to proceed with the formation and publication of the registers, the definitive administrative list of those freed on grounds of nonregistration was not drawn up until 1883, seventeen years after the passage of the law.[47] Years of unpaid labor had been extracted from those who were to have been freed at the time of the 1867 census.

Unregistered slaves obviously had not been freed automatically by the passage of the law, nor was there any guarantee that they would now obtain their rights. But the mere raising of the issue was disruptive, and some slaves moved to take advantage of a situation in which masters were losing their monopoly of authority. What masters feared was not just the loss of individual slaves, but the impact of making the evidence so public. Suddenly slaves could be part of the process of determining who was slave and who was free. Witness, for example, the case of Carlos, an unusually assertive slave belonging to D. Julián Ramos, of Cárdenas. When Carlos learned of the law that said that all unregistered slaves were free, he hastened to see whether he was registered and discovered that he was not. So

[46] For requests from masters for the inclusion of new slaves in the registers, see ANC, ME, legs. 3814-20.

[47] Expediente promovido por el T. Gob^r de Pinar del Río, 1878, ANC, ME, leg. 3814, exp. Bj. For a list of those freed in 1883 see Anejo a la carta oficial de fecha 5 de diciembre de 1883, Relación de los individuos a quienes . . . se ha espedido documento de libertad, AHN, Ultramar, leg. 4815, exp. 289.

he submitted a petition to the minister of Ultramar, expressing his delight at being unregistered and asking for his *carta de libertad.* As it turned out, he had been registered under the name of his previous owner, so his request was denied.[48] But it was precisely this kind of initiative that worried slaveowners. They might be able to hold the line in disputed cases, but they were not sure how to deal with changed attitudes and expectations.

The issue of registration illustrates the ambiguous significance of the Moret Law and its associated regulations. The law provided legal freedom for the very young and the old and created openings for the pursuit of freedom by some of working age. But in the context of highly unequal power relations, when the juntas, the consejo, and the governor were virtually unanimous on the necessity for maintaining social peace by minimizing change, it was very difficult for slaves to give substance to their freedom or their new rights. Moreover, planters holding fast to a system of forced labor took both formal and informal measures to prevent the rights of slaves from interfering with the owners' own freedom of action.

For example, two of the traditional rights of slaves who had obtained *coartación* were the right to work on their own account, keeping a portion of the wage earned, and the right to change masters. The civil government reiterated the right to earn wages in a resolution issued March 8, 1870. But on March 12, the resolution was suspended "in view of a petition from several planters of this capital." Then, on May 1, 1871, the governor declared that rural slaves who were *coartados* did not have the right to change masters. This was extended in August 1875 to include denial of permission to seek a new master to rural slaves about to be sold. Finally, in April 1875, the government ruled that *coartados* had no right to receive pay for Sunday and holiday work.[49] These official countermeasures suggest that slave attempts to make use of *coartación* may have been expanding in the countryside, and that both rural masters and the colonial government were eager to limit their spread. The measures were also an expression of hostility on the part of some planters to even such freedom of labor as partial wages or limited mobility brought.

[48] See the letter of "El pardo Carlos o Calisto, siervo de Dn. Fabián Barroso," in AHN, Ultramar, leg. 4759, exp. 59.
[49] Cano y Zalba, *El libro,* pp. 56-57, 59, 304-305.

Masters had multiple concerns about loosening the bonds of slavery. One proprietor argued before the consejo that allowing slaves to change masters would lead to "corruption," since a competitor might pay the slave the price of *coartación* in order to obtain his or her labor. This would undermine both the sacred right of property and the "moral force" that he saw as the basis of the "discipline and subordination" of African slavery in the island. He claimed that this was all the more dangerous in view of the "politico-social propaganda" and the other tendencies of "revolutionary vertigo" that afflicted the island.[50]

Most Cuban planters acknowledged, at least in theory, that slavery could not continue indefinitely and that free labor would eventually become the appropriate basis for the organization of production in the island. In this they were less rigid than their counterparts in the U.S. South.[51] The outcome of the U.S. Civil War had sobered slaveholders elsewhere in the New World, and the idea that free labor would bring development and modernization appealed to Cuban estate-owners who saw themselves as sugar manufacturers as well as planters. But their behavior during the period of the Moret Law reveals their concern not to lose non-economic "moral force" and their reluctance to accept the competition that would accompany a genuinely free market in labor.

Thus throughout the 1870s most Cuban slaves remained unequivocally enslaved. Moreover, planters held the children of slaves on plantations working without pay, attempted to deny unregistered slaves access to the lists that would enable them to verify their status, disputed the ages of the elderly, and lobbied for limitations even on the traditional entitlements granted to *coartados*. But slaves continued to seek their freedom, and the war in the east continued to create uncertainty and disruption. Furthermore, while the Moret Law did not immediately alter the structure of the slave labor force available to planters, the suppression of the slave trade threatened to do so. Willingly or not, Cuba's planters would have to adapt to a changing labor force and to changing attitudes and expectations.

[50] See the discussion in the case of María Jesús Hernández, parda, esclava, solicita libertad, AHN, Ultramar, leg. 4759, exp. 95.

[51] On attitudes of U.S. slaveholders toward the prospect of free labor, see James L. Roark, *Masters Without Slaves: Southern Planters in the Civil War and Reconstruction* (New York: W. W. Norton and Co., 1977).

IV

Adaptation, 1870-1877

The Cuban planters quite recognise now the probability,
almost certainty, of a coming abolition of slavery. They make
here no organised public objection to its eventual arrival;
but they demand time, and an immigration of labour
hands under Government sanction and aid, and also a
series of years of preparation of a very gradual description.
"How not to do it!" is their *môt d'ordre* . . .

—*British Consul-General Dunlop, Havana, 1871*[1]

The 1870s in Cuba were a period of political and social conflict. The civil war in the east drained Spanish resources and polarized Cuban politics. The struggle over the enforcement of the Moret Law—carried out almost unnoticed in small confrontations between slaves, masters, juntas, and government officials—helped to undermine the established social relations upon which slavery rested. In the economic realm, however, the decade appears at first to have been one of relative prosperity. The average annual output of sugar was up almost 25 percent from the previous ten years, despite a decline in production in the east.[2]

Cuba shipped this sugar to several major markets, the United States absorbing in 1875 approximately 65 percent, England 16 percent, France 8 percent, and Spain 3 percent. The role of the United States as importer would continue to grow through the decade. Beet sugar was becoming a more formidable competitor, with 36 percent of the world market in 1870, but cane would remain predominant for the rest of the decade. Most important, sugar prices remained relatively steady. Average quotations for fair refining sugar in New York City were 5.36 cents per pound in 1870, and 5.08 cents in 1880.

[1] Consul-General Dunlop to Earl Granville, Havana, Jan. 16, 1871. Extract printed in *Anti-Slavery Reporter* 18 (Jan. 1, 1873): 95.
[2] Moreno, *El ingenio* 3: 36-37.

Slave prices for the 1870s are difficult to determine, but seem to have remained relatively high.[3]

It can be argued that the mid-1870s represented a turning point, as the pressures for technical modernization, consolidation, and heavy investment pushed the industry into crisis. Manuel Moreno Fraginals asserts that by 1875 Cuban slave plantations "which for some time had been showing clear signs of crisis, started on the path to their definite disintegration." He carries the argument a step further and locates the source of emancipation in this process: "The 'industrial revolution' in the sugar industry also made it necessary to transform labor relations . . . having finally triggered the crisis of the slave system on which the old *ingenio* had been based."[4]

"Crisis" is an elusive concept. Moreover, a crisis of the sugar industry was not necessarily the same thing as a crisis of slavery, and would not necessarily bring about abolition. To determine the links between the economic state of the sugar industry and the actual process of slave emancipation, one must look directly at the structure of the slave population and the behavior of planters, slaves, and other workers. The evidence suggests that, despite the many pressures on sugar planters and on slavery, within the sugar estates of the central and western regions the institution of slavery proved remarkably resilient and adaptable. It appears that the numbers of slaves in the most productive age groups did not decline dramatically, at least on the larger plantations, and thus the more prosperous planters were not faced with an immediate crisis of labor supply. Furthermore, the introduction of technology had by no means automatically made slavery undesirable to planters, and they did not behave as if they had given up their attachment to servile labor. When they needed additional or replacement workers, they made

[3] On Cuban exports, see Moreno, *El ingenio* 3: 76. On beet sugar, see Noel Deerr, *The History of Sugar*, 2 vols. (London: Chapman and Hall, 1949-1950) 2: 490. On sugar prices, see Willett and Gray, *Weekly Statistical Sugar Trade Journal*, Jan. 3, 1896, and "The World's Sugar Production and Consumption," U.S. Congress, 57th Congress, 1st Sess. (1902), Doc. no. 15, part 7, serial set 4314, p. 2691. On slave prices, see notes 21-23, below.

[4] See Moreno, "Plantaciones," pp. 73, 59. (I have used the English translation of these quotations from the version of the essay that will appear in Manuel Moreno Fraginals, Frank Moya Pons, and Stanley L. Engerman, eds., *Between Slavery and Free Labor: The Spanish-Speaking Caribbean in the Nineteenth Century* [Baltimore: The Johns Hopkins University Press, 1985.]) In this essay, Moreno also argues that the 1880 law of abolition was "merely the de jure recognition of a situation characterized by the de facto disintegration of the slave system" (p. 80).

use of a variety of labor forms alongside slavery without repudiating slavery itself.

This evolution of labor patterns in the 1870s can be understood only within the framework of Cuba's changing population. The total slave population fell between 1862 and 1877 by about 46 percent, leaving somewhat fewer than 200,000 slaves in the island in 1877.[5] The rate of decline varied widely from province to province. Matanzas and Santa Clara, the major sugar producers and the provinces with the largest numbers of fully mechanized mills, stand out for their high rates of persistence of slavery. Along with Pinar del Río, a province with one-third of its slaves in sugar and one-third in tobacco, they show an 1877 slave population of over 60 percent of that in 1862, despite the decline due to the legal reclassification of children and the elderly. Havana, the province that contained the island's major urban area, showed a substantially more rapid decline. Its slave population in 1877 was less than half that of 1862. Incomplete figures on the numbers of slaves on sugar plantations in 1877 suggest that the great bulk of the decline in Havana's slave population took place in the city, with much greater persistence on the plantations.[6] Both Puerto Príncipe, a cattle-raising area, and Santiago

---

[5] The figures cited in this paragraph and in Tables 10 and 11 are based on several official tabulations. Those from 1862 are from Cuba, Centro de Estadística, *Noticias estadísticas*. They have been compiled into provinces by aggregating jurisdictions, as described in Chap. I, note 48. To reflect the redistricting done at the time of the establishment of the six provinces I have reduced the slave population of Havana province by 8,853, the slave population given for Alacranes district in 1862, and added that many to Matanzas. I have also added 394 to the slave population of Puerto Príncipe and subtracted the same from Santa Clara to adjust for the division of the jurisdiction of Sancti Spíritus.

Returns from the 1867 slave count are neither reliable nor consistent and are included here only for the purpose of comparison. They can be found in Resumen general de los esclavos que segun el censo de 1867 . . . existían a la terminación de ese censo en las jurisdicciones que componían el territorio de la Isla, AHN, Ultramar, leg. 4884, exp. 160. I have moved 9,760 slaves from the province of Havana to the province of Matanzas, based on the assumption that in 1867 Alacranes held the same proportion of the slave population of Güines that it had in 1862. In the case of the Sancti Spíritus redistricting, Morón, part of the area transferred, appears as a jurisdiction in the 1867 figures, and can be incorporated directly into Puerto Príncipe.

The 1871 figures are from Resumen de los esclavos comprendidos en el padrón de 1871, AHN, Ultramar, leg. 4882, tomo 4. They have not been adjusted because the totals for Güines in 1871 and for the adjacent jurisdiction of Matanzas suggest that the later formal redistricting is already reflected in the 1871 figures.

The 1877 census has often been considered unreliable, but the article by Fe Iglesias, "El censo cubano," presents new evidence on the compilation of results and suggests that in its final revision it was more accurate than previously imagined. I have used her totals for 1877.

[6] For the 1862 figures, see Cuba, Centro de Estadística, *Noticias estadísticas*, "Dis-

TABLE 10
Slave Population, 1862-1877

Province	1862	1867	1871	1877
Pinar del Río	46,027	44,879	36,031	29,129
Havana	86,241	84,769	63,312	41,716
Matanzas	98,496	102,661	87,858	70,849
Santa Clara	72,116	68,680	56,535	42,049
Puerto Príncipe	14,807	14,889	7,167	2,290
Santiago de Cuba	50,863	47,410	36,717	13,061
Total	368,550	363,288	287,620	199,094

SOURCE: 1862—Cuba, Centro de Estadística, *Noticias estadísticas*, "Distribución"; 1867—AHN, Ultramar, leg. 4884, tomo 8, exp. 160; 1871—AHN, Ultramar, leg. 4882, tomo 4, "Resumen de los esclavos . . . , 1871"; 1877—Fe Iglesias García, "El censo cubano de 1877 y sus diferentes versiones," *Santiago* 34 (June 1979): 167-211.

TABLE 11
Slave Population, 1862-1877
(1862 = 100)

Province	1862	1867	1871	1877
Pinar del Río	100	98	78	63
Havana	100	98	73	48
Matanzas	100	104	89	72
Santa Clara	100	95	78	58
Puerto Príncipe	100	101	48	15
Santiago de Cuba	100	93	72	26
Total	100	99	78	54

SOURCES: See Table 10.

de Cuba, an area of backward sugar mills and much small-scale farming, lost slave population rapidly after 1867. These were the two provinces most involved in the Ten Years' War, which brought about the destruction, both direct and indirect, of numerous plantations, the freeing of many slaves in smaller holdings, and the death or migration of many others (see Tables 10 and 11).

It is apparent that where sugar prospered, slavery persisted. Table 12 ranks the provinces in descending order of their significance and degree of development as sugar producers (though the positions of Havana and Pinar del Río could be reversed, depending on which

tribución." For approximate figures on the population on sugar plantations in Havana province in 1877, see the summary of the agricultural census in *Revista de Agricultura* 3 (March 31, 1879): 75.

TABLE 12
Sugar Production and Slave Population

Province	1860 Total Sugar Production (metric tons)	1860 Average Production Per Mill (metric tons)	1862 Number of Slaves on Ingenios	1862 Slaves on Ingenios as Percentage of Total Population	1877 Slaves as Percentage of 1862 Slave Population[a]
Matanzas	265,664	601	72,689	34%	72%
Santa Clara	145,163	368	44,106	15%	58%
Pinar del Río	38,644	379	16,830	11%	63%
Havana	38,999	310	19,404	5%	48%
Santiago de Cuba	31,953	161	14,181	6%	26%
Puerto Príncipe	15,434	151	5,461	8%	15%

SOURCES: Same as Tables 4, 5, and 10; Cuba, Centro de Estadística, *Noticias estadísticas*, "Distribución."

[a] Children and the elderly, roughly 20 percent of the earlier slave population, are excluded from the 1877 count.

measures take priority). Slavery can be seen to have declined most sharply in the three provinces where sugar was proportionately less important, and to have persisted in the three provinces with the highest average product per mill, and where slaves on *ingenios* had been between 11 and 34 percent of the 1862 provincial population.

As a result, slavery became increasingly concentrated in the major sugar zones. Matanzas and Santa Clara had 46 percent of Cuba's slave population in 1862; by 1877 they had 57 percent. Similarly, an increasing proportion of Cuba's slaves resided in the countryside. The 1871 slave lists divided slaves into those on rural estates and those in domestic service—an imperfect dichotomy, since some urban slaves did not do domestic work and some domestic slaves did not live in cities—but one which gives a rough idea of the rural-urban division. In 1871, 55,830 slaves were counted in domestic service, and they constituted about 20 percent of the total slave population of 287,620. By the end of 1879, the governor general, basing his calculations on 1877 figures, gave the number in domestic service as 29,992, down to 15 percent of the 200,440 slaves he believed to exist at the time.[7] Both of these tendencies strongly suggest

[7] For the 1862 and 1871 figures, see note 5, above. For 1877, see Telegrama al Ministro de Ultramar, Nov. 27, 1879, AHN, Ultramar, leg. 4882, tomo 5. The revised total for 1877 was somewhat lower.

88

that the causes of emancipation cannot be found solely within the sugar plantations, for as emancipation proceeded, these plantations held proportionately more, not fewer, of Cuba's slaves.

Thus during the 1860s and 1870s, when the "contradictions" within Cuban slavery were in theory becoming most apparent, the major sugar areas were nonetheless holding on to most of their slaves, or acquiring new ones to replace those lost. In Matanzas in 1862 the slave population was around 98,500. About 20 percent of these slaves would have been either under the age of ten or over the age of sixty, leaving approximately 78,800 of working age.[8] In 1877, as a result of the Moret Law, all slaves were by definition between the ages of nine and fifty-nine, but there were still about 70,850 slaves in Matanzas. The slave population of working age had fallen in the intervening fifteen years, but only by around 8,000, or 10 percent, an amount plausibly attributable to deaths and a shift in the age structure, partially counteracted by some in-migration. Planters in Cuba's most productive province were not abandoning slaves or slavery.

The persistence of high levels of slave population in the major areas of sugar production did not, however, mean that sugar in those areas was produced entirely with slave labor. Cuba recorded a product of 533,800 metric tons of sugar in 1861 and increased output to over 700,000 tons per year during the late 1860s and early 1870s.[9] Despite a diminishing total slave population, sugar production had expanded, either through the addition of nonslave workers or through increases in productivity, or both.

There is abundant evidence of the addition of new workers. Although the island's total population had grown only slightly between 1861 and 1877, the Chinese population had increased 35 percent. For example, in Santa Clara, whose portion of the island's total sugar crop continued to increase, the 1877 census listed 13,301 Asians, twice as many as there had been in 1861; in Matanzas, the total was

[8] The figure of 20 percent was arrived at from the age distribution of slaves reported in 1862, in which 22 percent of slaves were listed as over age sixty or under age 10. I have assumed that the proportion would be somewhat smaller in a plantation area, which would have a higher concentration of imported Africans. See Cuba, Centro de Estadística, *Noticias estadísticas*, "Clasificación por sexos y edades." This estimate also coincides with the age pyramids derived by Moreno from plantation accounts. See Moreno, *El ingenio*, 2: 90.

[9] Moreno, *El ingenio* 3: 36, 37.

TABLE 13
Chinese Population, 1861-1877

Province	1861	1872	1877
Pinar del Río	2,221	3,396	3,137
Havana	9,456	11,365	10,108
Matanzas	15,782	27,002	20,054
Santa Clara	6,274	15,878	13,301
Puerto Príncipe	341	297	94
Santiago de Cuba	754	462	422
Total	34,828	58,400	47,116

SOURCE: 1861—Cuba, Centro de Estadística, *Noticias estadísticas*, "Censo de población segun el cuadro general de la Comisión Ejecutiva de 1861"; 1872—Expediente General Colonización Asiática, AHN, Ultramar, leg. 87; 1877—Iglesias, "El censo cubano."

20,054, up from 15,782. For the island as a whole, the figures were 47,116 Asians in 1877 (the majority still under indentures) versus 34,828 in 1861 (see Table 13). The ratio of slave workers to Chinese in sugar production, however, was still over six to one in 1877. Total white population had increased by around 22 percent between 1862 and 1877 (more than offsetting a decline of 22 percent in the black population) and some discharged Spanish soldiers and other immigrants could be found working on the plantations. Evidence from account books and from the 1877 agricultural census nonetheless suggests that the numbers of whites doing field work on plantations continued to be relatively small.[10]

The question of productivity is more difficult to answer, since average product per worker is impossible to calculate with confidence on the basis of surviving evidence. However, planters did introduce new equipment for the boiling-houses of the larger plantations, and were able to increase the total output of sugar without increasing substantially the acreage planted in cane.[11] Clearly the

[10] The 1877 agricultural census, whose figures are only approximate, listed 90,516 slaves, 20,726 "alquilados y libres," and 14,597 Chinese in the *dotaciones* of sugar plantations filing reports. The category "alquilados y libres" would seem to indicate rented slaves and free workers. However, some owners who filed returns apparently interpreted it to include freed and sometimes nonworking slaves. The category still only totals 16 percent of the total in the *dotaciones. Revista de Agricultura* 3 (March 31, 1879): 75. Population figures are from the 1862 census and from Iglesias, "El censo cubano." For evidence from account books, see below.

[11] There were 1,190 *ingenios* listed in the 1877 agricultural census, claiming 17,701 *caballerías* of land under cultivation, as opposed to 1,365 with 20,758 *caballerías* in cane in 1860. It is clear from the detailed returns, however, that some plantations did not return figures on area planted, so the 1877 total of 17,701 understates the

existence of slavery was not incompatible, at least in the short run, with technological improvements and with the addition of supplementary forms of labor.

The strategy of large planters appears to have been to maintain control over their slaves, while expanding their labor force in other ways. Thus the contradictions of Cuban slavery (of which the failure of the slave population to maintain its numbers was the most urgent) did not have to impel abolition as such. An observer sympathetic to Cuban planters noted drily in 1873: "The slave-owners in Cuba are convinced of the necessity of manumitting their slaves; but readily as they acknowledge the evils of the slave system, they are not persuaded of the wisdom of any measure by which it may be brought to an end." He saw them pursuing a policy of substitution of free labor for slave, as such became necessary, rather than actual suppression of the institution of slavery.[12]

The most distinctive characteristic of the plantation labor force in the mid-1870s, then, was its diversity. Plantation slaves, rented slaves, indentured Asians, and black, white, and mulatto wage workers all labored on the estates. Plantation employers did not face a homogeneous supply of labor, but rather a segmented labor force, with different forms and quantities of payment due different types of workers. Wages were paid by the day, the task, the month, the trimester, or the year; the amount paid varied widely; workers sometimes did and sometimes did not receive maintenance; compensation occurred in coin, bills, credit, goods, or shares.[13]

This is the situation that has been interpreted as chaotic, symptomatic of the internal collapse of slavery.[14] But one must look carefully at the argument that the diversity of forms of labor in the 1870s was indicative of a disintegration of Cuban slavery in the face of unavoidable contradictions. The argument has at least two parts. The first part has to do with planters' response to the decline in the

---

total. For 1860, see Rebello, *Estados*. For 1877, see "Noticia de las fincas azucareras en producción que existían . . . al comenzar el presupuesto de 1877-78 . . . ," *Revista económica* 2 (June 7, 1878): 7-24, and *Revista de Agricultura* 3 (March 31, 1879): 75.

[12] A. Gallenga, *The Pearl of the Antilles*, pp. 96, 105.

[13] This picture emerges from censuses, account books, and observers' reports. See the 1877 agricultural census, the plantation records cited below, and the essay, "Estudios de Agricultura: II. El Trabajador, El Jornal," *Revista de Agricultura* 1 (April 30, 1879): 83.

[14] See Moreno, "¿Abolición o desintegración?" and "Plantaciones en el Caribe," in his *La historia como arma*, pp. 50-117.

slave trade. Aware that their supply of new slaves was being cut off, some Cuban planters were taking better care of their existing slaves and were encouraging reproduction. But, it has been argued, this policy of "good treatment" inevitably led to a decline in the productivity of the slave work force as the proportion of the very young and the very old increased, eventually making the enterprise unprofitable. Moreno's study of plantation records shows convincingly that the proportion of slaves of working age did decline on some Cuban estates through the first half of the nineteenth century.[15] (A parallel process was occurring in some areas of Brazil.)[16] But even if one accepts the argument that maintaining a self-reproducing slave labor force was bound eventually to be unprofitable for Cuban planters—in a way that it was not, for example, for those in the American South—the question remains: Given the very late cessation of the contraband slave trade to Cuba, how far had this process actually proceeded on Cuban plantations by the time of abolition?

We do not have enough surviving plantation slave lists for the 1870s to put together a truly representative sample for the entire island. For one district, however, there is a very comprehensive source: the manuscript returns of an 1875 slave count. The district is Santa Isabel de las Lajas in Santa Clara province. It was a prosperous area in the jurisdiction of Cienfuegos, one which contained both old and new plantations. In 1862 the *partido* of Lajas had a slave population of 1,930 and contained seventeen *ingenios*. In 1875, when the manuscript listing was drawn up, there were fifteen *ingenios* and a slave population of 1,852.[17]

The strong rate of persistence of slavery in Lajas—a drop of only about 4 percent in thirteen years—may have been due in part to the

[15] Moreno, *El ingenio* 2: 83-90. He states that the conscious policy of "good treatment," aimed at creating a self-reproducing slave force, was the "most visible symptom of the dissolution of slavery" (p. 90).

[16] Stanley J. Stein found in his analysis of the coffee-producing municipality of Vassouras that the fifteen- to forty-year-old sector of the plantation population "dropped from a high of 62 per cent of the total labor force in 1830-1849 to 51 per cent in the succeeding decade, and finally to 35 per cent in the last eight years of slavery." *Vassouras. A Brazilian Coffee County, 1850-1900* (Cambridge, Mass.: Harvard University Press, 1957; reprint ed., New York: Atheneum, 1974), p. 78.

[17] For 1862 figures see Cuba, Centro de Estadística, *Noticias estadísticas*, "Censo de población . . . por partidos pedáneos," and Enrique Edo y Llop, *Memoria histórica de Cienfuegos y su jurisdicción* 2nd ed. (Cienfuegos: J. Andreu, 1888), appendix, pp. 5, 6. The manuscript slave list for Lajas is in Capitanía Pedánea de Santa Isabel de las Lajas, Núm⁰ 3, Padrón general de esclavos, 1875, ANC, ME, leg. 3748, exp. B.

presence there of slaveholders who were also slave traders, and suggests that the district was not typical, even for a sugar area. It does represent a significant part of a significant region, however, and the major plantations in the area were owned by such proprietors as Agustín Goytisolo, an innovator in plantation transportation, Tomás Terry, a reformist sugar magnate, and the Spanish-owned company of La Gran Azucarera. Analysis of the slave population of this district can thus show the kind of labor situation faced by large and small planters in an important sugar area in the mid-1870s.[18]

Of the slaves on *ingenios* in Lajas in 1875, 58 percent had been born in Cuba and 42 percent in Africa; 61 percent were male and 39 percent female. It was a population that plainly had relied recently and heavily on imports, probably during the boom in the contraband trade in the 1850s. The age structure of the plantation population is also quite striking, considering the date—just five years before legal abolition. It was not an aged population: while 28 percent were between ages thirty-one and forty, only 6 percent were between ages fifty-one and sixty, even though one might have expected this latter group to include some slaves over age sixty whose ages had been falsified by their masters to evade the Moret Law. Nor was there a high proportion of young slave children. Those born since September 1868 were technically free, and those between ages six and ten constituted only 7.5 percent of the population. Even though those born since 1868 were still the responsibility of the plantation, the total burden was probably relatively small, for in some instances slave parents maintained their *liberto* children directly, or later reimbursed the master for their maintenance. What is most significant is that the sixteen-to-forty age group, of prime working age, constituted fully 63 percent of the plantation slave population, and 66 percent of the males (see Table 14 and the accompanying figure).

It is clear that this was potentially a quite productive population. One hundred percent of the legally enslaved population was between ages six and sixty—the Moret Law had streamlined it that much. And between those limits, the population was further weighted toward those of working age. The largest single group consisted of males thirty-one through thirty-five, followed closely by males thirty-six through forty and twenty-six through thirty. Lajas plan-

<hr>

[18] Names of owners are given in the slave list. Further information on Terry can be obtained from Ely, *Comerciantes cubanos*, chap. 5.

TABLE 14
Ages of Slaves on *Ingenios* in Santa Isabel de las Lajas, 1875

Age	Male Slaves	Female Slaves	All Slaves	Percentage of Total
6-10	49	51	100	7.5%
11-15	56	61	117	8.8%
16-20	51	58	109	8.2%
21-25	108	69	177	13.3%
26-30	120	64	184	13.8%
31-35	132	72	204	15.3%
36-40	124	46	170	12.8%
41-45	69	44	113	8.5%
46-50	45	24	69	5.2%
51-55	31	15	46	3.5%
56-60	29	10	39	2.9%
61-65[a]	2	1	3	.2%
Total	816	515	1,331	100.0%

SOURCE: ANC, ME, leg. 3748, exp. B. Capitanía Pedánea de Santa Isabel de las Lajas, Núm. 3, Padrón general de esclavos, 1875.

[a] All of those under 6 or over 60 should legally have been free under the Moret Law. Some of those age 6 were free.

tations were not carrying a terrible burden of young and old slaves. Masters were not sustaining the full cost of reproduction of their work force. They were still operating with a carefully selected labor force built up primarily through purchase. The difficult future of slavery now that the trade had ended was apparent in the small

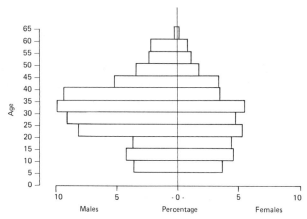

Age pyramid of slaves on *ingenios*
in Santa Isabel de las Lajas, 1875
(n = 1,331).

94

number coming up through the ranks—there were less than half as many males aged eleven through twenty as aged twenty-one through thirty—but the full effects of this would not be felt for a number of years. "Good treatment," if such there were in Lajas, had not had time to create either a self-reproducing slave population or one filled with young and old slaves.

The Lajas plantations did vary among themselves. The small *ingenio* of Destino, for example, with just twenty-eight slaves, was primarily Creole, and over half of its population was under age twenty-five. San Agustín, by contrast, with 110 slaves, was predominantly African, and only about a quarter of its population was under age twenty-five. To understand better the differences among plantations, one can rank by size the Lajas *ingenios* for which there are complete age data (see Table 15). One finds that all four of the predominantly African plantations were among the largest, although there were also two large plantations with majority Creole populations. All of the smaller plantations were predominantly Creole, probably, though not necessarily, reflecting fewer recent purchases of slaves. The percentage of the slave population that was between ages sixteen and forty also correlates slightly with size: on the six larger plantations, an average of 66 percent were between those ages; on the seven smaller, 56 percent. The large Caracas plantation stands out in the census, with fully 64 percent of its slave population concentrated between the ages of twenty-one and thirty-five, and 82 percent of those slaves African.

Although they were also using some Chinese laborers, free workers, and rented slaves, sugar plantations in Lajas remained heavily committed to slavery into the mid-1870s. Indeed, if one can trust the ambiguous figures from the 1877 agricultural census, it appears that the large Lajas plantations may have relied more heavily on slave labor than the small ones. Five of the six larger estates had a total of 701 slaves, 161 *alquilados y libres* (which could include rented slaves and *libertos* as well as free workers), and 89 Asians in their *dotaciones* in 1877, while six of the seven smaller estates held 235 slaves and 105 *alquilados y libres*. Further, all of the large plantations appear to have maintained or increased their slave holdings between 1875 and 1877, while on all of the smaller estates the number of slaves declined[19] (see Table 15).

[19] See Table 15 and "Noticia de las fincas," p. 13. Armantina and Manaca, excluded

TABLE 15
Populations on Specific *Ingenios*, Santa Isabel de las Lajas, 1875, 1877

| | 1875 | | | | 1877 | | |
Ingenio	Slaves	African	Male	Age 16-40	Slaves	Free & Rented[a]	Chinese
Santa Susana	283	43%	59%	56%	n.d.	n.d.	n.d.
Santa Catalina	181	51%	59%	66%	204	—	—
Caracas	154	66%	64%	71%	198	97	—
San Agustín	110	54%	61%	65%	113	19	—
Amalia	94	19%	48%	70%	102	—	29
San Isidro	84	60%	71%	89%	84	45	60
Sacramento	78	13%	68%	60%	70	20	—
Dos Hermanos	77	47%	77%	48%	68	30	—
California	62	2%	44%	47%	n.d.	n.d.	n.d.
Adelaida	38	40%	68%	63%	35	16	—
Santa Elena	32	31%	63%	53%	30	10	—
Maguaraya	30	43%	63%	57%	23	17	—
Destino	28	29%	79%	79%	9	12	—

SOURCE: Columns 1 through 4, same as Table 14; columns 5 through 7, "Noticia de las fincas," *Revista económica*, June 7, 1878, p. 13.

[a] This column must be considered only an estimate. In some cases, due to an apparent misunderstanding by those filling out the returns, some young and elderly *libertos* were included in the category "alquilados y libres," though they may not have been actual workers on the estate.

Clearly, then, large planters in Lajas were not yet facing an internal collapse of slavery. Though the demographic structure of their slave populations indicated trouble ahead, meaning that free laborers would have to be attracted sooner or later, this implied a theoretical acceptance of an eventual transition, not a willingness to give up control over the existing work force. In fact, *hacendados* in Cienfuegos, the jurisdiction in which Lajas was located, held meetings during the 1870s to oppose the immediate abolition of slavery.[20]

The evidence available concerning Cuban slave prices also gives grounds for caution against too quick an assumption of internal collapse. Though there do not yet exist sufficiently complete series of slave prices to permit confident generalization about the trends of the market, it is clear that prices remained relatively high in the 1870s. An American journalist visiting Santa Clara in 1873 reported the price of an able-bodied slave at $1,500 and "becoming dearer

from the comparison because their 1875 slave data are incomplete, had 122 slaves, 17 "alquilados y libres." Data are missing for Santa Susana and California in 1877.

[20] Edo y Llop, *Memoria*, p. 629.

every day."[21] The British consul estimated slave prices at the beginning of the decade at 500 to 650 pounds.[22] Hubert Aimes cites figures of $2,000 in 1872, $1,500 to $2,000 in 1873, and $1,600 in 1875 for Ladino slaves.[23] Similarly, slave rental prices seem to have remained constant and even risen at times.[24] These high labor costs presented a serious problem for planters, in the face of stagnant sugar prices, but they hardly signal a decay of slavery, if by that one means internal collapse and the rejection by planters of slave labor.[25]

A second part of the argument for the internal dissolution of slavery rests on the concept of slaves as instruments of production whose productivity depended on brute strength and coercion alone and who were therefore unsuited to certain kinds of skilled labor and became rapidly less valuable once they became physically less capable.[26] But is this indeed how slaves behaved—or even how they were viewed by planters?

In a pamphlet addressed to the Spanish minister of Ultramar in 1868, an owner of 300 slaves in Cuba estimated the average value of male slaves thirty-one to fifty years old as *higher* than that of slaves sixteen to thirty, remarking that in the older group were those with skills, such as machinists, carpenters, masons, blacksmiths, *paileros* (those who worked with open boiling pans in sugar processing), etc.[27] To corroborate this portrait would require the analysis of a large sample of sale prices and *tasaciones* (legal appraisals of price) in order to determine the influence of various factors on the

[21] O'Kelly, *The Mambi-Land*, p. 64.

[22] See Thomas, *Cuba*, p. 256. See also John V. Crawford to A. H. Layard, May 15, 1873, in B. M. Ms. Layard Papers, Add. ms. 39000, fol. 139v. Crawford writes from Havana: "The prices of negro slaves are very high."

[23] Aimes, *A History*, p. 268.

[24] On the *ingenio* Delicias, for example, prices paid for slave rental remained relatively constant at 11 pesos per month through the 1870s, though they rose for short-term rentals in 1878. Libro Diario del Ingenio Delicias, Años 1872-1882, ANC, ML, 10802. Monthly rental for slaves on the *ingenio* Santa Rosa in 1876 was 17 pesos, as it was on the *ingenio* Concepción in Matanzas in 1878-1879. ANC, Bienes Embargados, leg. 201, exp. 5 and leg. 206, exp. 7.

[25] A good example of the use of slave prices to analyze the decline of slavery is Jaime Reis, "The Impact of Abolitionism in Northeast Brazil: A Quantitative Approach," in Vera Rubin and Arthur Tuden, eds., *Comparative Perspectives on Slavery in New World Plantation Societies* (New York: New York Academy of Sciences, 1977), pp. 107-22. See also Moreno, Klein, Engerman, "The Level and Structure."

[26] See the earlier discussion of the assumption of a contradiction between slavery and technology in Chap. I, above.

[27] *Exposición del Exmo. Señor Conde de Vega Mar . . .* (Madrid: T. Fortanet, 1868), in AHN, Ultramar, leg. 4759.

market value of slaves. But even taken by itself the statement suggests that a slave work force with an age structure similar to that found in Lajas was not necessarily experiencing sharply declining productivity, and that planters did not invariably view slave labor as "brute" labor.

More important is the direct evidence that slaves were used extensively in the large, advanced mills. The *ingenio* España, for example, was one of the most advanced plantations in Cuba in the 1870s. Its work force in 1873 was composed of 530 slaves, 86 Asians, and just 19 whites. That is, the work force was over 80 percent slave, and 97 percent unfree labor, if the Chinese were, as is likely, indentured.[28] The *ingenio* Álava, whose technological apparatus Moreno has used to illustrate the industrial revolution on Cuban plantations, reported in 1877 a *dotación* of 550 slaves and 71 Asians. Though it undoubtedly employed some salaried workers, slaves clearly remained the basis of its operations.[29] The Las Cañas plantation has been described as "Cuba's most modern mill in 1850" which "up to 1880 . . . kept adding new machinery in a continuous process of renovation." Its work force in 1873 numbered 450 slaves, 230 Asians, and 27 whites. Again, the number of free white workers was very small, and they held the same jobs they had always held on Cuban plantations: administrator, *mayordomo*, machinist, and so forth. On Las Cañas, the Asians do seem to have been treated differently from slaves, and they were concentrated in the processing sector.[30] These examples do not really test the claim that technological advancement encouraged a shift to free labor—for that, one would need reliable statistics on the work forces of a cross-section of Cuban plantations and detailed information on the internal division of labor, data that do not appear to have survived. But the examples do suggest that technological advancement did not *require* the extensive use of fully free labor. One could go further and argue that the only substantial concession to the supposed necessity of a shift to

[28] Fermín Rosillo y Alquier, *Noticias de dos ingenios y datos sobre la producción azucarera de la isla de Cuba* (Havana: El Iris, 1873).

[29] See "Noticia de las fincas," p. 11. España, Álava, and Las Cañas were all located in Matanzas province.

[30] Moreno's description of Las Cañas as "Cuba's most modern mill" can be found in *The Sugarmill*, pp. 124-25. Figures on the work force are from Rosillo, *Noticias*. Observations on the treatment of the Chinese are from Juan Pérez de la Riva, "Duvergier de Hauranne," p. 107.

free labor made on many major Cuban plantations in the 1870s involved the employment of a relatively small number of Chinese workers, many of whom were still held under indentures. The reasons for the use of Chinese indentured workers in mechanized mills were complex, and need not be seen as inherent to their status as juridically free labor nor as evidence of a contradiction between slave labor and mechanization.

There is no question, however, but that planters were adapting. They did need new workers to make up for the decline in the slave work force, and if these workers could be hired for specific tasks, including technical ones, rather than bought, all the better. However, this was not the same thing as wanting fully free wage laborers to perform these tasks, and it was a long way from wanting a fully free wage labor force or abandoning already purchased slaves. Throughout the period one sees a conflict between the search for new forms of labor and an allegiance to the old methods of dealing with labor—an allegiance stemming not from mere traditionalism, but from a need and a desire to maintain certain kinds of social and economic control.

An outstanding example of this conflict was the institution of the Chinese *cuadrilla*, or gang. Chinese workers who had served out their terms, or had escaped from their masters, were often grouped together into *cuadrillas* by entrepreneurs, themselves Chinese, and hired out. Duvon Corbitt describes these *cuadrillas*, which first appeared in 1870:

Under this arrangement the chief of the gang . . . would enter into a contract with the owner of a sugar mill or other establishment for a certain piece of work. The chief not only supervised the work of his fellow countrymen, but he also arranged for their food and lodging. The Chinese *cuadrilla* proved to be especially useful in the hot and difficult work of the evaporating rooms of the sugar mills.[31]

This, finally, was a form of wage labor, economically very distinct from the coercive individual "contracts" under which the Chinese first worked. The flexibility it provided planters is suggested by a classified advertisement in a Matanzas paper in 1870: "A gang of Asians seeks work in the countryside, either by month or for the harvest; able to provide the number of workers requested."[32]

[31] Corbitt, *A Study of the Chinese*, p. 91, citing Antonio Chuffat Latour.
[32] *Aurora del Yumurí*, Matanzas, Oct. 18, 1870.

99

However well suited to certain requirements of sugar production, though, this arrangement was not entirely compatible with the maintenance of forced labor elsewhere in the system. Contractors were accused of accepting runaway coolies into their gangs, and thus undermining planters' control over their indentured workers. One Chinese witness before the Commission of Enquiry described the response of the authorities in his case:

holding a *cédula*, I procured for the owner of a plantation 20 laborers, all of whom possessed a similar document. Nevertheless the police accused me of hiring men whose terms of contract service had not been completed, seized me, deprived me of $70 in silver and $200 in paper, demanded another $200 as the price of my release, and, as I was unable to pay it, placed me in prison.[33]

The interests of control took precedence over those of economic flexibility, and at the end of 1871 the captain general forbade the use of such gangs.[34] The approach of the government and of planters continued to be one of compulsion, not one of free labor and mobility. Chinese not under contract to a specific master were often confined in municipal *depósitos centrales* in an effort to prevent them from behaving like free workers. These depots, similar to those in which runaway slaves were held, also became contracting agencies, hiring out Chinese workers to individual employers and to government projects under a prison-like discipline.[35]

During most of the 1870s, the majority of Chinese laborers were still serving out their original contracts or second contracts into which they had been lured or coerced. A *padrón* drawn up by the Comisión Central de Colonización in 1872 counted 58,400 Chinese in Cuba, of whom about 34,400 were serving out their contracts. Some 7,000 had fled their masters, about 1,300 had fled and were held in *depósitos*, and 900 were in *depósitos* pending recontracting. Only about 14,000 were free, either naturalized or as foreign subjects. By 1877, though, the proportion had become more equal: there were about 25,200 "Asiáticos colonos" and 21,900 "Asiáticos cumplidos," corresponding roughly to indentured and free (see Table 16). In the same year, Spain signed the Treaty of Peking with China, halting the further emigration of Chinese workers to Cuba under contract.[36]

[33] China, *Report of the Commission*, p. 56.
[34] Corbitt, *A Study of the Chinese*, p. 91.
[35] See China, *Report of the Commission*.
[36] On the treaty, see Corbitt, *A Study of the Chinese*, p. 72.

TABLE 16
Status of the Chinese Population, 1872 and 1877

Status	1872		1877	
Under contract	34,408	(59%)	25,226	(54%)
Free[a]	14,064	(24%)	21,890	(46%)
Runaways	7,036	(12%)		
Runaways held in *depósitos*	1,344	(2%)		
Cumplidos in *depósitos*, pending recontracting	864	(1%)		
In jails or prisons, or pending trial	684	(1%)		
Total	58,400		47,116	

SOURCES: Same as Table 13.
 [a] In 1877 the category used is "cumplidos," meaning those who had fulfilled their contracts.

Both slavery and the use of indentured Chinese workers made labor costs to a large extent a form of fixed capital, maintained year-round regardless of seasonal variation in the need for labor. The use of contracted gangs of free workers provided greater flexibility but risked undermining control over those in whom an investment had already been made—as in the case of the *cuadrillas* and runaways. One way to modify the structure of labor costs, without threatening existing arrangements, was to make a more flexible use of existing slaves by renting slaves from other owners. This was a common recourse for planters in the 1870s.

The records of the *ingenio* Delicias reflect this pattern. In the 1870s a few free persons of color were employed on Delicias, and were paid about seventeen pesos a month. But there were far more rented slaves, whose masters were usually paid eleven pesos a month for them.[37] The rental of field slaves—in contrast to hiring-out by *coartados* who kept part of their earnings—permitted the shifting of labor to areas of greatest profitability but did not weaken slavery as an institution nor loosen the constraints on slaves, though it did undermine claims to a paternalistic bond between master and slave.

Immigrant labor—white, black, Asian, or Mexican Indian—was another alternative. Throughout the 1870s, different sources of foreign labor were discussed, and individual entrepreneurs undertook various efforts at importation. But a notable feature of the immigration and colonization schemes proposed and carried out in Cuba in this decade was their similarity to slavery. Francisco Díaz Tor-

[37] Libro Diario del Ingenio Delicias, ANC, ML, 10802.

101

riente requested and was granted permission by the colonial government in 1871 to import Mexican workers on six-year contracts. Their contracts included an agreement by the worker to go anywhere he was sent and to submit to the prevailing system of punishment. He was to be paid just four pesos a month plus maintenance and was required to acknowledge that he accepted this wage, even if it were below those prevailing in Cuba, because of the advantages of the contract. The scarcity of slaves, particularly following a recent cholera epidemic, was cited in government discussions as a reason for approving the immigration of Mexicans. The "pacific" nature of Yucatecans, in contrast to Asians, was also invoked.[38]

Recruiters expected Spanish workers to accept similar conditions. The Sociedad Colonizadora in Sagua la Grande sought workers between the ages of twenty-two and forty in Spain, but offered them contracts that obliged them to submit to the "régimen correctivo" obtaining on plantations and to allow the holding back of fifty pesos from their wages to insure compliance with the four years of the contract. Wages were to be ten pesos monthly, and workers would be granted small plots to work on their own time and fifteen pesos toward return passage at the end of the term of service.[39] Daunting as these conditions were, some Spaniards did respond, as can be seen in the substantial volume of Spanish immigration and in individual appeals to the government in Madrid for passage to Cuba.[40]

Military colonization was another alternative, recommended for its political virtues as well as its discipline. An article in the *Semanario Militar* of 1873-1874 argued that combatting the insurrection had essentially become a war of "reconquest" and that military colonization was one way to guarantee loyalty.[41] But only in a modified form, in the release of some soldiers for work on plantations, was it adopted in the 1870s.

Another way to combine the economic flexibility of free labor

[38] Expediente general de colonización mejicana, AHN, Ultramar, leg. 90, exp. 39.

[39] Request for authorization from D. Joaquín Espinós y Julián, Valencia, April 25, 1874, AHN, Ultramar, leg. 91.

[40] See, for example, Solicitud de Man¹ Aguado Martínez pidiendo pasar a Ultramar en clase de colono, Jan. 11, 1873, AHN, Ultramar, leg. 91. There are also lists of immigrants in the same *legajo*. On the overall volume of Spanish immigration, see Carlos Trelles, *Biblioteca histórica cubana*, 3 vols., 2 (Matanzas: Andrés Estrada, 1924): 360-61, and Duvon Corbitt, "Immigration in Cuba," *Hispanic American Historical Review* 22 (May 1942): 280-308.

[41] "Colonización de la Trocha del Este," *El Semanario Militar*, 1873, 1874. Found in BNE, Manuscritos, 13228, fol. 225, Papeles relativos a las Provincias de Ultramar coleccionados por D. Eugenio Alonso y Sanjurjo.

with the coercion of slavery was to lease convicts from the government. Evidence of the use of convicts on plantations is abundant. In the personal histories of prisoners of the 1870s and early 1880s, plantations appear as places to which one is condemned, from which one escapes, or in which one dies. The mulatto José Barrera, for example, convicted for robbery, was condemned to three years in prison, part of which he served on the *ingenio* Josefita. But convict labor presented many of the same problems of control as slave labor. Barrera tried to flee not only from Josefita but also from the *ingenio* El Banco, from a quarry, and from road work.[42] The convicts' hostility toward plantation work was reflected in their repeated attempts at flight and also in the vivid example of Lino Portilla of Matanzas, who attempted in 1878 to commit suicide rather than be transferred to an *ingenio*.[43]

To the government and to employers eager for labor, these were disadvantages that could be overlooked. When Jorge Desage appealed to the government for permission to employ eighteen convicts on the *ingenio* Majana, the lieutenant governor of Jaruco thought this a good arrangement and reported that convicts had been substituted for slaves on that plantation for some time without any apparent disorder.[44]

Plantation records further reveal the range of adaptations undertaken on Cuban *ingenios* in the 1870s, and convey a sense of the nature and tempo of change. The work force of the *ingenio* Angelita, for example, owned by J. A. Suárez Argudín and located in the jurisdiction of Cienfuegos, was enumerated several times between 1868 and 1877. On June 10, 1868 the plantation had 414 slaves, 20 "empleados e operarios de la finca" (employees and operatives of the estate), most of them white, and 35 *colonos*, meaning in this case indentured Chinese laborers. Additional Chinese workers arrived later that month. In 1870 cholera caused many deaths, and by September of that year the *dotación* consisted of 397 slaves and 58 Asians. Children and the elderly legally freed by the Moret Law do not appear to have been excluded from the totals[45] (see Table 17).

Another document lists the work force in 1877, and an accom-

---

[42] Carlos de Urrutia y Blanco, *Los criminales de Cuba y D. José Trujillo* (Barcelona: Fidel Giró, 1882), p. 169.
[43] Ibid., p. 231.
[44] Expediente promovido por D. Jorge Desage . . . , 1874, AHN, Ultramar, leg. 4179.
[45] Libro Diario del Ingenio Angelita de la propiedad de Sr. J. A. Argudín, ANC, ML, 11536.

panying inventory confirms the impression that it was a well-mech-anized plantation, complete with steam-powered grinding apparatus and vacuum pans, centrifuges, and *montajugos* as well as the older Jamaica trains for processing. By this date the number of slaves had fallen to 247, and because of the Moret Law, 37 *libertos* over the age of sixty and 29 children under eight years of age were not counted, though they were clearly still part of the plantation pop-ulation. The total comparable to the 1871 figure of 397 would thus be 313, a drop of 84, or 21 percent, in six years.[46]

The 1877 work force also included eight free *negros acomodados*, all apparently former slaves of Suárez Argudín, earning between 8.50 and 34 pesos per month, and six rented slaves, for whom the estate paid 16 pesos a month. There were now 44 *empleados*, including the usual 20 or so white employees (administrators, overseers, ar-tisans) and also about 20 *movilizados*, soldiers presumably stationed on the plantation or released for employment there. Their numbers, however, fell sharply thereafter, and there were only three *movili-zados* left in December of the same year. A new category, *partidario* (sharecropper), had appeared by 1877, and included 11 heads of fam-ily. There were 45 *colonos asiáticos* employed at the time of the count, and at harvest time additional gangs of Asians were hired to cut cane[47] (see Table 18).

Despite the increased complexity and variety of the work force on Angelita by 1877, the importance of the nucleus of 247 slaves between nine and sixty years of age remains apparent. The share-croppers, though included in the plantation population, seem pri-marily to have been engaged in supplying food to the plantation rather than working in cane, though the evidence is not unequivocal. The increase in the number of free workers suggests that they were making inroads into some areas previously dominated by slaves, but it seems unlikely that either the temporary *movilizados* or the share-croppers were performing any of the more technical tasks. Nor does it seem likely that all of the Asians were in the more mechanized sectors, since this too was a fluctuating population, often rented out from the *depósito* and prone to flight. In short, it seems that at Angelita it was not the introduction of technology but the death of

[46] Libro Diario del Ingenio Angelita Argudín, 1877, ANC, ML, 10789.
[47] Ibid.

TABLE 17
Work Force on the *Ingenio* Angelita, June 1868

EMPLOYEES		SLAVES
Administrator	*Tachero* (works the *tacho*,	212 males
Doctor	or boiling pan)	202 females
Overseer	Sugarmasters (2)	
Mayordomos (2)	Mason	Total = 414 (all ages)
Machinist	*Montero*	COLONOS (Chinese laborers)
Cattle handlers (2)	Asian, job unspecified	35
Carpenters (3)		
Distiller	Total = 20	GRAND TOTAL = 469
(2 illegible)		

SOURCE: ANC, ML, 11536, Libro Diario del ingenio "Angelita" de la propiedad de Sr. J. A. Argudín, 1868-71, pp. 1-13.

TABLE 18
Work Force on the *Ingenio* Angelita, January 1877

EMPLOYEES		SLAVES
Administrator	*Montero*	126 males
Mayordomo	Messenger	121 females
Accountant	Head of the	Total = 247 (excludes 29
Overseer	volunteers	children and 37 elderly)
Cattle-handler	*Movilizados* (23)	
Overseer of the	Sugarmaster	COLONOS (Chinese laborers)
batey	*Tachero*	45
Person in charge	Plowmen (2)	
of *colonos*	Total = 44	OTHERS
Nurse (male)		Free blacks, jobs unspecified (8)
Machinist		Rented slaves, owned by
Carpenter		administrator (6)
Mason		Sharecroppers (11, plus 93
Barrel-makers (2)		family members)
Overseer of the		
potrero	GRAND TOTAL = 361 (or 454 including sharecropper families)	

SOURCE: ANC, ML, 10789, Libro Diario del Ingenio Angelita Argudín, 1877, pp. 2, 3, 17, 18.

slaves—and the necessity of replacing them—that initially brought the increased use of free labor.

After 1877, the decline in forced labor at Angelita accelerated. Asians persisted in fleeing, and replacements were not always available. Slaves became more likely to buy their freedom. While in the late 1860s such purchases were infrequent (just one man and his daughter obtained their freedom between June 1868 and September 1870), by the late 1870s they had become more common. In February

105

1878 four women and two children freed themselves, apparently after having visited the *síndico* (protector of slaves) to have their prices set. In April, Secundina, a thirty-year-old Creole, paid 750 pesos for herself and another 187 to free her *liberto* children. That same month the slave Gervasia went to Cienfuegos to have her price set at 700 pesos, and in August her mother, Jacoba Lucumí, aged fifty, made a down payment of 500 pesos on that amount. As this was going on, the plantation also began to increase the rewards given to slaves. At the beginning of the 1878 grinding season tobacco, token amounts of money, and bread were distributed.[48]

Reading through the daybook, one gets the sense that relations within the plantation were shifting; slaves, particularly women, found ways to buy their freedom, and the plantation increased its use of monetary incentives. Raising crops and pigs to sell to the plantation was a major source of money, and pigs were particularly significant. Sometimes raised on halves with the estate, sometimes independently, they brought in substantial sums when sold—from the twelve pesos paid to Silvestre in February 1877 to the forty-seven pesos paid to Juan de Mata some months later. Both women and men were involved in this business, as noted in November 1878, when piglets were given to be raised on halves to "Margarita lucumí, Martín prieto, y Carlota la lavandera."[49] When the plantation accepted 700 pesos from a slave as payment for freedom, it was thus recouping some of what had been paid to that slave for goods produced, as well as amortizing part of the investment in the slave. The master might well come out ahead. But a circuit of money exchanges had now been introduced to replace a relation of direct control—and not necessarily entirely at the planter's initiative.

Some money for the purchase of freedom may well have come from wages paid to other members of the estate's population. The daybook of Angelita records the births of at least two children described as "Asiatic" to women slaves—one of whom purchased her freedom shortly thereafter. It seems possible that in such cases money for self-purchase, or for purchase of the children's full freedom, came from the father as well as the mother.[50] As the estate came to employ more free male workers, these men provided visible

[48] Ibid.
[49] Ibid. See pp. 34, 162, 182, and 252, among others, for references to pigs.
[50] Ibid., pp. 130, 136.

evidence of the possibility of freedom, as well as contributing funds for their partners' and children's freedom.

The records of other plantations in the 1870s show many of the same characteristics. There were multiple forms of labor around a diminishing core of slave workers; "gratuities" were increasingly paid to slaves; the rental of slaves and the contracting of Asians provided additional flexibility. But none of these adaptations suggests a forthright repudiation of slavery, only a step-by-step adaptation as masters were forced to seek supplementary forms of labor and some modifications of the slave regime. The moves toward monetary compensation, moreover, do not appear to be closely correlated with work on machinery—money was as likely to be used simply as a bonus for Sunday work, or a general incentive at the beginning of the harvest.[51] Indeed, the repudiation of forced labor in this period comes not from planters but from the slaves and Chinese indentured laborers themselves, through self-purchase and through flight.

Cuban slaveholders by the late 1870s demonstrated a diminishing emotional attachment to the formal institution of slavery, and the possibility of abolition no longer put them up in arms. The Moret Law and demographic patterns were pushing in the same direction. There were not enough future slave workers to replenish the system; new sources and forms of labor had to be found.

This decay of slavery in the 1870s must, however, be interpreted with great care. Young and elderly slaves were freed by decree; others, particularly in the cities and in the east, obtained their freedom through litigation or self-purchase; and many slaves died or became free as a result of war. The gaps thus created were often filled with free workers. But although mixed work forces were common, it does not seem to be true that plantations were generally driven to repudiate unfree labor because of a decline in the quality of their slave labor force resulting from an excess of the young and the aged, as has sometimes been argued.[52] Plantations with available capital had often purchased Africans in the last years of the slave

[51] Other daybooks and slave lists for the 1870s include: Libro con la dotación de esclavos del ingenio La Crisis, APSS, Valle-Iznaga, leg. 27; Libro Diario del Ingenio Delicias, ANC, ML, 10802; Libro Diario al parecer de un ingenio, ANC, ML, 10806; and Libro Mayor del ingenio Nueva Teresa, 1872-1886, ANC, ML, 11245.
[52] For an example of this argument see Moreno, "Abolición o desintegración."

trade, and still had substantial *dotaciones* of young and middle-aged African and Creole slaves, not due for freedom under the Moret Law for years. Thus a core of slaves of working age continued to be held in bondage in the major sugar areas, helping to maintain high levels of production despite the sharp drop in the total number of slaves.

In the light of the regional pattern of the decline of slavery, and of the continued reliance of highly mechanized and highly capitalized plantations on slave labor, it also seems appropriate to view with some skepticism the notion of a rigid technological contradiction that impelled abolition. Indeed, perhaps the greatest danger in the idea of such a contradiction is the false image it may create of a force that mechanically brings about the destruction of a social system. For as striking as the contradictions within the slave system are, it is also clear that the process of emancipation took place at several removes from them, and played itself out in a complex dynamic of human initiative and response. Moreover, the improvisations developed to deal in the short run with the contradictions often succeeded in prolonging the slave system's life.

Chinese indentured laborers, contract workers, convict labor, rented slaves—these are the elements often cited as proof of the dissolution of the slave system in the 1870s. But they are just as much proof of its resilience. That such mixtures of labor forms could be brought together *without* the abandonment of slavery is remarkable. And that the men who ran these mixed plantations in many cases continued to be opposed to emancipation is further evidence of the difference between perceiving "contradictions" within slavery and identifying the forces actually driving abolition forward.

All of this is not meant to imply that Cuban slave society permitted, or would have permitted, economic development in its broadest sense. Both the class structure of the society and its links to specific international export markets tended to inhibit the kind of broad-based diversification and industrialization associated with such development. But Cuban slavery did permit a significant amount of technological innovation, and the specific role of slavery in blocking further development remains unproven.[53]

The arguments by Moreno Fraginals and others by no means ex-

[53] For an important discussion of these issues, see "The Debate over *Time on the Cross*" in Elizabeth Fox-Genovese and Eugene D. Genovese, *Fruits of Merchant Capital: Slavery and Bourgeois Property in the Rise and Expansion of Capitalism* (New

haust the possible variants on the theme of "internal contradictions" leading to abolition. One can envision forms of the argument that might focus on factors other than demography and technology, such as class structure or ideology. What I have tried to demonstrate here are the limitations of the most familiar form of the argument, while acknowledging some of its merits. There remains in the internal contradiction hypothesis a key insight about the difficulty of achieving capital-intensive development with forced labor, purchased at high price and maintained year round. But even this contradiction, perceived by some Cuban planters, did not compel them to abandon slavery. They sought instead to add flexibility through slave rentals, to add workers through immigration, and to maintain as much control as possible over their existing slaves.

It may have come as something of a surprise to them that this strategy could not work forever. But there *is* a sense in which these continued improvisations and innovations did undermine slavery. It is a social one, a kind of second-order contradiction. Free labor and indentured labor were *economically* complementary to slavery: indentured Chinese workers often dealt with the centrifuges while slaves handled other tasks; white woodcutters on contract would relieve the plantation of direct responsibility for providing fuel; the employment of free workers during the harvest diminished the problem of year-round maintenance of all workers. But the use of these complementary forms of labor had indirect effects on the social structure necessary to sustain forced labor.[54]

The importation of Chinese contract laborers, for instance, required the invention of a third category between slave and free. This often led to tensions in the work force by creating an invidious distinction between slaves and Chinese workers. The Chinese in-

---

York: Oxford University Press, 1983), pp. 136-71. They argue that the class structure and ideology accompanying slavery were key to the absence of development. One difficulty with applying their formulation to Cuba is that the "seigneurial" aspects of the slaveholding elite—such as they were—seem to have been less important obstacles to development than the continuing dependence of the Cuban economy, both before and after slavery, on a single export crop facing an uncertain world market. For an examination of these questions in a somewhat different context, see Richard Graham, "Slavery and Economic Development: Brazil and the United States South in the Nineteenth Century," *Comparative Studies in Society and History* 23(October 1981): 620-55.

[54] For a discussion of some of the ways in which resolutions of one contradiction within slavery can create another, see Sidney Mintz, "Slavery and the Rise of Peasantries," in Michael Craton, ed., *Roots and Branches: Current Directions in Slave Studies* (Toronto: Pergamon Press, 1979), pp. 213-42.

sisted on being treated differently from slaves, and the law—at least in theory—upheld this distinction. But the pattern of labor on the plantation could place the Chinese in situations that they felt obscured this distinction, and violence, flight, and conflict with slaves were frequent results. Similarly, the existence of *cuadrillas* of free Chinese, while providing needed flexibility, tended to weaken the bonds holding indentured Chinese to the plantation, since if they could escape the plantation they might be able to join a gang and be free of the direct supervision of plantation overseers and masters.

Planters found ways to adapt to the inflexibilities of slavery, but the ways they found had unintended social consequences. Much as they might have liked simply to add on free workers as needed to compensate for the decline in the slave population, this tactic carried its own risks. Plantation slavery as a social system depended to a large degree on isolation—as planters themselves acknowledged, for example, when they set up and explicitly defended plantation stores as instruments of social control.[55] The incorporation of free workers, beyond those supervisors and artisans rigidly and traditionally separated from the *dotación*, broke some of that isolation. It made obvious to slaves the existence of alternatives, created new sources of information, and made new alliances—both of individuals and of groups—possible. Such alliances could involve a union between a slave woman and a Chinese man, both interested in freedom for their children; communication between free black workers and those who remained enslaved; assistance from a newly freed slave to other members of his or her family. These alliances and examples aided slaves in their efforts at challenge and self-purchase and, in extreme cases (as in the east during the Ten Years' War), encouraged flight and rebellion.

One need not conclude from this that slavery in Cuba was always inherently socially brittle. But in this specific political context, when abolition was already on the agenda, when insurgency was a reality, and when there was division within the white population, innovations and adaptations carried serious risks.

[55] For the debate on plantation stores, see Sobre pago de contribuciones de las tiendas de los Ingenios, AHN, Ultramar, leg. 4818, exp. 84. For more general discussion of plantation stores, see Chap. VIII, below, and the essay by Manuel Moreno Fraginals, *El token azucarero cubano* (Havana: Museo Numismático de Cuba, n.d.) reprinted in his *La historia como arma*, pp. 145-61.

Ingenio Flor de Cuba, Casa de Calderas (Boiling House). At mid-century the boiling of cane juice on the more advanced plantations was done with the aid of imported vacuum pans. Cane continued to be hauled to the mill by oxcart. (Source: Cantero, *Los ingenios*.)

Ingenio Unión. This engraving from the 1850s shows a large *ingenio* in the Cárdenas region. The estate's machinery included steam-powered grinding apparatus, vacuum pans, and centrifuges; its work force consisted of 498 slaves. (Source: Cantero, *Los ingenios.*)

Ingenio Flor de Cuba. The large, rectangular *barracón*, which housed the estate's 409 slaves and 170 indentured Chinese workers, is visible at the far end of the estate. (Source: Cantero, *Los ingenios*.)

A group of workers on the Canal de Vento, photographed by Henri Dumont, a French doctor, in the 1860s. They were in all likelihood *emancipados*, Africans found on captured slave ships, nominally freed by the Spanish government, and put to labor on public works. (Source: Dumont, "Antropología.")

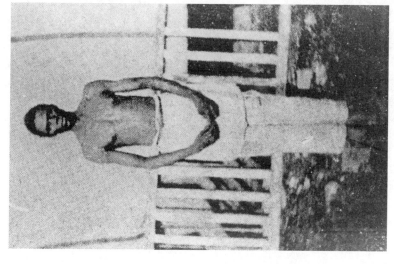
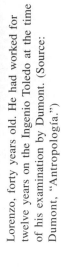

Lorenzo, forty years old. He had worked for twelve years on the Ingenio Toledo at the time of his examination by Dumont. (Source: Dumont, "Antropología.")

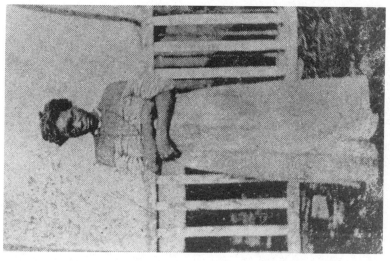

Juana, twenty-five years old, listed as *macuá* in origin. Recently imported from Africa, she worked on the Ingenio Toledo in the 1860s. (Source: Dumont, "Antropología.")

Two *emancipados* who labored on the excavations of the Canal de Vento. The man was identified as *mandinga* in origin, the woman as *lucumí*. (Source: Dumont, "Antropología.")

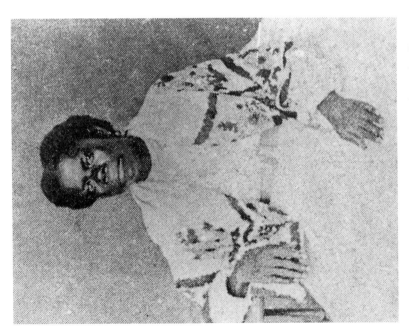

María Antonia, thirty years old. Originally from the Congo, she lived in the city of Havana. (Source: Dumont, "Antropología.")

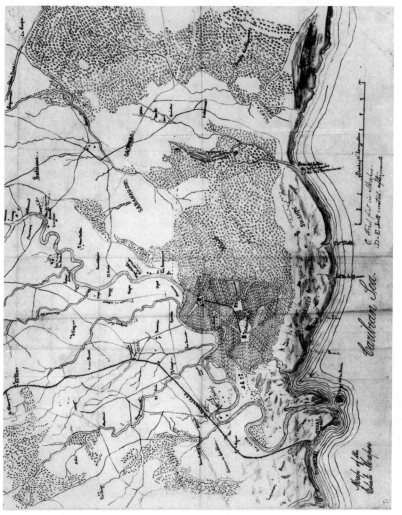

Map of the Mapos estate in Sancti Spíritus in the 1890s, showing cane fields, woods, and the rail line linking the three plantations owned by the Valle-Iznaga family: Mapos, San Fernando, and Natividad. (Source: U.S. National Archives, RG 76, Entry 352, Claim no. 121.)

A veteran of the Cuban insurgency of 1895 and his wife. (Source: Olivares, *Our Islands and Their People,* 1:91.)

A small farmer's tobacco patch, Havana Province, 1899. Some former slaves became renters or owners of small plots of land on which they grew crops for subsistence and for the market. (Source: Library of Congress.)

The noon rest in the sugar cane field, 1899. Women worked alongside men in the cane fields both during and after slavery, though after emancipation women increasingly engaged in paid field work only at harvest time. (Source: Olivares, *Our Islands and Their People*, 1:181.)

Mounted special police guarding cane cutters on the Soledad Estate, 1896. During the War for Independence, sugar *centrales* were vulnerable to attack from without and sabotage from within. (Source: Library of Congress.)

Three women returning from market, 1899. (Source: Olivares, *Our Islands and Their People*, 1:106.)

V

Challenge

Though Cuban planters hoped to avoid disruption through the gradual process of replacing slaves with free workers as the slave population declined, several converging and closely related pressures were building to force a more immediate resolution of the issue of slavery. One was the growth of antislavery sentiment in Spain and the prospect that the metropolitan government might take unilateral steps toward immediate abolition. Another was the Ten Years' War and its indirect effects, including the destruction of plantations and the liberation of many slaves in the eastern end of the island. A third arose from the actions of slaves and indentured Chinese workers themselves, as they pushed for concessions and challenged their masters, disrupting the normal order of things.

The antislavery movement in Spain achieved a major triumph with the abolition of slavery in Puerto Rico in 1873, and Cuban planters feared that Cuban slavery might be next.[1] Some prudent slaveholders hoped to fend this off with alternate forms of very gradual emancipation. In 1873 a group of *hacendados* drew up a proposed bill of emancipation that incorporated a ten-year apprenticeship or *patronato* in place of any indemnity for slaveholders, a small stipend for the apprentices, work regulations based on those in force for Chinese laborers, and state-supervised labor contracting after the expiration of the *patronato*. The law, it was suggested, should go into effect only after the end of the insurrection, at which time the island's economy could better stand the shock, and troops would be available to repress possible "outbreaks of joy" or the "desire for revenge."[2] One observer in Havana reported on the schemes for shifting slaves to the status of the indentured Chinese

[1] Crucial to this 1873 triumph was the activity of Puerto Rican abolitionists. See Corwin, *Spain and the Abolition of Slavery*, chap. 15.

[2] Great Britain, Parliament, *Parliamentary Papers* (Lords), 1875, vol. 23 (Slave Trade no. 2), "Correspondence Respecting Slavery in Cuba and Puerto Rico, and the State of the Slave Population and Chinese Coolies in those Islands."

and commented that the expressed aim of several Matanzas planters was that "the word abolition should be only a myth, dust to throw in the eyes of those English and American rogues who want to force themselves into our affairs; with this plan, with the problem resolved on paper, things might go on without greater novelty."[3] According to a British government representative in Cuba, however, planter delegates from Santa Clara, Cienfuegos, and other parts of the interior objected even to such a limited proposal and opposed all discussion of further emancipation, preferring to rest with the Moret Law.[4] The proposal was thus apparently not forwarded to Madrid, though the governor did communicate the idea of a set of regulations parallel to those designed for the Chinese.[5]

The threat of further action from Madrid abated somewhat in the mid-1870s. A military coup in Spain in 1874, the suspension of the Cortes, and restrictions on the right of assembly narrowed the field of action of antislavery activists in the metropolis. Between 1875 and 1879 the government denied the Spanish Abolitionist Society permission for public meetings, and during much of the decade the society was obliged to act primarily through its executive committee. Though its newspaper and pamphlets influenced public opinion, the society could not hope for immediate legislative action.[6]

The existence of the Cuban insurrection was invoked in Spain by those opposed to reform, and served as the all-purpose counterargument to abolitionist claims. At the same time, however, the reality of the war within Cuba increased the practical pressures on the institution of slavery.

Colonial officials saw blacks and Asians in the insurrection as a substantial threat to social order, even after they had been defeated in battle or had surrendered. In 1876 Arsenio Martínez Campos, chief of the Spanish forces, reported that a large portion—perhaps the majority—of the insurrectionists were slaves and that attempting to return them immediately to their masters and their plantations would only disturb the *dotaciones* and introduce more "seeds

---

[3] Letter signed Tricanga, Feb. 13, 1873, in Correspondencia de Wenceslao de Villarutia, ANC.

[4] Great Britain, Parliament, *Parliamentary Papers* (Lords), 1875, (Slave Trade no. 2).

[5] Extract of telegram from the governor general of Cuba, Aug. 7, 1873, AHN, Ultramar, leg. 4881, tomo 2.

[6] Rodríguez, "La idea y el movimiento antiesclavista."

of discord and more desire for emancipation."[7] Slaves' desire for emancipation had become, through the events of the war, a force that had to be reckoned with.

The Spanish government was unlikely to take any major steps to deal with this problem as long as the war continued, for to do so might disrupt order in areas still at peace, and risk alienating white loyalists. Spanish officials in the field, however, had to contend with the fact that slaves had a will of their own. An order to field commanders in 1876 outlined a procedure for dealing with slaves who came into Spanish hands from the insurrection. Commanders were to determine, as discreetly as possible, whether a slave was willing to return to his estate, the optimum solution. If he was not willing, if his "horror of slavery" was too great, then he was to be incorporated into the Spanish *guerrilla*. He was not to be led to believe that this would automatically mean freedom at the end of the war— for that would depend on his conduct—but he was to be given a hint of the possibility.[8]

The problem with such a policy was that, if officially acknowledged, it could produce precisely the opposite effect from the one desired, for it implied that slaves in the insurrection, even if captured by the Spaniards, might be more likely to gain their freedom than those remaining on the plantations. And when in November 1877 a commander in the field circulated a message to the effect that slaves coming from the insurrection would be freed, he was rebuked and relieved of his command by Martínez Campos. Public announcement of such measures, Martínez Campos wrote, would alarm private property in the island and have counterproductive effects on the plantations still in operation. The general question of slavery was, in his opinion, "the most difficult political and military problem" that the Spanish government had to resolve in Cuba.[9]

Though the issue of slavery grew increasingly difficult to resolve, the military threat from the insurgents was diminishing. By 1876 the insurrectionist forces were isolated, divided, and exhausted. The United States had never recognized the rebels' belligerent status.

[7] Capitanía General, Estado Mayor, Campañas, Circular, M. Campos, reservado, Nov. 7, 1876, AHN, Ultramar, leg. 4883, tomo 6.

[8] Esclavos fugados que sean aprehendidos por las columnas, Jan. 27, 1877, AHN, Ultramar, leg. 4759, exp. 91.

[9] Martínez Campos to Cortijo, Dec. 17, 1877, AHN, Ultramar, leg. 4883, tomo 6.

Conservatives within the rebellion had stalled the invasion of the west and undermined it when it finally took place. Radical leadership by Antonio Maceo and Máximo Gómez had been thwarted by campaigns against them by other insurgents, the first because he was a mulatto and was accused of wanting a "black republic," the second ostensibly because he was Dominican.[10]

A new Spanish offensive under Martínez Campos in 1877 further weakened the rebels militarily, while his offers of pardon and land affected morale.[11] At the same time, conservatives within the insurgent ranks were attempting to unseat the president of the rebel republic, Tomás Estrada Palma. Though the insurrectionists, particularly those under Maceo, continued to fight on, the situation had become extremely difficult. In Ramiro Guerra's words: "there was a general breakdown of organization, which undermined the force, discipline, and military morale of men who were fatigued and despairing in a terrible and endless war against a more and more aggressive enemy."[12] Vast areas of land had been laid waste, many of the best leaders had been killed, the Spaniards had marshaled yet more force, and the divisions among the rebels had reached the point where they interfered with military mobilization. In late 1877 the president of the republic was captured by the Spaniards, and in early 1878 his successor began to negotiate the terms of an armistice.[13]

On February 10 representatives of both sides signed the Pact of Zanjón, which granted Cuba the same political conditions that obtained in Puerto Rico (a concession falling far short of independence) as well as a general "forgetting of the past" concerning political crimes, freedom to those slaves and Chinese who were in the insurrectionist lines, and permission to leave Cuba for all those who so desired. The general question of slavery was left to be settled once Cuban delegates were seated in the Cortes.[14] The freeing of the slaves in insurrectionist lines did not constitute abolition—it was a partial emancipation made necessary by the fact that it would

[10] For a summary of these problems, see Thomas, *Cuba,* pp. 264-65.

[11] The strategy and character of Martínez Campos are discussed in Earl R. Beck, "The Martínez Campos Government of 1879: Spain's Last Chance in Cuba," *Hispanic American Historical Review* 56 (May 1976): 268-89.

[12] For a detailed discussion of the conflicts within the rebel ranks, see Guerra, *Guerra* 2: chap. 19. The quotation cited is from p. 343.

[13] Ibid., pp. 342-52.

[14] See ibid., p. 362, for the full text.

114

probably have been impossible to persuade rebel slaves to lay down arms otherwise. In gratitude and to secure their loyalty, the government also granted freedom to slaves who had served with the Spanish military. The total freed by the pact was estimated at 16,000.[15]

Though it was in some ways a conciliatory document, the treaty contained elements that provoked opposition. Insurgent leader Antonio Maceo, who took a principled stand in favor of full abolition, rejected it and attempted to reignite the war. Slaveholders loyal to Spain were indignant that slaves who had deserted their masters to fight against Spain should now receive freedom. To abolitionists and to slaves it seemed as though emancipation was being thwarted; to slaveowners it seemed that property rights were being ignored.

The ineffectiveness of the treaty in securing social peace quickly became clear in the eastern end of the island. In August 1878 the Spanish commandant of the region, Dabán, telegraphed the captain general that slaves were engaging in "passive resistance to work" and refusing to obey their masters and overseers. "They want their liberty like the convenidos," those who had come from the insurrection. Dabán asked for permission to intervene directly to punish them.[16] Permission was forthcoming: military forces were to be distributed among the ingenios, and, if any black rebelled, an immediate council of war was to be formed and he was to be shot.[17]

The maintenance of order on the plantations in the east had become a question of security. Slaves were a weak point in the pacification of the region, a frightening potential source of arms and men for further insurgency. Even the internal affairs of the plantation were a matter for concern, and the military promulgated orders regulating the issue of machetes to field workers.[18] The protection of slave property through the pursuit of fugitives and the maintenance of discipline on the plantation had become an active, worrisome, and time-consuming responsibility for the military. Armed force had long been the ultimate guarantor of order on plantations, and had thus conveyed a sense of Spain's indispensability to Cuban planters. The insurrection, in effect, changed that role from an indirect to a

[15] Trelles, Biblioteca histórica cubana 3: 553.
[16] Situación política del departamento oriental . . . 1878 . . . 1879 . . . (Santiago de Cuba: Sección Tipográfica del Estado Mayor, 1881), p. 6. The term convenidos seems to come from the title of the peace treaty that freed them, the Convenio de Zanjón.
[17] Ibid., p. 9.
[18] Ibid.

direct one. When warning a local officer of an anticipated slave uprising on a plantation, the commandant told the officer to advise his men to carry out their orders as though they were facing the enemy.[19]

On the 24th of August, 1879, the Spanish military indeed found themselves again face to face with the enemy, as groups of rebels from the previous insurrection rose in rebellion, in what would later be called the Guerra Chiquita, the "small war." The Pact of Zanjón had ended hostilities, but it had solved few of the problems that had led to war. There were still innumerable grievances among many Cubans, ranging from burdensome taxes to unemployment for artisans to a sense of betrayal on the part of slaves who had thought that the end of the war would mean freedom. The new rebellion was led by veterans of the Ten Years' War, Calixto García and Antonio Maceo, and fought by an army drawn primarily from the lower classes.[20] The Spanish tried to turn this characteristic to their advantage by charging that it was a race war, a plot to institute black rule. The rebels bitterly defended themselves against this charge, declaring that their defense of individual rights was made not on the basis of race, but of principle.[21]

At least one historian has claimed that the rebels did not in fact recruit among the slaves.[22] The issues of race and class, however, were inextricably bound together. To declare abolition and recruit among the lower classes was to mobilize blacks; to attack plantations was to threaten slavery. The war was not, however, as the Spanish charged, one of black against white. The list of rebels from a single locality reveals a varied cast: white and mulatto professionals and artisans, the overseer of a sugar plantation, the administrator of a coffee plantation, along with numerous blacks with no occupation listed. Some slaves did join the fight: the list included one Juan Bautista Chacón, who apparently gave himself up and then returned to the insurrection, taking with him the slaves of the *ingenio* San Miguel.[23]

[19] Ibid., p. 23.
[20] Rebeca Rosell Planas, *Factores económicos, políticos, y sociales de la Guerra Chiquita* (Havana: Academia de la Historia de Cuba, 1953). See also Thomas, *Cuba*, p. 269.
[21] See the handbill "Los negros y mulatos cubanos residentes en Jamaica . . . ," Oct. 26, 1879, in AGI, Diversos, leg. 7, Polavieja.
[22] Rosell, *Factores*, p. 49.
[23] Antecedentes de personas que han tomado parte en las insurrecciones de la Isla

The uprising was eventually suppressed by the urgent deployment of 19,000 extra soldiers, and pitiless repression of rebel and civilian alike.[24] Even after the Spaniards forced individual rebels and their followers to surrender, however, the question of the fate of the slaves among them remained. At stake was not just the disposition of the slaves under arms, but the tranquillity of the area. Slaves in the east had taken the step that the Spanish authorities had been dreading since the beginning of the Ten Years' War: mass desertions.[25] The threat of a rebel movement that would successfully use the battle cry of abolition to incorporate all slaves into a rebellion thus became more plausible. Something had to be done to undercut this appeal, while tying slaves to their plantations in order to maintain production. Planters and policy makers proceeded along different lines to attempt to solve the problem.

Planters in the east feared that they would never again be able to control their slave work force. Many slaves had either fought in or seen the insurrections at first hand and had been exposed for years to the abolitionism of the insurrectionists. The chance of their being passively reincorporated into the slave system was slight. Moreover, the idea of freedom for all, as for the *convenidos*, seems to have provided a focus for disappointment and resistance among plantation slaves who had not joined the insurgents. Neither group would be easy to deal with.

The *hacendados* of Santiago de Cuba province responded with a bargain: they promised that slavery would continue only four more years and that during those years the slaves would receive a wage— five pesos monthly for men from age sixteen to fifty, four for women, three for the old and the young. The exact mechanisms whereby this concession was communicated are unclear, but the seriousness of the agreement was reflected in the advice of the senator from Santiago de Cuba in his report to the Reform Commission of 1879. If these guidelines were ignored, he predicted, it would be extremely

de Cuba durante mi mando en el Departmento Oriental . . . , AGI, Diversos, leg. 7, Polavieja.

[24] Rosell, *Factores*, pp. 56-58.

[25] Telegram from the governor general to the minister of Ultramar, Sept. 11, 1879, AHN, Ultramar, leg. 4882, tomo 3, exp. 76. Polavieja believed that part of the problem arose from the Spaniards' policy of leading slaves to believe that full emancipation would take place once Cuban delegates had been seated in the Cortes. See his letter of July 4, 1879, in Camilo Polavieja, *Relación documentada de mi política en Cuba* (Madrid: Emilio Minuesa, 1898), p. 43.

difficult to impose any solution on that province. These were the terms under which slaves had remained on the plantations, or returned to them after fleeing, he reported, and the majority of *hacendados* had agreed to them.[26]

This confrontation between masters and slaves represented something between *marronage* (flight of slaves) and a strike, given added urgency by the presence of rebellion. Those slaves in the hills, in conjunction with those on the plantations, extracted terms from a frightened slaveowning class. Furthermore, the terms were substantially better than those the government was prepared to grant. For a second time, the actions of a group of eastern planters—in this case, their concession of wages and freedom in a few years—broke the solidarity of Cuban slaveholders.

The governor general recognized the urgency of the situation. It was not clear which course of action concerning slavery was least dangerous, he wrote to Madrid in September 1879, given that the slaves of Santiago de Cuba province were deserting in large numbers. It had become necessary to guard them with troops, and masters had been obliged to offer them wages and the promise of freedom.[27] According to other reports, there were fires in the fields of cane, some set by slaves who vowed: "Libertad no viene, caña no hay." No freedom, no cane.[28]

The minister in Madrid acknowledged that the situation required immediate and extreme solutions and asked the governor's advice on how to resolve the problem "lo menos mal posible" and with the least disturbance of production. The governor believed that abolition should be delayed until the first of the year, accompanied by a three-year period of apprenticeship, work regulations, and a law against vagrancy.[29]

If it were to undertake abolition, the Spanish government had to determine how slaveholders elsewhere in the island would react to such a move. In August 1879 the Spanish government convened a commission in Madrid, including Cuban planters, to report on pro-

[26] See the opinion of José Bueno y Blanco in Documentos de la Comisión creada por Real decreto de 15 de Agosto de 1879 . . . , AHN, Ultramar, leg. 4883, tomo 5.

[27] AHN, Ultramar, leg. 4882, tomo 3, exp. 76.

[28] Rosell, *Factores*, p. 18. See also José Martí, Lectura en la reunión de emigrados cubanos, en Steck Hall, New York, Jan. 24, 1880, in Pichardo, *Documentos* 1: 438-40.

[29] See the telegrams in AHN, Ultramar, leg. 4882, tomo 3, exp. 83 and exp. 87.

posed reforms for Cuba. The delegates discussed a variety of issues. On commercial relations, duties, and taxes, the commission issued unanimous reports. But about slavery there was dispute. Four separate proposals emerged from a subcommission with five members.[30]

All agreed that the institution would eventually have to be extinguished; most agreed that this should be done gradually. The aim was to avoid emancipation *en masse*, in favor of individual freeings. Some proposed following the lines of the 1870 law, and freeing slaves by age, working downward from age sixty, until all were free by 1890. Others suggested expanding the institution of self-purchase. The representative from Santiago de Cuba advised following the offer already made by planters in that province: freedom in four years, wages in the meantime. A minority of the delegates proposed immediate abolition, to be followed by the free contracting of *libertos*.[31]

The willingness of planters to consider some form of abolition seems to have been based in large measure on their perception of the social and political risks of maintaining slavery, rather than on any immediate collapse of slave-based production. According to the *Revista de Agricultura*, 1879 was a good year, thanks to high prices.[32] Total production of sugar that year was 775,368 metric tons, a peak for the decade.[33] In an article published in April 1879, F. de Zayas estimated the costs of different kinds of labor available to planters. Slaves, he believed, cost six or seven pesos a month to feed, clothe, and maintain. Chinese indentured laborers cost twelve pesos in wages, plus five pesos for food. Free Chinese, maintained by their contractors, cost twenty-one or twenty-two pesos. Free black or white workers were paid twenty-one or twenty-two pesos, plus five for food. Rented slaves were the most expensive workers of all, costing twenty-two pesos plus five for food, or twenty-seven pesos plus five for food if hired during the harvest. That employers were willing to pay premium prices for rented slave labor suggests that as late as 1879 slaves were still seen as the most appropriate form of labor for many tasks on plantations.[34]

However, while the estimated 170,000 rural slaves remained the

[30] See Documentos de la Comisión, AHN, Ultramar, leg. 4883, tomo 5.
[31] Ibid.
[32] F. de Zayas, "Economía rural," *Revista de Agricultura* 1 (Oct. 31, 1879): 249-53.
[33] Moreno, *El ingenio* 3: 37.
[34] F. Zayas, "Estudios de Agricultura, II. El Trabajador, El Jornal," *Revista de Agricultura* 1 (April 30, 1879): 83-87.

core of the agricultural labor force, planters had moved a considerable distance toward the acceptance of free labor.[35] This is clear not only in the increasing use of free white workers, particularly Spanish soldiers who remained in Cuba after the close of the Ten Years' War, but also in the changing status of the Chinese. The commission sent by China to investigate the condition of indentured Chinese laborers in Cuba in 1873-1874 had documented extensive abuses, and China had halted the immigration of contract laborers to Cuba. The last of the 125,000 Chinese indentured laborers landed in 1874. When the Ten Years' War ended, the Cuban government lifted the previous ban on the use of Chinese *cuadrillas*, gangs of free workers. The recontracting of indentured Chinese workers was now banned, though existing contracts and second contracts were allowed to stand.[36] Once again, a balance was being struck between the use of direct coercion and the use of market mechanisms. This time the balance was shifting toward free labor, both because there would be no further entry of indentured workers and because the *cuadrilla* was one of the few ways to keep the Chinese employed in agriculture once their contracts had expired.

Cuban planters, however great their continued reliance on slavery, were thus in quite a different frame of mind about free labor from that of their opposite numbers in the U.S. South prior to and during abolition.[37] Slaveholders in Cuba had seen sugar produced with, in part, free labor; they had seen former slaves working for wages; they had adapted to intermediate forms of labor like the indentured Chinese and, subsequently, the *cuadrillas*. Despite the destruction occasioned in the east by the war, they did not face the general economic devastation that had befallen southern planters in the United States. Though some slaveowners might persist in the belief that those who were now their slaves would not labor except under

[35] The figure of 170,448 was given by the governor general in a telegram to the minister of Ultramar, Nov. 27, 1879, AHN, Ultramar, leg. 4882, tomo 5.

[36] Corbitt, *A Study of the Chinese*, pp. 72, 91. Helly, *Idéologie et ethnicité*, p. 330.

[37] For a perceptive analysis of U.S. slaveholders' responses to emancipation, see Roark, *Masters Without Slaves*. For a comparative discussion, see Genovese, *The World the Slaveholders Made*, Part I. In discussing the Cuban case Genovese tends to overstate the eagerness of Creole planters to shift to free labor, mistaking the position of the insurgents for the desires of Creole planters as a group. The contrasts he draws among the levels of commitment of different slaveholding classes to the maintenance of slavery are, however, very important. See also Robert Brent Toplin, "The Specter of Crisis: Slaveholder Reactions to Abolitionism in the United States and Brazil," *Civil War History* 18 (June 1972): 128-38.

compulsion, there was ample evidence that some kind of transition was possible and even, under certain circumstances, desirable.

The prospects for the survival of slavery as a stable institution had also changed over the decade. Slowly, some of the provisions of the Moret Law and other legislation had taken effect. The government was finally obliging local authorities to undertake the long-delayed posting of slave registers. When the registers were made public, a cry of protest arose from masters and from public officials. The members of the Ayuntamiento of Guane in the western province of Pinar del Río wrote in August 1879 that since the lists had gone up they had observed "manifest tendencies" among blacks to "alter the public order." For the moment, this was expressed in "passive resistance," but there was fear that shortly they would rebel, "demanding their liberty which they believe decreed already by the simple fact of the publication of the lists." The same month the mayor of Sagua la Grande in Santa Clara province wrote that the names of some of those who had been considered slaves had appeared on the lists as free, and this was producing "great excitation" among proprietors. They feared a reaction among the other slaves upon hearing that "half their *compañeros* are now acquiring freedom without apparent justification." Proprietors were also apparently worried that credit would be cut off in view of the existing uncertainty.[38]

In several provinces, the number of slaves who were not properly registered was greater than the number who were. In Pinar del Río 20,000 slaves appeared on both the 1867 and 1871 lists, but 29,000 more appeared only on one or the other. When, in the late 1870s, the lists were posted, it became apparent that none of the latter could legally be held as slaves. Some of them were elderly, or very young, or deceased, but there were able-bodied adults among them as well. A similar situation existed in Santa Clara and Havana. Only in Santiago de Cuba and Matanzas had the records been filled out—or faked—in such a way as to avoid such discrepancies.[39]

The issue of registers illustrates both the impact of legal change and the ways in which that impact had been blocked. For years it had been law that anyone not registered as a slave was to be considered free. As a practical matter, though, the registration rules were not enforced, in part because everyone recognized the inac-

[38] See the petitions in AHN, Ultramar, leg. 4882, tomo 3, exp. 75.
[39] Ibid.

curateness of the lists, in part because of planter opposition. Contraband slaves had been slipped into the registers to replace those who had died, and had thus become legalized. At the same time, some legally acquired slaves were unregistered because their masters had been careless or had attempted to avoid paying the capitation tax, or because lists had been destroyed or misplaced. Estimates of the number of individuals held in bondage without registration reached 70,000.[40] The effort in the late 1870s to verify holdings against slave censuses was not a legal innovation, only a belated effort at compliance with an old law. Making such lists effectively public was nonetheless an important act. The law had been on the books without causing serious disruption because, although occasional individuals might sue for freedom on the basis of their absence from the lists, slaves had little access to those lists. Now matters of individual servitude and freedom, previously handled discreetly by masters and the Juntas de Libertos, as much as possible over the heads of those whose freedom was involved, could be thrown open to scrutiny. Posting the lists meant that both parties in a dispute could refer to them, that slaves had greater access to evidence on the basis of which they could claim their freedom.

There is little indication that the colonial officials who unleashed this furor were trying to strengthen the hand of slaves at the expense of masters. They were merely trying to enforce a rule that had been blatantly ignored for ten years, to the increasing embarrassment of the government. Both foreigners and abolitionists had protested that the law was being flouted, and Spanish officials were trying to strengthen the case for gradual abolition, not weaken it, when they sought to ensure that the laws were observed. But attempting to enforce the registration rules made it clear that it had long been the masters, not the government, who determined who should be held as a slave. Altering this would be disruptive—not only because it freed some slaves but because it would provide an example of government-sanctioned emancipation to others.

By 1879 the Spanish government was in a very difficult situation concerning slavery in Cuba. Within Spain, pressure from abolitionists was again increasing.[41] Within Cuba, desertions, passive resistance, cane burning, and the omnipresent threat of a new insurrection made the cost of retaining slavery look ever higher. In substance and

[40] Lionel Carden to Salisbury, April 29, 1880, PRO, FO 84/1568.
[41] Corwin, *Spain and the Abolition of Slavery*, chap. 16.

as a symbol slavery provided a continuing focus for antigovernment agitation and disruption of production; the half-hearted provisions of the Moret Law had not diminished that hostility. Because of the uncertainty about the future, lenders denied credit to planters, and the value of the Cuban currency against gold fell.[42] This had not turned most planters into abolitionists, for they feared the cost of abolition would be higher still, but it made them eager for some "resolución de la cuestión social."

At the same time, both the governor general and slaveholders emphasized the terrible disruption that might follow immediate abolition. The governor thought that freed slaves would head for the woods, languish, and die.[43] One observer predicted that abolition would alienate from Spain those who depended on the revenues of slave hiring-out, or who had a large proportion of their capital tied up in slaves.[44]

In such a situation, an apparently logical solution for Spain was to abolish the name of slavery without abolishing its substance, which is precisely what the parliament did. In November 1879 the minister of Ultramar announced the introduction of a bill of abolition, arguing that no one any longer defended slavery, that the only disagreement was on the method by which it should be ended. He proposed the establishment of a *patronato*, a kind of patronage or wardship, an intermediate relationship between master and former slave that would provide the master with indemnification in the form of labor, and provide the slave with "tutelage."[45]

The tone of the 1879-1880 parliamentary debates on the *patronato* was distinct from those of 1870 on the Moret Law. While there was now great unanimity on the inevitability of abolition, there was far less abolitionist zeal or liberal language. In keeping with the tenor of Spanish politics of the period, this was a conservative gathering to discuss problems of labor and social control, not an occasion for principled antislavery pronouncements. Barons, counts, and marquises loomed large in the advisory committee on the bill; Cuban

[42] See the opinion of José Bueno y Blanco in Documentos de la Comisión . . . , and the speech by Portuondo in Spain, Cortes, *Diario de las sesiones de las Cortes*, Congreso, 1879-1880, tomo 2, núm. 95, Feb. 4, 1880, p. 1666.

[43] Letter of Oct. 15, 1879, to the minister of Ultramar, AHN, Ultramar, leg. 4883, tomo 5.

[44] Dispatch, Consulat Général de France, March 13, 1878, in MAE-Paris, C.C., La Havane, vol. 22.

[45] Statement by the minister of Ultramar, Nov. 7, 1879, in AHN, Ultramar, leg. 4883, tomo 5.

slaveholders argued for indemnification and for regulation of labor; even the proponents of the law invoked the dangers of a return to "barbarism" if abolition were not carried out gradually. Obvious racism emerged in the interventions of Cuban delegate Fernández de Castro, who claimed that "anthropological science" had shown the differences between whites and blacks and that, in times of great turmoil, blacks historically reverted to barbarism and human sacrifice.[46]

Both the Constitutional Union party and the Liberal party of Cuba had accepted in principle the familiar idea of a *patronato*, however, and insistence on indemnification or on an even more gradualist solution abated. It was replaced by concern with the overall economic relation between Cuba and Spain, and much of the debate revolved around possible economic concessions to Cuba. Though these were not forthcoming from the government, the law establishing an eight-year period of *patronato* passed in the Cortes on January 30, 1880.[47]

This formal acquiescence to legal abolition did not necessarily reflect a widespread desire by the powerful in Cuba to loosen the bonds that held slaves under control. On the eve of the passage of the bill creating the *patronato*, municipalities were constructing new *depósitos* in which to hold runaways in order to use them on public works.[48] And months after passage of the bill, court edicts continued to refer to "slaves" and to call for individual runaways to surrender themselves or be declared rebellious and contumacious.[49] The creation of a new peculiar institution, the *patronato*, something between slavery and freedom, nonetheless accelerated the rate of change and affected the lives of masters and of slaves in unanticipated ways.

[46] For the debates, see Spain, Cortes, 1879-1880, *Discursos de la ley de abolición de la esclavitud en Cuba* (Madrid, 1879-1880). The reference to barbarism appears in the Dictámen de la Comisión, Appendix to the Senate session number 46. The statement of Fernández de Castro is from the Senate session of Dec. 15, 1880, p. 595.

[47] Spain, Cortes, *Discursos.* For additional discussion of these issues, see Corwin, *Spain and the Abolition of Slavery*, chap. 16. For an analysis of the Spanish political situation at the time of the debates, see Beck, "The Martínez Campos Government. . . ."

[48] Consulta del expediente promovido en el ayto. de Guamacaro para la creación de un depósito de cimarrones, Oct. 20, 1879, ANC, CA, leg. 58, exp. 602.

[49] *Gaceta de la Habana* (April 18, 1880), Edictos, Quinta Sección.

PART TWO

The Limits of Gradualism,
1880-1886

VI

The *Patronato*

The concept of the *patronato*, of an intermediate status between slave and free, bespoke a belief in gradual change. Fearful planters raised specters of Haiti, of Radical Reconstruction in the United States, and of barbarism in general to gain support for the idea that only a prolonged transition could avoid such evil consequences of abolition. Proponents of the *patronato* elevated gradualism to the status of a major virtue, the only way for slaves to become responsible free men and women and for society to withstand the shock of transformation.[1]

Underlying the *patronato* was a denial that interests were fundamentally in conflict; the needs of former slaves and those of former masters would be mediated and compromised to the benefit of both. The minister of Ultramar expressed this hope when he introduced the bill to establish the *patronato*:

Thus the present owners of slaves can organize the transformation of labor without flinging into the risks of a hazardous life as proletarians those who form a kind of large family of tenants (*colonos*) in intimate community of interests with the proprietor and manufacturer. He will continue to obtain their cooperation, but it will be rewarded, both through the stipend and through help, protection, defense—in short, guardianship.[2]

The fond imagery of family and tutelage was rarely echoed by masters themselves, except when they spoke for public consumption. They were far more concerned with maintaining authority and securing labor. But the notion of an institution that would mute conflicts and thereby ultimately serve the interests of those in power helps explain the appeal of the *patronato*.

Enacting such a law, of course, neither eliminated conflict nor fundamentally transformed social attitudes. But in the specific con-

[1] See, for example, the opinion of Coppinger, in AHN, Ultramar, leg. 4926, exp. 144. Gradualism was also a fundamental political principle of many of the reformists.
[2] Introduction to the Proyecto de Ley, in AHN, Ultramar, leg. 4883, tomo 5.

text of Cuba in the 1880s, the law nonetheless had a substantial impact. This impact is revealed in the rapidly evolving government interpretation and enforcement of the law, in the changed interactions of masters and slaves, and in the unanticipated early termination of the *patronato* in 1886.

The law that was promulgated in Madrid on February 13, 1880, left in place the fundamental legal relations of slavery. Although lawmakers renamed the owner *patrono* and the slave *patrocinado*, the master still had a right to the labor of the former slave, and was to represent him in all civil and judicial acts. He could transfer these rights to another *patrono*, subject to certain qualifications, by the usual legal means, including sale and bequest. He could mete out corporal punishment for misbehavior or failure to work. Runaways were to be returned to him, and in cases of severe resistance to his authority on the estate he could call in outside forces to restore order. These were the standard rights that had been exercised by slaveholders for centuries. The duties of masters toward *patrocinados*, however, were slightly greater than those that had been owed to slaves. Masters were obligated not only to feed and clothe *patrocinados* and their children but also to educate the young. They could not separate families or send domestic servants to the countryside against their will, and they had to pay each *patrocinado* aged eighteen and over a monthly stipend.[3]

The relationship was by no means a strictly contractual one. In the first place, slaves did not voluntarily contract into their "guardianships." Moreover, *patrocinados* had few of the rights of a free worker. They could not leave a master's estate without permission, refuse to labor, or seek another master of their own free will. At the same time, they suffered some of the disadvantages of free workers, since their pay could be docked for the time that they were ill or being punished. With the exception of minors, the aged, and the infirm, *patrocinados* were always vulnerable to being legally ejected from their residences if the *patrono* "renounced" his rights over them.

In some respects, the law establishing the *patronato* resembled a

[3] This discussion of the law establishing the *patronato* is based on the text of the 1880 law and its Reglamento and the text of the slave code of 1842 and subsequent regulations. These can be found in the appendix to Ortiz, *Los negros esclavos*, pp. 439-87.

liberal slave code, prescribing hours of rest and amounts of food, safeguarding the integrity of the family, and favoring domestic servants over field workers. It was also reminiscent of the insurgents' Reglamento de Libertos. In crucial respects, however, it departed from the standard provisions of a slave code.

First, it established an expiration date for legal servitude. One quarter of the *patrocinados* held by each master in 1884 were to be freed at the end of each succeeding year in descending order of age. (When several *patrocinados* of a single master were of the same age, a lottery would be held.) Each owner would thus lose one in four, then one in three, then one in two of his remaining *patrocinados* in 1885, 1886, and 1887. By 1888 slavery would end altogether, though each former slave would have the obligation to certify that he or she was gainfully employed for four years from the date of his or her freedom.

Second, the law and the Reglamento that followed it established a set of local and regional boards to oversee the operation of the *patronato*, to rule on disputes, and to act as an intermediary for self-purchase. The provincial governor was to preside over the provincial Junta de Patronato, composed of a provincial deputy, a judge of the district court, the district attorney, the *síndico*, and two taxpayers, one of whom had to be a *patrono*. The local juntas, organized in the appropriate municipalities, were to be presided over by the mayor, and to consist of the *síndico*, a principal taxpayer, and two reputable citizens. Primary authority rested with the local juntas, but cases could be appealed from there to the provincial juntas, and thence to the Consejo de Administración, an advisory body in Havana. As a last resort, cases could be referred to the ministry of Ultramar in Madrid.

Third, the law extended the right to self-purchase, establishing procedures and fixing amounts to be paid. Formal self-purchase, to be called "indemnification of services," was accomplished by paying a decreasing price for freedom, calculated as thirty to fifty pesos for each remaining year of the first five years of the *patronato*, plus half that much for each of the last three. This provision was not unlike the highly touted older institution of *coartación*, under which Cuban slaves had long had the right to buy their freedom by installments. But even during the period of the Moret Law few field slaves had ever succeeded in making use of *coartación*. Under the new law the price was fixed by regulation rather than by the market, and would diminish each year. Moreover, a *patrocinado* could deposit his or her funds directly with the junta rather than with the master.

Fourth, the law specified that infractions of Article 4, which specified masters' obligations, would be punishable by freeing of the *patrocinado*. While the penal code in force under slavery had called for a transfer of ownership as a penalty for abuse of a slave, and required manumission only in extreme cases, the law of the *patronato* would in theory grant full freedom for simple violation of the regulations.[4] One of the most important of these regulations was the required payment of a monthly stipend to the *patrocinados*. The Reglamento specified that stipend to be one peso to those who were eighteen years of age, two to those between nineteen and twenty, and three to those over twenty. The stipend was to be paid in gold or silver, or bills, and not in goods of any kind.

For these legal changes to have an effect, of course, they had to be enforced. The struggles between *patrocinados* and *patronos* over their rights under the law took place within the domain of several administrative systems, and in a climate of political debate on the wisdom of maintaining the *patronato*. Authorities at different levels had somewhat different goals and loyalties, leading to conflicts and reversals, and outside pressures increasingly impinged on the process of enforcement.

For the colonial government in Madrid, the maintenance of order appeared to require both the abolition of an institution called slavery, and its replacement by one designed to appear paternal and transitional. In order to disarm abolitionists and political opposition within Cuba, it was important for Spain to create a distinction between slavery and the *patronato* and to enforce, or appear to enforce, those parts of the 1880 law that expressed a departure from slavery. But at the same time officials in Madrid wished to avoid social upheaval or disruption of production and to prevent the alienation of powerful economic interests in the island, interests to which they, in some cases, had personal as well as political links.[5] The ministry

[4] On earlier penalties, see *Código penal vigente en las Islas de Cuba y Puerto Rico mandado observar por Real Decreto de 23 de Mayo de 1879* (Madrid: Pedro Núñez, 1886).

[5] See Miguel Martínez Cuadrado, *La burguesía conservadora (1874-1931)* (Madrid: Alianza Editorial, 1973), p. 55. For a discussion of Spanish domestic politics and the issue of slavery see Izard, *Manufactureros, industriales, y revolucionarios*, chap. 5.

of Ultramar was thus verbally emphatic that the laws be obeyed and that disputes be handled with dispatch and a semblance of fairness. Actual enforcement, however, was largely left to the officials in residence in Cuba. Although the ministry frequently resolved those rare appeals that reached Madrid in favor of *patrocinados*, on questions of general policy the government sought and heeded the opinions of planters.

Spanish officials within Cuba were also ambivalent. As representatives of the authority of Madrid and at the same time guardians of order within the colony, their position was delicate on any issue where the interests of their clients in Cuba and those of their superiors in Spain were at odds. Egregious abuses of *patrocinados*, if given publicity, reflected on Spanish administrators and could be used to discredit Spanish rule; rigorous enforcement of the protective provisions of the law, on the other hand, risked infuriating *patronos*.

These conflicts were further complicated by calculations of the strategy most likely to keep the social peace. In any decision, the possibility of popular discontent as well as elite anger had to be taken into account. The governor general in his report to Madrid in mid-September 1880 analyzed the situation in the following way. The attitude of the people of color, particularly the *patrocinados*, was for the moment satisfactory, he reported, and he believed that it would remain so if masters complied with all of the obligations that the law of abolition imposed on them. He therefore urged masters to cooperate with the law. Obviously he was keenly aware of the urgency of avoiding serious disaffection and possible cane burnings or uprisings by former slaves passing through the process of transition. For the governor of an island only recently pacified, the responsibility for preventing disorder was primary. But the interests of order could cut the other way as well. The ultimate sanction against masters who did not observe the regulations was the freeing of their *patrocinados*, and the use of this sanction could, in the governor's opinion, create far more trouble than the offense itself. The freeing of some *patrocinados* because of offenses committed by their *patronos* might provoke a "scandal" that could "alter the tranquillity" in which the other *patrocinados* lived.[6] This the governor wished very much to avoid. An obvious way to do so was to place

[6] Letter from the governor general, Sept. 15, 1880, AHN, Ultramar, leg. 4884, tomo 7, exp. 86.

planter interests above *patrocinado* claims. Thus even though one of the aims of gradual abolition was the reduction of tension and the elimination of a motive for insurrection, in moments of crisis the enforcement of the law of gradual abolition could stand in direct conflict with the perceived requirements for keeping the peace.

Even routine enforcement of some provisions of the 1880 law could on occasion lead to abrupt large-scale freeing of *patrocinados*, as in areas where nonregistration of slaves had been widespread or where registers had been destroyed, making *patronos'* claims to the services of *patrocinados* legally void. But when mass freeings of *patrocinados* seemed a possibility, governors tended to back off from or stall enforcement.[7] They were as apprehensive as planters about the consequences of rapid change in the status of former slaves.

The Consejo de Administración in Havana handled appeals from the provincial juntas, and was particularly concerned to minimize disruption of the economy. Some members were former slaveholders hostile to any initiatives by *patrocinados*; only a few believed that a smooth transition required rigid adherence to the protective provisions of the laws. When they had been consulted about the Reglamento governing the *patronato* at the time of its drafting, a majority of the members of the consejo had opposed it, which suggests that their zeal in enforcement may have been wanting.[8] As a body, they were generally willing to rule in favor of *patrocinados'* claims in those cases where it was clear that, by denial of wages or by physical abuse, masters had violated the basic notion of a transition away from slavery. But they were more likely to excuse infractions of the more demanding requirements of the law—such as the education of children or the payment of stipends precisely on time. The consejo's procedures were such, in any case, that winning an appeal was nearly impossible. Endless notarized depositions were necessary, and few appellants could keep up with the requirements and carry a case through to a ruling. The most frequent resolution seems to have been simply *"caducada"*—the case had lapsed because one or another deadline had passed. This had two effects. One was to

---

[7] A long debate over the legitimacy of various additional registers helped to prolong the process of verifying the old slave lists and to stall the freeing of unregistered *patrocinados*. See AHN, Ultramar, leg. 4814, exp. 270 for conflict over the delay, and leg. 4815, exp. 289 for the final resolution.

[8] Trelles, *Biblioteca histórica cubana* 2: 423.

stall the freeing of *patrocinados*, for they would not be issued freedom papers during the slow process of appeal. The other was to
uphold rulings of the local and provincial juntas by default.[9]

The local and provincial Juntas de Patronato, of which there were
over a hundred, were responsible for the day-to-day enforcement of
the law. Though not required to have a membership that was one-
half slaveholder, as the Juntas Protectoras de Libertos had been, they
were intended to protect former masters as well as former slaves.
The government called on them to follow careful procedures and to
avoid precipitate action. In practice, they showed no strong presumption in favor of the rights of *patrocinados*. For example, former
slaves who turned up in a district and claimed to be free were often
placed in the municipal *depósito* while the junta publicized their
descriptions in the local press for a month, in order to determine
whether anyone had legal rights over them. The former slave might
be freed after thirty days, but if the junta did not believe that the
individual had a right to freedom, despite the nonappearance of a
master, he or she might be sent to labor on public works.[10]

The most controversial and disruptive aspect of the juntas' activities was their responsibility for handling complaints from *patrocinados*. Legally, a *patrocinado* could leave his or her master's dom-
icile in order to bring a complaint before the junta. It was then the
responsibility of the junta to examine the evidence and rule on the
case.

It is difficult to generalize confidently about the behavior of juntas
when faced with complaints, for no complete set of their proceedings
has been found. Several general lines of evidence about their conduct
and sympathies do emerge, however. First, the possibility of conscious and unconscious bias against *patrocinados* was great. The
members of the juntas had been men of power and distinction in a
slave society, and they appear generally to have shared the dominant
beliefs of that society. Furthermore, there was considerable potential
for conflict of interest within an organization composed of officials
and citizens already enmeshed in local affairs. Abolitionists went
so far as to charge that the majority of juntas were composed of

[9] See ANC, CA, legs. 60, 64, 65, 69, 70, and 71 for numerous appeals to the Consejo
de Administración.
[10] See, for example, the *Boletín Oficial de la Provincia de Santa Clara*, April 9,
1881, and February 13, 1881.

recognized proslavery men, and that masters could simply arrange matters to their convenience with the juntas.[11]

Graft and collusion also occurred. The juntas were inadequately funded, and the temptation to mishandle funds deposited by *patrocinados* must have been great. Occasionally scandals would erupt, and there would be a flurry of dismissals of officials. Nor was this the only form of corruption. Unscrupulous members of the juntas were able to put *patrocinados* in their debt and thus obtain a claim to the *patrocinados'* labor for themselves or their friends.[12]

In the course of an investigation of corruption in the Junta of Rancho Veloz, in Santa Clara province, one member of the local junta complained that aside from himself all the members of the junta were linked by ties of family, and that this was prejudicial to the interests of both *patronos* and *patrocinados*. He charged that this junta rarely met, that it never carried out plantation visits, and that members assigned to themselves the services of *patrocinados*. In a case in the same district, a young woman who purchased her freedom in 1882 did not receive her *cédula*, or freedom papers, from the junta. Moreover, the junta's secretary called her in to demand two ounces of gold for himself, since he had helped her obtain her freedom. She did not have the money, and he threatened that if she did not find it, he would send the Guardia Civil to collect her and send her to an *ingenio*. She still had not received her *cédula* when the investigation began, and without it obviously was vulnerable to the demands of the corrupt official.[13]

Corruption, ironically, did not always work entirely against the interests of *patrocinados*, despite their vulnerability. During the investigation of the Junta of Rancho Veloz, for instance, there were accusations from *patronos* and administrators of estates as well as from *patrocinados*. They charged that junta members were inciting

[11] Exposición que al Excelentísimo Señor Ministro de Ultramar hace la Junta Directiva de la Sociedad Abolicionista Española, May 30, 1883, AHN, Ultramar, leg. 4814, exp. 279.

[12] Telegram from the governor general to the minister of Ultramar, Jan. 18, 1882, AHN, Ultramar, leg. 4813, exp. 235. For a case of corruption, see Don Juan Riús eleva recurso de alzada, AHN, Ultramar, leg. 4831, exp. 57.

[13] See Copia del expediente instruido en averiguación de los abusos cometidos por la Junta Local de Patronato de Rancho Veloz, and Copia del expediente instruido por la Junta de Patronato para averiguar los abusos cometidos por el Ayuntamiento de Rancho Veloz, in Don Juan Riús eleva recurso de alzada, AHN, Ultramar, leg. 4831, exp. 57.

patrocinados to file complaints against their masters, and that the junta failed to pay *patronos* the money due them when *patrocinados* purchased their freedom. Though justice was not being done for the *patrocinados*, the disorderly behavior of the junta in this case was worrying to planters, for they deeply resented the intrusion of the junta into their affairs. Two examples will illustrate the pattern. In one case, a mother offered her plantation's administrator a certain sum to free her daughter, and when he refused she made a separate agreement with the junta, and left the plantation along with her child. The administrator later complained bitterly that he had never received the money she had deposited, but a deeper grievance was perhaps the circumvention of his will. In another case, a woman deposited 200 pesos with the junta for her freedom, and the head of the junta urged her to file a claim for her daughter's freedom as well. It was probably this kind of initiative, rather than their exploitation of the labor of *patrocinados*, which brought a scandal down on the heads of the officials of Rancho Veloz.[14]

Even a corrupt and prejudiced junta would on occasion find it in its interest to rule in favor of *patrocinados.* A planter competing for labor could try to arrange for another *patrono*'s *patrocinados* to be freed in order to work for him. One proprietor expressed fury at a local junta because his *patrocinados* kept being freed and then turning up on a neighbor's plantation.[15] Though such competition could yield freedom for some *patrocinados*, as the least powerful parties they doubtless suffered in the long run from the corruption of the legal process.

There seem to have been two general patterns of variation in the behavior of juntas. First, there was a rural/urban difference that tended to mean better treatment for *patrocinados* in the city. Juntas in large towns were more likely to be staffed with officials less directly tied to the interests of former slaveowners and were therefore somewhat less subject to *patrono* influence. They also functioned within view of the press and of opposition politicians eager to charge mistreatment of *patrocinados*.[16]

---

[14] Ibid.
[15] Ibid.
[16] Great Britain, Parliament, *Parliamentary Papers* (Lords), 1882, vol. 24 (Slave Trade No. 3), "Report by Acting Consul-General Carden on the Number and Condition of the Slaves in Cuba."

This activism by politicians was one manifestation of a larger shift in Cuban politics that influenced policy on slavery at several levels. In the late 1870s and early 1880s, after the end of the Ten Years' War, electoral politics opened up considerably in the island. Martínez Campos, the new captain general, began a period of relative conciliation aimed at consolidating Spanish rule. Elections to municipal office and to the Spanish Cortes were finally permitted, though sharply limited by a property qualification. (Mayors, who were also the heads of the local Juntas de Patronato, were still appointed by the Spanish civil governors.) Reformism, eclipsed during the war, reemerged in the form of the Liberal or Autonomist party, pro-Spanish but also in favor of civil rights for Cubans. On the other side were the conservatives, the Constitutional Unionists, who wanted closer ties with Spain.[17]

Although the press law of Cuba specifically forbade writers to "defend or expound doctrines contrary to the organization of the family and property" or to excite the animosity of one class against another, the question of slavery remained alive, even after the establishment of the *patronato*.[18] Given the virtually unchallenged predominance of the planter and merchant elite, and the legal repression of public discussion of the issue of slavery, colonial Cuba never developed an above-ground abolitionist movement comparable to that of Brazil. Abolitionism was stronger underground, first among the anticolonial insurgents and later among certain veterans of the first struggle for independence. Nonetheless, some white politicians, professionals, and journalists, and some free persons of color, composed a small group openly in favor of abolition. Their critique of slavery was not only moral but also economic, social, and political. They differed on the appropriate mechanisms for ending slavery, but generally perceived it as a backward institution, due for replacement by a modern regime of free labor. Some viewed the freedom of black Cubans as essential to that of white Cubans, a prerequisite for social harmony and economic progress.[19]

[17] Thomas, *Cuba*, pp. 267-68, discusses the Liberals and the Constitutional Unionists.

[18] The text of Title II, Art. 16, of the Ley de Imprenta may be found in the *Boletín Oficial de Santa Clara*, May 7, 1881.

[19] On Cuban abolitionists, see Entralgo, *La liberación étnica*, pp. 84-101, and Cepero Bonilla, *Azúcar y abolición*, chap. 19. On Brazil, by way of contrast, see Robert Conrad, *The Destruction of Brazilian Slavery* (Berkeley: University of California Press, 1972), and Robert Brent Toplin, *The Abolition of Slavery in Brazil* (New York: Atheneum, 1972).

The island's Liberal party, formed in 1878, began by calling for indemnified abolition, a cautious step indeed. But in 1879 the party adopted a position of more explicit abolitionism and in the 1880s opposed the imposition of the *patronato*. The small Partido Democrático, with a liberal, anticlerical platform, supported abolition of the *patronato* and aimed their publicity at, among others, artisans and free persons of color.[20] In July 1882, the Autonomist deputies followed suit and proposed, unsuccessfully, the abolition of the *patronato*.[21] Issues concerning the enforcement of the laws of the *patronato* thus became part of the political conflict between the colonial government and its critics. A few *patronos* freed their *patrocinados* publicly and were hailed as "benefactors of humanity" in the Liberal press. Abolitionists also tried, unsuccessfully, to establish an abolitionist society in Havana.[22]

Although these politicians and publicists remained a small minority without full freedom of expression, they nonetheless helped to keep the issue of slavery alive, to put pressure on juntas, and, intentionally and unintentionally, to communicate information to *patrocinados*. Even in the absence of a strong or widespread antislavery movement, the question of endorsement of or opposition to the *patronato* became involved in party struggles, as each party sought support from free persons of color and charged the others with hypocrisy or opportunism.

Juntas in Havana thus operated under the watchful eyes of party propagandists and occasional abolitionists reporting back to Spain, and with the knowledge that appeals of disputed cases could be more easily relayed to the ministry in Madrid. In the province of Havana, over 3,000 *patrocinados* obtained their freedom by proving that their masters had violated the law or the regulations of the 1880 bill. By contrast, in Santa Clara, a more isolated sugar region whose provincial junta was reputed among abolitionists to be of proslavery sympathies, fewer than 500 *patrocinados* were able to obtain their freedom by proving their masters to be at fault. Unfortunately, fig-

[20] For the platform of the short-lived Partido Democrático, see *La Razón: Semanario Político Dedicado a los Artesanos*, June 26, 1881, in AHN, Ultramar, leg. 4807.

[21] On the evolution of the position of the Liberal party, see Trelles, *Biblioteca histórica cubana* 2: 426 and 3: 553, and Rafael María de Labra, *Mi campaña en las Cortes Españolas* (Madrid: Aurelio J. Alaria, 1885).

[22] For references to the freeing of *patrocinados* see *La Propaganda* (May 4, 1882), and Trelles, *Biblioteca histórica cubana* 2: 426. On attempts to establish an abolitionist society, see *La Discusión* (June 19, 1882).

ures on the total number of cases *initiated*—as opposed to requests granted—do not exist. Still, though the number of freeings was a function of the number of complaints and their accuracy, as well as of the inclinations of different juntas, such disparities almost certainly reflected the presence in regions like Santa Clara of juntas determined to hold the line against *patrocinado* appeals.[23]

Junta behavior also tended to reflect the level of tension in the surrounding region. In Santiago de Cuba, for example, where tensions were extremely high, the provincial junta functioned to some extent as a peace-keeping arm of the government. Its members worked with General Polavieja to draft repressive antivagrancy plans and to establish as much control as possible over *patrocinados*.[24] In fact, the junta in Santiago de Cuba behaved with such disregard for the rights of *patrocinados* that a royal order in December 1881 reprimanded it for violations of the regulations. The junta was charged with excessively high assessment of the price of self-purchase, with recalling a *cédula* of freedom already issued, and with approving a master's illegal discounting of stipends owed a *patrocinada*.[25]

It is clear that the juntas' dedication to the task of ensuring fulfillment of the law was compromised by other concerns. They tended to make their own interpretations of the "spirit" rather than the letter of the legislation on gradual abolition, in response to the prevailing views on the danger of rapidly altering the status quo.

In sum, the commitment to enforcement of the law of 1880 varied among the different levels of administration. Madrid was both abstractly sympathetic to the rights of *patrocinados* and deeply concerned about social stability, but in any event saw few cases. The governors of the provinces were sensitive to the needs of agriculture in their areas and extremely fearful of disruption of production or of social peace. The governor general of the island and the Consejo de Administración tended to be sympathetic to the interests of *patronos* and *hacendados*, and supported the enforcement of some

[23] For statistics on the number of *patrocinados* freed each year, see AHN, Ultramar, leg. 4926, exp. 144, and leg. 4814, exp. 273. For abolitionist denunciations of the biases of the juntas, see Exposición . . . de la Sociedad Abolicionista, AHN, Ultramar, leg. 4814, exp. 279.

[24] See *Conspiración de la raza de color descubierta en Santiago de Cuba el 10 de diciembre de 1880* . . . (Santiago de Cuba: Sección Tipográfica del Estado Mayor, 1880), pp. 145-55.

[25] Reales Ordenes, Dec. 2, 1881, AHN, Ultramar, leg. 4884, tomo 7, exp. 110.

provisions more than others. Local juntas were entangled in local affairs, providing an audience and a target for complaints, but no guarantee of justice.

The crucial questions about the *patronato*, however, cannot be answered by reference to its legal provisions and their enforcement alone. By simply examining the text of the law one could make either of two quite different cases. Judging by the protective clauses concerning *patrocinados*, one could argue that the law granted money, education, legal recourse, and eventual freedom to individuals who previously had rights to none of these things, and thus it fundamentally altered slavery. But judging by the provisions for the maintenance of authority through coercion and corporal punishment, and the absence of the civil rights of free workers, one could argue that there had been little change indeed, at least in the short run. The second argument could be strengthened further by an examination of the thinly veiled slaveowner mentality of the document, where the polite terms of "patronage" and "tutelage" are embedded in a language of punishment and authority that reflects an unremitting concern for domination. Indeed, contemporary abolitionists portrayed the *patronato* as simply another form of slavery: an institution that denied freedom to the *patrocinado*, kept him or her under highly personal control, and alienated the product of his or her labor in return for maintenance and a small stipend rather than a competitive wage.

To understand what actually took place between former slaves and former masters during the years of the *patronato*, however, one must recognize that, while the *patronato* was in some respects another form of slavery, it was not *just* another form of slavery. It was an ambiguous institution, one which attempted to eliminate, but could not, the tensions and contradictions involved in gradual abolition. To the extent that the law tried to resolve these contradictions, it either denied legal freedom, thus undermining the distinction between slave and *patrocinado*, or granted new rights, thus giving *patrocinados* potential leverage in determining the course of emancipation. The ambiguity of the institution meant that neither *patronos* nor *patrocinados* saw it as functioning fully in their interests, yet both attempted to use it to defend or advance their positions.

The *patronato* was designed to ensure a slow, smooth transition ending in 1888. The administrators charged with enforcing the law had no interest in freeing large numbers of *patrocinados* and were not particularly sympathetic to *patrocinado* efforts to free themselves. One would expect, then, that the number of *patrocinados* would remain relatively steady from 1880 to 1885, when the planned freeings began, and then drop at a regular rate to zero by 1888. The actual pace of emancipation, however, was quite different.

Within the first year after the establishment of the *patronato*, over 6,000 *patrocinados* had obtained full legal freedom. Then during the second year, 10,000 obtained their freedom, and 17,000 during the third year. In the fourth year over 26,000 *patrocinados*—almost 9,000 of them in the sugar province of Matanzas alone—became free. There had been almost 200,000 slaves in Cuba in 1877, but by 1883 there were just 99,566 *patrocinados* remaining in the registers, and by 1885 just 53,381.[26] Rather than spending five to eight years as *patrocinados*, slaves were rapidly exiting from their intermediate status. "Gradual" abolition seemed to be proceeding at an alarmingly fast pace as, in the words of a distressed observer, "every day they know their rights better and turn up at the juntas to exercise them."[27]

Any evaluation of the *patronato* must, then, capture this paradoxical combination of change and absence of change that marked the 1880s. On the one hand, any new room for maneuver for former slaves was significant. On the other, the prolonging of the promised emancipation was in itself a triumph of stalling and resistance by masters. It is to this interaction of *patronos* and *patrocinados* that we now turn.

[26] See the records titled "Estado numérico" in AHN, Ultramar, leg. 4926, exp. 144, and leg. 4814, exp. 273.

[27] Letter to the governor general from F. Ardenín, Nov. 12, 1882, AHN, Ultramar, leg. 4814.

VII

Patrocinados: Obstacles
and Initiatives

In the daybooks of plantations, the eighth of May 1880, the date of
the Reglamento putting into effect the law that abolished slavery
and established the *patronato*, passed without notice. The work
force did not decline, labor did not stop, the rhythm of life appeared
unaltered. Although stipends began to be paid, at first irregularly,
they seem often to have been used as a special incentive rather than
as wages, in much the same way that rewards or feasts had been
used under slavery. Laborers still worked at 4:00 A.M. in the mill.
There was still work on Sundays during good weather in harvest
season. There was, on the surface, little change.[1]

If one simply asks whether the 1880 law actually brought emancipation or protected *patrocinados* against abuse, the answer is quite
clear: it did not. As the Moret Law had not freed those whom it
declared free, the 1880 law did not protect those whom it declared
protected. But it provided, in part unintentionally, a set of weapons
with which those *patrocinados* willing and able to press their claims
could attack their masters. The cases brought before the juntas thus
offer not proof that the law was good and benevolent, but rare insight
into the tactics and values of those *patrocinados* actually able to
lodge complaints. More important, they show the inadequacy of
conceptualizing slave and *patrocinado* behavior in terms of "accommodation" or "resistance," and the necessity of analyzing that behavior in terms that reflect the complexity of *patrocinados'* goals
and strategies.

Patrocinados quickly learned to use their new weapons. In Santa
Clara province, for example, the first notice of the establishment of
the provincial junta came in May 1880. By the end of the month, a

[1] See, for example, Libro Diario del Ingenio Nueva Teresa, 1880-1886, ANC, ML,
10830, and Libro Diario del Ingenio Delicias, 1872-1882, ANC, ML, 10802.

variety of claims had already been made. Two men sought to legitimate their de facto freedom, one having been in the insurrection,
the other having fled an estate on the day of his master's death three
years before. Another *patrocinado* came to assert rights over some
livestock and to demand ten years' worth of Sunday pay for the time
he had been hired out. A woman claimed the wages of her free
children; another complained of ill treatment. Though the number
of *patrocinados* granted full freedom in response to complaints
against their masters was never large in Santa Clara, the number of
claims of one sort and another appears to have been substantial.[2]

Patrocinados were probably the most powerless individuals in
Cuban society, highly vulnerable to retaliation and exploitation. But
some of them clearly had a sense that the moment of formal abolition was a moment in which to assert rights, and thus took risks
they might not otherwise have taken. It was a gamble, for example,
to appeal for legal freedom if one already had de facto freedom, since
the supplicant would be held in a *depósito* and an announcement
run in the local paper calling for anyone believing he or she had
the right of *patronato* to come forward. Many made the appeal,
nonetheless.

The goal of those who brought complaints was not always immediate freedom. Sometimes the *patrocinado* sought initially to
protect himself against abuse. The case of Crecencio, a slave and
later *patrocinado* in the *ingenio* San Rafael, is an example. He had
been a *cimarrón*, a runaway, and as punishment had been forced to
wear leg irons for two years. He went to the authorities in Güines
to protest this treatment and won an order to have the irons removed.
The plantation overseer, however, did not want to remove the irons
immediately, and the *alcalde* (presumably also head of the local
Junta de Patronato) agreed to let the overseer keep them on for two
or three more days to prevent any "bad effect" the example of a
successful appeal might have on the other *patrocinados*. Crecencio
flatly refused to work unless the irons were removed. Sent to the
fields to plant sweet potatoes, he stopped and demanded that the
irons be taken off. His aim, according to the driver of the work gang,
was to get those who had previously protected him to come to the

[2] *Boletín Oficial de la Provincia de Santa Clara*, May 28, May 29, May 21, 1880.
For additional claims, and lists of those freed, see the regular reports of junta activity
in the *Boletín*.

estate. Instead, the plantation overseer was called to the field where Crecencio stood, hoe in hand. According to the testimony of the other *patrocinados*, the overseer kicked Crecencio, had him whipped, put him in stocks, and then hit him on the head. When this evidence emerged during an official visit to the plantation (prompted by other problems), the overseer was fined twenty-five pesos and Crecencio was ordered transferred to another *patrono*. He eventually won his legal freedom because the *patrocinados* on the estate were found to have been denied food, clothing, and stipends.[3]

The case is interesting in part because of the way a *patrocinado* was trying to use the local authorities. Crecencio was clearly a resister of long standing. The establishment of new laws and of the juntas did not create his resistance, it simply increased the number of strategies at his disposal and the likelihood that one of them might succeed.

The outcome of such a complaint depended a great deal on the particular officials with whom *patrocinados* dealt. A local judge granted Crecencio's request to have the leg irons removed, but the *alcalde* modified the ruling when faced with the overseer's desire to keep order. And in the larger dispute on San Rafael, visits to the plantation by the judge and the *síndico* yielded *patrocinado* testimony highly unfavorable to the master, while visits from the *alcalde* and the *celador* yielded *patrocinado* denials that they had received corporal punishment. Only the very unusual conditions on the estate—lack of food and near bankruptcy that had led to riots among the *patrocinados*—created a situation in which the junta was prepared to free a large number. Even then, the master contested the ruling and brought armed forces into the estate to repress those who had been freed.[4]

It was by no means merely the young, the urban, or the Creole among *patrocinados* who took legal initiatives. In fact, the simplest, most straightforward grounds for appeal was advanced age. Since the promulgation of the Moret Law, it had been illegal to hold as a

[3] Copia certificada del expediente instruido en la Junta Provincial de Patronato de la Habana sobre mal trato dado a la dotación del ingenio Armenteritos, de D. Nicolás de Cárdenas, 1883, ANC, CA, leg. 99, exp. 8864. This *ingenio* is also referred to as San Rafael.

[4] Rafael María de Labra, an abolitionist, refers to a "rebellion" on Armenteritos and the calling in of the army "to maintain in servitude blacks declared free by the appropriate authorities." Labra, *Mi campaña*, p. 301.

slave anyone over the age of sixty. An African-born *patrocinado*, a native of Guinea and a field laborer in the province of Santa Clara, showed his sense of his own rights when he "absented himself" from his masters and went to the junta, asking for liberty on the grounds of old age and compensation for twenty-six pigs that his masters had slaughtered for consumption on the estate. His initiative did obtain his freedom, though in the process he was swindled by a corrupt official of a local junta.[5]

The age limit already established by the Moret Law was unambiguous, but the disputes that arose about the actual ages of slaves could turn these appeals into slow procedures, filled with claims and counterclaims. Often there was no written record of age, and masters could argue that the man or woman was actually younger than sixty, whereupon a doctor might be called in to estimate age.

In some cases the very identity of the *patrocinado* was called into question. A man who called himself José Julián Pizarro appeared before a local junta to claim his freedom, bringing as evidence his baptismal certificate. It listed his mother's name (María de Regla, de Nación Gangá), his godmother's name (María Ignacia Conga Pizarro), and the name he was given at birth: José Julián. But the junta refused to accept the evidence, claiming that his real name was Timoteo, that he was called Timoteo on the estate, and that he was only in his fifties. They declined to give him his freedom unless he could prove he was the person listed in the certificate. He did not produce anyone who had known his godmother or his first master, but he protested in a handwritten letter from Havana to the ministry in Madrid that he had been named José Julián at birth, though as was the custom he had been called by a nickname, in this case Timoteo. The apparent discrepancy between formal naming practices and plantation custom led to a two-year delay in the settling of the case. In 1883 he petitioned the ministry for a second time, noting with discouragement that although he trusted in justice from Madrid, "since the distance is great, Sir, each one here does as he pleases and everything has remained as before." He finally won his battle when the ministry, with some impatience, ruled that in such ambiguous cases the decision should favor liberty.[6]

[5] Don Juan Riús y Font eleva recurso de alzada, AHN, Ultramar, leg. 4831, exp. 57.
[6] El patrocinado José Julián Pizarro suplica se ordene su libertad, como sexagenario, AHN, Ultramar, leg. 4809, exp. 55. The letter seems to be his own work: " . . . pº

Nonregistration was also a clear grounds for appeal. Anyone who had not been registered as a slave was legally free and had the right, in theory, to receive a certificate of freedom. This seemingly straightforward procedure, however, was made more complex by the fact that not all slave registers had been published as ordered in 1877, and masters continued to appeal for the inclusion of additional slaves in the lists. This stalling tactic, which had worked through the 1870s to prevent the granting of freedom en masse to unregistered slaves, also worked to delay appeals by individual *patrocinados* in the 1880s, as officials consulted back and forth on the appropriate principles to apply. Finally in 1883 the ministry ruled all additional lists invalid and ordered certificates of freedom issued to those *patrocinados* held without proper registration. When the list was drawn up in December 1883, 11,408 *patrocinados* were formally declared free, though without any compensation for the fact that they had been held illegally for years.[7]

Sevicia, or excessive cruelty, had long been grounds for obtaining freedom, but it was not an easy charge to prove. Technically, the charge of *sevicia* was a matter for the courts, not the juntas, though one could interpret the 1880 law as giving juntas authority to rule in any case of illegal punishment. In practice, a *patrocinado* was likely to appeal to his local junta. The junta would then call upon a doctor to examine the complainant and testify concerning the nature of his or her injuries. Processes of this kind involved considerable subjectivity, and the political, social, and economic influence of the master might well block a fair judgment. In some cases, the junta simply ruled the injuries to be trivial and sent the *patrocinado* back to the master. The possibility of such a ruling could easily inhibit a *patrocinado* who feared further retaliation and who realized the complaints of mistreatment were especially liable to be "fixed" by the master. The tendency of juntas to dismiss injuries as trivial may have been increased by the circulation of stories of *patrocinados* who faked bruises and successfully gained their freedom. Although it seems unlikely that such deception was widespread, given the difficulty of proving even legitimate charges, the prevalence of the

como la distancia es mucha ES cada cual ase aqui lo que le parece asi es que todo ha quedado en esta anterior. . . ."
[7] Relación de los individuos, AHN, Ultramar, leg. 4815, exp. 289.

idea of successful fakery reflected masters' apprehensions about dealing with both their *patrocinados* and with the juntas.[8]

It seems clear that the law did not protect the *patrocinados* against physical mistreatment. What it did instead was to give some *patrocinados* a way to increase the cost of that mistreatment. By marching to the junta and displaying their injuries, they could create problems for those who inflicted them, whether or not freedom was obtained in the particular case. A free black man, for example, appealed the case of a *patrocinado* named Juan all the way to the colonial office in Madrid, despite the refusal of the junta to treat the wounds as serious or to believe that they were inflicted by the master. The remarks of the governor general when the case was referred back to him are revealing. He complained that *patrocinados* and "those who advise them" erroneously believed that the existence of injuries would get them freedom. Although the governor thought the case should be sent back to the regular courts, his reference to such a widespread belief among *patrocinados* suggests the way in which information, or even misinformation, about the 1880 law could increase the initiatives taken by *patrocinados* to obtain their freedom.[9]

The extraordinary number of obstacles to be overcome makes the number of *patrocinado* appeals impressive. Long-standing assumptions and structures characteristic of a slave society, however, sharply limited the likelihood of their success. In José Julián Pizarro's case, for example, the proof of age the *patrocinado* supplied, a slave baptismal record, was challenged by the master, who had no written evidence beyond the registration records he had himself made. But the junta excused this lack on the master's part, noting that the purchase and transfer of slaves before 1867 had been "irregular" and that therefore it was understandable that the master should have no records. The ministry in Madrid later rebuked the junta for such an unquestioning acceptance of slaveholders' omissions. But the predisposition of this junta to rule in favor of a master, despite the evidence, doubtless reflects the attitude encountered by many whose cases were never seen in Madrid.[10]

[8] El consul general Crowe al Conde Granville, April 20, 1883, AHN, Ultramar, leg. 4815.

[9] Francisco de P. Rico, moreno libre, suplica la libertad de Juan, por malos tratamientos, AHN, Ultramar, leg. 4809, exp. 57.

[10] El patrocinado José Julián Pizarro suplica se ordene su libertad, AHN, Ultramar, leg. 4809, exp. 55.

Similarly, when a *patrocinado* filed a complaint, he or she was dependent upon the courts and juntas to weigh ex-slave testimony against ex-slaveholder testimony. In the right place at the right time, such as Havana during a period of abolitionist pressure, the *patrocinado* might receive the benefit of the doubt. In other times and places, the white neighbors of a *patrono* may have been hesitant to portray him as a brute. Again, expectations and standards of conduct formed under slavery were not likely to be radically altered by a law that permitted some corporal punishment and continued to rely on subjective judgments about the degree of cruelty ruled excessive.

Appeals based on age or cruelty, as well as those based upon non-registration, were founded on principles recognized by laws long in force. The "abolition" laws of 1880 made it easier to pursue freedom on these grounds by establishing juntas to which *patrocinados* could appeal and before which they could testify. The grounds for achieving freedom that were actually introduced, rather than simply reinforced, by the 1880 law, however, turned out to be more useful to *patrocinados*. These fell into three categories: "mutual accord" between *patrono* and *patrocinado*, "indemnification of services" or self-purchase, and challenges to the *patrono* charging him with failure to fulfill his obligations under the law.

Freedom through mutual accord covered any arrangement made without the intervention of a junta. In some instances mutual accord meant buying one's freedom for an informally agreed-upon price rather than through official indemnification. For example, in one case, a *patrocinada* named Petra gave 11.5 ounces of gold to obtain exemption from the *patronato* by *mutuo convenio*.[11] It is not possible to determine the actual content of most of the agreements for freedom by mutual accord precisely because, in the absence of junta supervision, no permanent record was created. In many cases, there was probably a contract of some sort signed or agreed to, similar to those masters had long made with manumitted slaves. Such agreements might incorporate whatever concessions a *patrocinado* could gain by making life difficult for the master or threatening to take him to the junta, or whatever concessions on future wages the master could gain with the tempting offer of legal freedom. "Mutual accord" was particularly common in the sugar provinces of Matanzas

[11] Don Juan Riús y Font eleva recurso de alzada, AHN, Ultramar, leg. 4831, exp. 57.

TABLE 19

Patrocinados Legally Achieving Full Freedom, by Province,
May 1881-May 1886

Terms of Freedom	Pinar del Rio	Havana	Matanzas	Santa Clara	Puerto Principe	Santiago de Cuba	Total
Mutual Accord	3,013	3,620	14,997	11,342	60	2,070	35,102 (31%)
Renunciation by Master	2,739	6,785	3,639	3,613	167	1,883	18,826 (17%)
Indemnification by *Patrocinado*	2,141	2,113	3,446	3,115	24	2,164	13,003 (11%)
Failure of Master to Fulfill Article 4[a]	1,022	3,398	2,097	429	103	374	7,423 (7%)
Other Causes	1,831	2,952	4,452	3,249	189	1,551	14,224 (12%)
Article 8 (1885 and 1886 only)[b]	4,190	3,642	10,468	6,286	32	691	25,309 (22%)
Total	14,936	22,510	39,099	28,034	575	8,733	113,887 (100%)

SOURCE: AHN, Ultramar, leg. 4814, exp. 273 and exp. 289; AHN, Ultramar, leg. 4926, exp. 144; Manuel Villanova, *Estadística de la abolición de la esclavitud* (Havana, 1885).
[a] Article 4 of the 1880 law listed the obligations of the *patrono*: to maintain his *patrocinados*, clothe them, assist them when ill, pay the specified monthly stipend, educate minors, and feed, clothe, and assist in illness the children of his *patrocinados*.
[b] Article 8 called for one in four of the *patrocinados* of each master to be freed in 1885, and one in three in 1886, in descending order of age. In the event that several *patrocinados* were of the same age, a lottery was to be held.

and Santa Clara, where in each case it accounted for about 40 percent of the provincial grants of freedom (see Table 19).

Although Cuban slaves had long had the legal right to buy their freedom, the provisions for "indemnification of services" under the 1880 law, by specifying new procedures and reducing the cost of freedom, seemed to bring self-purchase within closer reach. The key, however, was the accumulation of funds. One source of cash was the stipend, the token payment in lieu of wages that amounted to one to three pesos a month. This alone would be an impossibly slow means of accumulating enough to purchase freedom during the first years of the *patronato*, though if a *patrocinado* saved all of his or her stipend, he or she might by 1884 be able to indemnify a master. To do so, however, a *patrocinado* would have to spend virtually nothing in the interim, never be sick, and avoid the loss of work time through punishment. It was also possible for the master to pay the *patrocinados* in bills and then require indemnification in gold. Abolitionists charged that the junta of Santa Clara accepted deposits only in Spanish gold, while *patrocinados* there were paid in Mexican gold.[12]

Like slaves in the 1870s, *patrocinados* in the 1880s often sought to raise money through the sale of goods from their *conucos.* Though the *conuco* lands did not legally belong to them, their rights to usufruct were sometimes respected even under unusual circumstances, either as an incentive or to prevent discontent. There is an intriguing entry in the account book of an unidentified plantation near Cárdenas in 1880: "Gratuity to the blacks of Dn. H. González for the *conucos* they left at the Ing° Recurso . . . $227." A group of about two hundred *patrocinados* had been brought from another plantation to work during the month of July, and apparently were being compensated for the loss of crops on their provision grounds during that month.[13]

One problem with attempting to raise funds through the sale of provision ground products was the limited market. The plantation itself was the most likely purchaser, and the power relations on the plantation meant that the price could ordinarily be dictated by the buyer. The extensive tradition of independent slave marketing found in Haiti and Jamaica seems not to have characterized the sugar areas

[12] Exposición, May 30, 1883, AHN, Ultramar, leg. 4814.
[13] Libro Diario al parecer de un ingenio, ANC, ML, 10806.

of Cuba. Slaves and *patrocinados* could sell to transient buyers, although given masters' efforts to keep rural plantation workers out of contact with outsiders this may have been difficult in isolated areas. In some regions, however, it was apparently common. One observer, writing in 1885, described such sales:

During the hours which the slaves are allowed to themselves, they are oftenest seen working on their own allotted piece of ground, where they raise favorite fruits and vegetables, besides corn for fattening the pig penned up near by, and for which the drover who regularly visits the plantations will pay them in good hard money.[14]

Owners of stores on the plantations also carried out transactions with the *patrocinados*.

Even without full access to outside markets, the quantities of money that could come into the hands of *patrocinados* were substantial. In the account book of the *ingenio* Nueva Teresa, for example, it is striking how much of both the income and the expenses involved the blacks of the plantation. The estate frequently paid its *patrocinados* for pork, corn, and *viandas* as well as stipends; they in turn deposited funds for their freedom and that of their family members.[15]

As in earlier years, the key to self-purchase was often a pig. Since *patrocinados* were allowed to raise pigs on the plantation, and could feed those pigs with their own crops, with part of their ration of corn, or on plantation refuse and forage, the animal was in effect a form of savings and investment. Combined with money saved from stipends, the liquidation of this investment could yield the necessary sum for self-purchase. As time went on and the price of a pig became a larger and larger fraction of the "indemnity" owed the master, freedom became more accessible. One observer remarked that, when the two became equal, hardly anyone would be left in bondage. That time never arrived, nor did every man, woman, and child raise a pig, but the connection was a significant one.[16]

---

[14] On slave marketing systems elsewhere in the Caribbean, see Sidney Mintz, *Caribbean Transformations*, chaps. 5, 7. The 1885 observation on Cuba is from Maturin M. Ballou, *Due South or Cuba Past and Present* (Boston: Houghton, Mifflin, 1885; reprint ed., New York: Young People's Missionary Movement of the United States and Canada, 1910), p. 301.

[15] Libro Mayor del Ingenio Nueva Teresa, ANC, ML, 11245.

[16] Vice-consul Harris al consul general Crowe, Sagua la Grande, April 2, 1883, AHN, Ultramar, leg. 4815.

Although many self-purchases were carried out by private agreement, the role of the junta as a potential intermediary was an important innovation. Trinidad, a slave in the province of Santa Clara, worked on the Caridad estate in the district of Rancho Veloz. The plantation was a large one that produced over 142,000 pesos worth of sugar in 1877 with a work force which included 222 slaves and 62 Asians.[17] In February 1880, with the promulgation of the law of abolition, the slave Trinidad legally became a *patrocinada*. In March of the same year, before the law had been officially published in Havana, she gave 210 pesos to the estate's administrator, who agreed thereafter to pay her the wages of a free woman, withholding them until the full sum for her freedom was reached. She paid the additional 138 pesos in February 1882, when she left the estate with her "beloved Asian Eleuterio" and offered the administrator three ounces of gold for the freedom of her daughter, Rita. He refused the money and wanted to keep the child. At this point, Trinidad took the matter into her own hands, depositing seventy pesos with the junta to buy Rita's freedom and refusing to return her to the estate.[18]

The case suggests some of the goals that *patrocinados* sought. Trinidad was not avoiding labor or seeking to escape from the plantation above all else. She seems instead to have been attempting to constitute her family, perhaps to establish a separate household with her partner and child. This may have been a particularly important goal in Trinidad and Eleuterio's case, since blacks and Chinese were normally housed separately on large estates. She continued to work on the plantation until she had earned the sum necessary to purchase her child's full freedom (Rita, though legally a *liberta*, would have owed her mother's master unpaid labor until the age of majority), but when the administrator refused she would not be deterred. The option of depositing indemnification with the junta made it possible for her to comply with legal forms and achieve her purpose despite the administrator's opposition. The fragmentation of authority introduced by the law of 1880 had created mechanisms with which *patrocinados* could partially circumvent the will of their *patronos*,

[17] These figures are from the 1877 agricultural census, as reported in "Noticia de las fincas," p. 22.

[18] For the case of Trinidad, see the evidence in Don Juan Riús y Font eleva recurso de alzada, AHN, Ultramar, leg. 4831, exp. 57, and in Demanda de Dn. José Carreras, ANC, CA, leg. 95, exp. 8613.

enabling them to apply their labor and accumulated funds directly to the task of obtaining their freedom.

The case also reflects several of the ambiguities involved in dealing with masters and juntas after the proclamation of the 1880 law. The price Trinidad had agreed to pay for her freedom was considerably larger than that prescribed by law. She apparently learned enough about the new regulations to appeal to the junta and to win the freedom of her daughter for less than the administrator demanded. But it was far more difficult to renegotiate her own purchase price. The master insisted that the agreement to pay over 300 pesos was based on her value as a slave, prior to the publication of the law in Cuba, and that she had made the agreement when she was already free (i.e., after she had paid the first installment and they had granted her wages of a free person). The agreement was thus an inviolable contract, he argued. The Consejo de Administración did not agree, and ordered seventy pesos refunded to her from the junta. But to recover the overpayment already made to the estate she would have to go through ordinary courts.[19]

Individual cases are eloquent testimony to the importance of self-purchase, but it is not easy to determine how many *patrocinados* were able to take advantage of the provisions for buying their freedom. The official records are incomplete, counting only those recorded as freed through formal indemnification of services between May 1881 and May 1886, a total of about 13,000, or around 11 percent of those who received their freedom during those years (see Table 19). This is probably an underestimate. It covers only five of the six years of the *patronato* and seems to include only arrangements for self-purchase supervised by the juntas.[20]

A clearer idea of the importance of self-purchase to both *patrocinados* and *patronos* comes from plantation records. Records from the *ingenio* Nueva Teresa, in Bahía Honda, Pinar del Río, from September 1882 to July 1886 show self-purchase to have been a significant part of the life of the plantation in those years. Individual deposits reflected the variety of circumstances of "indemnification of services," from the 196 pesos in gold deposited by the *patrocinado*

[19] Demanda de Dn. José Carreras, ANC, CA, leg. 95, exp. 8613.
[20] This inference is based on the sharp discrepancy between the relative importance of self-purchase and mutual accord in government records, where the second predominates, and in estate records, where the first is very much in evidence.

TABLE 20
Purchases of Freedom Recorded on Nueva Teresa,
September 12, 1882-July 1, 1886

Dates	Number Freed		Amount Paid Pesos (gold)[a]	Average Amount Paid For Each Adult Pesos (gold)
	Adults	Children		
1882 Sept.-Dec.[b]	7	7	1,303	178[d]
1883 Jan.-April	5	0	901	180
May-Aug.	13	2	1,635	117
Sept.-Dec.	3	0	421	140
1884 Jan.-April	6	1	754	123
May-Aug.	10	0	789	79
Sept.-Dec.	0	0	0	—
1885 Jan.-April	4	0	305	76
May-Aug.	2	0	105	52
Sept.-Dec.	8	0	496[c]	62
1886 Jan.-April	0	0	0	—
May-July	11	0	654	59
Total	69	10	7,363	

SOURCE: Libro Mayor del Ingenio Nueva Teresa, fols. 431-535, ANC, ML, 11245, and Libro Diario, Nueva Teresa, fol. 229, ANC, ML, 10831.

[a] Some of the purchases were made in gold, others in bills, others in a combination of the two. I have converted the bills to gold equivalent at a ratio of two to one.

[b] Although eleven of these purchases are recorded in the Libro Mayor for September, when the lists began to be kept, some were actually made in March, June, and August.

[c] The amount paid for one of the purchases is unrecorded; I have estimated it at 60 pesos and added it to the total.

[d] Excludes a case in which payment is recorded for five adults and six children together.

Bernardino for his manumission; to the 117 pesos in gold and 134 in banknotes deposited by Clementina Argudín for the freedom of her husband Lino *criollo*; to the 50 pesos gold deposited by Mamerta *criolla* for her son Mamerto, and so on.[21] Seventy-nine purchases of freedom in four years on a plantation that had approximately 175 *patrocinados* in 1882 challenge the suggestion by one author that "The slaves, even when they had the money, appeared to be unenthusiastic about purchasing their freedom."[22] Interest in self-purchase at Nueva Teresa was strong, from the early years when it could cost 100 to 200 pesos, to the end, when it cost 50 or 60 pesos (see Table 20).

The unusual effort made by *patrocinados* to achieve their freedom

[21] Libro Mayor del Ingenio Nueva Teresa, ANC, ML, 11245.
[22] Knight, *Slave Society*, p. 177.

153

through indemnification of services suggests that the act of self-purchase had a particular importance for the man or woman who could achieve it. It had practical consequences, as in the case of Pánfilo Criollo, who in 1882 had the misfortune to have to deal with the corrupt Junta de Patronato of Rancho Veloz. He was part of the *dotación* of the plantation San Vicente, owned by Sres. Calvo and Co. Apparently his age was in doubt, and he hoped to achieve freedom as a sexagenarian. But he was also prepared to deposit 120 pesos for his freedom, in case the ruling should go against him. The junta gave him a receipt for the money in August 1882, and he began to work "por su cuenta," on his own account. Almost four months later he had still not been informed of any final decision and did not know whether he was legally free. When called to testify before the judge who was investigating the conduct of the junta, Pánfilo, who was illiterate, described his case but explained that he could not leave the receipt for his deposit with the judge as evidence, for it was the only document that established his claim to the freedom he now enjoyed. Pánfilo had managed to acquire a measure of mobility through his deposit of money, and on the possession of that receipt hinged his new identity. Without it, he could be picked up as a runaway and placed in a *depósito*.[23]

Self-purchase seems to have had a symbolic as well as a practical meaning for *patrocinados*. Practically, it gave mobility and the right to work on one's own account. Symbolically, it may also have yielded a sense of accomplishment and heightened worth. It is difficult otherwise to explain cases like that of Magín Congo, from the Mapos plantation in Sancti Spíritus, who in January 1884 paid 30 pesos for his freedom, just three months before reaching the age of sixty when freedom would legally have been his in any case, or the *patrocinado* Fernando of Nueva Teresa, who at age fifty-nine turned over 66 pesos for his.[24] Just before beginning a new life in which cash would be increasingly important, they were relinquishing a part of their savings to their former masters.

Sidney Mintz, analyzing the importance of the marketing of goods

[23] Don Juan Riús y Font eleva recurso de alzada, AHN, Ultramar, leg. 4831, exp. 57.

[24] Libro que contiene documentos del estado general de la finca Mapos, Núm. 29, Jan. 21-27, 1884, APSS, Valle-Iznaga, leg. 24, and Libro Mayor del Ingenio Nueva Teresa, July 8, 1884, ANC, ML, 11245.

from provision grounds, has suggested that "slaves saw liquid capital as a means to attach their paternity—and hence, their identity as persons—to something even their masters would have to respect."[25] This observation that money carries power, even in the hands of the weak, may help to explain why some *patrocinados* who would shortly be freed by law in any case struggled to put together the substantial sums of money necessary to buy their freedom.

The act involved several kinds of self-assertion. First, it was the giving of money in exchange for freedom, breaking with the system under which manumission would have been granted in return for deferential behavior. Second, self-purchase was not passive. In the same way that *convenidos*, those freed because they had fought in the insurrection, distinguished themselves from *libertos*, those freed by abolition, *patrocinados* could, through "indemnification of services," claim for themselves responsibility for their own freedom. Self-purchase was an intermediate kind of act, not as radical as fighting, but more assertive than waiting out the eight-year apprenticeship envisioned by the law. This may help explain the self-purchases of 1885 and 1886, when the date for full freedom for all was approaching, and exertions to raise money would buy fewer and fewer extra months of freedom. *Patrocinados* also had no way of knowing, of course, that final abolition would arrive prematurely—and no guarantee that it would arrive at all, for that matter—and may have preferred to rely on their own efforts.

These efforts were probably regarded with mixed feelings by masters and administrators. Self-purchase by the aged and unproductive meant additional profit from an investment that otherwise had little left to yield and thus was a net gain to the estate. Even self-purchase by able-bodied workers could have the effect of subsidizing the wage bill. On the *ingenio* Nueva Teresa this phenomenon is particularly striking. From January 1883 to August 1884 the plantation paid an average of 334 pesos a month in stipends to its *patrocinados*. During the same period, the plantation received an average of 225 pesos a month from *patrocinados* purchasing their freedom or that of members of their families. In other words, deposits from *patrocinados* covered about 67 percent of the amount paid on Nueva Teresa in

[25] Mintz, *Caribbean Transformations*, p. 155.

stipends in those years.[26] Though essential freed workers had to be replaced or paid wages, indemnities represented an aid in meeting the cash demands following upon the 1880 law and a substantial reallocation of money from slaves to masters, particularly given the small incomes of *patrocinados*. Self-purchase was a quite literal expression of the fact that slaves were paying for abolition, reinforcing the general character of gradual emancipation as "philanthropy at bargain prices."[27]

As long as the number of *patrocinados* seeking freedom on a given plantation was not high enough to deplete the work force seriously if they left, and particularly if those who sought freedom included the very old and the very young, the master stood to gain from self-purchase in the short run. Money thus deposited could smooth the transition from unpaid labor to stipends to wages. But if the movement accelerated and spread extensively among the more productive workers, the estate stood to lose a great deal.

The experience of the *ingenio* Mapos, in Sancti Spíritus, reflects the uneven pace of emancipation on a single estate. The plantation had 277 *patrocinados* in September 1881, along with 49 elderly, 21 minors, and 6 *patrocinados* listed as runaways. The plantation employed eight *braceros*, or day workers, many of whom seem to have been women former slaves. The total *dotación* was thus 361, similar to the plantation's slaveholding of 323 in 1877. The number of working *patrocinados* fell very little from September 1881 to September 1882, at which time the *patrocinados* numbered 269 and the *dotación* 351. Most of the decline came from deaths, though one *patrocinada*, Caridad Criolla, had purchased her freedom for 55 pesos through the junta in Sancti Spíritus. But on the night of February 12, 1882, during the harvest, came the first challenge. Thirty-five *patrocinados* fled the estate and presented themselves to the Junta de Patronato in Sancti Spíritus.[28]

We have only the administrator's account of the incident, which does not state the charges, only that twenty-two of the *patrocinados*

[26] Libro Mayor del Ingenio Nueva Teresa, ANC, ML, 11245, and Libro Diario del Ingenio Nueva Teresa, ibid., 10831.

[27] See Robert William Fogel and Stanley L. Engerman, "Philanthropy at Bargain Prices: Notes on the Economics of Gradual Emancipation," *The Journal of Legal Studies* 3 (June 1974): 377-401.

[28] The evidence on Mapos comes from Libro que contiene documentos del estado general de la finca Mapos, APSS, Valle-Iznaga, leg. 24.

returned to work the next day, and the other thirteen the following day. Several were then called back to the junta, and the *síndico* came to the plantation to review the work force. The results, however, did not appear until a year later in January 1883, again during the harvest, when suddenly the number of *patrocinados* dropped from 265 to 201. The plantation record notes that the difference represents the number freed by the junta, some through indemnification in cash, others because medical examination showed them to be over age sixty, even though they appeared in the records as much younger. Though the evidence is incomplete, it suggests a possible dynamic to the process: a group of *patrocinados*, after a Sunday's rest and conversation, but during the peak period of the harvest, decided to challenge their master and go to the junta. Their challenge was a limited one, however, and they returned to the plantation once they had stated their cases. The junta moved with customary slowness, delivering a result only a year later.

The success of these initiatives led to a further series of self-purchases on Mapos after the harvest of 1883. Some cases were individual and others were group, like the nine *patrocinados* who bought their freedom on one day in April 1884. Some went through the junta and others did not, and it seems likely that those who paid the plantation directly were never recorded in official government statistics as freed through self-purchase. The number of *patrocinados* at Mapos fell by 40 from the end of January 1882 to the end of January 1883, and by another 25 by the end of the record in August 1884, leaving only 135 *patrocinados*, less than half the number of three years earlier. The harvest of 1884 had to be carried out with a much reduced work force, since many had apparently left the plantation.[29]

The most daring—and most difficult—form of legal initiative by *patrocinados* was to charge their masters with a violation of the regulations of the 1880 law in hopes of winning their freedom as a result. This strategy broke with the basic social order of a slave society and often met with resistance from masters and juntas. It was attempted, nonetheless.

The regulations accompanying the 1880 law specified in detail those obligations of the master whose default would give the *patro-*

[29] Ibid.

cinado the right to freedom. Masters were required to: (1) provide food daily; (2) provide two changes of clothing per year; (3) pay the monthly stipend; (4) educate freed children; and (5) feed, clothe, and care for the children of *patrocinados*, in return for which masters could use their services without pay.[30] These provisions were similar to those of a reformist slave code, with the addition of a fixed "stipend" as part of the obligation of maintenance. But the penalty to masters of granting freedom, and the establishment of a board charged with enforcement, meant that there was one group, the *patrocinados*, highly interested in the rigorous application of the sanctions, and another, the juntas, obliged to listen to their appeals.

The charge of nonpayment of stipends could have been a frequent one, since payment was a new obligation for masters, and one which they were on occasion unwilling or unable to meet.[31] Abolitionists claimed in 1883, however, that in practice *patrocinados* rarely received their freedom on the grounds of nonpayment. They charged that masters were able to produce testimony from their friends or documents to prove that stipends had been paid, testimony the *patrocinado* often had no effective means of challenging. The junta of Santa Clara, in particular, was accused of refusing to hear challenges from *patrocinados* to masters' evidence.[32] This fits with the statistical evidence that very few *patrocinados* in that province obtained freedom by proving the master to have defaulted on his obligations (see Table 19).

The evidence on cases of nonpayment can be viewed in two ways. On the one hand, it illuminates the obstacles encountered by *patrocinados* who faced hostile juntas. Masters' falsification of documents and perjury could and did make it much harder for *patrocinados* to pursue a charge of nonpayment. On the other hand, if one is assessing the impact of the 1880 law, it is not simply the continuing injustices done to unfree labor that are important, but also the unintended opening up of new forms of conflict and challenge in labor relations. In some cases, for example, *patrocinados* seem to have manipulated the situation in an attempt to provoke a technical

[30] *Código penal*, 1886, pp. 248-49.
[31] For rulings on payment see AHN, Ultramar, leg. 4884, tomo 7, exp. 85, exp. 99, and exp. 110. For a claim of nonpayment, as part of a suit on other grounds, see La morena Encarnación Rodríguez suplica se ordene su libertad, AHN, Ultramar, leg. 4809, exp. 56.
[32] Exposición, May 30, 1883, AHN, Ultramar, leg. 4814.

violation of the rules. Antonio Brocal, an African-born field worker, who was convinced that he deserved freedom on several grounds, refused to accept stipends from his master and challenged the authenticity of receipts for past stipends. It may have been that he was illiterate, and, rather than authorize signatures to receipts he could not read, he preferred to refuse his stipends altogether while his case was pending. Or it may have been that, like some *patrocinados* on other estates, he refused the stipend in order to deny the legitimacy of his master's claim over him. His claim was rejected by the junta as being groundless. He appealed the ruling but did not complete all the required formalities, so the case was dropped.[33] Such instances nonetheless reinforce the impression that *patrocinados*, sometimes in alliance with others, attempted to develop their own tactics for dealing with masters.

In 1881 twenty-nine *patrocinados* of the *ingenio* Unión, many of them quite young, presented themselves to a local junta to claim freedom on the grounds that they had not been paid for two months. The lawyer for the plantation's owner protested that the owner of the plantation store was responsible for payment and that, if the *patrocinados* had not received the money they expected, it was because they had run up bills at the store. He claimed that they had initiated the credit arrangement, and he was indignant that they should now complain. Although acknowledging that paying stipends in goods or credit was against the law, he argued that it was within the spirit of the law.[34]

The *patrocinados* had quite a different view of the matter. They denied that the storekeeper was responsible for paying their stipends and claimed that they should have received them from the *mayordomo*. They did indeed take goods from the store on credit, they said, but paid for them "with the product of the pigs." The storekeeper confirmed that it was the responsibility of the *mayoral* or the *mayordomo* to pay stipends, and that his extension of credit to the *patrocinados* was not against the stipends. The *mayordomo* admitted that some *patrocinados* had not been paid on time, claim-

[33] Demanda del moreno Antonio Brocal, ANC, CA, leg. 69, exp. 7020. For a case of ten plantation *patrocinados* who refused stipends see Demanda de Dn. Francisco Revilla y Carrillo, ANC, CA, leg. 69, exp. 7033.

[34] Evidence on this case appears in Demanda de D. Esteban Suárez, ANC, CA, leg. 71, exp. 7066.

ing that the delays had arisen from their service on another plantation. The local junta upheld the master, but the provincial junta in Havana freed the twenty-nine *patrocinados*.[35]

The incident reflects several aspects of developing relationships within the plantation. First, the plantation store was emerging as an important source of credit, both for the master and for the *patrocinados*. While denying that he was personally responsible for paying stipends, the storekeeper noted that he did advance funds to the administrator for their payment. The *patrocinados* had individual accounts with the storekeeper, who mentioned that some were in debt to him and some were not. Second, although the case centered on the issue of stipends because that was the basis of their legal claim to freedom, the *patrocinados* in their testimony pointed out a second source of income, their pigs. Indeed, it was probably this second source of income that gave them room to maneuver in dealing with the administrator. Several, in fact, had refused cash advances when they were sent to another plantation. That they could pay their bills at the store without such an advance may have enabled them to take this position. Finally, it appears that the precision of the rules on stipends could be an obstacle to the planter's autonomy. Both before and after slavery, free workers could be forced to accept credit at the store in lieu of wages, and wages could be delayed or withheld. But for a brief period such abuses of *patrocinados* were illegal, and the penalty was the loss of legal rights over the victim. Ironically, once a *patrocinado* had gained freedom by proving such an abuse on the part of his or her master, the only way to recover pay was through the regular courts, a lengthy and expensive procedure.

Tactical maneuvering to catch masters in a violation was seen as "bad faith," in the words of one lawyer, or as the result of "bad counsel," in the words of innumerable *patronos*. What these maneuvers indicate is that *patrocinados* had their own sources of information about their rights under the law. At the beginning of 1882 *La Propaganda*, a Liberal paper published in Sancti Spíritus, announced new rules on the prompt payment of stipends, the violation of which would incur the loss of the right of *patronato*. The article

---

[35] Ibid.

noted: "Ya lo saben los patrocinados"—the *patrocinados* already know it.[36]

Usually illiterate, often living on estates distant from the nearest abolitionist center, *patrocinados* were somehow finding out about the laws affecting them. No government effort was made to get this information to *patrocinados*; on the contrary, the provisions of the law printed on their identity cards emphasized their duties far more than their rights. Free persons of color were probably a major source of information, but there were undoubtedly others, including local abolitionists and possibly some local shopkeepers. Lawyers with an interest in pursuing cases may also have been involved, though there can have been relatively little incentive for them unless they had a particular interest in abolitionism. Whatever their initial source of information, *patrocinados* developed an effective network, leading to challenges and complaints. Literacy was no prerequisite for such complaints, and the great majority of those who brought cases to the juntas could not sign their own names.

Rural slaves seem to have been more likely than urban slaves to make oral appeals en masse, presumably seeking safety in numbers. While urban *patrocinados* made more successful use of the juntas, the volume of activity in the rural juntas is striking. Over two thousand *patrocinados* in the sugar province of Matanzas obtained freedom through proving their masters to have failed to fulfill their obligations, representing 28 percent of the cases of freedom in the island through this charge. Furthermore, 51 percent of the self-purchases through the juntas took place in Matanzas and Santa Clara (see Table 21). This volume of activity stands in sharp contrast to the opportunities previously available to slaves in those areas. In 1877 they had held 36 and 21 percent, respectively, of the island's slaves, but only 13 and 5 percent of the slaves who were *coartados*, engaged in gradual self-purchase.[37]

To pursue a case on any grounds with the juntas, or even to obtain information about their legal rights, *patrocinados* needed allies. While literate urban *patrocinados* might successfully carry their cases through the steps of complaint, hearing, and appeal, illiterate

[36] *La Propaganda* (Jan. 15, 1882). For a master's charge that a complaining *patrocinada* had surely been "counseled by some malintentioned person," see Demanda de Dn. Juan Sands, ANC, CA, leg. 71, exp. 7076.
[37] For 1877 figures, see Iglesias, "El censo cubano."

TABLE 21
Patrocinados Legally Achieving Full Freedom in Each Category,
May 1881-May 1886. Percentage from Each Province

Terms of Freedom	Number Freed	Pinar del Río	Havana	Matanzas	Santa Clara	Puerto Príncipe	Santiago de Cuba	Total
Mutual Accord	35,102	9%	10%	43%	32%	0%	6%	100%
Renunciation	18,826	15%	36%	19%	19%	1%	10%	100%
Indemnification of Services	13,003	16%	16%	27%	24%	0%	17%	100%
Failure of Master to Fulfill Article 4[a]	7,423	14%	46%	28%	6%	1%	5%	100%
Other Causes	14,224	13%	21%	31%	23%	1%	11%	100%
Article 8 (1885 and 1886 only)[a]	25,309	17%	14%	41%	25%	0%	3%	100%
Total	113,887	13%	20%	34%	25%	1%	8%	100%

SOURCES: Same as Table 19. Some rows do not add to 100% because of rounding.
[a] See notes to Table 19.

field workers faced substantial barriers when they confronted the local junta. In the countryside, juntas were made up of local notables, likely to have social and family ties to at least some of the *patronos* in the district. A field worker might, on first try, simply be turned away on the grounds that his or her complaint was of no consequence.

Relatives were the *patrocinados'* most obvious potential allies. Each time a *patrocinado* was successful in gaining freedom, he or she could in turn help other family members. Husbands would appeal for the freedom of their wives, wives for that of their husbands, parents and grandparents for that of their children and grandchildren. In fact, nowhere is the persistence of family ties under slavery more apparent than in such series of initiatives. The greater mobility the first relative gained from full freedom could enable him or her to press a case with the junta more vigorously, to evade retaliation by masters, or even to go to Havana to pursue an appeal.[38]

An example is the case of Juana Domínguez, living in Matanzas, who appealed in 1883 for the freedom of her brothers Pánfilo, Pedro, Nicolás, and others, on the grounds that they were not registered in the 1867 or the 1871 censuses. She pleaded that she was too poor to name a lawyer to represent her in Havana, and in the end she won her case.[39] In such instances emancipation was experienced as a familial, rather than simply an individual, phenomenon, perhaps strengthening the bonds among family members while increasing hostility between the family and its former owners.

A *patrocinado* who had no free relatives could turn to other free blacks, people with whom he or she might have links through the *cabildos de nación* or ties of *compadrazgo* (ritual kinship). Some free persons of color, at times organized into mutual aid societies, felt a responsibility for those still in bondage. They wrote petitions in individual cases, raised money to purchase freedom, and pressured

[38] For a mother appealing for her son's freedom, see Demanda de la morena Francisca García, ANC, CA, leg. 71, exp. 7062. For a mother appealing for her daughter's freedom, see the case of the *morena libre* Paulina Sarria of Cienfuegos, described in the *Boletín Oficial de la Provincia de Santa Clara*, May 12, 1881. For the case of the *moreno libre* Joaquín Martínez pursuing the freedom of his consort the *mulata patrocinada* Clara, see Demanda de Dn. José Ma. Pérez Vizcaina, ANC, CA, leg. 69, exp. 7032. For two mothers appealing together for the freedom of their children who were still on an *ingenio*, see Demanda de la morena Engracia Hernández, ANC, CA, leg. 71, exp. 7073.

[39] Demanda de la morena Juana Domínguez, ANC, CA, leg. 82, exp. 7793.

the government for full abolition. In some cases the petitioners were urban as well as free, thus giving them greater access to the appeal process. While *cabildos* and mutual-aid societies were generally located in towns, these included provincial towns such as Santa Clara, where they might well be in contact with rural *patrocinados*.[40]

Abolitionists, white as well as black, were also potential allies. Though the government tried to limit their activities, in Havana abolitionists opened offices where they provided a kind of legal aid to *patrocinados*, a service that was apparently much used.[41] In some, though by no means all, of the petitions that reached Madrid, one suspects an abolitionist amanuensis. The abolitionist rhetoric incorporated into such appeals may or may not have helped the case, but certainly the tactic of going to the ministry was an intelligent one. The case would usually be referred back to the governor in Cuba with a stern query, and the result might be victory. Carrying cases to Madrid through individual petitions, abolitionist manifestos, and the press also contributed to the campaign for full abolition.

Within Cuba, the major contribution of abolitionists seems to have been their ability to break the monopoly on public information held by planters and the government. The impact of legal aid offices could be multiplied through the cooperation of the liberal press. In Havana, at least, direct pressure was sometimes placed on the juntas. The paper *El Demócrata*, for example, announced on the day of a junta hearing in August 1882 that it was watching a particular case carefully and proclaimed: "We call the attention of the tribunals of justice to this scandalous incident so that it will not go unpunished."[42] How much such publicity influenced the junta is impossible to determine, but the newspaper's act of holding the case up for public scrutiny may have been of assistance to the *patrocinado*. Since the paper would be read in Havana, and perhaps sent to Madrid, the junta had an incentive to rule in favor of the *patrocinado* simply to avoid future inquiries. Circulation of local liberal papers might

---

[40] See, for example, Francisco de P. Rico, moreno libre, suplica la libertad de Juan, por malos tratamientos, AHN, Ultramar, leg. 4809, exp. 57. For a complex case in which several children appear to have been supported, while still legally under the *patronato*, by their free grandmother and their godmother, see Demanda de Dn. Antonio Norma y Lamas, ANC, CA, leg. 69, exp. 7017. On mutual aid societies, see Chap. XI, below.

[41] *La Discusión* (June 19, 1882).

[42] *El Demócrata* (Aug. 2, 1882).

similarly influence local juntas, while communicating information directly to *patrocinados*.

Despite the fact that relatively few field workers were actually within direct reach of abolitionists, a fear of collaboration between abolitionists and *patrocinados* plagued some planters. They saw enemies everywhere intriguing to set their *patrocinados* against them. Wrote one group of planters in 1882: "It seems as though there were a hidden power which like the evil spirit has been in incessant persecution to predispose all minds against these proprietors."[43] Their plea was for the government to resist any further changes in the Reglamento; their fear was that the tide was turning against them. *Patronos* realized that the law was at times being used to challenge them and that any further concessions would result in its being used even more effectively. What they were expressing was not an accurate description, for there was no hidden power, but the anxiety of a class watching the decay of an institution they relied on, and experiencing the loss of unquestioned authority.

In one revealing case, the owner of a group of rural *patrocinados* in the province of Santiago de Cuba faced a challenge from one of his *patrocinadas*, who successfully charged that she had not received her stipend. The master lashed out in anger, charging that the juntas were biased and that their rulings encouraged a group of "exploiters, the majority of them of the proletarian class, to dedicate their time to and concentrate on demoralizing a class which before had not needed much, and which, with its ruin, will doubtless drag down the country that unfortunately produced them." His tirade suggests that he, at least, believed that communication between unfree and free members of the lower class accelerated the process of *patrocinado* appeals.[44]

The *patronos* who expressed these fears were also responding to a breakdown in white solidarity, to the realization that they might become isolated within society. The breakdown was not just political, as in the emergence of the abolitionists, but also economic. In the effort to find allies to assist them in their pursuit of legal freedom, *patrocinados* sometimes took the risky course of appealing to a potential employer for help, someone eager enough for labor that he

[43] Exposición de varios hacendados, March 2, 1882, AHN, Ultramar, leg. 4884, tomo 8, exp. 134.
[44] Demanda de Dn. Luís Garzón, ANC, CA, leg. 69, exp. 7016.

would support the *patrocinado*'s claim before the junta. This could be a shrewd maneuver by a *patrocinado* to take advantage of a local labor shortage to become a free worker or a shrewd maneuver by an employer to place a former slave in his debt. It carried with it the risks inherent in replacing a legal *patrono* with an informal patron and creditor. *Patronos* were fearful of this kind of undermining competition between employers and sought reaffirmation of the rules barring individuals from having any *patrocinado* not their own under their power without authorization. They obtained the order, but the problem did not go away, for as more and more *patrocinados* achieved freedom, and thus more labor entered the realm of market relations rather than involuntary legal obligations, this kind of deal became more attractive. Bitter complaints appeared, for example, from rural proprietors in Rancho Veloz, in Santa Clara province, whose corrupt local junta was apparently open to such arrangements.[45]

Some masters tried to slow the momentum of freeings, particularly the efforts of relatives to free other members of their families. A paradoxical conflict arising from the 1870 and 1880 laws assisted masters in this attempt. By the Moret Law all children born of slaves after 1868 were free, though the mothers' masters were obliged to support them. Despite the children's legal freedom, the fact that these masters were legally required to feed and clothe them created an obligation for them to work without pay. Between 1870 and 1880, as long as the parents remained slaves, this obligation tended to be fulfilled as those *libertos* old enough to work labored with their parents. But when, in the 1880s, these children had grown older and their parents had become *patrocinados* with greater opportunities to gain full freedom, conflict arose. Masters claimed that the children still owed labor, and so a freed parent was not allowed to remove "free" children from the plantation unless he or she indemnified the master.

The presumption that masters had maintained the children of *patrocinados*, and therefore deserved remuneration from parents who obtained their freedom and wished to retrieve their children, was based on the 1880 law and on the old models of slavery in which

---

[45] The text of the order is in AHN, Ultramar, leg. 4814, exp. 270. For specific complaints, see Don Juan Riús y Font eleva recurso de alzada, AHN, Ultramar, leg. 4831, exp. 57.

children were raised collectively at the masters' expense. In reality, some parents were supporting their own children even while the master had legal rights over them. The case of Gabriela Arenciba is illustrative: her quarrel with her former master arose when he deducted from her stipends the costs of maintenance of her two daughters when in fact, she claimed, she had borne these costs herself. She and the children's godparents had paid for baptism, clothing, medical care, and the bed in which the girls slept, she charged, while the master did not even provide the education required by law.[46]

Planters and administrators used the ambiguous status of children not only to obtain remuneration for their previous expenditures but also to tie both free child and freed parent to the plantation through the logic of slavery in which labor was in theory given in exchange for maintenance. But both parents and sympathetic observers were indignant at the de facto requirement that parents ransom their free children from former slave masters. Governmental authorities were divided on the question and initially proposed a sliding scale of indemnities, based on the age of the child. Under this provision the full freedom of children might cost as much as it would have had they been slaves all along. Only in October 1883 did the government finally rule that parents who had obtained their freedom could take their children with them without indemnity.[47]

The difficulty of freeing children was important, in addition to the drama and pain it involved, because of the way it influenced the experience of emancipation. Emancipation was gradual not only in the sense of involving an intermediate stage between slave and free person but also in the sense that each family was likely to experience full freedom as a slow and cumulative process. The first member of the family to achieve legal freedom might well continue working under identical conditions, for a wage, in order to free the next member. Alternatively he or she might use the measure of autonomy gained to challenge the master and fight for the freedom of children. The process, which in the case of the *patrocinada* Trinidad, for example, took three years, could influence future relations between the former slave and the plantation. For Trinidad, the laborious accumulation of money in order to comply with the legal requirements

---

[46] Gabriela Arenciba, morena, solicita el abono del salario que se le adeuda, AHN, Ultramar, leg. 4786, exp. 288.

[47] See the discussions of policy in AHN, Ultramar, leg. 4814, exp. 267 and exp. 294.

for freeing herself and her child eventually led to confrontation with the estate when the administrator refused to relinquish legal control over her daughter. Such confrontations may have increased the likelihood that a *patrocinado* would choose to leave the plantation once freed.

Despite masters' efforts, the pace of emancipation accelerated. Initiatives increased, information spread, *patrocinados* accumulated more funds, and the process of achieving freedom took on a momentum of its own. The absolute number of *patrocinados* freed increased each year through 1885, representing a larger and larger proportion of those still in bondage. The number of *patrocinados* freed each year through self-purchase grew from 1882 to 1884, declining in 1884 as the total number of *patrocinados* fell and Article 8 (gradual freeings by age) went into effect. The number freed through conviction of the master increased through 1885. Mutual accord, which reflected either self-purchase or a desire on the part of master and slave to reach some kind of agreement, peaked in 1883-1884. Renunciations of the *patronato* by the master, which tended to be concentrated in Havana, remained somewhat steadier, though there was a small peak in 1884-1885, the year of a major commercial crisis. While these trends in part reflect changing junta policies on *patrocinado* appeals, they also strongly suggest an accelerating rate of effort by *patrocinados* (see Table 22).

The statistical pattern of emancipation reflects both the successes and the failures of *patrocinado* efforts during the 1880s, as well as masters' responses. As one would expect, given the power of masters and the lack of commitment to enforcement at different levels of authority, *patrocinados* had no assurance that they would receive even a modicum of legal justice. Abolitionists' complaints and the apparent low rate of success of *patrocinado* appeals in areas like Santa Clara strengthen the impression of a stalled change. Outright pressures and corruption could block challenges entirely; simple appeal and delay could halt the granting of freedom papers for years.

At the same time, the vigor of the new initiatives taken by *patrocinados* emerges from the records of individual plantations and of junta proceedings. Efforts to collect back pay, prevent physical abuse, and achieve full freedom were not confined to privileged slaves, as they had tended to be under the Moret Law. Complainants in the 1880s included elderly African-born field laborers like Antonio

TABLE 22
Patrocinados Legally Achieving Full Freedom, by Year,
May 1881-May 1886

Terms of Freedom	1881-82	1882-83	1883-84	1884-85	1885-86	Total
Mutual Accord	3,476	6,954	9,453	7,360	7,859	35,102
Renunciation by Master	3,229	3,714	3,925	4,405	3,553	18,826
Indemnification by Patrocinado	2,001	3,341	3,452	2,459	1,750	13,003
Failure of Master to Fulfill Article 4[a]	406	1,596	1,764	2,431	1,226	7,423
Other Causes	1,137	1,813	7,923	2,514	837	14,224
Article 8 (1885 and 1886 only)[a]	—	—	—	15,119	10,190	25,309
Total	10,249	17,418	26,517	34,288	25,415	113,887

SOURCE: Same as Table 19.

[a] See notes to Table 19.

Brocal and groups of young Creoles like those on the *ingenio* Unión, as well as domestic workers and urban artisans. Though being in or near an urban area clearly made emancipation through one's own efforts easier, many rural *patrocinados* took the additional risk and made the additional effort, as revealed by the self-purchases on Nueva Teresa and Mapos, the challenges at San Rafael, and the overall statistics on freedom in the island.

Networks of family and community were mobilized in order to pursue appeals, with links to free persons of color being particularly important. Throughout the process, there was a dynamic that went beyond the limited protections intended by the law, a dynamic of family emancipation and in some cases collective action, of individuals investing their energy or their new earnings in the freedom of their spouses, their companions, and their children.

These initiatives challenge the notion that slave behavior can be fitted neatly into categories such as accommodation and resistance. It has become increasingly clear that slaves throughout the New World showed a complex range of responses to the fact of bondage.[48]

[48] See particularly Sidney W. Mintz and Richard Price, *An Anthropological Approach to the Afro-American Past: A Caribbean Perspective* (Philadelphia: Institute for the Study of Human Issues, 1976). For a recent examination of similar ambiguities in maroon societies, see Thomas Flory, "Fugitive Slaves and Free Society: The Case of Brazil," *The Journal of Negro History* 64 (Spring 1979): 116-30. On slavery in the

Examination of the *patronato* suggests that the ambiguities went even further when an intermediate status between slavery and freedom was created.

On the one hand, challenge to the master, resistance of a sort, became safer and more likely to yield results. The slave who resisted being whipped in the 1860s risked even greater punishment and stood little chance of permanently affecting his situation; the *patrocinado* who took a charge of cruelty to the juntas in the 1880s had some chance of winning freedom, and this possibility could help to counterbalance the threat of retaliation. On a day-to-day basis, *patrocinados* were still obliged to work for their former masters, but the means of compulsion had been restricted, thus making recalcitrance somewhat safer and potentially more rewarding. *Hacendados* in Sagua la Grande complained to a British consul that their former slaves "laughed in their faces" when threatened with punishment because if struck they could denounce the master to the authorities. They may well have been exaggerating, but they were expressing their own realization of the reduced risks of petty challenges and the changed bargaining positions.[49]

Access to third parties, such as free black mutual aid societies or abolitionist organizers, and access to courts of appeal, the juntas, enabled some *patrocinados* to test more safely the limits of resistance to their masters. Indeed, the very nature of resistance was altered as it came to incorporate completely legal activities in support of the radical goal of defeating the masters' authority. The thirty-five *patrocinados* who marched off the Mapos plantation one night, and then returned to await the outcome of their complaints to the junta, are a case in point.

The safety of such testing should not be exaggerated, however. Collective resistance to labor was still viewed as virtual mutiny and repressed with force. A North American visitor reported a case in Güines in 1880 where the army was called in to discipline *patrocinados* who refused to work on a customary holiday. Nine of the resisters were shot dead.[50]

U.S. South, see especially Eugene D. Genovese, *Roll, Jordan, Roll: The World the Slaves Made* (New York: Random House, 1974).

[49] Vice-consul Harris al consul general Crowe, Sagua la Grande, April 2, 1883, AHN, Ultramar, leg. 4815.

[50] Ballou, *Due South*, p. 63.

At the same time, activities of a traditionally accommodating sort took on a new edge. Working dutifully to collect one's stipend and growing crops for sale to the plantation were perfectly appropriate behavior in the eyes of masters. The rewards to laborers for such accommodation, however, were now potentially greater. Accommodation under slavery could yield privileges and favors, but it was more likely merely to stave off suffering. Under the *patronato*, accommodation that led to the saving of a few years' stipends and the sale of a pig might mean legal freedom. Those who put their money down at the juntas were acknowledging that the master had legal control, but they were challenging his right to keep it. The initiatives of *patrocinados* thus emerge as a hybrid activity, neither wholly accommodating nor wholly resistant.

In a general discussion of personal motivations for undertaking public actions, a modern economist has pointed out the value of the striving itself, as opposed to a mere calculus of costs and benefits.[51] Following this lead, one might see legal initiatives and self-purchase by *patrocinados* as having a similar quality. Such efforts were directed toward the significant, explicit goal of legal freedom, but they were also substantive and symbolic actions in themselves, even when the chances of achieving the goal were slight or unpredictable. Striving, challenging, and asserting responsibility were, in a sense, as much the essence of freedom as the uncertain legal victories. To the extent that the 1880 law inadvertantly increased this striving, it thus accelerated the achievement of freedom in both a direct and an indirect fashion.

The behavior of *patrocinados* not only refutes the implication that they were passive or "unenthusiastic" about accelerating their own emancipation through such means as self-purchase; it also calls into question the assumption that gradual emancipation guaranteed complete continuity of authority. Slaveholding proprietors had intended that it should, but maintaining that authority under changing circumstances proved more difficult than they had anticipated. Masters, too, were obliged to respond with a mixture of accommodation and resistance, though their strategies would reflect a far greater range of options and a close relationship with those who formed government policy.

[51] Albert O. Hirschman, *Shifting Involvements: Private Interest and Public Action* (Princeton: Princeton University Press, 1982), chap. 5.

VIII

Masters: Strategies
of Control

A gradual transition from slave to free labor was consistent, at least
in theory, with what many planters in Cuba saw as the future of
their economic activities and of Cuban society. But to say that planters supported some form of abolition is to say very little indeed. The
key question was: What would replace slavery? The ways in which
former slaveholders, now *patronos*, behaved during the period of
transition reflect their conceptions of how society and labor should
be ordered; also revealed are the means they were willing to use in
an effort to ensure control over those aspects of the labor system
that they saw as crucial.

In fact, it is in part because some planters were vocal and influ-
ential in the design and the enforcement of the law that it is possible
to study their attitudes. Planters expressed their opinions concerning
the provisions of the *patronato* in 1879 when the law of abolition
was being drafted, in 1880 when the Reglamento for its implementation was being written, and throughout the period 1880-1886
whenever its enforcement created conflicts.

By 1879 most masters had abandoned hope of maintaining intact
the institution called slavery, but as a group they wished to see no
interruption in the supply of labor on their own terms. Continuity
of labor had special meaning for former slaveholders: it presupposed
continuity of "order, subordination, and discipline."[1] As they saw
it, the key to the maintenance of these was what they referred to
as "fuerza moral," moral force. "Fuerza moral" had many dimen-
sions, but perhaps most fundamentally it was thought to depend on
the masters' ability to employ corporal punishment.

Immediately after the passage of the law of abolition, a group of
hacendados headed by the leader of the Conservative party in Cuba,

[1] AHN, Ultramar, leg. 4884, tomo 8, exp. 135.

172

the Count of Casa Moré, submitted a detailed petition criticizing features of the draft of the Reglamento that would govern enforcement of the law. Moré and his fellow planters were alarmed by the suggestion that the prohibition on whipping be printed on the certificate given each slave as he was freed. First, they argued, everyone knew that whipping had long been outlawed, so there was no need, and indeed it would be "highly impolitic" to inform each *patrocinado* of this fact. Second, slaves were already well aware of their rights in this sphere, and, indeed, many of them had gained freedom under the 1870 law by charging their masters with excessive cruelty. The logic of the planters' position was peculiar. If the whip was outlawed and not used, it could hardly do any harm to state that fact. If it was outlawed and still used, it was correct and necessary to remind freedmen of their rights. Indeed, the *hacendados'* complaint strengthened the case for notification, suggesting as it did what may have been common practice: masters taking a calculated risk when they used the whip, considering its efficacy worth the remote chance that an individual might gain his or her freedom by pressing charges.[2]

It is impossible to know how extensive the use of the whip was because no master would willingly record the commission of such a prohibited act. In an 1886 lawsuit in Havana it emerged that a young *patrocinada* on the *ingenio* España had died in stocks after being whipped by an employee and a slave *contramayoral*. The extremity of the case—a "weak and rachitic" child dying of an epileptic fit apparently provoked by whipping on one of Cuba's most important plantations—brought it into the courts. Doubtless, many cases of simple illegal whipping went entirely unrecorded.[3]

On the question of punishment generally, these *hacendados* wanted to have the right to free use of stocks and chains for up to thirty days at a time. They insisted on the use of these relics of slavery because they were openly afraid of the consequences of treating former slaves like free workers. Order could not be maintained, they predicted, if *patrocinados* believed from the beginning that they

[2] For planters' claims, see Observaciones que al proyecto de reglamento para el cumplimiento de la ley de abolición presentan varios hacendados, n.d., AHN, Ultramar, leg. 4883, tomo 5, exp. 69.

[3] Denunciando el hecho de haber muerto en cepo una joven patrocinada del ingenio "España," AHN, Ultramar, leg. 4831, exp. 46.

enjoyed numerous rights, that their duties did not go beyond a certain number of hours of work, and that the punishment for infractions would not be corporal.

Hacendados seem to have desired greater powers of coercion for two reasons. First, they implicitly recognized the need for extra-economic means of compulsion where the economic stimulus was slight. The stipend paid the *patrocinado* was only a fraction of the wage due a free worker. Second, and perhaps more important, there was a fear peculiar to men who had been slaveholders all their lives: the fear that there would be resentment, resistance, and perhaps even vengeance once the threat of physical coercion was removed. Another group of *hacendados* petitioning the government expressed it quite plainly: there is a necessity for "material force" when one is dealing with "abject men," they claimed. They hinted at the possible "spirit of independence" among those who had felt all of their lives "la prisión de la esclavitud," the bonds of slavery. Implicit in all this was a fear that the threat of forced labor on public works and incarceration within the plantation would have little deterrent effect on men and women subjected to forced labor and incarceration all their lives.[4]

Planters won the first round of the battle, and the use of stocks and chains was permitted by the Reglamento issued on May 8, 1880. Minor offenses could be punished with stocks for periods from one to four days, more serious offenses with stocks from one to eight days, and grave offenses with stocks and chains from one to twelve days. Masters had the right to repeat these penalties if the *patrocinado*'s behavior did not improve. The definition of the gravity of offenses reflected the concern with continuity of the supply of labor, and the faults ranged from solitary passive resistance (light) to disturbance of the order of work (more serious) to incitement of others to refuse work (grave).[5]

Within Spain, however, abolitionists denounced the keeping of "free" men and women in stocks and chains in Cuba, and the colonial office in Madrid tentatively suggested that such measures might be eliminated. In February 1882, planters met with the governor general in Havana to discuss possible changes in the regulations regarding punishment. It was clear that ex-slaveowners, having lost

---

[4] Instancia presentada, April 25, 1880, AHN, Ultramar, leg. 4883, tomo 5, exp. 65.
[5] *Código penal*, 1886, pp. 248-49.

the legal right to use the whip, were going to put up a vigorous defense of stocks and chains.[6]

Echoing the group that had initially and successfully argued for the inclusion of these punishments in the Reglamento, the planters argued that stocks and irons were absolutely essential for the maintenance of order. These, they believed, were punishments that the *patrocinados* "respected"; incarceration would be an inadequate substitute. What they meant, evidently, was that stocks and irons were something that *patrocinados* sought to avoid. They suspected that incarceration, by contrast, might even be welcomed as a way to avoid work. While this line of argument was an admission of the repugnance planters believed workers felt for labor on the plantations, it also reflected a deep, long-standing social fear. Planters alluded to the very special situation of the "solitude of the countryside" where "thousands of men of color" were governed by "a few of the white race."[7] The implication was that something rather more like terror and less like justice was needed to keep order. Masters wanted the freedom to punish with impunity when faced with recalcitrance.

The loss of the right to use the whip had already reduced this freedom. The planters who remarked to a British consul that slavery without the whip was a "farce" and complained that *patrocinados* laughed in their faces were probably not giving a description of circumstances on the plantations that was literally accurate; instead it should be seen as the way the world looked to masters whose relationship to their social inferiors had been changed.[8] Although as a practical matter they retained much of the power they were accustomed to, they had lost part of their authority and now had to face the possibility of being called to account by their former slaves.

Because the dominance of masters over *patrocinados* was closely linked in the minds of governmental authorities with racial dominance and with the maintenance of the social order, planters could successfully defend the provisions of the 1880 law that permitted them to continue acting like slave masters. Whatever the qualms of the Spanish government about violence against *patrocinados*, so-

[6] AHN, Ultramar, leg. 4884, tomo 8, exp. 135; Labra, *Mi campaña*, p. v.
[7] AHN, Ultramar, leg. 4884, tomo 8, exp. 135.
[8] Vice-consul Harris al consul general Crowe, Sagua la Grande, April 2, 1883, AHN, Ultramar, leg. 4815.

175

cial disorder was a worse threat, and masters managed to stave off modification of the rules. Only in November 1883 did abolitionist pressure in Madrid finally yield a ban on stocks and chains.[9]

The maintenance of "moral force" required more than the legal right to punish, however. It also required that masters and their administrators be the sole authorities within their plantations in dealing with matters that they considered strictly internal. The new law, however, logically required some procedures for enforcement, and a royal order of December 1881 called for visits to plantations by members of the juntas to see if *patrocinados* were receiving their stipends. Claiming that such visits would be highly disruptive during the harvest, planters immediately put pressure on the governor, and by February 1882 they had obtained a suspension of the order until further notice. However, the ministry in Madrid rejected the claims of the planters and ordered the visits reinstated. Still, this order was not obeyed by the governor general until May, and the circular informing officials of the reinstatement was not sent out until August, so planters in the end were able to harvest free from "interference."[10] Even after the reinstatement, inspection visits to the estates appear to have been infrequent.

Masters were sensitive about these visits for several reasons. First, to judge from the tone of their complaints and their own records, many planters were violating the rules regarding stipends.[11] Examination of estate account books confirms the impression that in the early years of the *patronato* stipends were not always paid on time.[12] Masters had also found other ways to use pay as a weapon. *Patronos* were authorized to deny pay to a *patrocinado* who was ill or being punished, and some carried this further. One master deducted from a *patrocinada*'s account the amount she had earned when, while she was still a slave, she had run away and he had been unable to find her. Although in this case the master was caught, and a ministerial order prohibited the practice, he had for some time been able

---

[9] *Código penal*, 1886, pp. 267-68.

[10] AHN, Ultramar, leg. 4884, tomo 8, exps. 152 and 170. Also ibid., leg. 4926, exp. 144.

[11] Exposición de varios hacendados, March 2, 1882, AHN, Ultramar, leg. 4884, tomo 8, exp. 134.

[12] See, for example, Libro Diario del Ingenio Nueva Teresa, fols. 44, 57, 100, ANC, ML, 10831.

to persuade the Junta de Patronato that such a settling of old scores was legitimate.[13]

Masters, even those who were paying stipends on time, had a more general reason to fear inspection visits to the estates. They sensed that it was dangerous to introduce a third party into relations between *patronos* and *patrocinados*. In their petitions, planters referred to the interruptions of work and the "demoralization" that might result from estate visits. Behind these complaints was a feared loss of the monopoly of authority. For an investigator to enter an estate and speak directly to the *patrocinados* undermined the social relationships upon which slavery had been based. One master's comments reveal his own lack of illusion about the *patrocinados'* satisfaction with their lot: it is practically impossible that the *patrocinados* will declare themselves resigned and content on the estates, he wrote, when they hope that after their declarations they may be given complete freedom. This master, D. Nicolás de Cárdenas, who had just lost his claim to 185 *patrocinados*, was pleading a particular case and trying to argue that the testimony against him (that the *patrocinados* had received insufficient food) was false. But the sense of loss of control that he expressed was not confined to those who had lost their entire work force.[14]

His plaint reflected the corrosive effect on slave structures of two features of the *patronato*: the possibility of taking testimony from *patrocinados*, and the fact that the ultimate sanction for the master was loss of his legal rights over his former slaves, and full freedom for them. Manumission had existed as a sanction under the old slave codes, but only for abuses so drastic that no slave would seek them out or be in much condition to enjoy freedom afterward (e.g., blinding, crippling, etc.). Now a mere violation of regulations regarding payday could in theory bring freedom, if the juntas were able to "interfere" sufficiently to find out that one had taken place.

The actual outcome of visits to the plantations depended in large measure on the attitude of the officials making the inquiry. In some cases, the *patrocinados* were simply brought out en masse and, in the presence of the master, asked if they had any complaints. One

[13] Real Orden del Ministerio de Ultramar, Dec. 2, 1881, AHN, Ultramar, leg. 4884, tomo 7, exp. 110.
[14] Dn. Nicolás de Cárdenas y Ortega al Gobernador General, Oct. 1, 1880, AHN, Ultramar, leg. 4884, tomo 7, exp. 101.

such exercise yielded testimony so deferential that one marvels that the judge taking the deposition did not question its accuracy. The *patrocinados* were reported to have said that they had nothing to complain about in matters of food, wages, or anything else. They received their pay annually rather than monthly because they wanted the master to keep it so that they would not waste it. Furthermore, they gave the master the cash from the sale of goods from the food plots that he generously allowed them to till because they had so much confidence in him. Those *patrocinados* from the plantation who had gone to the junta with complaints had been acting on "bad advice," for all was well on the plantation.[15] One suspects that in such cases the visit was a pure formality, in which master and investigators agreed to go through the motions.

In other cases, the visits were indeed disruptive, for they uncovered abuses and interfered with the autonomy of plantation authorities. On the *ingenio* San Rafael owned by D. Nicolás de Cárdenas, for example, things were going very badly in 1880. There was a shortage of food, and not only did the *patrocinados* complain, but the plantation administrator himself reported that he did not know whether he could control the plantation unless he had more food. Under these circumstances, a visit to the plantation turned up angry and detailed testimony from the *patrocinados* about the small rations and the absence of wages. They complained that they were always hungry and that no clothes had been given them in two years. Furthermore, some reported that, contrary to law, they were being whipped. Interestingly, they testified that the *mayoral*, but not the slave *contramayorales*, whipped them. One *contramayoral* said that he was ordered to whip the other slaves, but refused "por ser estos sus compañeros" (because they were his companions).[16]

In addition to challenging the right of juntas to visit plantations, masters could create risks for those *patrocinados* who complained to the juntas. Most instances of retaliation undoubtedly went unrecorded, but the antipathy of masters and plantation administrators to these challenges occasionally emerges in the record. The administrator of the *ingenio* San Rafael, for example, had beaten the *pa-*

---

[15] Expediente promovido por D. Joaquín Quiles, ANC, ME, leg. 3813, exp. Cg.

[16] Copia certificada del expediente . . . sobre mal trato dado a la dotación del ingenio Armenteritos, de D. Nicolás de Cárdenas, ANC, CA, leg. 99, exp. 8864. See also Demanda de D. Nicolás de Cárdenas, ibid., leg. 59, exp. 6143.

trocinado Crecencio when he had the temerity to invoke the protection of outside authorities.[17] Another master used a *patrocinado*'s
complaint as evidence of "insubordination" and asked that he be
sent to the municipal *depósito*.[18]

Juntas could be equally unsympathetic. In 1886 a newspaper report
charged that a *patrocinado* who claimed to have been denied his
stipend was sent by the junta in Havana to labor on the public
works.[19] Though the right to complain was in theory guaranteed by
the 1880 law, civil authorities and plantation administrators had no
desire to see complaints become frequent, and they often worked
together to maintain the basic framework of authority despite differences over procedures or particular actions.

Masters clung to authority not simply because of psychological
needs or social fears, but because they wished to maintain specific
rhythms of labor that they feared could not be sustained without
force. When it appeared that the Reglamento might restrict the hours
that *patrocinados* could be made to work, planters filed petitions
using arguments similar to those on corporal punishment. On the
one hand, the petitioners claimed to be doing everything up to the
highest standards already, and on the other, they did not want their
behavior regulated to compel them to meet those standards. Some
argued that developments in processing had diminished the hours
of work and that very few plantations engaged in night work. On
those that did have night work, they claimed, the work was done
in shifts renewed at specified hours. Rather than conclude that this
made regulation unthreatening, they argued that the need for regulation was thus obviated. Another group of *hacendados* offered up
a paean to the joys of labor in sugar, evoking the bustle of the mill
yard during the harvest, the song of the African, the steam of the
boiling *guarapo* (sugar syrup), and, interestingly, the happiness of
the slave who worked at night and thus could rest during the day
in the silence of his hut and in the "bosom of his family." This they
contrasted with the rigid and invariable limits that would be imposed by a Reglamento.[20] These were transparently self-serving ar-

[17] Ibid.
[18] Remitiendo al Gobr. Gral. para un informe recortes del periódico "La Tribuna
. . . ," AHN, Ultramar, leg. 4528 1º, exp. 176.
[19] *El Popular: Diario Radical* (Jan. 25, 1886).
[20] Observaciones, AHN, Ultramar, leg. 4883, tomo 5, exp. 69, and Instancia presentada, ibid., exp. 65.

guments, but planters won their point, and the Reglamento permitted masters to require of *patrocinados* "the necessary hours of work, according to custom" during the harvest.[21]

To understand why this was a critical demand of masters, one need not reject all of the considerations they adduced (paeans aside). The extreme hours of night work characteristic of the boom period of mid-century, which had resulted in exhaustion, inefficiency, and even death, had indeed been reduced on some plantations by the 1880s, though grinding remained an around-the-clock operation. But what masters were defending above all was their authority over the labor process. The 1880 law gave *patronos* the right to demand labor from their former slaves; masters wanted the Reglamento to interpret this as entitling them to demand however much labor they might need from each individual *patrocinado*. To codify the amount, even if the hours granted were generous to the employer, would be to restrict that freedom of action. Any formulation of limits would mean that violation would be grounds for complaint and appeal, and this was precisely what masters did not want. A free laborer might refuse to work long hours; *patronos* wanted to make sure that no *patrocinado* could do so.

As a result of the latitude allowed masters, a considerable degree of continuity initially seemed possible. For example, while in the British West Indies masters had often withdrawn traditional "indulgences" from slaves when apprenticeship was established, on at least some Cuban plantations the old rhythm of holidays and rewards was maintained. On the *ingenio* Nueva Teresa, the New Year arrived just as the 1881-1882 harvest was about to begin. On the thirtieth of December an ox was slaughtered, and the *dotación* was given the day off. The following day fresh meat, bread (a luxury), and salt were distributed, and "*criollitos*" were baptized in the *casa de vivienda* (plantation house). The first days of January were also given as holidays; on the fourth and fifth the workers began to cut and haul cane; and at 6:00 on the morning of the sixth day the grinding began.[22]

Patronos may have felt it appropriate to observe these customs in order to maintain their own sense of legitimacy or to encourage

[21] *Código penal*, 1886, p. 247.
[22] Libro Diario del Ingenio Nueva Teresa, ANC, ML, 10831. Not all masters, however, continued to observe holidays. See Ballou, *Due South*, p. 63.

productivity among the *patrocinados*. Since government regulations were not being strictly enforced in any case, masters may also have been less seized by a spirit of vengeance than their British West Indian counterparts. The usual rewards of the harvest could be maintained because the usual level and forms of exploitation were being maintained. Indeed, when one examines the rhythm of work during a sugar harvest, even as it is reflected in the terse account of a plantation daybook, it is not difficult to understand why masters clung to their right to set hours and to their forms of extra-economic compulsion. During the months of the harvest, there was work at all hours of the night, the principle of Sunday rest was abandoned, and *patrocinados* labored days on end without a free day of rest. During the *zafra* of 1880-1881 on Nueva Teresa, for instance, *patrocinados* received only one day of respite between March 17 and April 15. At the end of May, the harvest ended, and a cow was killed for the *dotación* along with a calf for the *operarios*. Stipends for the *patrocinados*, due weeks earlier, were finally paid. The withholding of stipends in this case seems clearly to have been a means for maintaining work discipline, not a problem of available cash, for the man who regularly brought the money for stipends out from Havana had arrived at the estate three weeks earlier.[23]

On the general issue of pay, masters framed their complaints in terms of the practical exigencies of running a plantation and the inappropriateness of government interference. Although paying wages in return for labor is generally conceived of as the very antithesis of slavery, Cuban *patronos* seem not to have viewed the idea of payment with much alarm, though they grumbled about the difficulties of getting cash to the plantations. A nominal wage did not seem to alter the old relations of slavery radically: it was acceptable to most masters as long as it remained nominal and as long as they controlled disbursement. Their concern was often not *whether* the *patrocinados* would receive a stipend, but who would determine *when* they received it.

Late pay was an offense for which masters could, in theory, lose their rights over a *patrocinado*. But by pleading the unreasonableness of so drastic a punishment for what they portrayed as a bookkeeping problem, masters sought to gain greater freedom of action. The Re-

---

[23] Libro Diario del Ingenio Nueva Teresa, ANC, ML, 10831. See folios 108-16 for the beginning of the *zafra*, folios 128-29 for the end.

glamento of 1880 had said that pay was due on the eighth of each month, but before the next harvest masters had obtained the concession of a fifteen-day grace period after the eighth of each month. Shortly afterward, the regulation was loosened still further with an order ruling that the fifteen days of grace were to be counted not from when the pay was due, but from the time the *patrocinados* claimed their late pay.[24] This reduced to nil the master's risk of inadvertent loss of the *patronato* because of postponement of the payment of the stipend, for now he would have fifteen days from the time his crime was discovered in which to make restitution and escape punishment. The requirement that he pay interest on the delayed stipends was a small price for the flexibility thus gained. All threat had been taken out of the requirement of punctuality, a fact that the government in Madrid belatedly recognized, and at the end of 1881 a royal order reinstated the original provisions for payment on time or loss of the *patronato*.[25]

Masters did not accede willingly to the change, and in March 1882 one group sent yet another petition to the minister, claiming that while they had no malice in the matter, it simply was logistically difficult to get the money out to the plantations each month.[26] Since many estates were in debt already, the problem of ready cash could be a real one. The British consul suggested that even such a small amount of money was difficult for former slaveowners to raise.[27]

Some masters attempted to substitute other forms of payment for the stipend—in a few cases, by trying to take formal credit for concessions that might have been granted informally during slavery. Since the 1880 law made masters' obligations overtly reciprocal—maintenance and stipend in exchange for labor—one strategy was to claim that the *patrocinados* were in fact compensated for their labor by other generous acts of the master. D. José Beltrán of Santiago de Cuba allowed one of his *patrocinadas* to keep the money she earned from washing and ironing, and allowed her mother the money she earned for selling *dulces* (sweets). When challenged for his failure to pay stipends, he claimed that these were more than adequate

[24] AHN, Ultramar, leg. 4884, tomo 7, exps. 85 and 99.
[25] AHN, Ultramar, leg. 4884, tomo 7, exp. 110.
[26] AHN, Ultramar, leg. 4884, tomo 8, exp. 134.
[27] Carden to Granville, Oct. 16, 1880, PRO, FO 84/1568.

recompense.[28] In a more complex case, a bankrupt master asked for exemption from the obligation to pay stipends, because he was allowing his *patrocinados* to devote the majority of their time to their food plots and animals, while he searched for someone to whom he could rent them out.[29] In a sense, he was saying that the traditional right to cultivate *conucos* should be seen as a payment for labor. But in letting them devote even more time to their *conucos* he was also moving toward a kind of semi-peasant adaptation, where workers would be allowed to support themselves on the employer's land in order to be available when their labor was needed. In neither of these cases were the arrangements in lieu of stipends judged legal by the authorities, once challenged. Similar patterns may nonetheless have persisted in areas where juntas were not within reach or where masters could persuade *patrocinados* that it was in their best interests for the enterprise not to go bankrupt.

Though stipends were part of the justification for the *patronato*, *patrocinados* under the age of eighteen were owed no money. This provided *patronos* with a continuing supply of unpaid labor, including the *libertos* "freed" by the Moret Law but who remained with their parents. Technically, *patronos* were supposed to be educating the *libertos* and young *patrocinados*, but cases brought before the juntas indicate that the conception of education could be limited indeed. One master interpreted this obligation to apply only to those between ages six and ten, the ages he thought appropriate for schooling. His description of the consequences that would follow upon too exigent an enforcement of the education requirement suggests the importance of unpaid child labor. If all young *patrocinados* had to be educated, he wrote, it would mean withdrawing from agricultural labor a large and select group of workers, thus interrupting the tasks of agriculture and turning the *patronato* into a burden.[30]

The value of child labor was also acknowledged by a junta in Matanzas in the case of a *liberta* appealing for freedom. The girl had deposited funds with the local junta to compensate her master for the cost of her upbringing, funds he rejected as too little. The provincial junta ruled that the master had no right to indemnification

[28] Demanda de D. José Beltrán, ANC, CA, leg. 70, exp. 7043.
[29] Demanda de D. Luís Garzón, ANC, CA, leg. 69, exp. 7016.
[30] Demanda de D. José Romay, ANC, CA, leg. 70, exp. 7051.

because the labor that this girl had provided him from age six to eleven compensated him for his expenses.[31]

To avoid challenges to the established order, masters struggled not only to maintain a monopoly of authority and control over wages and hours but also to close the plantation to outside information. One characteristic of a smoothly functioning slave society was that disputes, in theory, were handled over the heads of the slaves, without involving them in the process. The initiation of abolition and the installation of the Juntas de Patronato broke this pattern. Abolition, however gradual, recognized the illegitimacy of slavery and suggested the possibility of more rapid emancipation. The juntas, however biased, altered relations by admitting claims of right from *patrocinados* through which they might win their freedom. Maintenance of a master's autonomy, thus, could come to depend on the denial of information to *patrocinados*.

The government in Havana cooperated in this campaign to keep *patrocinados* in ignorance, following a policy identical in spirit to that of a slave society. The old laws had often barred discussion of slavery as an institution, and when slavery was replaced by the *patronato* the governor general tried to bar discussion of total abolition. His logic was simple: the knowledge that abolitionists were proposing an early end to the *patronato* would doubtless "delude the unfortunate blacks" and "produce excitement in them."[32] The governor's perception that information had to be kept from the *patrocinados* was astute, for the evidence of experience was that with information those "unfortunate blacks" would attempt to defend their own interests.

A more direct strategy for blocking the access of *patrocinados* to authorities who might compete with the master in his jurisdiction over the work force was to make the world of the plantation as nearly as possible a physically closed unit and prevent *patrocinados* from leaving it. The law required *patrocinados* to obtain written permission from their master if they wished to leave the estate, and the owners of large plantations quickly developed additional means for lessening mobility. They established or expanded plantation stores, called *tiendas mixtas* in this period, and encouraged the *patrocinados* to spend their money within the plantation. The plan-

---

[31] Demanda de D. Jacobo Pérez, ANC, CA, leg. 65, exp. 6595.
[32] Denuncia del periódico "Discusión," AHN, Ultramar, leg. 4810, exp. 101.

tation store was thus not only a tool of economic control, but also of control of information. The aim was to enclose the *patrocinados*, and if possible other workers as well, within the plantation, discouraging them from setting foot off the property to learn of their rights, of other jobs, of other wages, of other options.

This system of company stores, however, could not function entirely without notice from the outside world. As long as the rigid institution of slavery existed, no outsider had the right to intrude into the provision of rations and goods to slaves. But once the *patronato* was introduced, owners of stores in adjacent towns began to raise questions about the master's exclusive right to provision his workers. Town shopkeepers, well aware that they were being denied a potential market, complained bitterly of the masters' monopoly. In several municipalities in Santa Clara, Matanzas, and Havana, they tried to break that monopoly by challenging the tax-exempt status of the plantation stores. Local merchants knew that one benefit of a shift to wage labor ought to be a stimulus to the surrounding economy. When *patrocinados* began to receive stipends, shopkeepers had reason to expect business to improve correspondingly. But the effect of the introduction of cash would be dampened if the master transformed his *mayordomía* (dispensary) into a store, either owned by himself or rented to an entrepreneur. In either case, less money would circulate beyond the plantation. Shopkeepers charged that this was not only illegal, since the stores were neither licensed nor taxed, but also immoral, since employees were coerced into buying there.[33]

Despite the exchange of charges and countercharges, both sides were essentially agreed that the function of the stores was control; they simply disagreed on whether abolition of slavery implied that such control should be relinquished. Planters regarded the stores as elementary good business practice. The stores helped to keep the *patrocinados* and others from leaving the property of the estates and kept away itinerant vendors who might disturb the good order of the plantation. To a planter like D. Agustín Ariosa of Remedios, in the province of Santa Clara, who had two plantations with a work force totaling about 800 *patrocinados* and 400 free workers, these stores were self-evidently a continuation of slave *mayordomías*.

[33] Sobre pago de contribuciones de las tiendas de los Ingenios, AHN, Ultramar, leg. 4818, exp. 84.

Ironically, he himself argued the continuity most emphatically, in order to support his claim to tax exemption. They were open only during the hours that workers were given leisure, they were located next to the *barracones*, and they sold no bread or drinks, only the necessities of the work force. He noted ominously in his petition to the government that any disequilibrium of this order would bring "deep disturbances in the public tranquillity in which you are so interested."[34]

The president of the municipality of Nueva Paz saw the same phenomenon differently; he charged that the principal object of the *tiendas* was to make the law of abolition a dead letter by actually issuing the *patrocinados'* stipends in goods rather than money. He argued that everyone knew that workers who did not buy in the stores ran the risk of losing their jobs and that *patrocinados* similarly feared punishment. Shopkeepers added that the goods sold in such stores were actually more expensive than those sold in the towns, emphasizing that plantation owners were thus profiting from, not aiding, their *patrocinados*.[35] Whatever their position on slavery, the tone of the shopkeepers' denunciations suggests a deep hostility to *patronos*, perhaps a reflection of tensions between merchants and planters in the countryside, perhaps a simple and immediate conflict of interests. This hostility may have led such shopkeepers to aid *patrocinados* indirectly, by passing on information that broke the barriers surrounding the plantation.

It is not surprising that during this transitional period the government took a compromising attitude toward the conflict, finally ruling that planters who owned their own stores owed no tax, but that those who rented out their plantation stores would have to pay. The institution could thus survive, stalling some of the potential transformations in slavery contained in the 1880 law by limiting the mobility of *patrocinados*, as well as laying the groundwork for decades of payment in *vales* (scrip) for purchases at company stores.[36]

For masters, a central problem of the *patronato* was its ambiguity. Slavery was a system based on coercion and on a monopoly of authority, yet the law of 1880 and its subsequent interpretations diluted that coercion and fragmented that authority. Masters re-

[34] Copia del expediente relativo a la reclamación de D. Agustín Ariosa, in ibid.
[35] Copia del expediente instruido por el Ayuntamiento de Nueva Paz, in ibid.
[36] On later use of plantation stores, see Moreno, "El token," in *La historia*.

MASTERS

sponded to these contradictions in various ways. Some leading planters struggled in rear-guard actions, tirelessly lobbying for the maintenance or re-introduction of as many elements of slavery as possible. Conservative Spanish and pro-Spanish planters like the Conde de Casa Moré and Francisco Feliciano Ibáñez were conspicuous in this group, though no simple Peninsular/Creole division can account for the differences in attitudes among various groups of *hacendados*. Some owners, like Agustín Ariosa, simply tried to take full advantage of the *patronato*, locking the *patrocinados* into a closed plantation world in which as little changed as possible. Those whose estates were at some distance from Havana may have found this somewhat easier. Others, however, were willing to accelerate emancipation, and relinquish the idea of holding all former slaves in an intermediate status. This could be either a political gesture or an economic expedient, or both.

"Renunciation" of the *patronato* over individual slaves was one way to accomplish this, and was almost identical to manumission under slavery, carried out as a benevolent act reflecting the generosity of the master, while relieving him of the responsibility of maintenance. This seems to have been relatively more common among the masters and mistresses of domestic servants in towns, but it also took place on plantations. There were some 18,800 official renunciations between 1881 and 1886.[37] It was sometimes simply a face-saving device, a gesture of largesse to avoid a prosecution for holding a *patrocinado* illegally, as in the case of the master who "renounced" his rights to a *patrocinado* over the age of sixty, over whom he had no legal rights in any case.[38] But renunciation could also be a way to shift rapidly to wage labor or to divest oneself of unproductive *patrocinados*.

More important than such manumissions were the agreements of "mutual accord" under which *patrono* and *patrocinado* established the terms of freedom independent of the juntas. Over 35,000 such accords were registered between 1881 and 1886. These could involve payment by the *patrocinado* and/or agreement on the terms of future labor.[39]

[37] See Table 19.
[38] Documento referente a reclamación de su libertad del moreno Angel, ANC, GG, leg. 366, exp. 17525.
[39] See Table 19 and the discussion of mutual accord in Chap. VII.

187

Arrangements of mutual accord were a way for the master to provide a stimulus for the *patrocinado* to work steadily. In the case of Trinidad, discussed earlier, José Carreras had agreed to free his *patrocinada* from the time she made a large down payment on her purchase price, and to pay her wages until she made up the rest of the price. Such an arrangement provided a greater incentive for the *patrocinada* than the tiny stipends called for under the law, and thus was essentially a shift to wage labor, though it derived some of its effectiveness as a motivation for work from the desire of the *patrocinada* to escape a particular legal status. By placing her in debt, it also reduced her mobility and decreased the likelihood that she would choose leisure, household duties, or subsistence cultivation over wage labor.[40]

From the point of view of masters, one advantage of such arrangements may have been that the conceding of legal freedom generally removed disputes from the jurisdiction of the juntas. For all of their flaws, the juntas, because of their special mandate, had certain advantages for *patrocinados*. Their services were available without charge, and they were formally responsible for enforcing prompt payment of stipends. Once a *patrocinado* had gained full legal freedom, however, appeals had to be taken to the regular courts. Although litigation in front of the juntas was a weapon with which a *patrocinado* could obtain freedom, litigation in the courts to recover withheld wages could be a terrible burden. Court procedures were daunting and expensive. One woman reacted angrily when the *síndico* informed her that she would have to go to court to settle her account with her former master. This litigation would "embroil" her and cause her to make expenditures she could ill afford, she wrote, in addition to forcing her to leave her work, which she could not do because she was supporting herself and two children and paying their teacher.[41] Such deterrents can only have worked to the advantage of masters.

A master could also sell the rights over *patrocinados* to another employer, thus directly recouping some of his investment in slaves rather than waiting to be compensated by the use of their underpaid labor. In one somewhat devious case, the master sold his rights, then

---

[40] Demanda de Dn. José Carreras, ANC, CA, leg. 95, exp. 8613.

[41] Gariela Arenciba, morena, solicita el abono del salario que se le adeuda, AHN, Ultramar, leg. 4786, exp. 288.

illegally lured the *patrocinados* back to his plantation to work for wages. In effect, he liquidated the labor rights he had over them without losing access to their labor.[42]

An employer who needed workers could also offer to represent a *patrocinado* before a junta in return for the *patrocinado*'s promise to work for him, a strategy which seems to have become more common as the rate of emancipation increased.[43] This tendency illustrates the ambiguity of the *patronato* as an economic institution. As employers moved away from reliance on slave labor, it was logical for them to attempt to attract individual workers, but former slaves still under the *patronato* legally had to be bought or hired from their masters. Promising to represent *patrocinados* before the junta was a way to circumvent this rigidity by encouraging them to take the risk of abandoning their masters. Within a city with an increasingly large free population of color, the practice was difficult to halt, and even in the countryside successful appeals to the junta could shift *patrocinados* from one plantation to another.

These different patterns of response by masters indicate a fundamental uncertainty about the nature of labor. Was labor now fully a commodity, to be bid for or lured into employment; or was work still a legal obligation owed by one class of individuals to another? Put another way: was it the labor or the laborer that should be seen as the commodity? The *patronato* retained strict obligations between former slaves and former masters, transferable by sale. But as the maintenance of that system of obligations became more difficult, the incentive to hire and fire rather than buy and sell increased, and the shift to wage labor accelerated.

Some masters lost their *patrocinados* through unofficial mechanisms. One was flight, which became easier as the balance of slaves and free persons of color shifted increasingly toward free. The detection of runaways had become more difficult, at the same time that the movement toward free labor made it more likely that runaways would find employment. The other mechanism was abandonment, often following death of a master or the bankruptcy of an *ingenio*. The juntas, despite their official role as supervisors of the

[42] Informe del Consejo de Administración, Aug. 8, 1884, AHN, Ultramar, leg. 4926, exp. 144.

[43] For an 1883 ruling of the junta of the province of Havana that attempted to halt this, see AHN, Ultramar, leg. 4814, exp. 270.

189

TABLE 23
Patrocinados Legally Achieving Full Freedom
in Each Province, May 1881-May 1886.
Percentage in Each Category

Terms of Freedom	Pinar del Río	Havana	Matanzas	Santa Clara	Puerto Príncipe	Santiago de Cuba	Total
Mutual Accord	20%	16%	38%	40%	10%	24%	31%
Renunciation by Master	18%	30%	9%	13%	29%	21%	17%
Indemnification by *Patrocinado*	14%	9%	9%	11%	4%	25%	11%
Failure of Master to Fulfill Article 4[a]	7%	15%	5%	2%	18%	4%	7%
Other Causes	12%	13%	11%	12%	33%	18%	12%
Article 8 (1885 and 1886 only)[a]	28%	16%	27%	22%	6%	8%	22%
Total	100%	100%	100%	100%	100%	100%	100%

SOURCE: Same as Table 19. Some columns do not add to 100% because of rounding.
[a] See notes to Table 19.

transition, were thus ignorant of the fate or location of some *patrocinados*. Officially published lists of *patrocinados* who were due their freedom but could not be found by the juntas testify to this ignorance.[44]

The juntas' statistics on *patrocinados* who were freed are nonetheless a good rough guide to the pattern of emancipation. Formal procedures for acquiring freedom were supervised by the juntas, and some of the informal procedures might eventually be incorporated into junta statistics as cases of flight and abandonment came to the attention of local authorities. Junta records, therefore, permit a comparison of the patterns in the six provinces of Cuba (see Tables 19 and 23).

In the major sugar provinces of Santa Clara and Matanzas, the most frequent means of achieving freedom was "mutual accord" between *patrono* and *patrocinado*. (This procedure should be distinguished from renunciation, where the *patrono* unilaterally gave up his rights, and which occurred in only about 10 percent of the cases of freedom in the two provinces.) Freedom through formal "indemnification of services" was relatively less frequent in these

[44] Sociedad Abolicionista Española, *Exposición que al Exmo. Sr. Ministro de Ultramar dirige la Junta Directiva en 1º de Mayo de 1884* (Madrid, 1884).

190

provinces, and conviction of the master for a violation of the laws was less common still. The *absolute* number of workers who successfully challenged their masters' authority or purchased their freedom was large—over eight thousand—but small as a percentage of total freeings in the two provinces. This pattern suggests that the majority of the *patrocinados* achieving freedom in the major sugar areas did so by agreeing with their masters on the terms of freedom ("mutual accord") or waiting until the gradual freeings by age under Article 8 began in 1885, though a significant number found other ways out.

The province of Havana provides a contrast to this pattern. There, the single most important source of legal freedom was renunciation of the *patronato*, followed by mutal accord, Article 8, and conviction of the master for violating the regulations. The prominence of renunciation is noteworthy. Some masters clearly thought that it was in their interests to free themselves from both the obligations and the privileges of continued legal authority over their former slaves. Although the provincial totals do not indicate how much of the renunciation was taking place in the city itself, the contrast between Havana province, with 30 percent of freed *patrocinados* obtaining freedom through renunciation, and more rural Matanzas, with only 9 percent, is striking. Conviction of masters for violating the regulations also accounts for proportionately more emancipations in Havana than in Matanzas or Santa Clara.

The process of emancipation in Havana was apparently one of abandonment and attack—masters giving up or negotiating away their legal rights over *patrocinados, patrocinados* successfully prosecuting many of those masters who did not. Such abolitionist agitation as was possible under the circumstances undoubtedly accelerated these processes, both directly and indirectly. Those who favored abolition could free their own *patrocinados* and contribute funds toward self-purchase by other *patrocinados*. The significance of organized abolitionism should not be exaggerated, however. The movement labored under the disabilities of government obstructionism and press censorship, and some members of the Liberal party, which favored abolition in principle, continued to hold *patrocinados*.[45] But the actions of *patrocinados, patronos,* juntas, and abolitionists contributed to the undermining of the institution of

[45] For Conservative charges that Liberals held *patrocinados* while espousing abolitionism, see *El Parlamento* (Jan. 15, 1886).

191

the *patronato* in Havana, leaving in bondage in 1883 just 21 percent of the number of slaves that had existed in the province in 1862.

The province of Santiago de Cuba provides a sharp contrast in the means used by *patrocinados* to achieve freedom. There the single most important source of legal emancipation between 1881 and 1886 was indemnification of services. A quarter of those achieving freedom did so by depositing money with the junta to purchase their freedom from their masters. The other major sources of freedom were mutal accord, renunciation, and "other," almost certainly nonregistration. Many of the slaves in Santiago de Cuba had already won their freedom by 1878, so the *patronato* was important to a smaller fraction of the population. But the high number of self-purchases is significant, perhaps reflecting the particular access of slaves (and later, *patrocinados*) in the east to land on which to grow their own crops, and perhaps reflecting as well the close links between *patrocinados* and free persons of color, many of whom were smallholders themselves.

Pinar del Río followed its own pattern, with the sources of legal freedom divided between the post-1885 freeings by age, mutual accord, renunciation, indemnification of services, and "other." The significance of Article 8 in Pinar del Río—as in Matanzas and Santa Clara—reflects the fact that other forms of emancipation did not develop as rapidly there as they did in Havana and Santiago de Cuba, leaving a proportionately larger number to be freed by the manumissions beginning in 1885, and finally by general abolition in 1886. In this respect Pinar del Río, a substantial producer of sugar with a significant number of advanced mills, followed the two major sugar producers.

As it had in the 1870s, the degree of persistence of bondage in the early 1880s closely paralleled the significance of sugar production in each province. In 1883 masters in the most important sugar region, Matanzas, held 55 percent of their 1877 slave population as *patrocinados*; those in Havana held 44 percent of theirs; those in Puerto Príncipe held a tiny 11 percent. After 1883, the pattern became more uniform, as emancipation picked up speed across the island. (See Table 24, which ranks the provinces in approximate descending order of their importance as sugar producers.)

Within the world of the plantation, masters could to some extent insulate their operations from the corrosive effects of the new law,

TABLE 24
Slave and *Patrocinado* Population, 1877-1886
(1877 = 100)

Province	1877	1883	1885	1886
Matanzas	100	55	28	13
Santa Clara	100	55	31	13
Pinar del Río	100	48	28	14
Havana	100	44	25	14
Santiago de Cuba	100	39	13	6
Puerto Príncipe	100	11	7	4

SOURCES: 1877—Fe Iglesias García, "El censo cubano de 1877 y sus diferentes versiones," *Santiago* 34 (June 1979): 167-214; 1883—AHN, Ultramar, leg. 4814, exp. 289; 1885 and 1886—AHN, Ultramar, leg. 4926, exp. 144.

at least initially. As a class, they had the power to influence provincial governors and local juntas, as well as the government in Havana, thus delaying the intrusion of actual enforcement. When pressures for emancipation became unavoidable, "mutual accord" allowed for new contractual relationships and some continuity of authority. Masters could not, however, entirely control the process. In those areas where there was serious political fragmentation, or where *patrocinados* had access to funds and to outside authority, the nature of emancipation was different, with more self-purchase and more legal challenging of masters. In those same areas, such as Santiago de Cuba and Havana, masters then drew back from the *patronato* and renunciation became a significant source of freedom.

There was a dynamic to the process of emancipation that transcended the will of the individual participants, a dynamic whereby loss of authority led to further loss of authority, *patrocinado* initiatives created their own momentum, the approaching end of the *patronato* made self-purchase cheaper, and the decreasing importance of slavery made government enforcement of *patrocinado* rights less difficult. The changing population of slaves and *patrocinados* reflected this trend: according to official statistics, which can be viewed as first approximations, the number of slaves on the island was almost halved in the fifteen years between 1862 and 1877, halved again to leave 100,000 *patrocinados* in 1883, halved once more in the next two years, and then halved one last time in what was to be the final year of the *patronato*, leaving just 25,000 *patrocinados* to be freed in 1886 (see Table 25).

TABLE 25
Slave and *Patrocinado* Population, 1877-1886

Province	1877	1883	1885	1886
Pinar del Río	29,129	13,885	8,110	3,937
Havana	41,716	18,427	10,419	5,693
Matanzas	70,849	38,620	19,997	9,264
Santa Clara	42,049	23,260	12,987	5,648
Puerto Príncipe	2,290	246	153	101
Santiago de Cuba	13,061	5,128	1,715	738
Total	199,094	99,566	53,381	25,381

SOURCES: Same as Table 24.

The year 1880 can be seen as a kind of pivot point in the process of emancipation and the decay of slavery. This is not because "abolition" in 1880 in and of itself changed the lives of those whose legal status it altered from slave to *patrocinado*, but rather because it set in motion forces that would help to break slavery down. Nor was the process slow and smooth as the planners had hoped, but instead rapid and uneven. Some of these forces were mechanical: the enforcement of the registration laws would, sooner or later, give legal freedom to thousands of *patrocinados*, as it did for 11,000 in 1883. Article 8, with its gradual freeings by age, would decrease the number of *patrocinados* by a substantial fraction each year beginning in 1885. But the more important forces set in motion were social. From the point of view of masters, the law of 1880 contained innovations that could corrode the accustomed relations between master and slave. The law eventually limited punishment, thus removing a stimulus for forced labor, just as wage labor was becoming more important and creating an invidious contrast between the *patrocinado* and his wage-earning co-worker. The law provided local boards of appeal for *patrocinados*, to which they could take their complaints and their funds. However biased the juntas might be, they were a disruptive third party. These legal provisions could be fought and evaded; *patrocinados* could be threatened and cowed; but the terms of the relationship had been altered.

The initiatives of *patrocinados* gave meaning to this altered relationship as thousands in the early 1880s obtained freedom through one means or another. At the same time, pressure from abolitionists and autonomists repeatedly raised the question of abolition in

194

Madrid and Havana.[46] By 1884, discussion concerning the ending of the *patronato* had become widespread. A commercial depression coupled with a worldwide drop in sugar prices racked the island, and the suggestion of abolition brought forth contradictory responses.[47] The Consejo de Administración, frightened by the crisis buffeting the economy, was divided. The majority insisted that the *patronato* had to be maintained, and even regretted the "imprudent concessions" that had followed the Ten Years' War and the "notorious damage" thus done to "legitimate property." To give up the *patronato* would be to "shatter the last, scant remains of the productive forces of the country." The chief of the Sección de Fomento was more tactful, reiterating the wisdom of gradualism and arguing that to abolish the *patronato* would be to neglect the interests that legislators must defend.[48]

A minority within the Consejo de Administración, however, expressed a quite different position. They argued that, as long as this intermediate condition between freedom and slavery existed, the disadvantages of both systems would persist, without the advantages of either. Forced labor could not exist without physical coercion, which had been abolished by 1884, while free labor would work only with the stimulus that came from the fear of being fired, which *patrocinados* did not feel.[49]

By 1885, resistance to the idea of final abolition had diminished still further. In the aftermath of the financial crisis, a number of Cuban *ingenios* were going out of business. The English consul reported that there was "neither Capital, credit, nor confidence anywhere."[50] In July 1886, the Spanish Cortes authorized the government to abolish the *patronato*, after consultation with Cuban planters.[51] In August 1886, the Havana Junta of Agriculture, Industry, and Commerce called for an end to the *patronato* in order to "normalize the condition of workers and make possible the regu-

[46] See Labra, *Mi campaña*, for a chronology of abolitionist pressures.
[47] For a discussion of the positions of the various political parties in Cuba on the question of abolition of the *patronato*, see Juan Gualberto Gómez, *La cuestión de Cuba en 1884: Historia y soluciones de los partidos cubanos*, (Madrid: A. J. Alaria, 1885).
[48] See the various *informes* in AHN, Ultramar, leg. 4926, exp. 144, no. 300.
[49] Ibid.
[50] Crowe to Granville, Jan. 3, 1885, PRO, FO 84/1719.
[51] Entralgo, *La liberación étnica*, pp. 101-12.

larization of wages."[52] The members apparently had in mind the creation of a larger supply of wage laborers through emancipation and the attraction of white workers into sugar. At least one contemporary economic thinker had already predicted a fall in wages as a result of free competition between former *patrocinados* and wage workers following emancipation.[53] The Sociedad Económica de Amigos del País concurred with the junta and called for abolition.[54] Even the Planters' Association agreed to the end of the *patronato* if there were also a law on labor and immigration. The planters wanted large-scale, possibly subsidized, immigration to increase the labor supply, as well as the institution of some controls on labor.[55]

Eager to dispense with the issue once and for all and assured that the measure would no longer be disruptive, the Spanish government declared an end to the *patronato* by royal decree on October 7, 1886. By this time, the great majority of *patrocinados* had already obtained their freedom, and special control over the labor of the remaining 25,000 was not deemed worth the continued uncertainty and improvisation.

Just as the behavior of former slaves reflected their complex responses to the ambiguous status of *patrocinado*, so the behavior of masters reflected the wide range of their responses to that of *patrono*. Some fought, some stalled, some conceded ground. Though the notion of a reciprocal relationship between former slave and former master, embodied in the *patronato*, was initially appealing, as a practical matter masters tended to refuse any new obligations that seemed too threatening, too demanding, or simply too costly. At the same time, planters in particular were very reluctant to relinquish the traditional privileges of imposing corporal punishment and controlling work routines. *Patrocinados* lacked economic power or real civil rights, making it exceptionally difficult for them to enforce compliance, though on occasion their masters' negligence provided the needed grounds for a suit for freedom.

Whatever the strategy of the individual master, planters as a group

[52] Informe de la Junta Provincial de Agricultura, Industria, y Comercio de la Habana, Aug. 7, 1886, AHN, Ultramar, leg. 280, exp. 610.

[53] José Quintín Suzarte, *Estudios sobre la cuestión económica de la isla de Cuba* (Havana: Miguel de Villa, 1881), p. 66.

[54] AHN, Ultramar, leg. 280, exp. 610.

[55] Telegram from the governor general to the minister of Ultramar, Aug. 12, 1886, AHN, Ultramar, leg. 4926, exp. 144.

were obliged to adapt. They had used the *patronato* to ensure a degree of continuity, but when that was no longer practicable, they were, finally, willing to relinquish it. Once the *patronato* had been definitively suppressed in 1886, planters turned their attention to new modes of increasing the labor supply and asserting control over laborers. In this process, they drew upon mechanisms developed during the *patronato*, and they also pioneered new forms of organization.

PART THREE

Postemancipation Responses, 1880-1899

IX

Planters and the State

The abolition of slavery . . . forced many changes in
methods of business and manufacture. The old planters
were slow to adapt themselves to changing economic
conditions, but new blood and new capital were found;
new processes and new machinery were introduced to
offset the loss of slave labor; manufacturing and
agricultural departments were gradually separated, and
country people leased small pieces of land from the
estates and delivered cane to the mills or centrals.
—*Edwin F. Atkins*[1]

During the process of emancipation, Cuban planters had tried—often
successfully—to use the power of the state to reinforce their authority over their workers. At the same time, legal provisions en-
acted by that state had been used by *patrocinados* to undermine
masters' authority. This dialectic did not end with final abolition.
Planters, old and new, retained or obtained preponderant power
within Cuban society and continued to seek and receive state aid
in the task of reorganizing and disciplining labor. In their efforts to
restructure labor and social relations, however, planters had to face
divisions and competition among themselves, divisions that could
provide some room for choice on the part of former slaves. Furthermore, Spain's highest priority continued to be the maintenance
of the colonial tie, a consideration that did not always coincide with
the planters' interest in direct and immediate control of labor. With
the completion of abolition, the Spanish government lost whatever
legal interest in the welfare of former slaves it had manifested during
the *patronato*; it nonetheless continued to be highly concerned with
the avoidance of discontent and unrest among key sectors, including
the free population of color. The organization of production that

[1] *Sixty Years in Cuba: Reminiscences of Edwin F. Atkins* (Cambridge, Mass.: The
Riverside Press, 1926), p. 39.

eventually emerged thus followed the lead of those sugar planters prepared to embark on a restructuring of class relations in the countryside, but it was constrained both by the overriding political interests of the colonial state and by the responses to emancipation of former slaves and other workers.

In this final section I shall examine postemancipation interactions and adaptations from several vantage points. The present chapter addresses the changing organization of plantation production and certain broad strategies of planters and the government for dealing with the problem of ensuring an adequate supply of labor, particularly the encouragement of immigration and the implementation of restrictions on "vagrancy." The following chapter focuses on former slaves, their options and behavior after achieving legal freedom. It thus deals with specific strategies by which individual planters tried to control their labor force—such as the use of plantation stores and the manipulation of wages—in terms of their direct effect on workers. The final chapter of this section analyzes the consequences of these different interactions, describing the island as it stood at the end of the century.

The records of specific *ingenios* offer insight into the transformation of sugar production during and after the period of final abolition. The inventories, daybooks, and work records of estates reveal several important trends: (1) an increase in the seasonality of labor, (2) a multiplication and greater specificity of different forms of labor, (3) an instability in the work force from day to day and week to week, and (4) the emergence of increasing numbers of cane farmers or *colonos*.

The plantations of Mapos and San Fernando, owned by the Valle-Iznaga family and located near Sancti Spíritus in Santa Clara province, provide a useful example. In 1877, Mapos operated with 323 slaves and 88 Asians and produced about 157,500 pesos worth of sugar; San Fernando operated with 205 slaves and 35 Asians and produced 109,000 pesos worth of sugar.[2] The process of emancipation on Mapos (discussed in Chapter VII) involved a gradual decline in the *patrocinado* population up to 1883, followed by a much more rapid decline—in large part due to self-purchase and legal challenge—thereafter. The process of emancipation on San Fernando is

[2] "Noticia de las fincas," p. 21.

unrecorded, though it was probably in these respects similar, since the two groups of *patrocinados* had direct contact with each other and dealt with the same junta and the same masters.

By the 1890s, when the surviving records for San Fernando begin, the estate showed a very different organization of work from the one reflected in the 1877 agricultural census. Instead of a relatively homogeneous work force tied to the estate, there was a constantly fluctuating use of labor, recorded daily in terms of specific tasks. *Altas* and *bajas*—hiring and dismissal or departure—were frequent, sometimes affecting over half the work force in a given week. The estate showed a *dotación* ranging from 51 to 213 workers in the period between May 1891 and April 1892. These were divided into *braceros* (laborers), *operarios* (operatives) of various kinds (machinery, masonry, carpentry), a very few *operarios dependientes*, and several *empleados*. Many of the *braceros* worked in gangs, led by a specific individual and issued separate rations. A distinction between directly hired day laborers and contract laborers is confirmed by an entry in January 1892 noting that some of the sugar centrifuged was made with "jornales de la finca" (wages of the estate) and the rest (three quarters of the total) by the contractor Cecilio Acosta. There were also some *colonos* on the estate, presumably supplying cane, but mention of them is infrequent. (In 1888 the *colonos* of the *ingenios* Natividad and San Fernando were listed together, and totaled thirty-one.)[3]

Labor on San Fernando had become intensely seasonal and variable. The chart on p. 204 shows the number of workers listed in the work force at the end of each week between May 1891 and April 1892. Interestingly, the number of laborers did not divide into a uniformly low "dead season" and a consistently high period of *zafra*, though differences between these seasons are quite apparent. There were three periods of high labor use. One came in August, when workers were "cleaning" the cane (*limpiando caña*). Some of this cleaning appears to have been done on a contract basis: the *cuadrilla de Pomares* (Pomares labor gang) was hired and assigned to work on specific cane fields; their accounts were kept separate. The second

[3] Libro del Estado General del Ingenio San Fernando (hereinafter San Fernando), 1890-1892, APSS, Valle-Iznaga, leg. 24. For a list of *colonos* see Igualas de D. Francisco L. del Valle y de los colonos de Natividad y San Fernando, APSS, Ayuntamiento, leg. 3, núm. 64.

peak came in November, when the workers were cutting and loading wood. The highest period was in January through April when they were cutting and loading cane and working in the mill. Several new *cuadrillas* made their appearance for these last two tasks.[4] San Fernando had shifted from slavery to seasonal wage labor, though it was not yet relying heavily on *colonos* to supply it with cane, continuing instead to produce most of its cane under direct supervision.

A broader view of the shift in the pattern of production reflected in estate records may be gained by examining the evolution of an entire district. The jurisdiction of Santa Isabel de las Lajas, also located in the province of Santa Clara, may serve as an example. In 1862 Lajas contained seventeen *ingenios* and 1,930 slaves.[5] In 1875 it held 1,852 slaves, of whom 1,428 were living on the district's

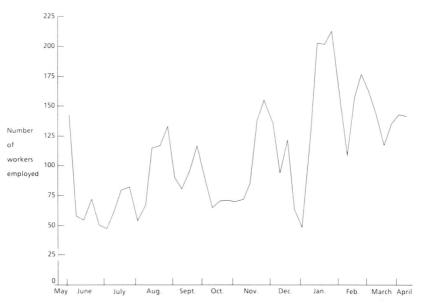

Work force on the Ingenio San Fernando, May 1891-April 1892. The figures are from the column "total" in the estate records at the end of each week. They include the categories *empleados, operarios de máquina, operarios varios, operarios de carpintería, operarios de albañil, braceros,* and *potrero.* They exclude five workers listed as *operarios dependientes* between September and April, a category that included a cook and assistants. (Source: APSS, Valle-Iznaga, leg. 24, Ingenios, Libro del Estado General del Ingenio San Fernando, 1890-92.)

[4] San Fernando, APSS, Valle-Iznaga, leg. 24.
[5] Cuba, Centro de Estadística, *Noticias estadísticas.*

fifteen sugar plantations.[6] In the early years of the *patronato* the planters of Lajas had held on to most of their former slaves, and in 1883 there were still 1,137 *patrocinados*.[7] But after 1883 the bound population fell sharply, from 1,137 to 299 in just two years.[8] This drop corresponded to a period of accelerating self-purchase and manumission in the island as a whole and to the economic crisis of 1884.

The subsequent evolution of Lajas is striking. In 1884, the district reported that it contained eleven *ingenios* "of importance."[9] By the beginning of 1888 it had only seven, about half the number thirteen years before. Of these seven, five had held over eighty slaves in 1875. One large plantation had been redistricted out of the area, and the remaining estates had been divided or converted into *colonias*, growing but not processing cane. The structure of the population had also changed. In 1862 Lajas held 5,564 inhabitants, including 3,252 whites and Asians, and 2,312 persons of color.[10] In 1883 it reported 7,548 inhabitants.[11] By 1887 there were 8,014 inhabitants: 5,186 whites, 2,554 persons of color, and 274 Asians.[12] In twenty-five years the population of color had increased somewhat (10 percent) while the white and Asian population had gone up dramatically (68 percent), strongly suggesting that immigration had taken place.

The transformation of Lajas reflects, compressed in time and space, the changes that many other sugar districts were undergoing as well. What is most remarkable about Lajas is the rapid transformation of its structures, in contrast to the prolonged legal process of emancipation. Legally, slave emancipation lasted sixteen years, but in Lajas the real shifts took place in a very few years at the end of that period. Lajas in 1875 strongly resembled Lajas in 1862, in terms of the number of plantations and their slave work force. Even in 1883, the number of *patrocinados* was still over 60 percent of the number of slaves in 1875. But by 1888 the district had ceased to be recognizable, both in the status of its workers and in the organization

[6] Padrón general de esclavos, ANC, ME, leg. 3748, exp. B.

[7] Edo y Llop, *Memoria*, p. 921.

[8] Ibid., appendix, p. 9. The figure of 299 is for 1885.

[9] Gobierno Civil de la Provincia de Santa Clara, Expediente sobre supresión de términos municipales en esta Provincia, AHN, Ultramar, leg. 4957.

[10] For names of plantations, see Edo y Llop, *Memoria*, appendix, pp. 11-12. For 1862 population, see Cuba, Centro de Estadística, *Noticias estadísticas*.

[11] Gobierno Civil . . . Santa Clara, Expediente sobre supresión, AHN, Ultramar, leg. 4957.

[12] Edo y Llop, *Memoria*, appendix, p. 14.

of production. Half of the 1875 mills were gone; cane was now grown on units that did not process it; all field workers were legally free; the population included twice as many whites as blacks.

The forces behind these changes on San Fernando and in Santa Isabel de las Lajas had as much to do with the international market for sugar as they did with the abolition of slavery in Cuba. Two developments were combining to force down prices of sugar in the last decades of the nineteenth century. First, the competition from beet sugar, long a threat, was gaining intensity. In the 1870s total world production of beet sugar had hovered around one to one and a half million tons. By the end of the eighties it was three and a half million, and by the end of the century it would be almost five and a half million. Not only did this mean an increase in the total world supply, it also meant direct competition by cane sugar producers with more highly technically developed European beet sugar producers.[13]

Of most immediate relevance to Cuba, however, was the North American market, which by 1880 absorbed over 80 percent of Cuba's sugar exports.[14] As U.S. consumption of sugar rose, the fate of the Cuban sugar industry came to be increasingly tied to markets and tariffs in the United States. Per capita U.S. consumption of sugar went from 52.55 pounds in 1886 to 66.04 pounds in 1894, while total consumption rose from 1,355,809 tons in 1886 to 2,012,714 tons in 1894.[15] During the Civil War the U.S. Congress had established a strongly prejudicial tariff that penalized sugars with a high proportion of sucrose, those that could be consumed directly. After the war, the power of North American refiners grew still further, and they finally united in the 1880s into a single trust producing a large volume for small marginal profit. Together these factors reduced the price margin between raw and refined sugar, exerted a downward pressure on the prices for raw sugar, and virtually destroyed the market for directly consumable sugar.[16] Average quo-

[13] Moreno, El ingenio 3: 37-38, and Leland H. Jenks, Our Cuban Colony: A Study in Sugar (New York: Vanguard Press, 1928), pp. 26-33.

[14] Moreno, El ingenio 3: 77.

[15] For figures on U.S. sugar consumption see Willett and Gray, Weekly Statistical Sugar Trade Journal, Jan. 3, 1896.

[16] See Jenks, Cuban Colony, pp. 28-29; Moreno, El ingenio 2: 186-209; and Alfred S. Eichner, The Emergence of Oligopoly: Sugar Refining as a Case Study (Baltimore: The Johns Hopkins University Press, 1969).

tations for fair refining sugar on the New York market fell from 5.08 cents per pound in 1880 to 3.05 cents in 1890.[17]

The impact on Cuba was twofold. First, mills that could not produce sugar cheaply could not survive, and the number of mills actually grinding dropped from over a thousand in 1877 to perhaps four hundred by 1894.[18] Second, for those who could produce sugar cheaply, the American market was vast, and in 1892 Cuban sugar production broke the one-million-ton mark.[19]

Cuban exports, however, were triply vulnerable: to U.S. tariff policy, to Spanish colonial policy, and to world prices. Though Cuba had long since ceased to be a classic colony in its trading patterns, it remained dependent on Spain for the negotiation of treaties with the United States. The Foster-Cánovas treaty of 1891 encouraged expansion of Cuban production for American refineries, but it was due to expire in 1894.

American control of the market for Cuban sugar was far more significant at the time than direct American ownership of sugar properties in Cuba. Edwin Atkins, whose family had long traded in Cuba, acquired the Soledad estate by foreclosure in 1883, and other American investors purchased land and developed a few *centrales* in the provinces of Santa Clara and Santiago de Cuba in the 1890s. Though this foreshadowed much more extensive foreign investment in the twentieth century, it had not as yet brought about substantial control over production, nor were American planters a sizable fraction of employers. Some Cuban planters—like the owners of Mapos in Sancti Spíritus—did, however, take out loans from North American firms to finance purchases of new processing equipment and thus increased the involvement of U.S. brokers and shareholders.[20]

Planters responded to this increased dependence in several ways.

[17] For year by year prices, see Willett and Gray, *Weekly Statistical Sugar Trade Journal.*

[18] Jenks, *Cuban Colony,* p. 31. There is, unfortunately, no reliable census for that date. H. E. Friedländer, in *Historia económica de Cuba* (Havana: Jesús Montero, 1944), p. 431, cites a figure of 900 mills in 1890 and 450 mills in 1894. The actual numbers may have been even smaller.

[19] Moreno, *El ingenio* 3: 38.

[20] See Jenks, *Cuban Colony,* pp. 36-37, and Atkins, *Sixty Years.* For testimony by U.S. investors, see Robert P. Porter, *Appendix to the Report on the Commercial and Industrial Conditions of the Island of Cuba* (Washington, D.C.: Government Printing Office, 1899). For investments at Mapos, see the claims made after the Spanish-Cuban-American War, found in USNA, RG 76 (Spanish Treaty Claims), Entry 352, Claim no. 121.

Some increased their personal links to the United States, even to the extent of investing in the United States and taking out U.S. citizenship in an effort to tie their fortunes to the dominant economic power of the region. Groups of planters also lobbied the Spanish government for favorable policies, emphasizing the importance of extending "reciprocity" to the United States in order to guarantee the entry of Cuban sugar into the U.S. market.[21] Finally, major planters sought to deal with low prices by increasing productivity in processing and shifting part of the responsibility of cane growing onto smaller farmers through the *colonato*.

THE COLONATO. The concept of the *colonia*—an estate that would grow cane to supply to a central mill—was not a new one. *Colonias* had long existed in Brazil, and modern *centrales* and *colonias* developed in the French West Indies after slavery. Projects for the separation of the industrial from the agricultural side of sugar production had frequently been propounded as the solution to the high capital requirements of processing.[22] Some Cuban *colonias* did begin to develop toward the end of the Ten Years' War, in the late 1870s. They remained limited in scope, however, and distinct in form. The *colonos* included both owners and renters who generally contracted directly with a central mill for processing and received a proportion of the sugar in return.[23] The extent of development of *colonias* in the 1870s is difficult to trace, for some estates continued to call themselves *ingenios* even when they no longer ground cane.[24] Problems of transportation, however, limited the spread of *colonias*, and in 1880 Francisco Ibáñez argued that the existing *ingenios centrales* did not merit the name because their scale was so small.[25]

[21] See Louis A. Pérez, Jr., *Cuba between Empires, 1878-1902* (Pittsburgh: University of Pittsburgh Press, 1983), chap. 1, and *Revista de Agricultura*, (August 5, 1894).

[22] See Ramiro Guerra y Sánchez, *Azúcar y población en las Antillas* (Havana: Editorial de Ciencias Sociales, 1976), pp. 73-79. On *colonias* in Brazil, see Stuart B. Schwartz, "Free Labor in a Slave Economy: The *Lavradores de Cana* of Colonial Bahia," in Dauril Alden, ed., *Colonial Roots of Modern Brazil* (Berkeley: University of California Press, 1973), pp. 147-97. On *centrales* in the French West Indies, see Christian Schnakenbourg, "From Sugar Estate to Central Factory: The Industrial Revolution in the Caribbean (1840-1905)," in Bill Albert and Adrian Graves, eds., *Crisis and Change in the International Sugar Economy 1860-1914* (Norwich: ISC Press, 1984), pp. 82-93.

[23] See Guerra, *Azúcar y población*.

[24] Gloria García suggests that some of the 1,190 estates listed as *ingenios* in 1877 may already have been *colonias*. Personal communication, June 1979.

[25] See Francisco Feliciano Ibáñez, *Observaciones sobre la utilidad y conveniencia*

208

The destruction resulting from the Ten Years' War added impetus to the development of the *colonias*. In the area of Sancti Spíritus, which was among the most seriously hurt by the war, the local press reported with approval in 1882 that Sr. D. Ángel Ortiz, owner of the ruined *ingenio* S. Antonio Polo, had undertaken to reconstruct it in the form of a *central*, dividing its lands up among *colonos* for them to plant cane. The newspaper saw this as an excellent precedent for the recovery of the area.[26]

In areas where war damage was less severe, the *colonia* also became important, for by using *colonos* a mill could enlarge its supply of cane without the direct planting of additional fields. This development, which spurred the expansion of mills in a period of scarce capital, is revealed by several kinds of evidence.[27] First, a few *colonos* appear in the account books of individual plantations, even while these plantations were functioning primarily with their own unfree labor force. In 1883-1884 on the *ingenio* Nueva Teresa, which still had perhaps one hundred *patrocinados*, there were about a dozen *colonos*—one Asian, one *moreno* who was evidently a former slave, two whose race was not specified but who were not given the title "Don," and the remainder listed with "Don," indicating that they were white. The whites took responsibility for one, two, or three *caballerías* each; the blacks and the Asian had just one each.[28]

Second, references to *colonias* begin to appear in the general descriptions of specific localities. Rancho Veloz, in the province of Santa Clara, for example, had sixteen *ingenios* in 1877.[29] In 1884, it still had fifteen *ingenios*, but also boasted fifty-five *colonias de caña*, whose crop was ground in different mills.[30] The district of Santa Ana in Matanzas illustrates the process even more clearly. In 1881 the district reported eleven sugar plantations, with a total cultivated area of 172 *caballerías*, producing 580,000 pesos worth of sugar. In 1884-1885 the district reported twelve sugar plantations, with a cultivated area of 240 *caballerías*, and an additional 114 "colonias en

---

del establecimiento en esta isla de grandes ingenios centrales (Havana: Imprenta y Litografía Obispo 27, 1880).

[26] *La Propaganda* (Feb. 9, 1882).

[27] Guerra, *Azúcar y población*, p. 76.

[28] ANC, ML, 10831 and ML, 10879.

[29] "Noticia de las fincas," pp. 22-23.

[30] Gobierno Civil de la Provincia de Santa Clara, Expediente sobre supresión, AHN, Ultramar, leg. 4957.

terrenos de Ingenios," with a cultivated area of 98 *caballerías*. Together they produced 530,400 pesos worth of sugar—the lower amount presumably reflecting the low sugar prices of that year. There were another 50 *colonias* located on *potrero* land. The compilers of the report commented on the development in a very short period of time of over one hundred and fifty *colonias* devoted exclusively to the growing of cane.[31]

At the same time, contemporary analysts began to recognize the growing importance of the *colonia*. In 1888 an article in the *Revista de Agricultura* argued that the division of labor was saving Cuban agriculture, and cited the example of the zone of Alfonso XII, where the *centrales* of Las Cañas and Conchita were maintaining the area's sugar production, which had threatened to decline under the impact of abolition and the economic difficulties of the period.[32] Edwin Atkins linked the development of the *colonato* to abolition, noting that, after emancipation, "country people leased small pieces of land from the estates and delivered cane to the mills or centrals."[33]

While the need to expand and modernize production by separating cane growing from cane processing seems not to have been a major factor directly causing the end of slavery, such a separation certainly accelerated after abolition. The *colonia* was an apt solution to some of the problems of the postemancipation period, precisely because it made possible the mobilization of new sources of labor and capital. *Campesinos*, especially whites, who would not have worked for wages alongside slaves were willing to undertake the cultivation and cutting of cane on their own. In 1888 one observer wrote that *colonias* were growing "in the shadow of the centrals that buy and pay well for cane," and that mills did not have to advance funds to the *colonos*, because town shopkeepers were willing to invest in the small farms.[34]

Edwin Atkins's comment that the "old planters were slow to adapt themselves to changing economic conditions, but new blood and

[31] The 1881 figures are from Provincia de Matanzas, Exma. Diputación Provincial, *Censo agrícola. Fincas azucareras. Año de 1881* (Matanzas: Aurora del Yumurí, 1883). Those for 1884-1885 are from Provincia de Matanzas, fol. 60, AHN, Ultramar, leg. 4957.

[32] See the selection from Juan B. Jiménez, *La Colonia*, printed in *Revista de Agricultura* 8 (July 15, 1888).

[33] Atkins, *Sixty Years*, p. 39.

[34] *Revista de Agricultura* 8 (May 6, 1888).

new capital were found" suggests one reason for the apparent disparity between the causes of abolition and its results. The modernization accelerated by an increasing separation of growing and processing displaced many *hacendados*, who found their estates swallowed up in the new central mills and either lost their land entirely or became growers of cane rather than producers of sugar. It is not surprising that those who foresaw that abolition might be followed by such a change in their own status would have opposed emancipation. But even those who stood to benefit from the development of central mills apparently saw little reason to relinquish any control over their workers along the way. Indeed, some of the planters who had stalled and evaded the actual steps taken toward slave emancipation—such as Ibáñez—paradoxically benefited from the growth of *centrales* that followed abolition.

Factors having little to do with abolition also spurred the development of the *colonato* in the 1880s. A drop in the prices of steel for rails, the construction of narrow-gauge railways to take cane directly from the fields to the mills, and the opening of public railroads to cane transport in 1881 increased the radius within which *colonias* could supply a given mill. This led not only to expansion but also to competition among mills. A newspaper article in Matanzas in 1881 noted that planters with modern processing apparatus were bidding for the cane of neighboring growers.[35]

Ramiro Guerra's classic account of the development of the *colonato* notes that this competition, ironically, doomed the *colono*. At first, of course, competition increased the amount the *colono* could ask for as payment from the mill. In the long run, however, expansion made the *central* more eager to control its sources of cane in order to ensure predictability of supply—something it could accomplish only by reducing the independence of the *colono* and tying him to the mill. Indeed, this process seems to have begun earlier than Guerra realized.[36] Contracts between *colonos* and mills from the 1890s show the efforts of estates to extend control over the *colono*

---

[35] Guerra, *Azúcar y población*, p. 78. On railroads, see Thomas, *Cuba*, p. 273, and Patria Cok Márquez, "La introducción de los ferrocarriles portátiles en la industria azucarera. 1870-1880," *Santiago* 41 (March 1981): 137-47. The observation on competition is from *Las Noticias* (Matanzas) quoted in *La América Latina* (November 9, 1881).

[36] Guerra's view, expressed in *Azúcar y población*, p. 75, is that the early *colonos* were relatively independent.

and guarantee that he would sell only to a single mill.[37] Such dependency, in turn, made possible abuses at all stages of the process—from the advancing of goods against a promise of cane in the future, to the weighing of the cane produced, to the settling of accounts.[38] Some *colonos* responded by joining together to insist on minimum rates for cane or to refuse payment in tokens and scrip.[39]

Colonos were, however, by no means a homogeneous group. They included former slaves who had been granted or leased small plots of land in order to keep them from leaving the estate, smallholders who turned to cane growing as the expansion of railways improved access to the mills, tenants and entrepreneurs who rented land and contracted to supply a specific mill, and former planters for whom new investments in modern processing machinery were not possible or prudent. The term *"colono,"* therefore, does not imply a specific class status or a particular relationship to the means of production. *Colonos* ranged from persons who were in effect working piece-rate on land owned by vast estates to investors who owned land and employed large numbers of workers.[40]

The transformation of some former slaves, peasants, and landowners into *colonos*, however, would not necessarily provide all of the labor needed to permit expansion in the sugar industry. Nor did the development of the *colonato*, in and of itself, ensure that wage workers would be available as needed. In analyzing the development of postemancipation societies in the Caribbean, Sidney Mintz identifies the "two jaws of Caribbean plantation discipline." One was the increase in the total labor supply; the other was the "reduction of economic alternatives available to the already existing labor supply."[41] In the Cuban case, there was an obvious means of bring-

[37] For examples of contracts, see Central Natividad, July 1, 1887-May 31, 1888, Libro de Cuenta 39, APSS, Valle-Iznaga, leg. 23. This volume shows indebtedness of *colonos* to the mill and to the store, and one case of a *colono* putting up an ox as security against an advance. For other examples of contracts, see USNA, RG 76, Entry 352, especially claims no. 121 (Mapos Sugar Co.) and 387 (Atkins).

[38] For a statement of *colono* grievances, see Juan Bautista Jiménez, *Los esclavos blancos, por un colono de Las Villas* (Havana: A. Álvarez y Comp., 1893).

[39] On *colono* strategies, see the testimony of José Badío in USNA, RG 76, Entry 352, Claim no. 97 (Central Teresa), Pt. 2. On *colonos'* refusal to accept scrip, see Moreno, "El token."

[40] A sense of the range of *colono* activities may be gained from examination of the contracts in the claims of millowners in USNA, RG 76, Entry 352.

[41] Mintz, "Slavery and the Rise of Peasantries," p. 215.

ing about the first—immigration; the second posed more serious difficulties.

IMMIGRATION. Immigration had long been propounded as the way for Cuba to develop, diversify, and prosper. Those who attempted to implement immigration schemes in the mid-nineteenth century, however, quickly discovered that as long as slavery persisted, free immigrants were unlikely to want to labor in sugar. As abolition neared, planters' hopes for free immigration increased, and they undertook various projects to encourage it.[42]

One of the most ambitious of these projects was proposed in 1879 by the Count of Casa Moré, a slaveholder and member of the Consejo de Administración, and signed by 1,500 planters, merchants, and manufacturers. They argued that the government should underwrite the immigration to Cuba of 10,000 Spaniards and Canary Islanders, and 30,000 Asians. The obvious purpose was to keep wages low and to provide substitutes for slave laborers—some of whom, Moré's backers believed, would cease working once slavery was ended.[43]

Responses to the proposal reflected the range of opinion on the subject of immigration. The Consejo de Administración, which included powerful planters, supported the proposal, though they thought it somewhat expensive for an experiment. They approved of Asian immigration because they believed white immigration would be inadequate; Spaniards had shown little inclination to choose Cuba over the republics of Argentina or Uruguay. They also argued—in a classic statement of "divide and rule"—that the society would be more secure against racial conflicts if there were three rather than two "races" on the island. Other interest groups, such as the Junta of Agriculture, Industry, and Commerce, and the Sociedad Económica de Amigos del País, opposed Asian immigration. The Sociedad Económica also challenged the idea of subsidized im-

[42] See Trelles, *Biblioteca histórica cubana* 2: 353-69, for an annotated list of immigration proposals. For a description of different party positions on immigration, see Juan Gualberto Gómez, *La cuestión de Cuba en 1884*. He associated the Constitutional Union party with free immigration, protected by the state, to fulfill the need for *braceros*; the Liberal party with exclusively white immigration, preferably by families; and the Democrats with free immigration.

[43] Expediente promovido por El Conde de Casa Moré, 1879, AHN, Ultramar, leg. 278, exp. 606.

migration, citing the principle that all that affected the private interest of individuals should be left to private initiative.[44]

The colonial office in Madrid, expressing its opinion in 1884, was puzzled by the desperate search for immigrants, and wondered why the former slaves would not be available for work after abolition. If slaves had been granted *conucos*, why could not former slaves be rented land or granted usufruct and persuaded to grow cane? Beyond that, if the planters wanted immigrants, they would have to put together the capital themselves.[45]

The firmest statement of the primacy of the free market, and its adequacy for solving the labor problem, came from Rafael Cowley, of the Sociedad Económica. The important element in attracting workers was freedom: "In the time of slavery, the degradation of work distanced whites from the cane fields; no one worked; with the *patronato* there were already 50,000; with freedom the number who will irrigate the fields of cane with the sweat of their brow is incalculable."[46]

The reactions to Moré's proposal reflected deep disagreements on several issues: (1) To what extent might the former slaves be expected to work in sugar after abolition? (2) What would happen to wages after the end of slavery? (3) How much direct coercion and discipline were necessary to ensure regular labor? (4) What kind of immigration was most socially desirable—white or nonwhite, single or family, contract or free? (5) Whose responsibility was the cost of such immigration—that of the planter, the government, or the immigrants themselves? The answers offered to these questions reflected the interests and the ideologies of the relevant parties. The Spanish government shied away from heavily subsidized immigration as expensive and divisive (smallholders would have to be taxed to support immigration for the benefit of large planters). Those concerned with white racial predominance on the island—or, alternatively, liberals fearful of a de facto reopening of the slave trade—opposed nonwhite immigration. Groups committed to development through free labor, like Cowley, did not want to see interference with the labor market. And most planters, eager to hold down wages, increase the supply of labor, and avoid dependence on their former

[44] Ibid.
[45] Ibid.
[46] AHN, Ultramar, leg. 280, exp. 610.

slaves, wanted to flood the labor market, if possible at someone else's expense.

Neither extreme triumphed. Moré could not get his huge subsidy; Cowley could not get planters to think in terms of the advantages of a fully free labor market. Instead, various intermediate tactics, some governmental, some individual, were attempted.

One such intermediate solution was the *colonia militar*, or military settlement. Francisco Ibáñez, the same Spanish planter interested in *ingenios centrales*, attempted in 1881 to establish *colonias militares* employing Spanish soldiers. This effort reflected the assumption that Spanish workers could best be persuaded to labor in cane under the discipline of a military colony.[47] Ibáñez's efforts did not succeed, but the idea was taken up again by the Spanish general Camilo Polavieja in the 1890s. His goals were more explicitly political: Spanish soldiers, settled in Cuba, would acquaint themselves with the terrain, make use of uncultivated land, diversify agriculture, and increase the ties between Cuba and Spain. These settlements would be, in a sense, counterinsurgent enclaves as well as economic enterprises.[48] The implementation of such projects, however, always ran up against competing military needs, and more urgent efforts at direct counterinsurgency. This was particularly true in the eastern end of the island, where 1880 saw another "conspiracy"—real or imagined—whose repression Polavieja took upon himself.[49] These schemes also faced the problem that land alone, without capital investment, was seldom sufficient for prosperity. Some military colonies were established, but they never became an important factor in the development of the Cuban labor force, though individual Spanish soldiers did settle in Cuba.[50]

An alternative form of immigration was colonization by entire families from Spain and the Canaries. The image of family immigration appealed to those who for racial and social reasons opposed the immigration of Asians, Africans, or unattached workers in general. One of the most successful of these efforts was the settlement of families from the Canaries on tobacco lands in the province of

[47] See *El Eco de las Villas* (Aug. 9, 1881), and Colonias militares, AHN, Ultramar, leg. 4802, exp. 272.
[48] Cuba, Colonias militares, AGI, Diversos, leg. 10, Polavieja, núm. 11.
[49] See *Conspiración de la raza de color.*
[50] See AHN, Ultramar, leg. 34, exp. 20.

Santa Clara; Canary Islanders were also among the first *colonos* on some sugar plantations.[51] Among the proponents of this kind of immigration were avowed white-supremacists, who called for the immigration of Spaniards, Canary Islanders, Italians, Greeks, Maltese, and Corsicans, so that the future of Cuba would be saved by "the predominance thus assured to the descendants of aryans."[52]

Successive Spanish administrators, more directly interested in social stability, also advocated family immigration. Governor general Salamanca, in 1889, expressed the hope that day laborers from Spain, the Canaries, and possibly Puerto Rico, might become smallholders in Cuba, where there was vacant land and the possibility of profit in sugar farming. Salamanca organized the sending to Cuba of Spanish families to establish colonies in the provinces of Puerto Príncipe and Santiago de Cuba. His project stood in opposition to the immediate interests of planters, for he saw family immigration as preferable precisely because "in the face of the abundant need for work of individuals obligated by necessity comes the abuse of proprietors who convert into slaves those unfortunate ones who come seeking a day's work." This presented, he believed, a problem for public order. He saw himself as serving the long-term interests of the colony because family settlements would provide a flexible source of labor, avoiding both the coercion by employers that came from extreme labor surplus and the high wages and irregularity of work that came from shortage, when *braceros* could earn enough in one week to live for two. His project was plagued by difficulties, however, including bad weather and a decline in private support for the colonists.[53] These schemes, which did not serve the immediate needs of planters, and which depended on grants of land and investments of capital, were not destined to become the predominant form of immigration.

In the end, the direct importation of able, single, male fieldworkers was the solution around which the greatest support could be mobilized. Those who had wanted nonwhite and coerced labor were thwarted both by political opposition to such immigration and by the closing off of sources of supply. While the British planters of

---

[51] See José A. Martínez-Fortún y Foyo, *Anales y efemérides de San Juan de los Remedios y su jurisdicción* (Havana: Pérez Sierra y Comp., 1930-31) 3: 281-82, 286.

[52] See José R. Montalvo, "El problema de la inmigración en Cuba," *Revista Cubana* 8 (December 1888): 524-38.

[53] See Envío de 250 familias a Cuba, AHN, Ultramar, leg. 173, exp. 131.

Guiana and Trinidad had adapted to the transition to free labor by importing indentured Asians, Spain could provide no such expedient from elsewhere in its diminished empire. After an investigation of abuses, the Chinese had ended contract labor for Cuba, and the British were hostile to the idea of anyone's engaging Indians for labor in the island.[54] There was insuperable domestic opposition in Cuba to free African labor, both from those who feared the creation of a new slave trade and from those who wished to ensure white supremacy in Cuba. Even the luring of workers from other Caribbean islands was for the moment blocked by their respective colonial powers.[55]

Spain and the Canaries were thus the logical source, and planters mobilized capital and initiative in the form of various Sociedades Protectoras to import workers. The government provided partial subsidies to private contractors.[56] Thousands of men, particularly from Galicia, embarked for Cuba. Though some importers brought families, the lists of passengers reveal the preponderance of male day laborers. In one such list, every passenger is male, and all are listed as "braceros."[57]

The total volume of the immigration was substantial. In 1861 there had been around 116,000 Spaniards in Cuba; in 1887 there were 140,000. Thereafter tens of thousands of Spaniards entered each year. Although many also returned to Spain, an average of about 6,900 remained each year between 1882 and 1894 (omitting 1888 for lack of data). This immigration accelerated fairly steadily throughout the period prior to the outbreak of the War of Independence. In the five years from 1889 to 1894 there was a net influx of about 58,700 Spaniards.[58]

Spanish immigration served several functions. It provided new workers, helping to counteract the supposed "labor shortage" and to hold down wages. It introduced more whites into field work, both as *colonos* and as day laborers, breaking down the old ethnic ster-

[54] Sobre la introdn de trabajadores libres de la India Oriental, MAE-Madrid, Cuba, Ultramar, leg. 2941, 1880.
[55] Letter from the consul to the minister of foreign affairs, Dec. 19, 1883, fols. 317 and 317v, MAE-Paris, CC, La Havane, Vol. 22.
[56] Sobre conducción de emigrantes a la isla de Cuba por las Sociedades de inmigración, AHN, Ultramar, leg. 175-6, exp. 155. See also Corbitt, "Immigration."
[57] Instancias presentadas en 22 de Marzo y 19 de Julio del mismo año, AHN, Ultramar, leg. 175-6, exp. 156.
[58] Trelles, *Biblioteca histórica cubana* 2: 348, 361.

eotypes about labor in sugar. As Edwin Atkins wrote approvingly: "Spanish immigration was encouraged, and constantly increasing numbers of native whites, following the example of these immigrants, worked with the negroes in the cane fields."[59] Finally, it introduced what was thought to be a politically more reliable element into the plantation population—reliable both in its adherence to Spain and in the inhibition it provided to plantation-based black conspiracies.

VAGRANCY. Mass immigration was not, however, the only way to deal with the problem of labor; direct coercion was another. Cuban planters, during the period of the *patronato*, had generally not relinquished the extra-economic control the law gave them over their former slaves. It was an open question whether they were prepared to let it go once emancipation was complete, and accept the rules of the game of a fully free labor market. The history of the debate over "vagrancy" illustrates their ambivalence.

Discussion of the issue of vagrancy, like discussion of white immigration, had a long history in Cuba. It was, however, a notably vague subject, and one about which opinion varied widely. The notion of vagrancy itself was not well defined, and the term was used to refer to the existence of unemployment or underemployment within certain sectors of the population, or to the refusal of workers to labor at the wages offered, or to their choice of subsistence over wage labor. The discussion of vagrancy was rarely characterized by clarity as to which of these phenomena was at issue, and it often involved the expression of general social fears and racial prejudices, as well as an equation of vagrancy with a predilection for criminality.

Prior to the final abolition of slavery, there had been several inhibitions to the enactment of laws specifically suppressing vagrancy. First, there seemed a danger that such laws would reduce white workers to something very like the status of slaves. While employers might not have minded that, the tactic could inhibit immigration, vitiating one of the hoped-for consequences of the move toward abolition, an increased supply of white labor. Outlawing vagrancy in an economy with a highly seasonal demand for labor was also in a sense contradictory, since some workers were bound to be un-

[59] Atkins, *Sixty Years*, p. 39.

employed in the dead season. As an astute member of the Reform Commission in 1879 observed: "to establish by law or by regulation the obligation to work under such conditions, carries with it inevitably the *right to work*, a socialist principle which this commission rejects absolutely."[60]

However, the law in the 1870s did authorize government officials to fix the residence of "vagos y gente de mal vivir" (vagrants and disreputable persons) under certain circumstances. This practice was expanded to include fixing their residence in the Isle of Pines, in a Protectorado de Trabajo where they were put to work alongside convicts. In the Protectorado, which operated in the 1870s and 1880s, the inmates apparently processed tobacco and made bricks, as well as performing field work.[61]

The issue of vagrancy took on new importance in the early 1880s. Slave emancipation was widely expected to lead to vagrancy, in the sense of a floating population that did not work, as well as to problems of labor supply. There was also a judicial reason for the new concern. Spain had recently decriminalized vagrancy, making it only an aggravating circumstance in the commission of another crime, and extended this reform to the island of Cuba. Among other things, the legality of the Protectorado de Trabajo on the Isle of Pines was now in doubt. Thus at the same time that social factors seemed to increase the risk of widespread vagrancy, metropolitan policy had reduced the basis for legal repression of it. This problem did not go unnoticed by authorities in Spain and they, in two royal orders, one of June 5, 1881, and the other of May 3, 1884, directed the governor of Cuba to draw together materials on the question. In 1889 an *informe* was finally completed and forwarded to Madrid. In it, different groups expressed their opinions on vagrancy and, in the process, revealed a good deal about their conception of the transition from slavery to free labor.[62]

Some of the commentators proposed the idea of an expanded institutionalization of vagrants. The *fiscal* (prosecutor) of the Audiencia of Puerto Príncipe suggested the construction of *casas de cor-*

---

[60] Statement by Julio I. Apezteguía, Documentos de la Comisión, 1879, AHN, Ultramar, leg. 4883, tomo 5.

[61] For information on the Protectorado, see Minuta a los Comandantes de Presidio, April 17, 1884, AHN, Ultramar, leg. 1833, exp. 451. See also Fondo de utilidades de 1877 a 1883 in ibid., exp. 466.

[62] Medios de estirpar la vagancia, AHN, Ultramar, leg. 4952, exp. 345.

rección (houses of correction) in every provincial capital. As a lawyer, he had some initial qualms about the denial of liberty without proof of commission of a crime, but he rationalized the procedure by pointing to the institutionalization of beggars and orphans as a precedent. The inmates of these *casas de corrección* would be confined for two years, during which time they would work under contract in the fields, in factories, or in individual homes, with half of their pay going for the maintenance of the *casa* and the other half to them. Those who after release were again vagrant would be confined for increasing lengths of time, up to lifetime incarceration for incorrigibles.[63]

The intendancy of Hacienda (Treasury), by contrast, was doubtful of the wisdom of such institutional solutions. Confinement of vagrants on the Isle of Pines, their report suggested, might pose a threat to security. Instead, it emphasized preventive measures: increases in public works, education, and religion. The intendancy also suggested an idea that others were to take up: an effort to "create necessities in these social groups, and even require them, obliging them among other things to wear clothes that cause less offense to public morals." The problem, the report argued, was that in warm climates people had few needs, and thus less impulse to work. If their needs could be increased, so then would their desire to work.[64]

The Consejo de Administración recognized an essential fact about vagrancy: that severe laws did not eliminate it. The councillors argued for the creation of new wants and needs among the freed slaves and against the idea of forced labor. They clearly had in mind political considerations when they wrote that not only would forced labor not work but it might create severe disturbances. The people of color of Cuba should not be alienated: "It is important to the nation to maintain them tranquil, loyal, and submissive to the laws."[65]

Rafael Cowley, writing for the Sociedad Económica de Amigos del País, took a liberal tone. He argued that the whole problem was much exaggerated and challenged the notion that abolition had led to vagrancy. He denied that there had been any substantial diminution of work performed and cited production statistics to support

[63] Informe del fiscal de la Audiencia de Puerto Príncipe, 1885, in ibid.
[64] Informe de la Intendencia General de Hacienda de la Isla de Cuba, Oct. 28, 1885, in ibid.
[65] Informe del Consejo de Administración, Sept. 13, 1888, in ibid.

his case. He went through a careful examination of the legal problems involved in the direct repression of vagrancy and concluded that "every direct measure against vagrancy is ineffective and vain or unjust and oppressive."[66]

Finally, some local officials displayed an intense racial hostility and suggested draconian solutions. Nicolás Serrano wrote an *informe* for the municipality of Havana in which he declared that the causes of vagrancy were born above all in the "bosom of the colored race" and that abrupt abolition had created an alarming crisis in Cuba. The remedies he suggested included drafting all blacks between eighteen and twenty-eight years of age into an army that would be used on public works and on plantations "under the severe regime of military rules."[67]

In the end, no comprehensive plan for the repression of vagrancy was developed. *Casas de corrección* were not installed in every province; nor was a workbook or *libreta* system for rural workers established.[68] Instead, the government used existing laws selectively through the 1870s, 1880s, and 1890s to prosecute individuals who were, among other things, perceived as vagrant. Although vagrancy had been discussed largely in terms of the problem of making former slaves work and saving agriculture from crisis, in practice authorities seem to have been concerned to attack more specific ills. Examining the investigations of cases of vagrancy prosecuted in 1881-1882, after formal abolition of slavery but while a Junta for the Repression of Vagrancy was still active, one gets a picture of who the targets for repressive action were.

First, the majority of those charged were white. Second, of the persons of color charged, most were mulatto rather than black, and thus less likely to have been field slaves. Finally, the actual operation of the prosecution was highly subjective, primarily preoccupied with the accused's "antecedents" and standing in the community.[69]

[66] Informe de la Sociedad Económica de Amigos del País, Feb. 1886, in ibid.

[67] Statement by Nicolás Serrano, May 24, 1888, in ibid.

[68] Puerto Rico had a *libreta* system that coexisted with slavery and was abolished with it. See José A. Curet, "De la esclavitud a la abolición: Transiciones económicas en las haciendas azucareras de Ponce, 1845-1873," in Andrés A. Ramos Mattei, ed., *Azúcar y esclavitud* (San Juan: Universidad de Puerto Rico, 1982), pp. 59-86, and Mintz, *Caribbean Transformations*, pp. 82-94. There were attempts in the city of Havana in the late 1880s to repress vagrancy more vigorously. See Pérez, *Cuba between Empires*, p. 25.

[69] Examples of such cases can be found in Negociado de O. P. y Policía, AHN,

The case of Máximo Gamboa is an example. He was a mulatto and testified that since the end of the insurrection he had worked to support his wife, son, and an "agregado" (who was his nephew) by growing coffee on a small *finca*, owned with his brother. But his neighbors said that he was of "mala conducta" and fond of drink, and that they knew of no goods that he owned. The fact that he had been in the insurrection was mentioned. While this case might be viewed as an effort to force smallholders into wage labor, the circumstances make that interpretation unlikely: Gamboa claimed to be in his sixties and "inútil" because of having broken his arms and legs. He would hardly be the most logical candidate for field work. He was nonetheless convicted of vagrancy, despite the newly reformed law. One suspects that, in the tense atmosphere of the eastern end of the island in 1880, his political background was a major factor.[70]

The case of Tomás Rodríguez y Bernal illustrates another typical sort of prosecution. He was white, twenty-one years old, from Havana, a *tabaquero*, without permanent home or family. By his own account, he had spent March and April 1882 cutting cane in the *ingenio* San Carlos, where he claimed to have earned forty-eight pesos gold a month. He then worked part of May and June as a cook's assistant in a restaurant, and July in another *ingenio*, earning thirty pesos a month. At the end of the summer he had come to Havana, where he had not found work. He had a police record of "malos antecedentes," assaults, and threats, and the administrators of the two plantations cited denied that he had worked there. The Junta for the Repression of Vagrancy concluded that he was lying, that he had worked only one month out of the past six, and so should be sent off to the Isle of Pines.[71]

Many of those prosecuted for vagrancy in the early 1880s were like Tomás Rodríguez—white, young, urban, single males, often with police records. Few seem to have been former field slaves who

Ultramar, leg. 3859. A minority report of the Consejo de Administración in 1884 called attention to the very low rate of prosecution of persons of color for vagrancy and banditry. Voto particular de Mendoza y Azcárate, Informe del Consejo de Administración, Aug. 8, 1884, AHN, Ultramar, leg. 4926, exp. 144.

[70] Negociado de O. P. y Policía, 1881, núm. 7511, Expediente promovido . . . contra el pardo libre Máximo Gamboa, AHN, Ultramar, leg. 3859.

[71] Año de 1882, núm. 22810, Expediente promovido . . . contra D. Tomás Rodríguez y Bernal, AHN, Ultramar, leg. 3860.

had migrated to the cities; few were laborers in the countryside who declined to work for wages.[72]

In the 1890s, when banditry had become a problem that aroused considerable concern, officials once again consigned selected "vagrants" to the Isle of Pines. Camilo Polavieja, the governor general, sent the wife of the famous bandit Manuel García there, among others. One analyst of the campaign suggests that those incarcerated by Polavieja were not vagrants at all, merely individuals living in the area frequented by García. There were also charges that people were being denounced and deported to the island simply for refusing to do business with local "caciquillos" (bosses).[73]

This range of cases suggests a mixed function for the campaign against what was referred to as vagrancy. It was related to mobilizing the work force: the driving of smallholders into wage labor or the forcing of young men to settle down were part of forming and expanding the working class. But the campaign was even more closely connected to direct forms of social control, and the charge of vagrancy was widely used to round up suspected criminals without having to convict them of any specific crime, to detain former insurgents, and to undercut the basis for banditry.

Much as the idea of a generalized repression of all vagrancy might have appealed to officials and employers when they were in a law-and-order mood, it posed numerous problems. First, any wholesale effort to regulate labor would require an immense amount of administration. As the economy was shifting toward ever more seasonal, flexible work, and thus to a necessarily mobile labor force, any pass-book scheme for field laborers would become increasingly unworkable. To keep track of workers, many of whom were hired and fired each week, would require a great deal of effort on the part of employers, and vast record-keeping schemes by local officials. It was one thing to compel a few thousand *emancipados* to contract to work in the 1860s—they were non-Spanish-speaking Africans, under direct control of the government, treated almost exactly like slaves and employed in a limited number of enterprises. It would be quite another to keep track of several hundred thousand field workers all

---

[72] See cases in AHN, Ultramar, legs. 3859 and 3860.
[73] See María Poumier, "Bandolerismo y colonialismo. Manuel García: ¿Rey de los campos de Cuba?" The charge concerning *caciquillos* is from *La Lucha* (Oct. 6, 1892), and is cited in Poumier.

over Cuba. Even the requirement that former *patrocinados* attest to their gainful employment for four years after their emancipation had been loosely interpreted and even more loosely enforced.[74] And what was one to do with them if they were indeed vagrant and unemployed? The government could hardly take responsibility for putting them all to work without entering into massive state intervention in the economy, nor could it easily keep them all at work on private plantations if they chose to leave. It was far more difficult to distinguish a runaway worker than a runaway slave.

This is not to say that the state remained aloof from the enforcement of work discipline. Sending a few hundred men to the Isle of Pines, for whatever real reason, was doubtless thought to help discipline the rest. The law banned any "combination" to alter the price of labor, and the government intervened to try to suppress strikes of urban workers and of coopers throughout the island in 1886. The coopers' strike, which involved Spaniards, white Cubans, and mulattos, was nonetheless successful in bringing about wage increases. It was followed by a strike of lightermen and weighmen, also successful. In view of these events, the U.S. consul in Matanzas expected strikes on the plantations the following year, but they do not seem to have occurred.[75]

Rural guards, both public and private, provided an extra measure of security in the countryside. D. Manuel Calvo, in a letter to the government requesting permission to employ guards on his estate, stated his purpose as "vigilance in the fields" and "better order among the employees and workers of the estate." The official order in 1881 authorizing the formation of such groups of guards mentioned only the first purpose—presumably out of discretion, not out of reluctance to aid in the pursuit of such "good order."[76] Esteban

[74] For the interpretation of the work requirement, see Ministerio de Ultramar, Subsecretaría, Sección de Política, Expediente que se pone al despacho del Exmo. Sor. Ministro, n.d., AHN, Ultramar, leg. 4815.

[75] Title XIII, Chap. VI, Art. 567 of the Penal Code prescribed the penalty of *arresto mayor* for those who "wrongfully combine to enhance or lower the price of labor or regulate its conditions wrongfully." See U.S. War Department, Division of Customs and Insular Affairs, *Translation of the Penal Code in Force in Cuba and Porto Rico* (Washington, D.C.: Government Printing Office, 1900), p. 115. For information on the 1886 strikes, see Report of Frank H. Pierce, Consul at Matanzas, March 5, 1886, in U.S. Congress, House, *Reports from the Consuls of the United States, April-December, 1886*, 49th Cong., 2nd Sess., 1886-1887, *House Misc. Docs.*, vol. 4, pp. 265-67.

[76] Creación de guardas de campos, municipales y particulares, AHN, Ultramar, leg. 154, exp. 44.

Montejo, a former slave, also recalled that workers who failed to carry their identification documents with them were on occasion subjected to physical punishment during Polavieja's tenure as governor general in the 1890s.[77]

In general, however, the state had moved away from the business of directly guaranteeing masters' powers of coercion over labor on specific estates. Under slavery, the power of the state was available, if necessary, to repress resistance to work on plantations, for any such resistance directly threatened the social order. As emancipation was taking place, the state shifted its role in labor relations toward that of an arbiter: a biased arbiter, to be sure, far more concerned with order than with justice, but no longer an unqualified supporter of every slaveholder.

This shift represented, in part, a response to the changing character of the work force. Prior to abolition, planters had dealt with a sharply segmented labor force, composed of different categories of workers, the distinctions among which were maintained through the legal system and through the direct power of the state. Employers had, in effect, faced several distinct sources of supply of labor—one that responded (roughly) to the level of wages offered free workers; one that was determined by the cost and number of available Chinese contract laborers; one that reflected the supply of slaves for rent; and one shaped by the market value of slaves. Total expenditures on labor resulted from a complex combination of these different elements. With final abolition, the labor supply was consolidated. Wage rates varied depending on the region, the task, the season, and the individual, but they were not rigidly divided by ethnic or juridical categories. Thus the labor system was no longer directly dependent on the maintenance of such distinctions. At the same time, the development of the *colono* system opened up new sources of labor and new forms of organization, forms that required a very different kind of support by the state: the enforcement of contracts rather than of discipline, the provision of subsidies to immigration rather than connivance at the illegal slave trade.

These shifts carried profound implications. First, with the reduction of employers' reliance on direct state support, the basis for Spanish colonial rule was altered. Throughout the period of the sugar

[77] Miguel Barnet, *Biografía de un cimarrón* (Havana: Instituto de Etnología y Folklore, Academia de Ciencias de Cuba, 1966), p. 89.

boom, slaveholders had perceived Spain as the ultimate guarantor of slavery on their estates. Once the need for such a guarantee was eliminated, the question could arise with greater urgency: now that the United States was by a wide margin Cuba's major market, and trade with Spain was much reduced, was there any need for Spanish rule at all? It benefited Spanish exporters, but did it serve the interests of Cuban producers and consumers? Slavery and colonialism had so long been linked that the removal of the one was bound to affect the other.

Second, once slavery had ended entirely, the task of creating labor discipline shifted further toward the employer. In this task employers were aided, paradoxically, by the fact that the last years of the *patronato* had coincided with a period of low sugar prices, lack of credit, and widespread economic difficulty. There was thus less total demand for labor than had been anticipated, and therefore somewhat less need systematically to coerce former slaves.

To understand fully the labor supply that employers faced, and the mechanisms they developed to control and shape that supply, one must look more directly at former slaves themselves. After emancipation, planters and workers stood, as masters and slaves had during slavery, in a reciprocal—though by no means symmetrical—relationship. Former slaves were constrained by the limited economic opportunities presented by planters and by the planters' direct political dominance. Planters in turn had to adapt their strategies of production and labor control to various aspects of the behavior of their workers.

X

Former Slaves

> The locks had been taken off the *barracones* and the
> workers themselves had cut windows in the walls for
> ventilation. There was no longer any effort to prevent
> people from escaping, none of that. By this time all the
> blacks were free. They called it freedom, but I am
> witness to the fact that the horrors continued.
>
> —*Esteban Montejo*[1]

Cuban plantation slaves achieved legal freedom through a variety
of mechanisms including war, self-purchase, individual manumission, litigation, and government decree. Their responses to that freedom also varied widely, ranging from a decision to leave the plantation world entirely to a persistence in dependence on the old
estates. Their different efforts to make something of their new freedom, however, did not simply fall along a continuum from passivity
to activity, or from peacefulness to violence, or from plantation to
peasantry. Rather they involved a mixture of such features, within
the limitations imposed by the economic and political system, as
well as by direct coercion.

Examination of the fate of former slaves is made difficult by a
change in the nature of surviving sources. It is an irony of nineteenth-
century social history that slave societies, while legally denying the
slave's individuality, left written traces of that individuality in lawsuits, complaints, registers, and account books; while the nominally
free societies that followed, in which employer and worker were
tied primarily by the exchange of a wage, often left sparser records
of the lives of individual workers. This is not surprising, for master
and slave were entangled in each other's lives in multiple ways and
committed to each other over long periods of time, while employer
and worker were often linked only by anonymous and ephemeral
ties. The lack of records, however explicable, poses a problem for

[1] Barnet, *Biografía*, p. 62.

the construction of a portait of postemancipation society, and one must rely disproportionately heavily on inference from statistical sources and on the inevitably subjective observations of contemporaries. (While the records of the Juntas de Patronato are in some ways comparable to those of the United States Freedmen's Bureau in their reflection of the process of emancipation, they cannot provide a similar portrait of the free labor system, for they end with full emancipation.)

With these limitations in mind, it is possible to sketch out the options that former plantation slaves faced, dividing them into rough categories. A freedman or freedwoman might: (1) remain on the plantation, move to another plantation, or join a labor gang to work in sugar by the day or by the task; (2) undertake the growing of sugar as a *colono*; (3) seek to achieve a certain distance from the plantation through a family division of labor or through part-time wage labor and part-time cultivation; or (4) migrate out of the sugar regions, either to the city, the hills, or the more open land of the east. Of course, not all of these options were available to every slave, and the degree of access to different alternatives varied both geographically and across time.

WAGE LABOR. Returning to, or remaining on, the plantation as an agricultural worker often meant continuing the same kind of labor, under the same direction, that one had experienced as a slave. It might also mean living in the same dwelling. Esteban Montejo, the idiosyncratic and individualistic former slave whose oral "autobiography" was compiled in the mid-twentieth century, looked back upon this with a certain disdain:

The blacks who worked at Purio had almost all been slaves. They were used to life in the *barracón*, so they did not even go out to eat. When lunch-time came they went into their rooms with their women to eat, and the same with dinner. They did not go out at night. They were afraid of people, and said they would get lost.[2]

For such freedmen and freedwomen, the major changes in their work lives would be the receipt of wages and some shifts in living

[2] Ibid., p. 64. The reliability of the Montejo memoir as a historical source is open to some question, given its format and its very recent compilation. It seems best to view it as reflective of individual attitudes and recollections, rather than as a source for evidence on matters requiring strict chronology or precision.

conditions. Young children could be withdrawn from field work and women might choose when to offer their labor for a wage and when to work at domestic tasks. Family life could be constituted or reconstituted, though under the stress of heavy and often insecure labor for the parents. Many of the male laborers on estates nonetheless remained at least legally unmarried, continuing the pattern of a community of single males living in barracks within the plantation. This pattern now incorporated white immigrants as well as former slaves, however, and differed in its intensity from the prison-like concentrations of male slaves that had existed during the earlier booms in the sugar industry.[3]

Rather than remain on their old estates, some former slaves joined *cuadrillas* or work gangs. Planters had become familiar with contract labor gangs through their experience with Chinese laborers and seem readily to have adopted *cuadrillas* of other workmen after slavery. Some observers criticized this trend, pointing out that employers had to pay an intermediary, the contractor, and might also find workers abandoning one gang for another that paid higher wages. Records of payments to *cuadrillas* are nonetheless frequent in the account books of the immediate postemancipation period.[4]

It is virtually impossible in retrospect to penetrate these gangs and determine their internal organization. They may have been under the strict control of the contractor, or they may have exhibited some of the internal democracy that has been attributed to comparable work squads in parts of the United States in the years immediately after emancipation.[5] The most that can be said is that they moved the former slave one step away from the estate's own overseer and tied his fate in part to the other members of the gang.

Whether hired individually or as part of a *cuadrilla*, workers received rations similar to those issued under slavery: rice, beans or

[3] On the shift in female participation in the labor force, see "Report by Consul Pierce, Cienfuegos," in U.S. Cong., House, *Labor in America, Asia, Africa, Australasia, and Polynesia*, 48th Cong., 2nd Sess., 1884-1885, House Exec. Doc. no. 54, vol. 26, pp. 255-56; and "Statement by P. M. Beal, manager of Colonia Guabairo," in Porter, *Appendix to the Report*, p. 252. On the marital status of laborers, see, for example, "Statement of L. F. Hughes, assistant manager of Ingenio Soledad," in ibid., p. 268.

[4] See "La cuestión de brazos," in *El Español: Diario Político de la Tarde*, Jan. 5, 1886. For payments to *cuadrillas* in the 1890s, see, for example, Cuadernos con relación de los contratos de tiro de caña y otros, APSS, Valle-Iznaga, leg. 7, exp. 19.

[5] For observations on work squads in the U.S., I am grateful to Gerald Jaynes, personal communication, 1984.

chickpeas, and *tasajo* (jerked beef), with occasional fresh meat when an old ox was slaughtered, supplemented by *viandas* (starchy vegetables and edible roots such as *boniato, malanga, ñame*, etc.) and cornmeal. Some estates apparently also issued bread, pork, *aguardiente* (sugar cane brandy), codfish, olive oil, and lard to their employees. One *colonia* manager asserted that he provided coffee, oil, bacon, and spices in addition to basic rations, and cabbage, tomatoes, and turnips during the winter.[6] The food a worker actually received seems to have depended in part on the category of work being performed and sometimes on race as well. The American consul in Cienfuegos wrote in 1884:

> The owner of one of the largest plantations in the island, which during the crop season employs about five hundred persons, tells me that by cooking for them, which he does by steam, he is enabled to feed the skilled laborers at 33 cents a day, the unskilled white laborers at 22 cents a day, and to feed the unskilled negro laborers at 16 cents a day. A distinction is usually though not always drawn between white and negro laborers of the same class.[7]

There was no guarantee that the food supplied would even consistently conform to the familiar description of *tasajo* and rice. In the records of the *ingenio* San Fernando toward the end of 1890, one finds that the rations, which had consisted primarily of *tasajo* and rice, suddenly contained less *tasajo*, and on November 17 the *tasajo* disappeared altogether. From then until January 11, 1891, the *raciones para braceros* consisted only of rice, lard, and coffee. While it is possible that during this period fresh meat may have been substituted for dried, it is unlikely, as there is no record of any substitution, nor had the *zafra*, the traditional occasion for slaughtering an animal, begun.[8]

On some estates workers could now exercise a degree of freedom in food preparation, obtaining permission from their overseer to collect their food uncooked and prepare it in their rooms. Receiving one's rations uncooked could also be a burden, however. An article in *El Productor* in 1889 reported that in Trinidad cutters and loaders of cane were paid eighteen pesos monthly and food, but that they had to pay three pesos to whoever cooked it for them; they had no

[6] On food, see Barnet, *Biografía*, pp. 63-64; "Report by Consul Pierce," p. 254; and U.S. War Dept., *Report on the Census*, p. 531.
[7] "Report by Consul Pierce," p. 254.
[8] San Fernando, APSS, Valle-Iznaga, leg. 24.

time to cook it for themselves since they worked from 4:00 A.M. to 11:00 A.M., and from 12:00 noon to 7:00 P.M.[9]

The work itself continued much as before. "One passed the hours in the fields and it seemed as though the time never ended. It went on and on until it left one exhausted," reported Montejo.[10] That the rhythm of work had changed little was also attested to by planters. An article in the official publication of the Cuban Planters' Association in 1888 described a worker's day on a plantation or cane farm (*colonia*) as beginning with a 2:00 A.M. rising, followed by work until 11:00 A.M., a break for lunch, and then work from 1:00 to 6:00 P.M.[11] The manager of a large American-owned *colonia*, founded in 1889, gave much the same picture of conditions for his work force of 350 during the *zafra* and 150 during the "dead time," though he cited 4:00 A.M. as the rising time.[12]

Within a plantation, work fell into different categories. Both employers and employees had opinions about the desirability of various jobs and the appropriate kind of worker for them. P. M. Beal, the *colonia* manager cited earlier, expressed a preference for Canary Islanders and Spaniards for "stowing cane on the cars, plowing, ditching, road repairing, and railroad work." But he argued that, for "cane cutting, carting, planting, and cultivating, native labor—in particular negro labor—is preferable, because, being experts, the work progresses more rapidly, the cane plant suffers less injury, resulting in more remunerative returns, and its life is prolonged, which is a big item to the farmer." Another employer concurred: "One negro in cutting cane can do as much as two of any other class."[13] Freedmen themselves preferred some types of work over others. An observer in the Sancti Spíritus region reported in 1882 that when *libertos* returned to work on the *ingenios*, they chose the task of *machetero* (cane-cutter) over that of *alzador* (loader).[14]

Interestingly, specific tasks had different overtones in Cuba and in Puerto Rico, where emancipation had taken place some years before. In Cuba, ditching, for example, was not a highly skilled job

[9] See Barnet, *Biografía*, p. 64, and *El Productor* (Feb. 7, 1889).

[10] Barnet, *Biografía*, p. 63.

[11] Cited in Julio Le Riverend, "Raíces del 24 de Febrero: La economía y la sociedad cubanas de 1878 a 1895," *Cuba Socialista* 5 (Feb. 1965): 8.

[12] U.S. War Dept., *Report on the Census*, pp. 531-32.

[13] Porter, *Appendix to the Report*, pp. 253, 267.

[14] "Macheteros y alzadores," *La Propaganda* (Jan. 8, 1882).

231

and was likely to be given to new immigrants. In Puerto Rico, because of the importance of irrigation, ditching was a skilled and relatively prestigious job within field labor. Many ditchers there are reported to have been *libertos*, trained under slavery, and their descendants. Indeed, in the case of Puerto Rico, *libertos* were apparently crucial in a variety of skilled sectors within the sugar industry in the years immediately following emancipation, and employers sought them for both field and factory labor.[15]

Prior to abolition, some Cuban planters had imagined that an apartheid-like distinction between black agricultural workers and white factory workers would emerge after slavery. Indeed, they had seen this as part of a strategy for rapid development of the sugar industry.[16] One modern historian has asserted that such a division did exist and that the industrial work in the new *centrales* was performed exclusively by whites. Those who had been slaves on estates absorbed into *centrales*, he argues, ceased working in the processing of sugar and were employed exclusively in the agricultural tasks of cane growing and harvesting.[17]

The evidence on this point, however, seems inconclusive. If a sharp ethnic distinction between the agricultural and the manufacturing sectors were emerging in the 1890s, one would expect to find evidence of it on estates like Soledad, the modern *central* owned by Edwin Atkins. In a set of comments on the estate workers, the manager of Soledad, L. F. Hughes, did not address the question directly, but he did describe his work force as it stood in March 1898, the last month of crop time. Of the 1,600 men employed, there were "from 150 to 200 Chinamen [*sic*]; of the balance of the laborers probably there were more negroes than Spanish, with the white Cubans in a distinct minority." He went on to generalize about the different categories of workers: the Chinese he saw as steady but weak, the blacks and the Canary Islanders as the best labor, and so on. But particularly revealing is his comment that "The white men are mainly employed as stevedores in the batey, though they are

[15] On ditchers, see Mintz, *Caribbean Transformations*, p. 114. On the role of *libertos* in the Puerto Rican sugar industry, see Andrés Ramos Mattei, "El liberto en el régimen de trabajo azucarero de Puerto Rico, 1870-1880," in Ramos Mattei, *Azúcar y esclavitud*, pp. 91-124.

[16] See Ibáñez, *Observaciones*. He argued that whites would prefer the "industrial" work of the *batey*, and that fieldwork could be left to persons of color.

[17] Moreno, "El token," p. 151.

also good laborers in the field." He did not single them out as mill workers.[18]

There may well have been a concentration of blacks in fieldwork and whites in mill work, but several factors militated against absolute segregation. First, many Spanish immigrants were rural workers, some specifically imported for the harvest. One would expect most of them to be assigned to the field or the millyard where demand for seasonal unskilled and semiskilled labor was high. Second, some former slaves undoubtedly possessed skills that were of value in the mill, particularly if they remained in residence on the estate and could be expected to be available year after year.[19]

The differentiation that the American consul had noted in 1884 between black and white "unskilled" workers seems to have diminished in importance, while others grew. In the same way that there had been distinctions under slavery between indentured and free Chinese, and between owned and rented slaves, a distinction was now made between the categories of permanent and temporary worker. Esteban Montejo described the options for individual agricultural wage laborers in Santa Clara: one could sign on as a fixed laborer, contracted for several months, or one could work free-lance, agreeing on a price for weeding or clearing a specific area of land. Montejo viewed the free-lancers as having more autonomy because they were able to pace their own work, subject only to approval of the final job, and he described them as "muy vivos" (very sharp). But they also were transient, lodged in the smallest rooms of the barracón (to which they did not bring women, Montejo noted), and obliged to move on if they ran out of money before there was more task work to be done.[20]

Even among those who worked regularly for wages on a single estate, there were further distinctions. On one plantation cited by Montejo, in order to receive one's pay in cash one had to go to the

[18] Porter, *Appendix to the Report*, p. 267.
[19] Walter Rodney singles out the category of "pan-boilers" as a group of Creole Africans in the Guianese sugar industry whose skills were essential to the factory, and argues that they were able to gain some autonomy as a result. It is difficult to determine whether former slaves in Cuba held a comparable position prior to the introduction of fully mechanized controls on the vacuum pans. If they did, their importance would have been an inhibition to segregation within the factory. See Walter Rodney, *A History of the Guyanese Working People, 1881-1905* (Baltimore: The Johns Hopkins University Press, 1981), p. 161.
[20] Barnet, *Biografía*, pp. 65-66.

office and collect it from the *mayordomo*. Montejo preferred to collect his pay half in cash, half in credit from the storekeeper, in order to avoid going to the office to be "looked up and down." Others had no choice about dealing with the plantation store. The *Revista de Agricultura* in 1889 reported that one group of workers in the Trinidad area of Santa Clara province planned to emigrate because their wages were low and because they were obliged to buy in the stores established by the plantation owners.[21]

During the early stages of the ending of slavery wages had generally been calculated to include maintenance, and rations were issued to most workers. On the *ingenio* Nueva Teresa in the late 1870s and early 1880s, for example, many wage workers signed on agreeing to take their meals with the appropriate group on the plantation: slaves, Asians, or white employees.[22] As the transition to wage labor advanced, workers (such as those in the *cuadrillas* of Chinese) took on more of the responsibility for their own maintenance, or transferred it to contractors, and the role of the plantation store changed. Instead of merely issuing rations, it sold goods. Purchases there on credit could thus take the place of some of the cash wage. Once emancipation was complete, the role of the store changed again. In place of cash payments, many planters issued *vales* or tokens good only at the store.[23] Others simply maintained an account for each worker and subtracted his or her purchases from the final payroll. Their motives seem to have included concern to limit mobility, desire to confine expenditures to the estate, and response to a lack of coinage.

The records of the plantation store at the *ingenio* Natividad in Sancti Spíritus reveal a wide variation in the degree to which its workers contracted debts with the store. Some never bought anything at the store; indeed eighteen out of thirty-two workers on one such list kept the amount they purchased below one peso. Others bought considerably more, though the only ones actually to exceed their cash wages were a *capataz* (foreman) and one temporary worker.[24] Rather than revealing an entire work force held by debt

---

[21] Ibid., pp. 67-68. The *Revista* article is cited in LeRiverend, "Raices," p. 10. For a general discussion of plantation stores, see Moreno, "El token."

[22] See the account books of the *ingenio* Nueva Teresa, ANC, ML, 11245, 10879.

[23] Moreno, "El token."

[24] Negocios 1857-1896, APSS, Valle-Iznaga, leg. 7, exp. 19.

and credit, the *ingenio* Natividad presents a more complex picture. Those workers who grew enough for their own subsistence or who dealt with outside markets might avoid becoming indebted to their employers. Those who lacked resources or mobility or who preferred to avoid the *mayordomo* might deal extensively with company stores.

Factors beyond individual idiosyncrasy determined these differences. For some—perhaps particularly those who had struggled to purchase their freedom—refusing to deal with the company store could be an assertion of self-respect.[25] Temporary workers without either family or provision plots would probably be more likely to deal with the stores. On estates where payment was given in scrip, however, workers had little choice. An investigation carried out in 1883 in the sugar zone of Guanajayabo apparently revealed that within five days after the payment of monthly wages, 90 percent of the money paid out had returned to the estate through the *tienda mixta*.[26] This pattern of keeping wages almost entirely within the plantation may well have been uncharacteristic, but government authorities estimated in 1888 that hundreds of Cuban *ingenios* were issuing wages in *fichas*. They also cited reports of workers trying to use the plantation scrip at town stores.[27]

In areas where the demand for labor exceeded the supply, workers sometimes turned credit to their own advantage, extracting an initial payment prior to signing on. This obviously was a risky business, since it could lead to lasting debt. For temporary workers who left before their term was up, however, it meant an effective increase in wages. Thus employers were likely to be hostile to the extension of credit when they could not be sure of continued control over the workers. Articles in the Liberal press of Sancti Spíritus inveighed against workers who asked for advances to purchase goods to give to their families and then did not work or return the advance.[28] The Junta de Agricultura of Santa Clara in 1881 went so far as to claim

[25] For such sentiments expressed by a Puerto Rican sugar cane worker in the twentieth century, see Sidney W. Mintz, *Worker in the Cane: A Puerto Rican Life History* (New Haven: Yale University Press, 1960), p. 142.

[26] Moreno, "El token," pp. 154-55.

[27] See the letter from the alcalde of Guara to the governor of Havana, Sept. 18, 1888, in Expediente . . . sobre el pago de jornales a braceros en forma de fichas que representan valor estimativo, ANC, ME, leg. 4330, exp. AH.

[28] "Trabajadores," *La Propaganda* (Feb. 26, 1882), and "Hacendados y trabajadores," ibid. (Dec. 1, 1884).

that one could not find workers unless one extended advances, which were often not repaid. However, a newspaper article reporting this complaint expressed some skepticism about the claim and denied that the phenomenon was extensive.[29]

The problem of credit was, from the point of view of masters, part of the more general one of ensuring the continuity of labor. Another article written in Sancti Spíritus complained of workers who left the plantations to go to town and participate in the *parrandas*, putting music and sociability above labor.[30] (The *parranda* was a party or gathering of singers and musicians for improvisations, and in Sancti Spíritus it was apparently likely to be an interracial gathering.)[31] The *Revista de Agricultura* in 1888 echoed this plaint, saying that there were too many holidays during the harvest and that workers left at crucial times in order to go to town for the festivities.[32]

The editors of *La Propaganda* in Sancti Spíritus and of the *Revista* in Havana professed to believe in freedom of movement. In an ominous passage, however, an author for *La Propaganda* wrote that while it would be regrettable if the government were forced to introduce a system of *cartillas* (workbooks) for rural workers, as had been done for domestic servants, if this happened it would be the fault of the workers themselves, who had made ill use of their individual guarantees. The author called on workers to fulfill their obligations and forsake their immoderate desire for entertainment in order to aid the reconstruction of the country. "Entertainment as a habit degrades; work always ennobles," he intoned.[33] The *Revista de Agricultura* was more cautious, calling only for a limit on the number of fiestas permitted and for restrictions on cockfighting.[34] For one *colono* quoted in a newspaper article, musical instruments themselves came to symbolize workers' unwillingness to labor steadily. Significantly, the instruments he cited were the drum and the accordion—one African, one European.[35]

---

[29] *El Eco de Cuba* (Jan. 15, 1881). For a general discussion of debt and peonage see Arnold J. Bauer, "Rural Workers in Spanish America: Problems of Peonage and Oppression," *Hispanic American Historical Review* 59 (Feb. 1979): 34-63.

[30] *La Propaganda* (Feb. 26, 1882).

[31] Personal communication from Edelmiro Bonachea Jiménez, Director Provincial de Cultura, Sancti Spíritus, May 1979.

[32] "Las fiestas en los campos," *Revista de Agricultura* 8 (Sept. 2, 1888): 385.

[33] "Trabajadores," *La Propaganda* (Feb. 26, 1882).

[34] "Las fiestas en los campos."

[35] *La Propaganda* (May 17, 1885).

For more conservative observers, what was at issue was the social order itself. An article in the journal of a local "artistic and literary society" criticized workers' belief that they did not have to tolerate instructions when they were performing their tasks, and attributed this flaw to "an exaggerated concept of one's own personality." Workers, the author argued, had to understand that they were part of one class in society, and that because of their position they were dependent on another. Their spirit of independence would have to be "harmonized" with their subordination. Though the article did not mention freedmen specifically, some of the perceived "exaggerated concept of one's own personality" may have been an expression of autonomy by former slaves reacting to orders from their former masters. At the same time, the author's critique of this autonomy reflected a more generalized concept of hierarchy, applicable to whites as well as blacks.[36]

In addition to exhorting the rural working class to be deferential and work harder, employers tried to exercise control directly through the wage system. One *ingenio*, for example, advertised a "good wage" for fieldworkers—sixty cents per one hundred *arrobas* cut and loaded, thirty cents per day charged for food—but noted that pay would be given only after a month's work and that no advances would be issued.[37] Both the amount and the manner of payment on plantations varied widely according to the relationship of supply and demand across geographical areas and between seasons, the nature of production in each region, and the strategies of employers and workers.

In Trinidad, a severely depressed region in the province of Santa Clara that contained *ingenios* producing *mascabado* sugar but no *centrales*, monthly wages for day laborers did not go above nine or ten pesos during the summer of 1888; they had been ten to fourteen a few months earlier.[38] In Cienfuegos, which was undergoing development, a worker in 1888 might expect fourteen to seventeen

[36] *La Fraternidad*, Sancti Spíritus (Aug. 17, 1890). One could go a step further and argue that employers' attitudes were in part a legacy of Iberian seigneurialism, reinforced by the institution of slavery. To demonstrate this convincingly, however, would require a tracing of elite ideology and its roots that is well beyond the scope of this study. For a discussion of Cuban slavery that employs the concept of seigneurialism, see Paquette, "Conspiracy."

[37] *La Propaganda* (March 26, 1882).

[38] *Revista de Agricultura* 8 (Sept. 16, 1888): 142, and 8 (July 8, 1888): 279.

237

pesos in gold, including maintenance, and some fresh meat. In Sagua, wages were twelve to fourteen pesos, with worse food. In Matanzas, where there were numerous former slaves, pay was thirty-five to forty pesos a month in depreciated bills (around half the value of gold) and maintenance was not included.[39]

An *informe* from the Sociedad Económica de Amigos del País, issued just before the abolition of the *patronato*, had estimated wages at from forty to seventy cents a day, or ten to eighteen pesos per month. The Círculo de Hacendados at the same time estimated a range of fifteen to twenty pesos per month without maintenance in "dead time," twenty-five to forty during the *zafra*. This latter estimate probably included some specialized workers.[40] In practice, pay varied widely, even on the same plantation. In July 1889, monthly pay to the over two hundred *braceros* working on the *ingenio* Natividad in Sancti Spíritus ranged roughly from nine pesos for some cane haulers to thirty for some cane cutters. Most tasks earned around fifteen to twenty pesos.[41]

Wages were at roughly similar levels in the 1890s. One manager cited an average for field laborers during the summer months of seventeen pesos, although higher amounts (twenty-one pesos) were paid to cane cutters and cane loaders during crop time.[42] The *ingenio* Natividad recorded wage rates of twelve to twenty-six pesos to *braceros* during the *zafra* of 1895-1896.[43] The American-owned Soledad *central* in Santa Clara province reported paying from fourteen to twenty pesos Spanish gold in 1895.[44]

This cataloguing of general wage levels in different regions is not intended as a precise statement of the wages earned by former slaves who remained on plantations. If tied to a plantation store, they could find their real purchasing power as well as their freedom much reduced; if hired only part of the year, or part of each month, their income was correspondingly lower. The point is that the wages paid the freedmen and freedwomen were certainly higher than the wages paid to Chinese and other contract laborers in the 1870s, but they

[39] *Revista de Agricultura* 8 (July 8, 1888): 279.
[40] Informe, Sociedad Económica de Amigos del País, Aug. 22, 1886, and Informe, Círculo de Hacendados, Aug. 7, 1886, AHN, Ultramar, leg. 280, exp. 610.
[41] Relación de pagos, Natividad, July 31, 1889, APSS, Valle-Iznaga, leg. 7, exp. 13.
[42] U.S. War Dept., *Report on the Census*, p. 531.
[43] APSS, Valle-Iznaga, leg. 7, exp. 19.
[44] Porter, *Appendix to the Report*, p. 268.

were not markedly higher than wages paid to free workers in the 1870s. Planters' total expenditures on wages had risen sharply with the shift of workers into the wage-earning sector, but the wages paid to individual workers had not.

Planters seeking subsidized immigration or laws restricting workers' rights tended to speak in terms of a "scarcity" of workers, but other observers noticed that in absolute numbers there was not a general "labor shortage." José Quintín Suzarte wrote in 1881 that there was in fact an abundance of *braceros*, and that they would have to reduce their "pretenciones" when faced with competition from the work forces of those plantations that had gone out of business, from released soldiers, from urban workers displaced by released soldiers, and from freed *patrocinados*.[45]

Nonetheless, as in virtually all postemancipation societies, planters in Cuba complained that former slaves spent too much time in leisure. Indeed, former slaves did at times choose to place domestic labor, the cultivation of food crops, and companionship with friends and family above the endless hoeing, cutting, and lifting of cane. But observers also noted that workers migrated in search of higher pay, and shifted from one estate or gang to another in pursuit of better wages. In such cases, there was no denying former slaves' responsiveness to monetary incentives. The "labor shortage" bemoaned by planters should thus be seen in the context of employers' desire for an expansion of the total work force to drive down the cost of labor and their unwillingness or inability to offer higher wages. One planter, recalling the nineties, wrote simply that "planters, who were very poor, due to the low price of sugar and the excessive taxation, could not afford to employ all the laborers that presented themselves."[46] Under these circumstances, the leisure of some former slaves was an enforced one.

Whatever the fears of employers, it is clear that abolition did not trigger a catastrophic flight of former slaves from plantation labor, thus crippling production. Although levels of sugar production in the 1880s were below those of the peak years of the 1870s (when prices were higher), they did not plummet, but remained comparable to earlier figures, averaging just 8 percent below the amounts for the previous decade. In the 1890s they began to climb again, and

[45] Suzarte, *Estudios*, p. 66.
[46] Porter, *Appendix to the Report*, p. 263.

TABLE 26
Cuban Sugar Production, 1870-1894

Year	Metric Tons	Year	Metric Tons	Year	Metric Tons
1870	702,974	1878	553,364	1887	707,442
1871	609,660	1879	775,368	1888	662,758
1872	772,068	1880	618,654	1889	569,367
1873	742,843	1881	580,894	1890	636,239
1874	768,672	1882	620,565	1891	807,742
1875	750,062	1883	601,426	1892	1,000,797
1876	626,082	1884	626,477	1893	945,035
1877	516,268	1885	628,990	1894	1,110,991
		1886	657,290		

SOURCE: Manuel Moreno Fraginals, *El ingenio: complejo económico social cubano del azúcar*, 3 vols. (Havana: Editorial de Ciencias Sociales, 1978) 3: 37-38.

reached the unprecedented one million ton mark by 1892 (see Table 26). While technical innovations and the attraction of new workers accounted for some of the recovery, former slaves of necessity provided much of the labor.

THE *COLONATO*. This expansion of production relied not only on continued growing of cane on the *ingenios* but also on the extension of the *colonato*. Former slaves could, in theory, have participated both as workers and as *colonos*. Indeed, the *colonato* had on some estates arisen in part as a mechanism to keep freedmen on the plantation. A Cuban planter recalled the development of the *colonato* on the Hormiguero estate after abolition:

> We adopted the system of giving out grounds to some of our slaves, building houses for them, and starting them raising sugar cane. Then we got their families, some Canary Islanders, and some of the people of the country, and commenced in that way. They went very nicely for a while, and then commenced to abandon the thing, and we had to take up the cultivation of cane ourselves again. Their work was intermittent, and we could not rely on them.[47]

It is impossible to know, from the employer's account, just why the arrangement ceased to work in this instance. But low prices for sugar in the mid-1880s—and thus low prices to the *colono* for cane—may have been a major factor. The need of the *central* for strict control over the supply of cane could also make coexistence with semi-

[47] Ibid., p. 129.

independent farmers difficult. Other plantations had much better luck with the *colono* system, though it always contained the potential for conflict over prices and how the cane was being grown.

As time went on, however, it became clear that cane farming would be a predominantly white occupation. By 1899, the census counted 4,541 sugar "plantations" (including cane farms) in the island with white owners, and just 520 with "colored" owners. There were 6,730 plantations in the hands of white renters, 2,645 in the hands of colored renters. Together the farms with colored owners or renters comprised less than 4.5 percent of the total land of plantations devoted to the growing and/or processing of cane.[48]

When in the early 1890s a *colono* in the province of Santa Clara composed an angry tract criticizing the exploitation of *colonos* by millowners, he chose as his title *Los esclavos blancos (The White Slaves).*[49] He was acknowledging, in effect, that the *colonato* was now perceived as a largely white institution. There were in his province in 1899 4,350 white owners and renters of sugar farms and just 1,003 colored owners and renters, though 30 percent of the provincial population of agriculturalists was classified as "colored." The only other province with a substantial number of colored owners and renters of sugar farms was Santiago de Cuba, with 1,708.[50] In both cases many of the colored *colonos* may have been the descendants of free persons of color rather than recently emancipated slaves, for these were provinces that throughout the late nineteenth century had counted noticeable populations of black and mulatto smallholders. For smallholders of all groups, the expansion of the *colonato* was, however, a mixed blessing. It provided a new mechanism for producing a cash crop, but at the same time put pressure on the supply of land.

The concentration of *colono* lands in the hands of white owners and tenants may have resulted in part from overt ethnic favoritism by planters, as occurred in some coffee regions of Brazil, but it was undoubtedly also exacerbated by a lack of capital and of access to credit on the part of freedmen.[51] Indeed, the two factors were inter-

[48] U.S. War Dept., *Report on the Census,* p. 560.
[49] Jiménez, *Los esclavos blancos.*
[50] U.S. War Dept., *Report on the Census,* pp. 560, 448-49.
[51] On discrimination by planters in Brazil, see Warren Dean, *Rio Claro: A Brazilian Plantation System, 1820-1920* (Stanford: Stanford University Press, 1976); and Florestan Fernandes, *The Negro in Brazilian Society* (trans. Jacqueline D. Skiles,

twined, since planters were both major grantors of rented *colonias* and a major source of initial credit. Whatever the mix of reasons for the relative exclusion of freedmen from the *colonato*, it meant that most of them would participate in the sugar boom of the 1890s only as sellers of their labor. Selling one's labor to white *colonos*, often immigrants, may have been preferable to selling it to former slave-holders, but at least one freedman remembered those *colono* employers with bitterness: "What they were was sons of bitches, meaner and stingier (*más bravos y tacaños*) than the *hacendados* themselves. They were very tight with wages."[52] Rather than being an inherent trait of personality, this stinginess probably reflected the pressure on *colonos* as they shared with millowners and passed on to their workers the burden of falling sugar prices in the nineties.

FAMILY STRATEGIES. Both wage labor in sugar and tenantry on a *colonia* meant remaining to a large extent within the orbit of the plantation, though not necessarily the one on which one had been a slave. Some freedmen and freedwomen took still further steps to lessen their commitment to the plantations. This was sometimes involuntary: if laid off during the dead season, they had no choice but to look for other work or cultivate a provision ground. It could also be a conscious strategy, however, aimed at increasing one's opportunities and reducing one's dependence on a former master.

In 1886 Rafael Cowley, a member of the Sociedad Económica de Amigos del País, reported that many freedmen had gone to the towns to find the "social life" that had previously been denied them. Cowley then described the evolution of a familial division of labor: women would live in the town, occupied in domestic work and their own household duties, while their partners continued to work in agriculture. Logically, then, men preferred to work on plantations that were close to towns, and they were even willing to work for less than they would have obtained on more distant plantations.[53] This account suggests a new kind of stratification in the supply of labor after emancipation. First, some women withdrew from year-

A. Brunel, and Arthur Rothwell) (New York: Columbia University Press, 1969), esp. pp. 17-18. On early efforts to attract European immigrants to Brazil, see also Emília Viotti da Costa, *Da Senzala à Colônia* (São Paulo: Difusão Europeia do Livro, 1966), pp. 65-123.

[52] Barnet, *Biografía*, p. 105.

[53] AHN, Ultramar, leg. 280, exp. 610.

round labor in agriculture, following a pattern observed in one slave society after another, and could be attracted back into field work only when wages were relatively high.[54] Second, by moving to the towns, these women affected the supply of male labor as well, since male workers whose partners were in town would avoid work on isolated plantations.

Descriptions of plantation life after slavery often noted a separation of men from their families. The assistant manager of the American-owned *ingenio* Soledad believed that most of his male workers were not married, and reported that the families of those who were married lived in the nearby villages. "Most of the laboring men, if they have families, when they are paid off, go away for a day or a day and a half and take their money to their families, and then come back to work." This family division of labor thus appears as a consequence of the orientation of the employers on large plantations toward bachelor laborers, and the resulting provision of barracks-like living arrangements for workers, as well as the preference of some families for residence in towns. Another observer of Soledad and neighboring estates wrote simply that "the families prefer to live in the towns and the planters do not care to have the families on the estates."[55]

Women did, however, often return to field work at harvest time, when demand was up and wages were higher. P. M. Beal, manager of the Guabairo *colonia*, reported in 1899 that "During the harvest I give the negro women preference, and pay them the same salaries as the best male labor. They are the most constant, their work is usually well done, and each one keeps her man straight, which is an appreciable item."[56] A description of labor on sugar estates in Cienfuegos in 1884 described the drying of *bagazo* (cane stalks) specifically as women's work.[57] Montejo noted that women's domestic work was not seasonal, that "there was no such thing as a dead time for them." He cited washing, mending, sewing, and raising pigs and chickens among their responsibilities.[58]

[54] For evidence on the change in female participation in agricultural labor, see note 3, above. On Brazil, see Stein, *Vassouras*, p. 262.

[55] The assistant manager is quoted in Porter, *Appendix to the Report*, p. 268; the other observations are from Pedro Rodríguez, in Porter, p. 195.

[56] U.S. War Dept., *Report on the Census*, p. 530.

[57] "Report by Consul Pierce," p. 251.

[58] Barnet, *Biografía*, p. 94.

Despite the predictions of fearful whites that former slaves would wander, languish, and die, or the claims by some scholars that plantation slaves knew nothing of family or economy and that many were therefore traumatized by abolition,[59] it is evident that some former slaves did organize and perpetuate family economies, involving shared and complementary wage and household labor. The ties may not always have been legal or permanent, but neither were they all aimless or ephemeral. The strength of these ties should not be surprising; they were already apparent in the efforts of large numbers of parents and others to purchase the freedom of children or spouses during the period of gradual emancipation.

SMALLHOLDING. Throughout the Caribbean, the plantation and nonplantation sectors had long competed for many of the same resources. Owners of plantations in some instances sought to block the development of possibilities that would allow former slaves to become self-sufficient away from the plantation. But the two sectors could also, under certain circumstances, be complementary, exchanging goods and sharing labor, however uneasily. This was particularly likely if the seasonal labor needs of the crops cultivated did not overlap directly, as in the case of maize and sugar. In Cuba after emancipation a classic Caribbean "reconstituted peasantry," in which former slaves became small-scale cultivators, did not emerge, but smallholding of one kind or another was apparently sought by many former slaves.[60]

The major precedent for the growing of crops other than sugar by former slaves was the *conuco* or provision ground. During slavery, masters found that some labor could profitably be dedicated to food crops, reducing the estate's dependence on imported foodstuffs, and slaves found that *conuco* cultivation provided access to capital. The

[59] Moreno, "Aportes culturales y deculturación," p. 22.

[60] The phrase "reconstituted peasantry" is Sidney Mintz's. For a recent discussion of some of these issues, see Sidney W. Mintz, "Reflections on Caribbean Peasantries," *Nieuwe West-Indische Gids/ New West Indian Guide* 57 (1983): 1-17. See also Franklin W. Knight, *The Caribbean: The Genesis of a Fragmented Nationalism* (New York: Oxford University Press, 1978). For a clear instance of explicit planter efforts to stymie the development of a peasantry, see Alan H. Adamson, *Sugar Without Slaves: The Political Economy of British Guiana, 1838-1904* (New Haven: Yale University Press, 1972), esp. chaps. 2, 3. For a contemporary instance of conflicts between plantations and smallholding in Cuba, see Brian H. Pollitt, "Agrarian Reform and the 'Agricultural Proletariat' in Cuba, 1958-66: Some Notes," University of Glasgow, Institute of Latin American Studies, Occasional Paper no. 27, 1979.

conuco had thus persisted despite adversity, and provided a basis for the survival of a kind of family economy. Some who turned to wage work after emancipation may have abandoned their *conucos*, as the existence of overtime pay competed with subsistence cultivation and changing patterns of mobility drew freedmen away from their plots. The *conuco* nevertheless remained a model for subsequent agricultural activity, even for those who continued to work at least part of the time for the plantation. As the employer lost his ability to enforce all of the terms of labor, freedmen could shift the balance between time spent on their own crops and time spent on the plantation's. An American observer wrote in 1899:

The Cuban negro has a marked trait in the instinct of landownership. It is one of the standard complaints of the sugar planters that he clings to his cabin and his patch of ground to the detriment of successful cane-raising. He does not care to be swallowed up in the big plantation, and usually his wish for a *bohío* or palm-hut of his own in preference to quarters in the plantation barracks has to be gratified.[61]

This account appears to depict a situation in which the cultivation of cane and the cultivation of food crops coexisted, despite the employer's greater interest in cane, because of the employee's insistence on access to a small amount of land as a condition of employment. Concession of this right could have multiple consequences. On the one hand, the worker was attached to land close to the plantation and therefore was more accessible at harvest time. On the other hand, with the possibility of applying his energies to a provision plot, he might well not offer his labor for as many days per week, or as many weeks per month, as the employer would wish.

The transition from a slave *conuco* to a freedman's plot sometimes involved an intermediate stage. A slave who had grown crops on his *conuco* might obtain freedom by self-purchase, based on the product of that plot, during the 1880s. If he remained on the same plantation he might, instead of hiring on as a day worker, plant on estate land and receive the value of a portion of the crop each year. Justo Argudín, for example, a former slave on the *ingenio* Nueva Teresa, obtained his freedom and began to grow corn on halves with the plantation. His account was kept in the plantation books and he

[61] Charles M. Pepper, *To-Morrow in Cuba* (New York: Harper and Bros., 1899; reprint ed., New York: Young People's Missionary Movement of the United States and Canada, 1910), p. 151.

apparently collected no cash for years on end, but he had made a half-step from slave toward peasant.[62]

It is difficult to reconstruct the precise mixture of motivations that lay behind these choices. The cultivation of food crops provided a more reliable guarantee of the family's subsistence and was a form of work not directly controlled by the plantation. As such, it may have had an appeal beyond its yield in strictly economic terms. An American visitor wrote at the end of the century that Cubans in the countryside "seem to prefer the cultivation of small patches of ground for themselves, rather than working for wages, although the net result to them may not be so favorable." He suggested that "the colored Cubans, at least, seem to consider that the course which they follow in this respect especially demonstrates their personal independence, which they have been anxious to establish since they have been freed from slavery."[63]

The shift into some form of smallholding also often reflected a specific decision to apply one's energies to *cultivos menores*, "lesser crops." In his 1886 report, Rafael Cowley wrote that there had been a move by *libertos* to small farms, reflecting the freedmen's preference for other crops over cane growing and sugar production. He claimed the shift had been significant enough to be reflected in overall production figures for grain, pineapples, and potatoes. This increased production could eventually satisfy the demand both for internal consumption and for export to the United States, he predicted.[64]

Cowley's report points up the complexity of interpreting freedmen's attraction to smallholding. Small plots could yield subsistence crops for family consumption or for sale, but they could also yield cane or crops intended for export. Observers alarmed by the withdrawal of some black workers from wage labor in cane tended to blur the two, and to perceive a total retreat from the market economy. Enrique José Varona wrote in distress in 1888: "The black country person, who lives with very little, is slowly drawing away from the *fincas*, to form a great mass of inert population, which

[62] For the account of Justo Argudín, see fol. 226 of Libro Mayor del Ingenio Nueva Teresa, ANC, ML, 11245.

[63] William J. Clark, *Commercial Cuba* (New York: Charles Scribner's Sons, 1898), p. 39.

[64] AHN, Ultramar, leg. 280, exp. 610.

consumes strictly what it produces."[65] From the point of view of those concerned with the island's exports and productivity for the market, a retreat into subsistence by former slaves was unacceptable. But the evidence of crops actually planted on smallholdings owned or rented by persons of color suggests that Varona's portrait was overdrawn.

The majority of the holdings rented or owned by persons of color were located in the provinces of Santiago de Cuba, Santa Clara, and Pinar del Río. In Santiago de Cuba in 1899, "colored" owners and renters planted their lands primarily in bananas, Indian corn, sweet potatoes, cacao, coffee, and sugar cane. In Santa Clara, colored owners and renters planted most of their land in sugar cane, while also growing sweet potatoes and corn. In Pinar del Río, both owners and renters concentrated on tobacco, while planting sweet potatoes and *malangas* as well. Some squatters occupying tiny plots undoubtedly escaped the census reports, but the overall picture is one of a commitment to the market as well as to subsistence.[66]

To employers seeking laborers on estates, the withdrawal of freedmen from the plantation might appear a stubborn refusal to cooperate, a retreat into leisure and inertia. But for freedmen who managed to find land, such withdrawal could actually multiply their possible activities, for they could combine subsistence cultivation, market gardening, and the growth of export crops with periodic wage labor. The returns on these activities might be exiguous indeed, but the multiplication of activities could mean an important increase in autonomy.

Land was hard to find, however, and the growth of *centrales* made the task harder still. To escape from the orbit of the estates, some former slaves found that they had to flee the sugar regions entirely. A growing problem, however, was the difficulty of staying more than one step ahead of the expanding *centrales*.

MIGRATION. The eastern region seems to have held the greatest attraction for potential migrants. Indeed, a major shift eastward in the population of color can be discerned in the pattern of population distribution at different census dates between 1862 and 1899. The

[65] Enrique José Varona, "El bandolerismo," *Revista Cubana* 8 (June 1888): 481-501.
[66] U.S. War Dept., *Report on the Census*, pp. 558-59. Landholding and crop patterns will be discussed further in Chap. XI, below.

TABLE 27
Distribution of the Population of Color
by Province, 1862-1899

Province	1862		1877		1887		1899	
Pinar del Río	64,063	(10.8%)	59,496	(12.6%)	59,213	(11.2%)	46,836	(9.3%)
Havana	143,805	(24.2%)	111,096	(23.6%)	116,146	(22.0%)	108,328	(21.4%)
Matanzas	110,450	(18.6%)	108,750	(23.1%)	117,538	(22.2%)	80,321	(15.9%)
Santa Clara	114,442	(19.2%)	96,959	(20.6%)	109,025	(20.6%)	106,574	(21.1%)
Puerto Príncipe	26,158	(4.4%)	8,472	(1.8%)	13,208	(2.5%)	17,375	(3.4%)
Santiago de Cuba	135,570	(22.8%)	86,799	(18.4%)	113,668	(21.5%)	146,109	(28.9%)
Total	594,488	(100%)	471,572	(100%)	528,798	(100%)	505,543	(100%)

SOURCES: 1862—Cuba, Centro de Estadística, *Noticias estadísticas*, "Distribución"; 1877—Iglesias, "El censo cubano," Appendix; 1887—Spain, Instituto Geográfico y Estadístico, *Censo de población de España segun el empadronamiento hecho en 31 de diciembre de 1887* (Madrid: 1891-92); 1899—U.S. War Department, *Report on the Census of Cuba, 1899* (Washington, D.C.: Government Printing Office, 1900), p. 195 (includes figures from census categories "Negro" and "Mixed").

number of blacks and mulattos in the island had dropped sharply following the closing of the slave trade and before full emancipation. This decline was particularly marked in the two eastern provinces where the Ten Years' War hit hard, causing many deaths and encouraging slaveholders to move their slaves out of the area. This population recovered somewhat after 1877, especially in the east, where emancipation was completed first and where it is likely that wartime losses were in part recouped through new births. After full emancipation, there was a striking increase in the portion of the population of color located in the east. Much of this change seems to have been due to migration of population out of sugar areas. Matanzas, for example, lost some 17 percent of its white population and 32 percent of its population of color between 1887 and 1899. The province of Santiago de Cuba, by contrast, increased its white population by fourteen percent, and its population of color by 29 percent[67] (see Table 27).

The east offered greater access to land for a variety of reasons. Its hilly and mountainous interior had long been inhospitable to sugar production, leaving room for the development of a nonplantation sector removed from the region's sugar-producing areas of Guantánamo and the district around the city of Santiago de Cuba. Moreover, in some of the territory devastated by the Ten Years' War, the government had undertaken the distribution of state-owned land to aid in reconstruction. Among those applying for land were blacks and mulattos, though it is not possible to determine whether they were former slaves.[68] In 1885 the government reported that over 1,000 hectares had been distributed in the area of Manzanillo, part of the old *finca* Monte.[69] The scale of the operation, however, was far too small to provide land to substantial numbers of individuals or to

[67] Juan Pérez de la Riva argues that an analysis at the level of municipalities also shows migration out of sugar regions and into nonsugar regions, though he does not elaborate on the method used to establish this. See his "Los recursos humanos de Cuba al comenzar el siglo: inmigración, economía, y nacionalidad (1899-1906)," *Anuario de Estudios Cubanas*, Tomo 1: *La república neocolonial* (Havana: Editorial de Ciencias Sociales, 1975), pp. 7-44. Figures on white population may be found in the sources listed in Table 27.

[68] For a decree authorizing the distribution of land to soldiers, to those who remained faithful to Spain and suffered damages, and to insurrectionists who surrendered and were pardoned, see *Memorias de la Sociedad Económica de Amigos del País*, Series 8, 1 (Dec. 1877): 119-22. For applications for land, see ANC, GG, leg. 48.

[69] See Libro de Actas, proyectos de Decreto de Ley, y demás documentos, AHN, Ultramar, leg. 280.

bring about the recovery of areas damaged by the war. Indeed, it is unclear how many of the anticipated titles were ever distributed.[70]

At the same time, private North American investment was attracted to parts of the east damaged by the war, and several large American-owned *centrales* began to develop in the 1880s. As processing was centralized, ruinate *ingenios* became *colonias*. These promised a very different kind of future for the region that the small farms growing tobacco and *viandas* envisioned by those who petitioned for individual plots from the government.[71]

Thus the east, while offering an internal frontier in which some elements of a "reconstituted peasantry" might develop, was itself already under the pressure of change. It would not offer a refuge to all freedmen, and increasingly its own inhabitants would find themselves drawn or pushed into closer ties with plantation society.

In addition to expressing concern that freedmen might withdraw into subsistence cultivation, some policy makers had, prior to emancipation, raised the specter of a mass flight of freedmen to the cities and an accompanying increase in vagrancy and criminality. Some former slaves did migrate to the cities and towns, but the magnitude of the phenomenon appears to have been limited. The proportion of the island's population of color resident in the province of Havana, for example, did not increase dramatically during the period of emancipation. The city of Havana itself held an estimated 47,000 residents of color in 1877, 54,400 in 1887, and 64,800 in 1899. The increase between 1887 and 1899 was a substantial 19 percent, but it was less than the increase in the province of Santiago de Cuba (29 percent). The city contained 10 percent of the island's population of color in 1877 and again in 1887, 13 percent in 1899. The percentage of the island's total population of color living in the five largest cities had been around 19 percent in 1877, and was around 23 percent in 1899. (The proportion of the white population living in these cities in 1899

[70] Robert Hoernel argues that many of the titles were never distributed. See "Sugar and Social Change in Oriente, Cuba, 1898-1946," *Journal of Latin American Studies* 8 (Nov. 1976): 225.

[71] Hoernel points out that the destruction, in effect, assisted in the modernization of the sugar industry in the east, since large *centrales* could directly supersede the ruined estates. Ibid., p. 225. For testimony by several operators of the new North American *centrales*, see Porter, *Appendix to the Report*.

was comparable: around 24 percent.)[72] Of course, these figures are difficult to interpret because of the intervening years of war and the Spanish policy of "reconcentration." Nonetheless, they do not seem to reflect a mass flight to the cities.

Indeed, most Afro-Cuban city-dwellers of 1899 are likely to have been descendants of the pre-abolition urban population of color rather than themselves post-abolition migrants. The free population of color had already been strongly concentrated in the cities prior to abolition, and its relatively high rate of growth was regularly commented upon by observers. In 1877, in the city of Matanzas, for example, there were 7,013 free persons of color and another 2,321 urban slaves. Twenty-two years later the city's population of color was 11,456, and primarily female. Again, it is difficult to make direct inferences because of the turmoil of the intervening years, but it seems that relatively few of the province's tens of thousands of field slaves would have had to migrate to the city in order to make up the 2,122 person increase in the interim.[73]

Migration to the cities and towns did not invariably indicate a total departure from agriculture. As we have seen, it was sometimes part of a familial arrangement combining female urban labor and male rural labor, and sometimes a seasonal movement in response to shifting demand for workers. As such, urban migration did not necessarily carry with it the connotations of rootlessness and potential criminality that fearful observers had anticipated. Indeed, an examination of the biographies of a group of Havana criminals in the 1880s does not support the idea that a large proportion of them were former field slaves, at least judging by their places of origin.[74]

Occasionally former slaves attempted an even more drastic migration away from plantation society. In 1883 one group apparently

<hr>

[72] Figures on the 1877 population are from the *Boletín Oficial de la Hacienda de la Isla de Cuba* 1 (Sept. 15, 1881 and Oct. 15, 1881), and *Boletín Oficial de Hacienda y de Estadística de la Isla de Cuba* 2 (Aug. 30, 1882). Figures for 1887 are from Spain, Instituto Geográfico y Estadístico, *Censo de la población de España, segun el empadronamiento hecho en 31 de diciembre de 1887* 2 vols. (Madrid: Impr. de la Dirección General del Instituto Geográfico y Estadístico, 1891, 1892). Those for 1899 are from U.S. War Dept., *Report on the Census*, pp. 194-99.
[73] The 1877 figures are from *Boletín Oficial de la Hacienda de la Isla de Cuba* 1 (Oct. 15, 1881). The 1899 figures are from U.S. War Dept., *Report on the Census*, p. 196.
[74] Urrutia, *Los criminales*.

embarked for "Angoué" (probably in coastal equatorial Africa), and oral tradition holds that as late as 1897, during the war, an important group of *lucumíes* also left for Africa.[75] A somewhat better documented case is that of Francisco Cuevas, who proposed to the queen of Spain in 1887 that the Spanish government support a group of Cubans in their effort to establish a colony on the west coast of Africa. He asked the government to pay their transportation and first four months' maintenance. Their avowed aim was to save their "brothers" from "the ignorance and savagery in which they live submerged, bringing them the Light of progress and the consolation of our Holy Roman Catholic Religion." They intended to work collectively and share their wealth, but they wanted government protection from the "savages." Five of the ten signers of the proposal were named Terri. One suspects that they had been slaves of Tomás Terry, a planter whose estates received African slaves until very late, but whether they were African or Creole is impossible to determine. The actual aim of their project and degree of their aversion to the "savagery" of Africa remain a mystery. In any case, the proposal was evidently ignored by the government.[76]

Though the possibility of a voluntary "return to Africa" had been envisioned by the 1870 legislation on gradual abolition, there is no evidence that it was ever systematically undertaken. The colonial government would have had little interest in funding such ventures unless it sought to drastically "whiten" the population, and planters expressed no interest in facilitating the departure of potential workers.

A few former slaves seem to have opted for a kind of internal exile, setting up independent communities comparable to the *palenques* that had long existed in the eastern part of the island. A local newspaper referred in 1882 to a *palenque* in the hills near Sagua, in the province of Santa Clara. One is initially tempted to suggest that

[75] Juan Pérez de la Riva, "Antiguos esclavos cubanos que regresan a Lagos," in Juan Pérez de la Riva and Pedro Deschamps Chapeaux, *Contribución a la historia de la gente sin historia* (Havana: Editorial de Ciencias Sociales, 1974), pp. 165-67. Fernando Ortiz expressed skepticism about reports of former Cuban slaves returning to Africa, but noted one case in 1895, which is possibly the same one that was preserved in oral tradition, and repeated to me by Pedro Deschamps Chapeaux. Ortiz, *Los negros esclavos*, pp. 302-303.

[76] AHN, Ultramar, leg. 146, exp. 35.

some freed slaves were following a model from slavery and establishing settlements along the lines of maroon communities. The context of the report, however, suggests that the term may have been used somewhat loosely. A conservative newspaper was bemoaning the "vicious, vagrant habits" of recently freed slaves, and cited the capture of some of the inhabitants of this *"palenque,"* who were accused of supporting themselves by marauding nearby estates. So there is little way to determine whether a real *palenque* had been established, or whether the word—evocative of fugitive slaves and illegality—was used to add to the vividness of the argument for more law and order.[77] In any event, the growth of autonomous villages comparable to the "free villages" of Jamaica was thwarted both by the absence of groups like the Protestant churches who might aid in the amassing of capital, and by the lack of available land. While former slaves in Jamaica could establish new farms in areas of marginal or declining sugar estates, those in Cuba were faced with an aggressive and expanding plantation agriculture.[78] They might for a time incorporate themselves into existing, predominantly Afro-Cuban communities in the east, but eventually the plantations would threaten much of that world as well.

Like former slaves throughout the Caribbean, Cuban freedmen and freedwomen sought in various ways to increase their autonomy, either rural or urban. Those who had been slaves were not mere elements in an abstract transition to "free labor," but individuals and families who tried to make something of their new juridical status, however constrained they might be by the policies of the state and of planters or by their own lack of capital.

In analyzing these work patterns, one must seek the actual circumstances that gave rise to different outcomes, and question the implications hidden within the terminology adopted by employers. Thus the "unreliability" of former slaves as agricultural workers in one region could reflect their access to land and preference for work

[77] For information on *palenques* and the Ten Years' War, see Franco, *Palenques,* pp. 115-16. For the 1882 reference see Resumen del espíritu de la prensa, Dec. 25, 1882, AHN, Ultramar, leg. 4807.

[78] On the development of the postemancipation peasantry in Jamaica, see Douglas Hall, *Free Jamaica, 1838-1865: An Economic History* (New Haven: Yale University Press, 1959), especially chap. 1; Mintz, *Caribbean Transformations,* chap. 6; and Thomas C. Holt, "The Problem of Freedom."

in crops other than sugar, while their much-appreciated "constancy" in another might be achieved by forcing them into virtual landlessness.[79] The patterns of landholding and social relations that characterized Cuba in the final decade of the nineteenth century were thus both cause and effect in this dialectic of striving and constraint, and it is to these that we now turn.

[79] For an example of this kind of distinction, made by a contemporary, see the statement of Pedro Rodríguez of Caibarien: "Our blacks at Las Villas and Matanzas are better than those in the eastern part of the island. They are more in the habit of working." Porter, *Appendix to the Report*, p. 195.

XI

Land and Society

En el año '44   In the year '44
yo 'taba en el ingenio   I was on the plantation
En el año '44, negra,   In the year '44, *negra,*
yo 'taba en el ingenio   I was on the plantation
Ahora, ahora   Now, now,
negro con blanco   black with white
chapea cañaverá   weeding in the canefields

*Lyrics of a slow rumba sung in Matanzas after emancipation.
(1844 was the year of the repression of a reputed
slave uprising.)*[1]

The transition to free labor in Cuba meant a fundamental reorganization of labor, landholding, and social relations. Owners of slaves and *ingenios* became employers on *centrales* and *colonias*. Slaves became legally free workers, in sugar and elsewhere. The interaction of employers and laborers, and of available land and available capital, however, was by no means geographically uniform. The result was a regional diversity in patterns of land use and landholding at least as striking as that which had existed under slavery.

At the same time, emancipation altered several aspects of the social and political environment of the island. Abolition transformed the Afro-Cuban community in ways that affected Afro-Cuban attitudes toward political activity and toward Spanish rule. It also changed the political equation for the Spanish colonial government, leading it to court Afro-Cuban support as part of its larger strategy for the maintenance of colonial rule.

Together these changes shaped Cuban society on the eve of the outbreak of a new anticolonial struggle. This chapter will examine the changes in landholding and in social relations affecting the Afro-Cuban community, while the conclusion and epilogue will trace some of the consequences for the growing political conflict.

[1] I am grateful to Rogelio Martínez Furé for providing the text of this song.

LANDHOLDING AND LAND USE. By the end of the century, access
to land varied dramatically from province to province, particularly
for persons of color. The 1899 census is a somewhat anachronistic
source, since it was compiled after the War for Independence, but
its figures are nonetheless revealing of provincial patterns: landowners and renters varied as a percentage of the white population
in agriculture from 11 percent in the cattle-raising area of Puerto
Príncipe to 29 percent in Santiago de Cuba, while for persons of color
the range was from 2 percent in Matanzas to 30 percent in Santiago
de Cuba[2] (see Table 28). A brief examination of landholding in each
province reveals the complex situation that had yielded these ratios.

The eastern province of Santiago de Cuba represented an extreme
case, a special variation in the pattern of black and mulatto occu-
pancy of land. Some 30 percent of both white and "colored" agriculturalists apparently rented or owned land in the province. With
their family members, they comprised a group with a remarkably
high degree of access to small plots of land. This pattern of landholding was later to influence the development of the rural proletariat and peasantry in eastern Cuba, for native workers with access
to land were less willing to work for the developing *centrales*, and
planters responded both by importing immigrant workers and by
expanding their landholdings at the expense of renters, owners, and
squatters. The three major crops, in terms of area planted, of the
colored owners and renters in the province in 1899 were bananas,
Indian corn, and sweet potatoes, suggesting that they were in part
engaged in subsistence farming. Their fourth crop, however, was

[2] U.S. War Dept., *Report on the Census.* I have used two major kinds of evidence
from the census in this chapter. First, pages 403-506 of the census contain information
on occupations, divided by "race," and incorporating into one major category agriculture, fisheries, and mining. Since in most areas of Cuba the latter two activities
were only of slight significance, I have used these aggregate figures to stand for
agriculturalists alone.

Second, pages 553-64 contain information on landholding and crops cultivated.
Again, there is some imprecision. I have used the figures for rented and owned
holdings to stand for individual landholders, though it is likely that there was some
multiple rental and ownership. I have not included the figures on tenure other than
rental or ownership because these are not broken down by race. Such tenure appears
most significant in Puerto Príncipe and Santiago, and may well represent *precaristas*
or squatters. These represent some 4.5 percent of holdings.

In my discussion of these data I have used the term "colored" as it is used in the
census, to refer to those perceived by the census takers (who were Cuban, not North
American) as black, mulatto, or Asian. In the island as a whole, the "colored" population included 234,738 persons listed as Negro, 270,805 listed as Mixed, and only
14,857 listed as Chinese (p. 195).

TABLE 28
Landholding among Agriculturalists, by Province
and by Race, 1899

	Whites			Blacks, Mulattos, and Asians		
Province	Agricul-turalists	Holdings Rented or Owned	Holdings as Percentage of Agriculturalists	Agricul-turalists	Holdings Rented or Owned	Holdings as Percentage of Agriculturalists
Pinar del Río	37,163	8,527	23%	11,534	1,775	15%
Havana	25,200	5,533	22%	6,788	336	5%
Matanzas	24,912	3,470	14%	25,892	537	2%
Santa Clara	57,188	13,015	23%	24,763	2,737	11%
Puerto Príncipe	13,951	1,602	11%	3,107	171	6%
Santiago de Cuba	39,816	11,488	29%	28,883	8,783	30%
Total	198,230	43,635	22%	100,967	14,339	14%

SOURCE: U.S. War Dept., *Report on the Census of Cuba, 1899*, pp. 403-405, 555-56.

cacao, and they also cultivated a disproportionately large amount of coffee. Working 26 percent of the land in the province, they planted 59 percent of the total coffee acreage.[3]

The colored owners in Santiago de Cuba had quite different patterns of planting from those of the renters. They focused on cash crops, planting approximately 40,000 *cordeles* in cacao, 33,000 in coffee, 28,000 in bananas, 18,000 in coconuts, and 14,000 in corn. (One *cordel* equals approximately 400 square meters or about one tenth of an acre.) Colored renters, by contrast, planted their land in sweet potatoes, corn, bananas, yucca, and sugar cane, in that order.[4] These figures suggest quite different resources and priorities across the two groups, presumably reflecting, among other things, the way that planting decisions—particularly for tree crops—depended on the degree of security of tenure. Land owned by persons of color was perhaps also more likely to be poor, hilly terrain, suited to coffee and unsuited to cane, while rented land was likely to be closer to mills and thus could be used for cane in conjunction with provision

[3] See Victor Clark, "Labor Conditions in Cuba," *Bulletin of the Department of Labor* 41 (July 1902): 663-793. For crop areas, see U.S. War Dept., *Report on the Census*, pp. 558-59.
[4] U.S. War Dept., *Report on the Census*, p. 559.

crops.[5] Whatever the mix of factors influencing crop choice, there had evidently developed in the east a pattern of agriculture with a distinct peasant character and a considerable degree of market orientation.

Many of these owners and renters, however, would also have worked as wage laborers. Theirs were generally very small holdings, often too small to support a family. Eighty-two percent of the plots of colored owners and renters in the province measured less than one quarter of a *caballería*, or less than 8.3 acres, and in 1899 had under cultivation an average of just .11 *caballerías*, or about 3.6 acres, each.[6]

Several interrelated characteristics distinguished the province of Santiago de Cuba from the rest of the island, and in different degrees gave rise to this pattern of landholding. First, the province was characterized by a relatively large free population of color before emancipation. Thirty-three percent of the provincial population in 1862 were free blacks and mulattos, many of them working on small holdings.[7] Second, the agricultural organization of the east before the Ten Years' War had been distinctive: much of the economic activity of the province was not devoted to sugar, and within sugar, small-scale, technologically backward planters found themselves at a disadvantage in competition with more advanced western planters.[8] Third, as the Ten Years' War progressed, the province's distinctiveness increased. Many slaves achieved their freedom, sugar declined in importance, and blacks, mulattos, and whites fought together in the ranks of the insurgent army. By the end of the war, the rigid patterns of a slaveholding society were to a large extent broken.

[5] I would like to thank Brian Pollitt for suggesting the ecological dimension to the owner/renter differences in crop choice. The owner/renter distinction may also in part have reflected the different opportunities of former free persons of color and postemancipation migrants.

[6] For acreage, see U.S. War Dept., *Report on the Census*, pp. 556-57. In his essay, "A Note on the Definition of Peasantries," Sidney Mintz argues that one must examine Caribbean peasantries in relation to agricultural wage laborers, and calls attention to the interpenetration of the two categories. Brian Pollitt further argues that in many cases in prerevolutionary Cuba the distinction barely existed. See Sidney Mintz, "A Note on the Definition of Peasantries," *Journal of Peasant Studies* (October 1973): 91-106, and Brian Pollitt, "Agrarian Reform."

[7] Cuba, Centro de Estadística, *Noticias estadísticas*, "Censo."

[8] For more detailed discussion see Chap. I, above, and chap. 2 of Guerra, *Guerra*, 1.

The actual interaction of the process of emancipation and the development of access to land in Santiago de Cuba was a complex one. It was not simply a question of former slaves fleeing to the hills, though the tradition of rebellion and flight was strong. On the one hand, nonslave agriculture and the prevalence of smallholdings helped create the classes that backed the insurgency during the Ten Years' War, and that more directly supplied the material base to sustain that effort, including manpower and food. On the other hand, the war itself had shaped the pattern of emancipation in the eastern end of the island, and after the end of the war, in 1879, former insurgents and those who remained in slavery joined to confront planters using, among other tactics, passive resistance to labor. Because of the political climate (an unpacified rebel province) and the geography (hilly and mountainous areas adjacent to sugar lands) flight from slavery remained a plausible threat, strengthening the 1879 challenge, which further accelerated abolition in the province and in the rest of the island. The relationship between the towns, the estates, and the *monte* (hills) became increasingly fluid. General Polavieja, commander of the region, complained bitterly in 1879 that "separatist committees" in the towns were responsible daily for sending both slaves and free men into the *monte*.[9] During the 1880s, *patrocinados'* access to *conuco* lands within the estates and to the products of additional lands through free relatives who were owners or renters may well have accelerated the rate of self-purchase.

It is thus not surprising that this province, which was also geographically difficult to control and in which large-scale plantations did not yet have a monopoly of the land, was the one in which slaves and their descendants had the greatest opportunity to obtain access to small plots of land by ownership, rental, or de facto occupation.

The eastern province of Puerto Príncipe, though also the scene of a rapid decline of slavery, showed a different pattern of landholding. In 1899 there were only 3,104 male agriculturalists of color in the province, compared to 12,473 native white males, reflecting in part the small preemancipation population of color, and in part their occupational distribution. (By 1899 over 10 percent of the province's colored males were engaged in "manufacturing and mechanical in-

---

[9] On the events of 1879, see Chap. V. For Polavieja's view see his *Relación documentada*, p. 50.

dustries" in the city of Puerto Príncipe itself.)[10] Just 30 farms were operated by colored owners, 141 by colored renters. Together they occupied 42 *caballerías* of land. Thus perhaps 6 percent of the province's colored agriculturalists were renters and owners of land. They grew little sugar, concentrating on bananas, sweet potatoes, and corn. As before abolition, the major activity of the province was cattle raising, but the colored owners and renters had few of the calves, steers, or bulls, owning instead pigs and chickens.[11]

In central Santa Clara province almost 25,000, or some 30 percent, of the agriculturalists were persons of color, but only about 11 percent of them were owners or renters of land. The approximately 2,700 colored owners and renters constituted about 17 percent of the total number of owners and renters in the province and cultivated 7 percent of the land. They planted more of their land in sugar cane than anything else, after which came sweet potatoes, corn, and bananas. Clearly at least some of them had become *colonos*, growing cane to be ground at nearby mills. Some 134 of what the census referred to as sugar "plantations" (which included *colonias*) were owned by persons of color, and another 869 were rented, though these colored owners and renters planted only 5 percent of the province's cane acreage. The average size of the sugar holdings owned by persons of color was just 93 *cordeles*, and of those rented was 86 *cordeles*, compared to 481 *cordeles* and 307 *cordeles* for white owners and renters.[12]

The situation in Santa Clara province reflected, in part, its distinct pattern of transition away from slavery. Free blacks and mulattos had been a minority of the population of color before the 1870s, but there had been a significant free, smallholding population of color. Slavery had remained strong in Santa Clara up to the time of abolition, and emancipation had proceeded relatively slowly. However, the pressures for adaptation had been considerable, and plantations in the province had early turned to demobilized Spanish soldiers, Chinese contract laborers, and contracted Spanish workers. This utilization of immigrants, begun to ease the transition, continued, and by 1899 Santa Clara showed the highest proportion of foreign-born in the agricultural labor force of any province (see Table 29).

[10] U.S. War Dept., *Report on the Census*, pp. 424-26.
[11] Ibid., pp. 556-57, 563.
[12] Ibid., pp. 556-60.

TABLE 29
Composition of the Agricultural Work Force, 1899

Province	Total Number in Agriculture, Fishing, and Mining	Percent Native White	Percent Foreign White	Percent "Colored"[a]	"Colored" Population as a Percentage of Total Population
Pinar del Río	48,697	65%	11%	24%	27%
Havana	31,988	66%	13%	21%	26%
Matanzas	50,804	40%	9%	51%	42%
Santa Clara	81,951	56%	14%	30%	31%
Puerto Príncipe	17,058	73%	9%	18%	20%
Santiago de Cuba	68,699	52%	6%	42%	45%
Total	299,197	56%	10%	34%	33%

SOURCE: U.S. War Dept., *Report on the Census of Cuba, 1899*, pp. 403-405.

[a] "Colored," according to the definition of the 1899 census, included blacks, mulattos, and Chinese.

By the 1880s, the province represented a kind of middle ground. There was room for a small amount of black and mulatto landholding and some cultivation of crops other than sugar. But the great majority of the former slave population remained in wage labor. Foreign workers competed with native; North American and other *centrales* bought up the land of ruined *ingenios*; and for some laborers migration seemed the only prospect for breaking out of the old ways.

Matanzas, the archetypical province of large plantations, represented an extreme in the range of patterns of transition. Most of its *ingenios* had already become steam-powered by the 1860s, and the province contained the majority of the heavily capitalized plantations of that period. It was, at the same time, the province that had clung most persistently to slavery. The slave population still outnumbered the free population of color in 1877, and plantations still showed a heavy reliance on slave labor. Chinese indentured labor, the most tentative step toward free labor, was used extensively. But as late as 1883 Matanzas had the largest proportion of its 1862 slave population remaining in the status of *patrocinado* of any province (see Tables 10 and 25). The debate over the status of company stores gives further evidence that many planters in Matanzas continued to model their plantations along the lines of slavery into the 1880s, restricting the mobility of workers and attempting to isolate them from outside influences.[13]

The transition to free labor in Matanzas province had taken place slowly, to a large extent under the control of planters. Emancipation, when it finally arrived, depended heavily on mutual accord and the gradual freeings by age mandated under the law. Even those *patrocinados* who successfully challenged their masters or purchased their freedom had few choices once that freedom was obtained, given the domination of plantations over the land.

Not surprisingly, this was the province that by the end of the 1890s showed the smallest proportion of landowners and renters among the population of agriculturalists of color—just 537 holdings occupied by colored owners and renters, in a province with a colored agricultural population of 25,892. Colored owners and renters were thus only 2 percent of the total colored agriculturalists, and they occupied just 189 *caballerías*, less than 4 percent of the province's agricultural land.[14]

The few colored renters and owners in Matanzas planted most of their land in sugar cane, followed at a distance by bananas, sweet potatoes, and corn. There were many fewer *colonias* owned or operated by persons of color than in Santa Clara. The overwhelming majority of the people of color of Matanzas were landless agricultural workers and their families. Interestingly, Matanzas also shows the largest number of women of any province listed as agriculturalists—some 4,160 women of color along with a very few white women. This seems a clear survival from slavery; most of the women were between ages thirty-five and sixty-four, born before emancipation.[15]

The situation in Matanzas reflected in part the oligopolistic structure of land ownership in that province. There were 96 estates of 10 *caballerías* or larger (66 of them owned and operated by whites, 27 rented by whites, one rented by a person of color) representing just 2 percent of the total number of farms and controlling over 40 percent of the farmland in the province. By contrast, 1,603 farms in the province were of less than one fourth of a *caballería* and comprised just 3 percent of the total farmland.[16]

---

[13] See Chap. VIII, above, and Sobre pago de contribuciones de las tiendas de los Ingenios, AHN, Ultramar, leg. 4818, exp. 84.

[14] U.S. War Dept., *Report on the Census*, pp. 556-57, 443.

[15] Ibid., pp. 560, 404-405, 443.

[16] Ibid., pp. 556-57.

Matanzas had become the home of a true rural proletariat, hemmed in by extremely limited opportunity. Many Afro-Cubans were quick to show their dismay with this development, migrating out of the province in substantial numbers. By 1887 the proportion of the island's population of color resident in the province had fallen to 22 percent, and by 1899 to 16 percent, representing a drop of almost one third in the provincial population of color in just twelve years (see Table 27).

The rural areas of Havana province also offered little opportunity for land ownership or rental by Afro-Cubans. There, colored owners and renters numbered only 336 out of a total of 6,788 colored agriculturalists, and they cultivated just 98 *caballerías*, 3 percent of the farmland. They planted mainly sweet potatoes, sugar cane, and corn.[17] The city itself seemed to hold greater promise, and its population of color increased. This situation in part resulted from the province's dichotomous transition from slavery to free labor: slow and controlled in the countryside, relatively rapid in the city in response to pressures from slaves and their allies. As in Santiago de Cuba, the relationship between emancipation and economic opportunity went both ways: greater economic opportunity sped the transition, and the demise of slavery further increased opportunities—in this case for urban employment rather than access to land.

In Pinar del Río, at the western end of the island, the 1,775 colored owners and renters constituted 17 percent of all renters and owners and held 11 percent of the land. They grew mainly tobacco, sweet potatoes, and *malangas*. The renters and owners had roughly similar priorities in planting, except that again the few owners, as contrasted with renters, grew a disproportionately large amount of coffee and no sugar. Pinar del Río had been primarily a tobacco-producing area, and most of the colored renters and owners seem to have come from that background. There were 1,260 tobacco "plantations" rented by persons of color in 1899, equivalent to over three-quarters of the total holdings rented by persons of color. Thousands of former slaves in Pinar del Río, however, ended up without land—there were 11,534 colored agriculturalists and only 121 owners and 1,654 renters of land among them.[18]

In sum, the province most committed to sugar and to slave labor—

[17] Ibid., pp. 405, 555-58.
[18] Ibid., pp. 405, 556-60.

Matanzas—became the area most characterized by wage labor. The region least committed to slavery and sugar—the east—became the one least committed to wage labor; there peasant and semipeasant adaptations developed to the greatest extent. When, in the twentieth century, sugar plantations penetrated extensively into Oriente, they had to create and import much of their work force; they could not simply rely on continuity from the days of slavery. Santa Clara, the middle ground, showed a mix of different patterns, containing both an ethnically mixed working class and substantial numbers of *colonos*, smallholders, and subsistence farmers, often in relatively close contact with each other.

These new employment patterns of rural workers were the most obvious consequence of the shift from slavery to juridically free labor. The patterns of work, in turn, however, helped to shape the evolution of the wider Afro-Cuban community, in ways that reflected both the specific historical experience of gradual emancipation and the rapidly evolving political situation of colonial Cuba.

THE TRANSFORMATION OF THE AFRO-CUBAN COMMUNITY. During slavery, the rural and urban sectors of Afro-Cuban society had been quite distinct. In rural areas, particularly sugar regions, plantation slaves lived in relative isolation and were subjected to extreme exploitation and extreme control. Very few free persons of color lived on the sugar estates, though rural free persons of color were numerous in the small farming sector in the east and, to a lesser extent, in tobacco cultivation elsewhere. In urban areas slaves worked at a broader range of occupations, under a broader range of conditions, than their rural counterparts. Urban free persons of color suffered sharp social and economic discrimination, but they also constituted an important social group, crucial to the functioning of the economy.

With emancipation, the sharp lines dividing these groups became blurred. Free Afro-Cubans were now to be found laboring in sugar; previously free and previously bound urban workers now held the same legal status. Moreover, the links between urban and rural sectors were tightened with the advent of greater mobility for rural laborers, increasingly seasonal demand for cane workers, and a family division of labor that often saw wife and husband residing separately in town and country for part of the year.

These changes occurred within a rapidly shifting economic and political environment. The sugar industry's increasing orientation toward the U.S. market, combined with the growth of discontent and nationalist sentiment in several sectors of the Cuban population, threatened Spain's colonial hold over the island. The evolution of the Afro-Cuban community figured into this process both as cause and effect. Afro-Cubans provided a substantial pool of potential support for, or hostility to, Spanish rule, thus obliging Spain to calculate its policy on social and racial issues with an eye to the political consequences. At the same time, members of the Afro-Cuban community could take advantage of concessions made by the metropolitan government and push for further incorporation into the island's political, educational, and social life.

The transformation of the Afro-Cuban community may usefully be examined from several different perspectives. First, substantial changes occurred in the institutional basis of Afro-Cuban public life, most noticeably in the decline of the *cabildos de nación* and the growth of new forms of association. Second, social relationships, both those between the existing free population of color and the newly freed slaves and those between Afro-Cubans and whites, shifted noticeably. Third, a full-fledged political struggle for civil and political rights, carried out primarily in the towns but with echoes in the countryside as well, unfolded during the last decades of the century.

The major institutions into which Afro-Cubans could incorporate themselves during slavery were the *cabildos de nación*, semireligious organizations that grouped the African-born by their place of origin. Although part of the ideological justification for slavery had long been the Christianization and "civilization" of Africans, in practice the efforts to fully Hispanize African slaves in Cuba had been limited. Planters generally viewed serious missionary activities as expensive and possibly dangerous and blocked efforts to undertake them on plantations.[19] Moreover, for the purposes of social control the government permitted the development of *cabildos de nación*, nominally Christian groups with strong African content. Organized along "tribal" lines, composed of slaves and free blacks, these groups owned property, engaged in rituals, festivities, and activities of mu-

[19] See Hall, *Social Control*, and Martínez-Alier, *Marriage*.

265

tual aid, and received patronage from colonial officials.[20] Both slave-holders and the government apparently viewed the *cabildos* as functional under slavery because they could provide an outlet for energy and a means of self-expression that might undercut potential resistance; at the same time they isolated Africans from other sectors of society.

From the point of view of the authorities concerned with social order, however, once emancipation had begun the significance of the *cabildo* changed. The identification of former slaves with their African origins was now a threat, a countervailing loyalty that might prevent freedmen from feeling themselves to be Spaniards. Furthermore, both liberals and conservatives saw the extinction of African culture as necessary if freedmen were to be incorporated into society and become "worthy" of the rights that had recently been granted them.[21]

Cabildos now appeared to be potentially separatist organizations in which free blacks could rule themselves, isolated from the dominant culture. With their structures of leadership and their ownership of property, they might become threateningly autonomous class, ethnic, or political institutions. The police inspector of Sagua la Grande, for example, denounced the form of organization of the local *cabildo* Congo, whose constitution, he charged, resembled that of a state.[22]

The connection between emancipation and this shift in perception is quite clear. The issue that brought it into relief was the question of whether Creole children should be allowed to join African *cabildos*. In an attempt to prevent Creoles from being influenced by Africans, the government had ruled in 1868 and again in 1877 that they could not. In 1879, however, members of the *cabildo* Arriero, "de Nación Gangá Mongoba," petitioned to allow members of their *cabildo* to bring their children, who were Creoles, to participate in the activities of the group. They cited the *cabildo*'s need to raise funds, the civilized nature of their activities (which included dances with an orchestra rather than drums), the Christian precepts of the

[20] See Rogelio Martínez Furé, *Diálogos imaginarios* (Havana: Editorial Arte y Literatura, 1979), pp. 118-31; Ortiz, "Los cabildos"; and Paquette, "Conspiracy."

[21] Consulta del expediente relativo a regularizar la situación de los cabildos de negros de Africa, 1879-1881, ANC, CA, leg. 58, exp. 6105.

[22] See his statement, March 11, 1881, in AHN, Ultramar, leg. 4787, exp. 309, del. 3.

cabildo, and the desire of parents that their Creole children be incorporated into *cabildo* activities rather than associate with "gentes de mala conducta."[23]

Officials initially viewed the request as reasonable because of the respectability of the organization, and the mayor and civil government recommended approval. Allowing Creoles into the *cabildos* was thought preferable to risking their joining the *ñáñigos*, secret societies widely perceived as violent and criminal.[24] Discussion of the request, however, continued through 1880 and formal abolition, whereupon the tone of government comment shifted markedly. Instead of simply keeping the *negros de nación* (the African-born) separate from Creoles, the aim was now suppression of the *cabildos*. The *cabildos* and their dances had been allowed as a form of "compensatory" relaxation and as such were appropriate during slavery but should disappear after abolition, wrote a member of the Consejo de Administración.[25] The majority of the consejo, which still supported the *patronato*, agreed in principle that the *cabildos* should disappear, but were fearful of causing "excitation" among the *negros de nación* by forcing the rapid extinction of their organizations. Maintenance of the *cabildos*, they pointed out, had come to be seen by Africans as a right. Therefore the government should only aim at a gradual elimination through the prohibition of new members who would prolong the life of the institution.[26]

There was basic consensus within the government in Havana that the *cabildos* should cease to exist, to eliminate the memory of Africa and of slavery, and thus to ensure loyalty to Spain. Interestingly, it was Nicolás Azcárate, who believed that the *patronato* was merely a disguised form of slavery and should be abolished, who was most emphatic about the necessity for a cultural offensive against the *cabildos* and the extinction of the African heritage. His more cautious colleagues defended both the continued coercion of the *pa-*

[23] For the rationale given in the 1860s, see ANC, CA, leg. 8, exp. 562. For the subsequent petitions, see the request from Liborio Molinet and others, June 3, 1876, and Oct. 22, 1879, ANC, CA, leg. 58, exp. 6105.

[24] Opinion of the Consejo de Administración, Jan. 25, 1880, AHN, Ultramar, leg. 4787, exp. 309. For a brief description of the society of *ñáñigos*, see Moreno, *El ingenio*, 2: 38.

[25] See statement by Nicolás Azcárate, July 14, 1881, in AHN, Ultramar, leg. 4787, exp. 309, and discussion in ANC, CA, leg. 58, exp. 6105.

[26] Opinion of the majority of the Consejo de Administración, July 14, 1881, AHN, Ultramar, leg. 4787, exp. 309. See also ANC, CA, leg. 58, exp. 6105.

tronato and the continued availability of the relaxation offered by the *cabildos* and their celebrations. They did advise, however, that provincial authorities encourage the foundation of new associations with "higher" goals than those of the *cabildos*.[27]

The government in Madrid, to whom the matter was finally referred, was less sympathetic to the idea of repressing the *cabildos*. First, the ministry viewed the question of entry of Creoles as moot, since the Creole children of Africans had long taken part in *cabildo* activities without incident. Second, it was reluctant to violate the recognized rights of association of Afro-Cubans. Therefore it ruled that there should be no resolution on the request of the members of the *cabildo* Arriero, since no special permission was necessary. Laws already existed to repress any serious problems or dangers that might arise, the ministry noted, and it was to be expected that the *cabildos* would naturally evolve into different forms of association.[28]

As a result, the *cabildos* faced hostility but no legal ban and persisted in their special role as patronized Afro-Cuban organizations, subject to government supervision of their elections and meetings. One newspaper report of a *cabildo* celebration in 1882 noted that the fiesta was celebrated "with less animation than in previous years." The description of the fiesta revealed its double function, first as a form of expression, of "expansión" as the article put it, for those of African origin, and second as an occasion of ritual submission. At midday the *cabildos* appeared before the governor general, "swearing submission to the government of His Majesty in the person of its representative" and receiving gifts of money and tobacco in return.[29] The close supervision of the *cabildos* by the government, and the advanced age of their members, doubtless contributed to their conservatism and decline, as younger Afro-Cubans sought other forms of association.

Although the *cabildos* left their mark on Cuban life and culture, and some survived into the twentieth century, the predominant form of association increasingly became the mutual aid society. These

[27] Opinion of the Consejo de Administración, June 21, 1881, and opinion of Azcárate, July 7, 1881, ANC, CA, leg. 58, exp. 6105.

[28] Discussion and ruling of Feb. 13, 1883, AHN, Ultramar, leg. 4787, exp. 309.

[29] On supervision of leadership, see Expediente sobre solicitud del moreno Victor Dilemo para nombrar nuevos capataces y matronas del Cabildo Santo Rey Melchor, 1884, ANC, GG, leg. 584, exp. 28864. On the 1882 celebration, see *El Eco de Cuba* (Jan. 15, 1882).

societies were organized along various lines, sometimes still tied to particular African origin; sometimes divided by occupational status, such as artisan; sometimes founded for a particular charitable purpose, such as the aiding of children. They were by no means confined to Havana or to the cities generally: in the province of Santa Clara alone there were thirty-two Sociedades de la Raza de Color in 1889, including many in predominantly rural areas. Their names suggest both the philosophy and the purpose of such groups: El Trabajo, El Amparo, Socorros Mutuos, La Fraternidad, El Progreso, La Amistad, La Igualdad, La Luz, Las Hijas del Progreso, and so on.[30] This trend was accompanied by the proliferation of newspapers and journals written by and for members of the black and mulatto communities.[31]

The main focus of both the organizations and the new periodicals tended to be education, recreation, and social welfare, though some also had strong political overtones. Associations with an explicit political identity ranged from groups closely allied to those who would subsequently become revolutionaries (such as Juan Gualberto Gómez and the periodical *La Fraternidad*) to associations that sought approval from the Spanish government both in the old form of patronage and in the newer form of explicit political alliance. Distinctive among the latter were the various Casinos Españoles de Hombres de Color, supported by the government and the Conservative party, and led by such men as the Afro-Cuban Rodolfo de Lagardère.[32]

In addition to political divisions, there were also divisions between *pardos* and *morenos* (mulattos and blacks). Although the mulatto/black distinction did not necessarily correspond to a free person of color/freedman distinction, the two often overlapped, aggravating the social differences between those who had long been free and those who had recently been freed. Mutual aid societies could either join or separate the two groups. José Martínez-Fortun, for example, cites 1878 as the date of founding of a specifically mulatto Sociedad

[30] On the lasting effects of the *cabildos*, see Martínez Furé, *Diálogos*, pp. 126-27, and Odilio Urfé, "La música y danza en Cuba," in Moreno, *África en América Latina*, pp. 215-37. On the mutual aid societies in Santa Clara, see *La Antorcha* (Feb. 24, 1889).

[31] Pedro Deschamps Chapeaux, *El negro en el periodismo cubano en el siglo xix* (Havana: Ediciones R., 1963).

[32] See AHN, Ultramar, leg. 4884, tomo 8, exp. 140, and leg. 4884, tomo 7, exp. 131. See also Deschamps, *El negro en el periodismo*.

de Instrucción y Recreo in Remedios, with the aim of arranging education for children of color.[33]

The experience of the society for persons of color that was founded in the city of Santiago de Cuba in 1879 reflects the range of tensions and manipulations to which such groups were subject. A year after its founding the group split into two societies, one for blacks and one for mulattos. The incident that provoked the conflict was a dance to which blacks were not initially invited. The colonial government, concerned that a unified organization of persons of color might become a locus of agitation for independence, became deeply involved in the affair, as did conservative politicians who "counseled" the seceding black members of the society.[34] The government's reason for wishing to see such organizations remain weak can easily be inferred from commandant Camilo Polavieja's report from Santiago de Cuba that "the societies of recreation, instituted by persons of color" were "conspiring day and night."[35] Polavieja's own role in the split within the society is obscure. His barber was one of the main leaders of the mulattos, though Polavieja himself was not in town the night of the divisive ball. The commandant later arrested one of the leaders of the blacks as a participant in the Conspiración de la Liga Antillana, a "conspiracy" whose suppression may simply have served as a pretext for deporting prominent black and mulatto leaders.[36]

Many of the new Asociaciones de Instrucción y Recreo explicitly rejected the *pardo/moreno* distinction, and viewed themselves as representative of a larger "class of color." Nonetheless, their leaders remained ambivalent about the behavior of some of their members. Distressed organizers repeated the familiar refrain that young people were too interested in dancing and not enough in studying. Further, the absence of legal marriage among many Afro-Cubans troubled the editors of journals such as *Minerva: Revista Quincenal Dedicada a la Mujer de Color*, who entitled one article "Raza negra elévate! La Familia" and urged marriage. *La Antorcha* of Trinidad argued for a "noble crusade" to legalize black families through "in-

[33] José Martínez-Fortun, *Anales*, 3: 176.

[34] See Emilio Bacardí y Moreau, *Crónicas de Santiago de Cuba* 3 vols. (Barcelona: Carbonell y Esteva, 1908-1913; reprint ed., 10 vols., Madrid: Breogán, 1972-1973) 6: 253, 327-32, 340. See 7: 168 for identification of the Conservative party politicians.

[35] Polavieja, *Relación documentada*, p. 43.

[36] Bacardí, *Crónicas*, 6: 340, 379-81.

dissoluble unions of the sexes" and cited as areas where marriage was strongest Santiago de Cuba and Camagüey (Puerto Príncipe). *La Fraternidad*, led by Juan Gualberto Gómez, was also concerned with "moralization" but noted with satisfaction in 1889 that the "numerous marriages" that had been taking place between persons of color over the last few years proved the "moralizing tendency" of the "much slandered race."[37]

While the freeing of slaves provided a large new membership for mutual aid organizations, it created at the same time a potentially disruptive new element. *La Antorcha* of Trinidad, which identified itself as a weekly "for the defense of freedmen" and supported racial unity, decried in 1889 the recent decline of many of the Centros de Instrucción y Recreo, deploring the fact that

A multitude of men who barely if at all knew what it meant to join together in societies, without knowing any other agreeable pastimes except "banquets" and "dances," entered into the societies and there were received and gratified with the same practices. What could one expect from such individuals?[38]

Despite this patronizing attitude toward the new members, *La Antorcha* continued to urge people of color to join such societies.

Postemancipation social relationships within the Afro-Cuban community, and between Afro-Cubans and whites, reflected the previous history of such relations in Cuba as well as the nature of the process of emancipation. Cuba's social structure had long been a complex mixture of class and caste, in many ways encouraging free persons of color to minimize their ties with slaves, though the division had never been fully effective or absolute.[39] The process of gradual emancipation had probably, on balance, strengthened the ties between slaves and free persons of color. Certainly in the eastern end of the island, the shared experience of war helped to break down distinctions, though tensions still persisted in the social hierarchy of the city of Santiago de Cuba. Elsewhere, the processes of self-purchase and litigation against masters encouraged cooperation and

[37] *Minerva* (Nov. 30, 1888); *La Antorcha* (April 14, 1889); *La Fraternidad* (May 13, 1889).

[38] *La Antorcha* (Jan. 13, 1889).

[39] See Chap. I, above; Martínez-Alier, *Marriage*; Knight, *Slave Society*; and Paquette, "Conspiracy."

made for gradual incorporation of family members into the category of free persons of color.

The choices of issues and activities by the new associations could either exacerbate or minimize tensions between blacks and mulattos, or between free men and freedmen. Two of the most distinctive incidents of mulatto/black separation are illustrative. In the first situation, the divisions within the society of persons of color in Santiago de Cuba focused around an event, a ball, which quickly raised the possibility of social exclusivity and resulting bitterness. Furthermore, the conflict seems to have been much exacerbated by the opportunistic behavior of white politicians seeking both a split in the Afro-Cuban community and alliance with its fragments. The second incident was the establishment of an exclusively mulatto Círculo de Obreros in Santa Clara, which reflected the eagerness of artisans to distinguish themselves as well as to assert social hierarchy.[40] When categories of occupation and ethnicity overlapped, the possibility of exclusivism in trade groups was heightened.

Two powerful forces worked against disunity in the Afro-Cuban community, however. The first was the existence of widespread white prejudice against persons of color, both black and mulatto, and the second was the possibility of benefits for all Afro-Cubans through concerted political action, sometimes in partial alliance with sectors of the white community. Both of these forces emerge clearly in the struggle for civil rights that emerged in the very late 1870s and continued into the 1880s and 1890s.

Education was the initial focus of this struggle. In choosing to work on the issue of education, the new Afro-Cuban associations and societies expressed their own vision of mobility and uplift through self-improvement and responded to the drastic inequality of educational opportunity existing in Cuba. (Afro-Cubans were underrepresented in primary education, even less numerous in secondary education, and virtually absent in the private schools to which many white parents sent their children.)[41] For both free per-

[40] See the discussion in *El Horizonte* (June 10, 1884).

[41] Black children attended public schools in disproportionately small numbers. In the province of Matanzas in 1884 there were 4,993 white children enrolled in schools and 1,118 children of color, though the provincial population of color was around 45 percent of the total. There were similar imbalances in other provinces. In Santa Clara in 1881 the numbers were 5,858 white children, 1,296 of color; in Santiago de Cuba in 1882, 2,952 versus 1,133. For enrollment figures, see Memoria semestral de la

sons of color and former slaves, the struggle for education seemed to promise an avenue to social and occupational mobility.[42] For some white liberals, asserting the importance of education for Afro-Cubans was a means of arguing for the primacy of social over racial factors in the existing disparities of status, opportunity, and "culture."[43] And for conservative Spanish administrators, granting concessions on this front might gain valued political support from a significant portion of the population.

Social relations had not, however, evolved to the point that such integration would be easily accomplished. In 1878 the Junta Superior de Instrucción Pública had ruled that persons of color could be admitted into secondary schools, professional schools, and the university, and in 1879 the society *El Progreso* of Guanabacoa won a ruling to allow children of color into the local public schools.[44] In Cienfuegos persons of color petitioned the provincial governor for the founding of schools for children of color, and rather than convert existing schools for whites, the governor ordered children of color admitted into the municipal schools.[45] In 1888, however, *La Fraternidad* attacked the government for failing to enforce the ruling that allowed men of color to attend secondary schools and the university.[46] And in 1889 it was still news that the Junta Provincial of Santiago de Cuba had ruled that children of color could attend municipal schools.[47]

A continued pattern of official concession followed by non-enforcement set the tone of the struggle over integration in Cuba. The colonial government had every reason to seek the support of the leadership of the very substantial population of color. Initially hostile and fearful of moves toward integration, the government quickly

Diputación Provincial de Matanzas, AHN, Ultramar, leg. 4819, exp. 142; *Boletín Oficial de la Hacienda de la Isla de Cuba,* Feb. 15, 1882, and April 30, 1882; *Boletín Oficial de la Provincia de Santa Clara,* June 5, 1881; and Bacardí, *Crónicas* 6: 351.

[42] On the importance of this goal for former slaves and their descendants elsewhere in the Caribbean, see, for example, Rodney, *A History,* p. 116.

[43] Enrique José Varona was an important proponent of this view. Manuel Moreno Fraginals, personal communication, 1982.

[44] For references to the 1878 ruling see "Las razas ante las leyes y las costumbres," *Estudios Afrocubanos* 1 (1937): 148. On the petition in Guanabacoa, see *La Fraternidad* (May 18, 1879).

[45] Edo y Llop, *Memorias,* p. 814.

[46] *La Fraternidad* (July 9, 1888). This reference is from Tomás Fernández Robaina's forthcoming bibliography on Afro-Cuban history.

[47] *La Fraternidad* (Feb. 21, 1889).

found that this was an issue on which virtually all of the organizations of color felt strongly. Even the tame Casino Español de Hombres de Color raised the question.[48] Formal agreement, it was evidently hoped, might quiet this agitation. Real enforcement, however, was not to be expected.

The opportunism of the government's behavior, however, was transparent and did not quiet the agitation of the Sociedades. As the colonial government increasingly came to view maintenance of Afro-Cuban loyalty as a key to avoiding the outbreak of revolution, official pronouncements became more favorable to their petitions. In 1893 men of color were legally empowered to use the title "Don," though white public opinion in some areas still scoffed at such a pretention. The same year the governor general ruled that children of color should be admitted to primary schools and called for general school integration to reduce race prejudice.[49]

Enforcement of these rules, too, was ineffectual. Conservative sectors continued to support segregated education, drawing on the U.S. example. Though liberal newspapers such as *La Discusión* upheld integration, even some Afro-Cuban societies turned in despair to segregated schools. One newspaper published in Cienfuegos lamented the fact that children of color were the targets of hostility in the municipal schools, and called for the setting up of separate schools. In 1889 they wrote that social preoccupation with race was every day becoming more intense and that "it is not possible for us to send our children to a place where if they are admitted by the law, they are the target of foul old prejudices."[50]

On the question of the integration of public places, members of the Sociedades and others were also quick to bring suit. Again, the government attempted to concede the point while avoiding the issue. The Consejo de Administración wrote in 1881 that the government should not force the owners of cafés and public establishments to accept persons of color, because it should not attempt to impose

[48] Consulta sobre lo promovido por D. Casimiro Bernabeu, July 27, 1881, ANC, CA, leg. 68, exp. 6799.

[49] Trelles, *Biblioteca histórica cubana*, 2: 428, and (Rafael María de Labra), *La raza de color en Cuba* (Madrid: Fortanet, 1894), p. 34.

[50] The citation from the Cienfuegos newspaper may be found in Deschamps, *El negro en el periodismo*, p. 14. Debate on integration and segregation may be found in the *Diario de la Marina* of March 1, 1879, and *Discusión* of March 4, 1879, according to Manuel Moreno Fraginals. Personal communication, 1982.

equality by force on existing customs. In a remarkable though inadvertent commentary on Cuba's particular combination of class and racial distinctions, they predicted that third- and second-class cafés would thus continue to admit persons of color, and first-class cafés would admit those persons of color distinguished in letters or arts, "as we have seen many times." Thus, they claimed, café owners could avoid "confusion" that would alienate their white clientele. They advised free men of color to trust in time and the growing culture of their class to bring about social equality.[51] In 1885, however, the governor general ruled that, except in cases of scandal, persons of color could not be prohibited from entering parks or establishments open to the public. And in 1887 the Consejo de Administración ruled that persons of color could not be excluded from the first-class coaches of trains.[52]

In the absence of concerted government efforts at enforcement, blacks and mulattos had to attempt to carry out these rulings themselves. Hostility and confrontation sometimes resulted, giving the lie to the notion of a perfectly peaceful incorporation of the descendants of slaves into Cuban life. La Fraternidad in 1888 regretted the hostility to school integration that had been encountered, a hostility so substantial that it effectively blocked children from entering schools to which they had a right of access.[53] The periodical La Igualdad reported in 1892 that merchants were refusing to obey the ruling that obliged them to do business with persons of color, and that certain "agents of authority" had refused to enforce it.[54] There were also echoes of the kind of violence associated with a search for greater rights by former slaves in other societies: La Fraternidad reported in 1888 that there had been an attack on men of color by the "guardians of order" in Havana, with the result that the streets of Havana were almost empty of blacks, "they being fearful that such an event might be repeated with them."[55]

Though they were able to a limited extent to make some of their views felt through their organizations and the press, Afro-Cubans did not have full voting rights. In addition to other restrictions or:

[51] ANC, CA, leg. 68, exp. 6799.
[52] (Labra), La raza, pp. 33-34. See also "Las razas" in Estudios Afrocubanos, pp. 146-47.
[53] La Fraternidad (July 9, 1888), p. 2.
[54] La Igualdad (Dec. 30, 1892), p. 2, cited in the Fernández Robaina bibliography.
[55] La Fraternidad (Feb. 20, 1888), cited in the Fernández Robaina bibliography.

the franchise, the electoral law of 1882 held that those who had been in slavery did not have the right to vote until after they had been exempt from the *patronato* for three years.[56] By 1888, however, this distinction was rapidly becoming moot, and political parties were vying for the votes of those Afro-Cubans who could meet the criteria for suffrage.

El País, the organ of the Liberal party, argued that it recognized no distinction between black and white and supported the elimination of the distinctions that still remained in the legal code (such as that making the commission of a crime by a black person against a white an aggravating circumstance in determining punishment). *La Fraternidad*, edited by an Afro-Cuban, however, was dubious of the commitments of the Liberal/Autonomists, and charged them with discrimination. *El País*, in a somewhat curious defense, regretted that there had ever been black immigration to Cuba and cited Montalvo's call for exclusively white immigration; it argued, nevertheless, that given the fact that there *were* persons of color in Cuba they should have the same civil and political rights. The Liberals further tried to win Afro-Cuban support by calling on them to remember who had fought battles for them in the past.[57]

An accurate recalling of the Liberals' past record might or might not win them Afro-Cuban support. While their party had eventually endorsed abolition and supported some *patrocinados'* efforts, they had also maintained an attitude toward persons of color that was both condescending and authoritarian. Believing in a civilizing mission for whites, and insisting that whites would have to exercise a "benign and generous tutelage" over an "incapacitated" black race, Cuban liberals showed considerable prejudice in the 1880s. Historian Raúl Cepero Bonilla wrote bitterly: "The autonomists continued thinking in the same racist terms as the ideologues of the class of slaveholding *hacendados*. The black was either eliminated or dominated."[58]

Conservatives, on the other hand, carried a long legacy of reactionary, pro-Spanish thought. Though occasionally effective at

---

[56] See article 34 of the electoral law of 1882 in AHN, Ultramar, leg. 4928, exp. 239.
[57] *El País* (Dec. 8, 1888).
[58] See the quotations from *El Triunfo* on pp. 216, 217 of Cepero Bonilla, *Azúcar y abolición*, and his own judgment on p. 217. For a more favorable view of the Liberals, see Entralgo, *La liberación étnica*.

pointing out liberal inconsistencies on racial issues, they had little basis on which to argue that they had served the interests of Afro-Cubans. Their hope for gaining votes lay in the efforts of the Spanish government to ally with select groups of Afro-Cubans, and they carried on a campaign through loyalist newspapers, a variety of which were edited by Lagardère.[59] Persons of color thus found themselves courted politically, and had the opportunity to take advantage of divisions among the white ruling groups, though always at the risk of finding their support manipulated by new patrons.

The struggle for civil rights in Cuba in the latter part of the nineteenth century was a remarkable phenomenon that soon took on a distressingly familiar pattern: multiple initiatives from Afro-Cubans followed by nominal concessions by officials, all within a framework of continued economic hardship and social discrimination. What is perhaps most distinctive about the struggle is that it took place in the context of a colonial society in which many civil rights were not granted to white Cubans either. Instead of a society with a tradition of popular participation or an ideology of democracy, this was a society that placed strict limitations on political and civil rights.[60] The particular political climate of the last decades of the century gave to the Cuban civil rights movement some of its special character, including the participation of otherwise highly reactionary individuals, like Lagardère, who sought to guarantee colonial domination through racial integration.

The evolution of social relations after emancipation in some ways paralleled the dynamics of emancipation itself. One reason for the government's willingness to abolish slavery had been a desire to avoid the further development of support by Afro-Cubans for revolutionary movements. Once abolition was granted, however, the problem of order did not go away. Spain, in the closing years of the nineteenth century, was in the process of conceding certain reforms and a degree of autonomy to Cuba in hopes of staving off further conflict. This trend toward increased formal rights created a situation in which some specific advances could be made toward the legal

[59] Deschamps, *El negro en el periodismo.*
[60] For some general observations on civil rights in postemancipation societies, see Magnus Mörner, "Igualdad legal, desigualdad social," in his *Historia social latinoamericana (Nuevos enfoques)* (Caracas: Universidad Católica Andrés Bello, 1979), pp. 271-91. He emphasizes the importance of a prior democratic tradition.

equality of the races. But concessions that were intended simply to stave off conflict presented the same problems in the 1890s that they had in the 1880s, when an astute governor had noted that although persuading masters to treat their *patrocinados* well was the best way to ensure peace, punishing masters for treating their *patrocinados* badly was distinctly dangerous.[61] Conceding the rights of Afro-Cubans to enter schools and restaurants seemed one way to ensure their loyalty; enforcing such rights, however, might raise a host of other problems that the Spanish government had no desire to face.

By the end of the century, then, Afro-Cubans faced limited and highly uneven opportunities for landholding and employment combined with partial social advancement and continued social discrimination. How they would interpret and respond to this situation would help determine whether Spain could maintain control over the island of Cuba itself.

[61] Letter from the governor general, Sept. 15, 1880, AHN, Ultramar, leg. 4884, tomo 7, exp. 86.

XII

Conclusion and Epilogue

The gradual abolition of slavery in Cuba, involving an intermediate status and a prolonged transition to free labor, resulted from the special circumstances of Cuban slavery and its particular domestic and international context. The Cuban sugar economy needed new workers to compensate for the ending of the international slave trade, while at the same time planters wished to maintain control over their enslaved work force. Spain sought to safeguard the colonial tie and to resolve the volatile issue of slavery in a way that was minimally disruptive. Gradual abolition was designed to meet these needs. The Moret Law and the *patronato* prevented mass freeings and sudden changes in the number of available workers, while opening the way for immigration and the reorganization of the labor force. Moreover, by incorporating slaves into elaborate—if ad hoc—legal processes, the government attempted to give gradualism a kind of legitimacy in the eyes of slaves. Freedom was to remain something one earned or achieved, not something to which one was simply entitled.

To a degree, the gradualist strategy worked. Disruption in the supply of labor was largely avoided, and many planters did not have to face a labor supply that was primarily composed of free workers until 1882 or 1883. The artificially low wages of *patrocinados* and the unpaid labor of minors, in conjunction with the continued legality of corporal punishment until 1883, meant that much of the system of slavery was maintained until almost the last minute. The gradual reincorporation of some freed *patrocinados* into the plantation labor force, the replacement of others by Chinese workers, convicts, demobilized Spanish soldiers, and *colonos* facilitated adaptation on plantations. While the total wages paid by planters increased as the free sector of their work force expanded, the amount paid to individual workers did not increase as sharply as it might have had emancipation led to a widespread labor shortage created

279

by abrupt withdrawals of labor by former slaves in the absence of adequate replacement workers. The more marked seasonality that characterized the employment of free labor also operated to planters' advantage, relieving them of the direct maintenance costs of their workers during the dead season. At the same time, of course, it made them vulnerable to a shortage of laborers during the crucial months of the harvest—a vulnerability they were able to mitigate in part as long as they could maintain the *patronato*.

Gradualism also partially achieved its goal of incorporating slaves into legalistic processes for achieving freedom. Many *patrocinados* were drawn into the "legal culture" through the mechanisms of complaint, appeal, and self-purchase.[1] An episode involving worker grievances after abolition reflects the lasting effects of this partial incorporation: Following a disturbance on the *ingenio* Roque in Matanzas in 1889, the laborers went to the *alcalde* of the nearby municipality to complain that they had been fired without receiving the wages owed them. The event in some ways resembled an uprising on a slave plantation—the workers were reported as being *amotinados* (rioting) and the Civil Guard was called in. Yet in other ways it resembled an appeal to a Junta de Patronato—the workers reported to the mayor that they had neither food nor lodging, and they were then cared for at the municipal offices.[2]

The importance and, ultimately, success of gradualism in achieving an incorporation of former slaves into the rules of the game should not, however, be exaggerated. *Patrocinados'* alternatives were few. Running away remained a difficult and dangerous option under the *patronato*, and collective resistance to labor was treated as virtual mutiny, as in the case of the plantation in Güines in the early 1880s where the army was called in to suppress *patrocinados* who demanded the right to leisure on a customary holiday, with the result that nine of the resisters were shot.[3] To the extent that gradualism simply concealed or relied upon continued repression, it fooled almost no one.

Cuban abolition thus left another conflictual legacy, for masters had been allowed to determine much of the nature of the transition.

[1] I am grateful to Thomas Flory for suggesting the term "legal culture" in this context.
[2] *El Productor* (April 11, 1889).
[3] See Ballou, *Due South*, p. 63.

By forestalling real change through the *patronato,* and maintaining corporal punishment, gradual abolition did not require planters to break their habits of direct coercion. Physical punishment of workers persisted even after emancipation, as did economic coercion through company stores. In some cases the coercive patterns were so severe that workers emigrated rather than be subjected to them, with the embarrassing result that employers were driving workers away in the midst of an alleged "labor shortage."[4]

Even as the *patronato* drew many former slaves into legal procedures and self-purchase, perhaps in ways that discouraged overt conflict, it also provided openings for challenge and contention. When *patrocinados* took seriously the limited opportunities the *patronato* offered for extending their rights, they called into question the legitimacy of their masters' rule and gained experience in confronting it. To the extent that *patrocinados'* behavior involved elements of resistance as well as accommodation, the government strategy of gradualism cannot be said to have fully accomplished its goal of preserving authority intact.

This experience of challenging the established order shaped postemancipation political responses as well. Those Afro-Cubans who pressed for full civil rights in the aftermath of final abolition were not, in the main, recently freed field slaves. Yet among them were undoubtedly some of the earlier free black and mulatto allies of *patrocinados,* individuals who had learned in the juntas the tactics of complaint, challenge, and appeal. The movement for civil rights in turn drew some of its strength from the incorporation of former slaves into the new mutual aid and educational societies. (One might draw a parallel with Louisiana, where free persons of color in New Orleans lobbied the federal government during the Civil War to hasten the transition to free labor in the occupied zones of the state and then subsequently emerged with new potential allies in the campaign for fuller civil rights.)[5]

By providing a measure of autonomy and room for challenge on the part of *patrocinados,* gradual emancipation also raised their expectations. Had abolition been accompanied by substantial improve-

[4] For evidence of emigration from Cuba to work on the Panama Canal, see Edo y Llop, *Memoria,* p. 976. He mentions the departure of 200 workers in December 1885.
[5] See C. Peter Ripley, *Slaves and Freedmen in Civil War Louisiana* (Baton Rouge: Louisiana State University Press, 1976), especially chaps. 4 and 9.

ments in other areas of economic and political life, it might conceivably have brought about a willing incorporation of former slaves into the existing society. The conclusion that must be drawn from the Afro-Cuban struggle for civil rights and from the pattern of postemancipation adaptations and access to land, however, is that such improvements were few. Certain choices could now be made that were not previously available; some families were reconstituted; new modes of life took shape. But the vast majority of former slaves remained landless and powerless.

To evaluate the full meaning of emancipation for former slaves requires a careful attention to perspective. From the vantage point of the study of slavery, emancipation is by definition a liberation. Even if the freedom of former slaves is highly compromised, nonetheless there has been a crucial change in legal and social status. The means by which their labor is commanded have also shifted in ways that are important to their employers and to the larger economic system. If, on the other hand, one approaches emancipation from the vantage point of the study of labor systems in Latin America, where the succession of forms of slavery, disguised slavery, peonage, contract labor, and so forth is depressingly familiar, it may seem that the changes in the institutions under which labor is extracted are almost epiphenomenal, for the essential facts of coercion and hardship remain.

Neither perspective is fully adequate, for slavery was at once a labor system and a social system. Its weight was felt by its victims both as a forced obligation to perform unpaid labor in tasks not freely chosen and as a series of abuses and restraints on personal mobility, autonomy, and dignity. Emancipation involved different degrees of escape from different aspects of bondage, and no simple comparison of "standards of living" before and after can capture the process.[6] Moreover, as we have seen, the range of postemancipation experiences was wide, even among former field slaves, and was marked by sharp regional variations.

It is thus by no means easy to attempt a comparison between

[6] The claim by Louis Pérez, Jr., for example, that "the decline of the standard of living for former slaves after emancipation was as immediate as it was dramatic," thus misses part of the point: that many of the elements that a full definition of "standard of living" comprises were incommensurate before and after slavery. See Pérez, *Cuba between Empires*, p. 23.

emancipation in Cuba and emancipation elsewhere. One may compare specific aspects of the process, but the variety of patterns within Cuba and within other slave societies tempers any attempt at broad generalization.[7] Ideally, one might narrow the field of comparison, drawing out precise parallels and divergences between the experience of emancipation in different regions that shared the same major crop as Cuba and experienced abolition in the second half of the nineteenth century. But to do so effectively would require an entirely separate empirical study of, for example, sugar-producing regions of Brazil, Cuba, and the United States. In the absence of such a full-scale comparative study, however, it is worth highlighting several aspects of Cuban emancipation that emerge as distinctive when compared with the transition to free labor elsewhere. I shall not reiterate here the particular importance of gradualism itself or the complex combination of intransigence and adaptability that characterized the Cuban planter class, which have been discussed throughout this study. I shall focus instead on the political context of Cuban emancipation, the character of Spanish and Cuban abolitionism, and the status of the Cuban sugar industry.

The political context of abolition in Cuba was distinctive in several important ways. As Spain's major remaining New World colony, and at the same time an island with an increasingly vigorous anticolonial movement, Cuba posed a political problem for its mother country that often overshadowed the issue of slavery itself. Emancipation legislation was thus designed and implemented with an eye to its effect on rebels and potential rebels as well as on slaves and masters. At the same time, because the island's sugar industry was a major source of revenue to Spain, colonial policy on slavery was very sensitive to the real or imagined effects of abolition on output. One could contrast this with the situation of the British government in Jamaica, which, while often deferential to the needs of planters, was prepared to contemplate a degree of decline in the sugar industry. Britain's role as a consumer of sugar grown elsewhere, and as

[7] For a work on the U.S. that emphasizes both the daunting variety of experiences and the existence of certain patterns within emancipation, see Ira Berlin, Joseph P. Reidy, Leslie S. Rowland, eds., *Freedom: A Documentary History of Emancipation, 1861-1867.* Series II: *The Black Military Experience* (Cambridge, England: Cambridge University Press, 1982). Further volumes forthcoming. See also Leon Litwack, *Been in the Storm So Long: The Aftermath of Slavery* (New York: Alfred A. Knopf, 1979).

an ideological champion of the notion of free labor, could transcend the specific claims of a particular colonial planter class.[8]

The ideological atmosphere in Spain also contrasts with the situation in Britain. Spain's liberals had long been prepared to overlook the apparent anomaly of the existence of slavery in Spain's colonies, and only in the 1860s and 1870s did an abolitionist movement arise in Spain itself. Even then, the movement's effectiveness was hampered by the overwhelming importance of the colonial question. The reasons for this reticence on the part of Spanish liberals are not entirely clear, and one of the interesting questions that remains is to trace the links between this reticence and the political and economic situation of Spain. But "free labor" in the colonies was in any event not an essential component of prevailing economic thought in Spain, and the nature of discussion on the issue of slavery was somewhat narrow: moral imperatives were counterposed to colonial interests, and as such carried only limited weight.

Similarly, within Cuba the abolitionist movement was small and late to develop. Here Brazil provides a contrast, for there both the relative economic eclipse of some slaveholding regions and the growth of important nonslave sectors combined to permit the development of a domestic abolitionist movement. Although this movement was strong only in the very last years of slavery, it nonetheless stands out as a far more vigorous and extensive domestic phenomenon than the small-scale and informal Cuban abolitionist movement. While some Cuban abolitionists were willing to provide legal advice to some *patrocinados*, Brazilian abolitionists actively encouraged slaves to flee from the plantations.[9] It is not that Cuba lacked radicals, but rather that uncompromising opposition to slavery tended to be found among anti-Spanish rebels, who expressed it in conjunction with views entirely unacceptable to the colonial political system. Again, the links between colonialism and slavery served to narrow the field of politically accepted debate.

The Cuban sugar industry may also be contrasted with the Brazilian. While Cuba attempted with notable success to meet an ex-

[8] My thinking on the question of Jamaica is much influenced by Thomas Holt, "The Problem of Freedom," and by conversations with Thomas Holt and Sidney Mintz.

[9] See Conrad, *Destruction*; Toplin, *Abolition*, and Viotti da Costa, *Da Senzala*. I am also grateful to Peter Eisenberg for various personal communications on the Brazilian case.

panding U.S. market, Brazilian sugar producers languished under the difficulties of high transportation costs, limited markets, and lack of capital. The effects were felt both during the process of abolition and during postemancipation adaptations, when former slaves in the sugar regions of Brazil tended to become personally dependent on their former masters, in a situation already characterized by surplus population.[10] While the move toward central mills faltered in Brazil, it took hold with remarkable speed in Cuba, transforming the economic landscape, though not necessarily for the better, for ex-slaves and other workers.

The political outcomes of emancipation in the Cuban case are difficult to disentangle from the larger political conflicts surrounding the island's colonial status. But it is apparent that the government made no effort to influence and mediate the integration of former slaves into the new society comparable to the efforts of the Freedmen's Bureau or the legislation that accompanied Reconstruction in the United States. There did not exist within the Cuban and Spanish elite a significant body of strongly abolitionist thinking that might carry with it socially radical implications; nor was there a sufficiently powerful competing fragment of the elite interested in reordering society to diminish the role of planters; nor had Cuba's slaveholders been defeated in war. While race relations immediately after slavery in Cuba did not generally show the virulent racism for which the United States became infamous, neither did Afro-Cubans have major allies among local officials in their efforts to improve their social and economic status.

As the island entered the final decade of the nineteenth century, it was the colonial question that emerged as the major point of overt conflict, linking as it did political, social, and economic grievances. Planters were increasingly aware that high production did not invariably lead to prosperity and that prosperity when it came was tenuous. Spain had negotiated the 1891 Foster-Cánovas treaty to improve the access of Cuban sugar to U.S. markets, but upon expiration of that treaty in 1894 the United States imposed heavy new tariffs in the Wilson-Gorman Tariff Act, and Spain reimposed its own tariff barriers on Cuba. Spain was thus reactivating and inten-

[10] See Peter L. Eisenberg, *The Sugar Industry in Pernambuco, 1840-1910: Modernization without Change* (Berkeley: University of California Press, 1974), especially chaps. 2, 3, 8.

sifying the *pacto colonial*, increasing its protectionism and its exactions from the island at an exceptionally sensitive moment. Moreover, the process of consolidation that had yielded the huge new *centrales* also put pressure on smaller units, and hundreds of *ingenios* were going out of business. In a general report on the economy in 1894, the *Revista de Agricultura*, organ of the Planters' Association, expressed an increasing sense of desperation.[11]

The crisis, of course, threatened small-scale growers as well as major planters. Falling prices meant lower returns to *colonos*, whose contracts had usually been designed to shift to them some of the risk associated with uncertain sugar prices. Some *colonos* had responded to their dependence on the *centrales* with efforts to organize common bargaining units among themselves. Juan Bautista Jiménez, a prosperous *colono* with inherited lands, was an early proponent of such organizations.[12] Perhaps more representative was José Badia, a former *colono* on the Central Teresa, in Santiago de Cuba. When asked during court testimony about grievances on the estate in the 1890s, he explained that he had disagreed with the estate owner about prices and that around 1895 the owner had bought him out "to avoid misunderstanding." Under cross-examination he was queried: "The disagreement about prices that you mention arose from a Union of the Colonos on all the estates; did it not, and which Union demanded an increase over the prices which had been theretofore agreed upon, isn't that so?" "Yes," he replied, "that's it."[13]

It would be wrong to assume that all *colonos* shared the contentiousness of Jiménez and Badia. *Colonos* were a heterogeneous group, some clearly identifying with other employers of labor, others on the margin between the status of worker and that of farmer. But continued conflicts over prices and contracts strained relations between estates and their tenants and suppliers, making it less likely that *colonos* would close ranks behind the established order when it faced attack from certain directions.

[11] See *Revista de Agricultura*, Special number (1894), particularly pp. 334-72, 442-44. For an excellent discussion of the atmosphere of the 1890s, see Pérez, *Cuba between Empires*, chap. 1. On the reinvigoration of the *pacto colonial*, and its consequences for Cuba, see Jordi Nadal, *El fracaso de la revolución industrial en España, 1814-1913* (Barcelona: Ariel, 1975) pp. 215-17.

[12] See Jiménez, *Los esclavos blancos*.

[13] Deposition of José Badia, USNA, RG 76, Entry 352, Claim no. 97 (Central Teresa), Pt. 2.

The economic crisis affected others in Cuban society as well. A decline in the sugar industry meant unemployment for a wide range of workers. Increased tariffs meant higher prices for consumer goods. Moreover, the sugar industry was so central to the Cuban economy that other sectors inevitably suffered. Though planters could not claim to speak for the whole society in their complaints, their distress was undoubtedly widely shared.

It is seldom easy to establish a simple chain of causation between crisis and grievance, on the one hand, and social upheaval, on the other. Most planters frustrated by Spanish economic and political policy were in no mood to unleash revolution; many of those seeking revolution had done so since long before the crisis. But it was into this tense atmosphere that in 1895 insurgency erupted once again in the eastern part of the island. It was led this time by the Cuban Revolutionary Party, unified under the leadership of José Martí, Máximo Gómez, and Antonio Maceo. The eastern region, traditionally an area of resistance to Spanish rule, responded to the insurgent call to arms, and by February 1895 the insurrection had a stronghold on the island.[14]

It is far beyond the scope of this study to analyze in detail the history of the Cuban War for Independence and its social base. There are, however, at least two features of that conflict relevant to the theme of emancipation and postemancipation society: first, the participation of Afro-Cubans in the insurrection; and second, the effects of the reorganization of production on the possibilities for popular political mobilization.

It is hardly surprising that former slaves and other Afro-Cubans were potential recruits for an insurrection in the 1890s. While it is difficult from the limited evidence available to infer actual motivations and grievances, the expectations of Afro-Cubans seem to have been increasingly disappointed. Slaves in Cuba had often been the agents of their own emancipation, and had reason to believe that their lives would change significantly as a result. But while they now had greater physical mobility, the opportunity to earn cash wages, and greater access to urban centers, they had little opportunity to acquire land or increase their incomes. They found their way blocked by the new forms of plantation production, by the influx

[14] See Pérez, *Cuba between Empires*, chap. 2.

of immigrants, by frequent unemployment, and by the persistence of racial and ethnic barriers. Political organizers willing to face the issue of race, to repudiate continued Spanish domination and the hierarchical distinctions such domination brought, and to challenge the prevailing economic order, had strong arguments with which to win Afro-Cubans over to participation in an anticolonial struggle.

At the same time, the experiences of former slaves and other Afro-Cubans had increased their capacity to mobilize politically. The family strategy whereby many couples divided their residence, with the woman employed in town and the man working on an estate during the week, helped to develop ties between the town and the country and decreased the isolation that had characterized life on the *ingenios*. The spread of mutual aid societies and Afro-Cuban newspapers provided experience in cooperative action and exposure to new ideas. Not surprisingly, some Afro-Cuban leaders from these organizations moved into openly anti-Spanish positions in the last years of the century.

The new insurgency was considerably less ambiguous on social and racial issues than the Ten Years' War had been. The great ideologue of the new struggle, José Martí, explicitly rejected annexation to the United States, criticized the island's elite, and repudiated racial divisions. The Manifesto of Montecristi, signed by Martí and Máximo Gómez as the fight began, hailed the unity between those who had been slaves and those who had not, and noted the progress made away from the "hatred with which slavery was able to divide them." Though the document also reflected some uneasiness about the potential "censurable haste" of a small minority of "discontented freedmen," its predominant tone was one of egalitarianism.[15] The charismatic Antonio Maceo, moreover, a leader of the earlier struggle, brought to the leadership of the new one a long record of uncompromising rejection of both slavery and racism.

The concept of "Cuba Libre" espoused by the insurgent leadership appealed to Afro-Cubans through both nationalism and an ideology of universal manhood suffrage and racial equality.[16] The insurgent force itself was clearly multiracial and multiclass, with a very strong popular character. Afro-Cubans often rose to positions of leadership within the rebel forces and experienced an equality with white

[15] For the text, see Hortensia Pichardo, ed., *Documentos para la historia de Cuba* 1: 483-91.
[16] See Pérez, *Cuba between Empires*, chaps. 16-18.

troops that transcended that which had been possible in the Ten Years' War. Those who opposed the insurrection described the rebels with a contempt that reveals both their own class prejudices and the class divisions they perceived. Edwin Atkins, a North American planter, recalled: "... of the insurgents—I personally knew very little. They were composed of men entirely outside my circle of acquaintance, very many of them being negroes, and a very large part of them being ignorant white Cubans."[17] Indeed, one of the leaders of a band raiding Atkins' Soledad estate was a former slave on the estate, Claudio Sarria.[18]

The earlier insurrection had also drawn in part on poor whites and free persons of color for its support, but in crucial respects the larger environment had now changed. Class relations on the new *centrales* lacked the rigidity and isolation of those on the slave *ingenios* of the 1860s and 1870s. In the normal course of events men now came and went to the *batey*, the fields, and the outlying *colonias* from both within and without the estate. Instead of controlling large numbers of bound workers who were locked in at night and prohibited from setting foot off the estate during the day, estates now relied on a fluctuating population of artisans and laborers. The shift to seasonal wage labor, combined with the decentralization of growing inherent in the system of *colonias*, had made the complex of fields and mill penetrable and vulnerable.

Even when estate owners were hostile to the rebels, insurgents were able to approach the plantations for recruits, for goods, for horses and oxen, and for weapons. Once they had moved into the sugar zones, insurgents could thus count upon estate populations for various kinds of informal support—a crucial change since the Ten Years' War. Some estate owners drew the contrast explicitly, complaining that they had been able to grind without interruption during the earlier conflict but now could not protect themselves against cane fires, financial exactions, and the "demoralization" of their work force.[19] Furthermore, the disruption of production freed still more workers as potential recruits for the insurgents.

[17] For a general discussion of the insurgent force, see Pérez, *Cuba between Empires*, pp. 106-108. The quotation from Atkins is in Deposition of Edwin F. Atkins, p. 7, USNA, RG 76, Entry 352, Claim no. 387 (Atkins), Pt. 1.

[18] See Deposition of Ydelfonso Cires, RG 76, Entry 352, Claim no. 387 (Atkins), Pt. 2.

[19] On the flow of goods and recruits, see the deposition of Máximo Cisneros, USNA,

L. F. Hughes, manager of the Soledad estate in the province of Santa Clara, described the situation in the early months of the war as one in which small parties of insurgents "frequently entered the batey, purchased supplies at the tienda and conversed freely with the employes whom they knew." The administration of the estate notified the Spanish authorities but was not able to prevent the contacts, although they did try to assure that sympathizers with the insurrection among their workmen remained unarmed. Later, Spanish troops were stationed on the estate and blocked the overt entry of rebels into the heart of the *batey*, but much of the estate remained vulnerable.[20] Emiliano Silva y Placeres, also a manager, described the presence of insurgents on *colonias* serving the Hormiguero estate in Cienfuegos: ". . . they used to be around there every day—sometimes to get clothes, sometimes to get saddles, and at other times to get food."[21]

In the eastern province of Santiago de Cuba, the situation was even more extreme. A Spaniard testifying about conditions on the Los Caños estate in the region of Guantánamo noted that after the end of 1896 the estate had ceased grinding and virtually all of the estate's workers had gone to the insurrection.[22] Central Teresa, located near Manzanillo, actually employed insurgents as cane cutters during the harvest.[23] While during the Ten Years' War parts of the east had been under rebel control and some estates had been burned or raided, now even the region's most productive sugar districts were highly vulnerable.

The sympathy of the employees on estates was crucial to the insurgent strategy of burning cane to halt the harvest. In some cases, workers actually set the fires.[24] In others, the desertion of workers

RG 76, Entry 352, Claim no. 240 (Central Tuinucú), Pt. 1. The owners of the Mapos estate also contrasted their situation during the Ten Years' War with that of the War of Independence. See the deposition of José M. del Valle Iznaga, p. 43, USNA, RG 76, Entry 352, Claim no. 121 (Mapos Sugar Co.), Pt. 1.

[20] See Deposition of L. F. Hughes, April 21-24, 1906, pp. 5-6, Entry 352, Claim no. 387 (Atkins), Pt. 1, and other depositions in the same file.

[21] Deposition of Emiliano Silva y Placeres, USNA, RG 76, Entry 352, Claim no. 293 (Hormiguero), Pt. 3.

[22] Deposition of Marcos Margadas, p. 5. USNA, RG 76, Entry 352, Case no. 120 (Sheldon), Pt. 2.

[23] Deposition of Alejandro Quesada, p. 7. USNA, RG 76, Entry 352, Claim no. 97 (Central Teresa), Pt. 2.

[24] See the testimony concerning the *colonia* Dos Hermanos, in Deposition of Emiliano Silva y Pláceres, p. 6. USNA, RG 76, Entry 352, Claim 293 (Hormiguero), Pt. 3.

blocked defense against attack. In the case of the Central Teresa, the link was made clear: "If the estate had not been raided, and many employees had not joined the raiders, any ordinary fire, caused accidentally or otherwise, could have been got under control."[25]

The reasons Spanish troops were unable to defeat the insurgency, or even to protect property, were many, including weakness in their preparedness and strategy. But the task they faced had also changed qualitatively since the Ten Years' War: a larger and more unified insurgent force now challenged the security not only of the open countryside but also of sugar estates—estates that themselves had relinquished a measure of social control when they made the transition to free labor. The owners of slave plantations in the 1860s and 1870s had feared uprisings, and eastern estates during the first war had on occasion faced passive resistance. But overt resistance and rebellion had been largely blocked in the west. By the 1890s the new *centrales* based on free labor did not need to fear that their workers would rebel in search of their personal freedom, but those workers now had far greater opportunity to use their own resources, and in some cases those of the estate, to promote separatist goals.

The loosening of controls was not an inevitable concomitant of the shift to juridically free labor. The government could have attempted, during and immediately following emancipation in the 1880s, to institute measures that might have thwarted some of this mobility. But, as we have seen, state-supervised controls on rural labor were not forthcoming from Madrid or Havana, where they were generally perceived as politically dangerous and economically unnecessary.

Only after the new insurrection was well under way and had extended across the island did the government institute direct labor controls. Now, however, they were part of a brutal effort at rural pacification through the forced movement of population into Spanish-controlled camps, or "reconcentration," a strategy as disruptive of normal work as it was terrifying to the populace. Though the policy was directed in large measure at the dispersed rural population of smallholders, it also brought some estate owners into conflict with the Spanish government, as their estates were shorn of workers and left open to insurgent attack. Requiring estate residents to move

[25] Supplementary memorandum, USNA, RG 76, Entry 352, Claim no. 97 (Central Teresa), Pt. 4.

into concentration camps and leave for work only with daily government passes obstructed the normal functioning of cultivation, harvesting, and grinding. The owners of the Mapos estate, for example, found their work force evicted from the estate and driven into camps in October 1896.[26]

During the Ten Years' War the repressive structure of plantation slavery, already in place, had reinforced Spanish military strategy by facilitating the isolation and fortification of estates; at the same time, this military strategy made possible the continuation of production over most of the island. Now, by contrast, a major aspect of the military strategy for securing territory and blocking insurgent access to the population—reconcentration—was in potential conflict with the continuance of economic activity, even by planters entirely sympathetic to the Spanish cause. The result was a weakening of both the strategy and the economy. Sympathy for the insurgents grew and production shrank as rebellion and reconcentration combined to halt the working of the estates.

One way and another, emancipation had transformed Cuban society, dismantling the most rigid of the barriers that had separated whites and blacks: the institution of slavery. Racism was by no means eliminated, but the caste-like labor system on which it had initially rested was now gone, replaced by a pattern of tenantry and wage labor within which racial distinctions were less significant. Postemancipation adaptations had altered authority relations between former masters and former slaves, while the development of the *colonato* had created an intermediate social group, a group sharing some of the concerns of planters, but often more closely linked socially to other smallholders and laborers than to large-scale processors and sellers of sugar. Thus while prejudice and inequality persisted, new possibilities for alliance also came into being, possibilities that began to be realized when the new movement for independence emerged.

During the long process of transition from slavery to free labor, and from *ingenio* to *central*, those planters and entrepreneurs prepared to invest in new equipment and to restructure class relations in the Cuban countryside achieved, within limits, their goal of cen-

[26] For a description of the effects on Mapos of the policy of "reconcentration," see the testimony of Rafael Meneses, USNA, RG 76, Entry 352, Claim no. 121 (Mapos Sugar Co.), Pt. 1.

CONCLUSION

tralization and increased production. Aided by government-assisted immigration programs, they prevented most workers and small-scale *colonos* from establishing economic autonomy or substantial bargaining power over wages and rates of payment. In the process, however, they permanently changed the social stucture of the island, contributing to the growth of classes whose labor they might for the time being employ as they chose, but whose political actions they could not in the end fully control.

Afterword to the New Paperback Edition

Marcelino Iznaga, who lives on the Pepito Tey sugar plantation, recalls that his uncle Rafael Iznaga often spoke of having served in the Cuban Liberation Army of 1895–1898, fighting for Cuba's independence from Spain. Like his neighbor and rebel officer, Captain Claudio Sarría, Rafael Iznaga had been born into slavery on a plantation in the Cienfuegos district, on the southern coast of the island. But Marcelino Iznaga is quick to point out that by the time of final abolition in 1886 his uncle was no longer a slave: Rafael Iznaga's father and mother had purchased their son's freedom some years earlier. For this family, emancipation had come as the result of a collective effort, not thanks to a decree issued by the Spanish government.[1]

Marcelino Iznaga recalls these features of his uncle's life history clearly and directly. I am somewhat chagrined to realize how oblique a route I traveled in order to discern the role of slave initiatives and anticolonial warfare in shaping the dynamics of slave emancipation and the development of a postemancipation society in Cuba.

The problem of freedom, the puzzle of how it was achieved and what it meant, was in the air in the 1970s, as I began graduate study. My approach to sources was shaped by two years spent reading account books and local judicial records for a master's thesis on the role of women in the seventeenth-century English economy, followed by seminars on Latin American history with Stanley Stein, combined with a stint as a research assistant for Ira Berlin and Herbert Gutman. I envisioned a doctoral thesis aimed at determining the causes of the end of slavery in Cuba, evaluating the competing hypotheses of technological change, metropolitan calculation, and nationalist accomplishment. Then I would go on to examine the process of proletarianization, trace the rise of a postemancipation peasantry, and find out what freedom meant to those who had been enslaved.

Though I did not realize the intellectual hubris of my proposal, I did notice one obvious *inconveniente*: the island of Cuba itself was largely off-limits to researchers from the United States. Local records might well be out of reach. Never mind; the footnotes to Franklin

Knight's *Slave Society in Cuba during the Nineteenth Century* suggested that there was rich documentation from the late colonial period in Madrid's Archivo Histórico Nacional.[2] I could anchor the study in Spanish archives, try to persuade the Cuban Ministry of Foreign Affairs to allow me to do additional research on the island, and hope that the U.S. State Department would ignore my travel to its "closest of enemies."

By a fortunate coincidence, President Jimmy Carter momentarily ended restrictions on travel to Cuba for U.S. citizens. Senior Cubanists generously introduced me to a member of the Cuban mission to the United Nations, whom I proceeded to barrage with my seminar papers, my dissertation prospectus, and an altogether irrelevant critique of U.S. foreign policy in Bolivia, written years earlier on the basis of my undergraduate thesis. The Cuban delegate apparently concluded that I really was an overeager graduate student wishing to read nineteenth-century documents in the Cuban archives, not an intelligence agent. A two-week visa was issued and then extended; additional visas were subsequently granted.

The research on the island was an adventure in itself. Pedro Deschamps Chapeaux, Manuel Moreno Fraginals, Fe Iglesias, John Dumoulin, and other historians in Havana welcomed me as a colleague, despite my inexperience. A succession of representatives of the Cuban Ministry of Foreign Relations assigned responsibility for scholarly visitors graciously left me more or less to my own devices. After some weeks in Havana, I headed for the provinces, where the director of the archives in Sancti Spíritus let me continue to read documents each evening while he wrote reports.

The more archives I consulted in Spain and in Cuba, however, the clearer it became that I was not getting very close to capturing the "meanings of freedom." The documentation on emancipation itself was rich: parliamentary debates, petitions for freedom, voluminous judicial appeals, plantation daybooks, captured insurgent records. The documentation on previously bound laborers in the *post*-1886 period, however, was alarmingly thin. Former slaves seemed to vanish into a vast rural population and were almost never identified in the records by previous condition of servitude. How was I to figure out where they had gone and what their lives beyond slavery had involved? Had emancipation truly erased the distinction between those formerly enslaved and those long free, or was it merely the written record that was opaque on this question?

When in the fall of 1978 I sat down at my desk in Ann Arbor to reread my note cards and begin to write, I had the queasy sensation that I was about to fail of my goal. For several months I worked to patch together a portrait of the postabolition period using the 1899 Cuban census, the daybooks I had found in Sancti Spíritus, and assorted fragments from provincial records. But the results did not ring with the voices of the freedpeople. To get any sense of the experiences of individuals, I needed to move back well before the end of slavery itself and examine the voluminous and detailed material on the unfolding of the 1870 Moret Law and of the *patronato*, the period of apprenticeship established in 1880. These laws, however manipulative their intent, had unleashed numerous challenges and appeals, thus generating records filled with names and stories.

As I shifted my focus to emancipation itself, the end of slavery began to look less and less like a single event called abolition, to be explained by one or another unified causal mechanism. It now appeared as a long and intricate process involving dynamic interactions among slaves, masters, anticolonial rebels, and agents of the state. Moreover, self-purchase and challenges by slaves seemed to have become widespread by the last years of bound labor, accelerating and transforming the planned gradual transition. The relationship between law, slave initiatives, and economic change was complex, and the maintenance of the social relations of slavery distinctly precarious.

In the spring of 1979 I went back to the Archivo Nacional de Cuba to review systematically the appeals files of the Consejo de Administración for the 1870s and 1880s. The evidence of challenge and contestation by slaves that had first surfaced in the Spanish colonial archives was now more than confirmed in the testimony by and about slaves and *patrocinados* at the local level. As best I can recall, use of the term "agency" had not yet become common among historians, but I was certainly struck by the importance of all this activity by slaves, male and female, young and old. Initiatives by slaves began to take center stage in the chapters I was drafting.

As a result of his own work on Brazil in a similar period, however, my advisor, Stanley Stein, was appropriately skeptical of any implication that slaves had managed to achieve meaningful freedom within the context of grudging metropolitan reforms. He shocked me by referring to self-purchase by slaves as "a sucker's game," and he wondered aloud whether more slaves had actually achieved their freedom than had died during the period of gradual emancipation. Maybe death, not the slave, was the agent of abolition. Evidence of emancipation by self-purchase, lawsuit, and negotiated agreement would have to be checked against broader demographic trends, and one would have to look carefully at the paths to freedom taken by slaves on individual plantations. I began final drafting of my thesis with this in mind.

Manuel Moreno Fraginals, after years of studying the technology of sugar production, also remained skeptical, though for different reasons. He was convinced that the end of slavery in Cuba could best be understood in terms of the internal contradictions of the slave system in a period of technological innovation and falling commodity prices. After hours spent side by side coding manuscript censuses, we agreed to disagree about causation while collaborating in the unearthing of evidence and the elaboration of the debate.

While I was preoccupied with digging deeper into the historical ground on Cuba, teachers and colleagues helped broaden my perspective and clarify my thinking. Sidney Mintz urged me to put Cuba into the context of Caribbean peasantries—even if it seemed that I was having a hard time finding the necessary details on those slaves who had become peasants. Charles Gibson warned me not to take judicial records at face value, however appealing their evidence of initiative, and urged me to be alert to the role of the lawyers and notaries who helped produce them. Frederick Cooper talked me out of using the term "proletarianization" on the grounds that it was both infelicitous and teleological. Other words ending in "-ation"—so tempting to a newly trained scholar—fell away as Thomas Holt and Ira Berlin reminded me of the risks of writing about categories rather than about people.

The final manuscript proposed a reciprocal relationship between legal reforms and slave initiatives; it engaged—though it did not attempt to resolve—the questions about causal mechanisms; and it sketched a postslavery countryside neither peasant nor proletarian. I had been able to trace the experiences of various men, women, and children who had pushed the process of emancipation forward in one way or another. But what of the ambitious idea of finding the meanings of freedom, the goal that I had postponed in order to concentrate on the dynamics of emancipation itself?

By 1984, when I handed the manuscript to the publisher, it had finally dawned on me that the study of postemancipation society in Cuba was going to require a longer-term collective effort. First, there was an immense evidentiary challenge. Once the status of slaves as property was ended, the quality of written records revealing the activities of individuals and families changed. Lists of slaves, for example, were easy to find; lists of *former* slaves were very rare. It would take years of digging in local records to piece the picture together.

Second, the question of how to understand the many meanings of freedom had burst the bounds of slavery studies and of social history as I had originally envisioned them. Thomas Holt put it bluntly: there was no point in simply championing social history to the exclusion of political. One could not hope to understand changes in the nature of citizenship without plunging into politics, and often comparative politics at that. Among other things, this would mean engaging the 1895–1898 Cuban War for Independence, a historiographical minefield that I had heretofore studiously avoided.

Third, questions of meaning and social identity did not lend themselves particularly well to national-level, aggregate analysis. Selecting illustrative examples would not solve the problem, since any skeptic could legitimately ask just how representative Rafael Iznaga, for instance, actually was. A microhistorical analysis, focusing in detail not just on individual cases but on different life trajectories within a particular social field also seemed to be called for.

Over the next fifteen years, I went in all three of these directions at once—an exhilarating if somewhat reckless research strategy. As a result, when I look back at *Slave Emancipation in Cuba*, I tend to view it in light of this ongoing work and in light of the now quite extensive new historiography on societies after slavery.[3]

The stunning documentary volumes produced by the Freedmen and Southern Society Project at the University of Maryland, under the directorships of Ira Berlin and Leslie Rowland, have transformed the study of emancipation and postemancipation society in the United States South.[4] The penetrating work of Brazilian historians, including Sidney Chalhoub and Hebe Castro, has demonstrated that even in societies that had no Freedmen's Bureau, and no institution comparable to the Stipendiary Magistrates of the British West Indies, archival sources nonetheless survive with which to reconstruct postemancipation experiences.[5] The work of these and numerous other scholars encourages optimism about the possible uses of the additional manuscript material that is emerging in Cuba.[6] Moreover, a rich comparative discussion with a strong monographic foundation has now become possible.[7]

At the opposite end of the spectrum from transnational comparison lies microhistorical research, both the newest and perhaps the oldest strategy for postemancipation studies. Stanley Stein's *Vassouras*, published more than forty years ago, was a model of what is now often referred to as microhistory, precisely because it posed major interpretive questions within a tightly bounded region and layered different kinds of local evidence.[8] Several Brazilian scholars have resumed this approach, producing gems of detailed research.[9] For Cuba, local history is abundant, but rigorously problem-oriented microhistory is uncommon.

Recently, however, it has begun to emerge. Several historians, for example, have converged on the coastal city of Cienfuegos, where the presence of an excellent provincial archive in a major sugar-producing region creates ideal conditions for both archival and oral-historical work, through which documents and memories can be juxtaposed and brought into dialogue.[10] The written request by Rafael Iznaga for a veteran's pension rests in an archive only a few miles from the present home of his nephew Marcelino Iznaga at Central Pepito Tey, formerly Soledad Plantation.[11] With a sturdy vehicle, one can even locate the small farm on the banks of the Arimao River where Rafael Iznaga settled after the 1895–1898 war. In this setting, the "exceptional ordinary" can become more than anecdotal, and the nature of memories themselves can become part of the picture of freedom.[12]

One of the things that I learned in writing *Slave Emancipation in Cuba* was that the question of the meanings of freedom has no easy answers—or even reasonably difficult answers. There are only *very* difficult ones. But that, of course, is part of what sustains the historian's enterprise. It is also part of what makes reflecting on race, freedom, and nationhood an engrossing challenge for citizens of Cuba and the United States alike.

October 1999

NOTES

1. Rafael Iznaga's brother Victoriano was freed in the same way and later became a messenger for the Cuban rebels during the 1895–1898 war. Marcelino Iznaga Suárez Román, Central Pepito Tey, interview with the author, June 1999. I would like to thank Ira Berlin, Ada Ferrer, Thomas Holt, Aims McGuinness, Sidney Mintz, Peter Railton, and Anne Scott for their very helpful comments on an earlier draft of this afterword.

2. These were primarily located in the Sección de Ultramar. See Franklin W. Knight, *Slave Society in Cuba during the Nineteenth Century* (Madison: University of Wisconsin Press, 1970).

3. For a bibliographic overview, see Rebecca J. Scott, Thomas C. Holt, Frederick Cooper, and Aims McGuinness, eds., *Societies after Slavery: A Select Annotated Bibliography of Printed Sources on the British West Indies, British Colonial Africa, South Africa, Cuba, and Brazil*, forthcoming, 2001, University of Michigan Press.

4. The volumes of *Freedom: A Documentary History of Emancipation, 1861–1867,* are published by Cambridge University Press and include Ira Berlin, Joseph P. Reidy, and Leslie S. Rowland, eds., *The Black Military Experience* (1982); Ira Berlin, Barbara J. Fields, Thavolia Glymph, Joseph P. Reidy, and Leslie S. Rowland, eds., *The Destruction of Slavery* (1985); Ira Berlin, Thavolia Glymph, Steven F. Miller, Joseph P. Reidy, Leslie S. Rowland, and Julie Saville, eds., *The Wartime Genesis of Free Labor: The Lower South* (1990); and Ira Berlin, Steven F. Miller, Joseph P. Reidy, and Leslie S. Rowland, eds., *The Wartime Genesis of Free Labor: The Upper South* (1993).

5. See Sidney Chalhoub, *Visões da liberdade: Uma história das ultimas decadas da escravidão na Corte* (São Paulo: Companhia das Letras, 1990), and Hebe Maria Mattos de Castro, *Das cores do silêncio: Os significados da liberdade no sudeste escravista—Brasil século XIX* (Rio de Janeiro: Arquivo Nacional, 1995).

6. The location and consultation of Cuban manuscript materials will be facilitated by the guide to Cuban regional archives being prepared by a team of Cuban and U.S. scholars, coordinated by Louis A. Pérez Jr., Marel García, and myself. The guide is scheduled for publication in Spanish in Cuba and in English by the University of Pittsburgh Press.

7. For one comparative discussion, see Frederick Cooper, Thomas Holt, and Rebecca Scott, *Beyond Slavery: Explorations of Race, Labor and Citizenship in Postemancipation Societies* (Chapel Hill: University of North Carolina Press, 2000). Others have framed comparisons in other terms. See Mary Turner, ed., *From Chattel Slaves to Wage Slaves: The Dynamics of Labour Bargaining in the Americas* (London: James Currey, 1995); Frank McGlynn and Seymour Drescher, eds., *The Meaning of Freedom: Economics, Politics, and Culture after Slavery* (Pittsburgh: University of Pittsburgh Press, 1992).

8. Stanley J. Stein, *Vassouras: A Brazilian Coffee County, 1850–1900* (Cambridge, Mass.: Harvard University Press, 1957; reprint ed., Princeton, N.J.: Princeton University Press, 1985).

9. See the secondary works on Brazil cited in Scott, Holt, Cooper, McGuinness, *Societies after Slavery.*

10. The key initial figures in this collaboration were Orlando García Martínez, the director of the Provincial Archives of Cienfuegos, and Michael Zeuske, a historian from Germany. I joined them around 1996, and we organized a scholarly conference there in 1998. A volume of papers from that conference, titled *Espacios, silencios y los sentidos de la libertad: Cuba, 1879–1912,* edited by Fernando Martínez Heredia, Orlando García Martínez, and Rebecca Scott, will be published in Havana by Ediciones UNIÓN in late 2000. Several doctoral students have recently developed research projects with a significant Cienfuegos component, including Alejandra Bronfman of Princeton University, David Sartorius of the University of North Carolina, and Frank Guridy and Adrian Burgos of the University of Michigan. Aims McGuinness of the University of Michigan has collaborated on oral historical interviews in the region. A group of seventeen young researchers, Cuban- and U.S.-based,

spent ten days in June of 1999 in the Cienfuegos archives, engaged in research and debate on questions of race and nationality in Cuba.

11. This document is among the pension requests in the judicial holdings of the Archivo Provincial de Cienfuegos, Cienfuegos, Cuba.

12. On the concept of the "exceptional ordinary"—which might also be rendered as the "ordinary exception"—see Jacques Revel, ed., *Jeux d'échelles: La micro-analyse à l'expérience* (Paris: Gallimard/Le Seuil, 1996), p. 31. The phrase that Revel uses, drawing on the work of Edoardo Grendi, is *exceptionnel normal.* Revel notes wryly that it exercises the fascination of a concept that one would love to be able to use if only one knew how to define it. For my own effort to revisit the question of freedom through a microhistorical study, see "Reclaiming Gregoria's Mule: The Meanings of Freedom in the Arimao and Caunao Valleys, Cienfuegos, Cuba, 1880–1899," *Past and Present,* forthcoming. An earlier version appeared in Spanish as "Reclamando la Mula de Gregoria Quesada: El Significado de la Libertad en los Valles del Arimao y del Caunao, Cienfuegos, Cuba (1880–1899)," *Illes i Imperis: Estudis d'història de les societats en el món colonial i post-colonial* (Barcelona) 2 (Spring 1999): 89–108.

Select Bibliography

MANUSCRIPT COLLECTIONS

Cuba

ARCHIVO NACIONAL DE CUBA, HAVANA
This archive, as one would expect, is the best source of documentation on nineteenth-century Cuban history. Many of its holdings are indexed and catalogued.

Consejo de Administración—This collection includes essential policy discussions and numerous legal appeals. Most useful for the study of emancipation were the bundles containing lawsuits involving slaves or *patrocinados* and their masters (legs. 59, 60, 64, 65, 68, 69, 70, 71, 76, 82, 85, 92, 95, 99) and those containing discussions of the *cabildos de nación* (legs. 8, 44, 58, 76).

Fondo Valle—This section contains materials complementary to those in the Fondo Valle-Iznaga of the Archivo Provincial de Sancti Spíritus (see below). A typed inventory of the Valle family papers in this *fondo* is available at the ANC.

Gobierno General—This section duplicates some of the political material in the Sección de Ultramar of the Archivo Histórico Nacional in Madrid (see below). But it also includes detailed supporting data relevant to policy discussions between Havana and Madrid. Particularly useful were *legajos* containing information on the *patronato* (legs. 163, 271, 272, 273, 275, 366), those containing population lists (legs. 271, 275), and those concerning Afro-Cuban organizations (leg. 100).

Miscelánea de Expedientes—This extraordinary "miscellany" contains legal case files, manuscript returns of censuses, governmental papers, and assorted other materials. A multivolume, typed inventory of its contents is available at the archive. The most important *legajos* for this study were those containing population statistics and censuses (including legs. 25, 3748, 3820, 4119), appeals of cases where slaves or *patrocinados* had claimed freedom (including legs. 3813 and 3814), reports on activities of the *sindicaturas* (leg. 3814), records of payment in scrip (leg. 4330), and information on convict labor (leg. 3954).

Miscelánea de Libros—This section contains numerous bound manuscript volumes. Most important for this study were the daybooks and account books of sugar plantations, including numbers 10789, 10802, 10806, 10831, 10879, 11245, 11247, 11518, and 11536.

ARCHIVO PARROQUIAL DE LA IGLESIA MAYOR DEL ESPÍRITU SANTO,
SANCTI SPÍRITUS
The archive of the main church of the town of Sancti Spíritus contains the
registers of baptisms, marriages, and burials for the area in an excellent
state of preservation. See the volumes Matrimonios, Pardos y Morenos,
Libro núm. 3, 1812-1891, and Bautismos de Pardos y Morenos, Libro 16,
1866-1880, for the Iglesia Mayor, and the volumes Defunciones de Color,
Libro 1º, 1875-1898, and Bautismos de Color, Libro 1, 1875-1901, for San
Antonio Abad, Jíbaro.

ARCHIVO PROVINCIAL DE SANCTI SPÍRITUS, SANCTI SPÍRITUS
This provincial archive contains, in addition to municipal records, many of
the papers of the Valle-Iznaga family, large landowners of the region. For
this study, the most important documents were the accounts, inventories,
and payrolls of sugar plantations owned by the family. They are primarily
found in leg. 24 of the Fondo Valle-Iznaga, though there are relevant materials in other *legajos* of the same *fondo*. The Fondo Ayuntamiento also
contains information concerning the Valle-Iznaga sugar holdings, particularly in legs. 3 and 4.

BIBLIOTECA NACIONAL JOSÉ MARTÍ, HAVANA
Colección Cubana—The manuscript section of the Colección Cubana con-
    tains materials relevant to the study of slavery, particularly in the col-
    lections titled Morales, Pérez, and Suárez R. Their contents are indexed
    in the card file of the Colección Cubana.
Colección Julio Lobo—This as yet uncatalogued mass of documents con-
    tains materials from various sugar plantations. Caja 7, for example, in-
    cludes lists of *patrocinados* and employees on the Central Rosalia.

Spain

ARCHIVO HISTÓRICO NACIONAL, MADRID
Sección de Ultramar—The documentation on slavery, emancipation, and
    related issues in this rich collection of material from the old Ministerio
    de Ultramar and from Cuba is widely scattered. The original Libros de
    Registro are an important guide, for they help one to locate *expedientes*
    on specific topics. The typed inventory available at the archive is also
    essential for the identification of relevant *legajos*. In general, the following
    groups of *legajos* proved most useful for this project:
    Fomento: (information on colonization projects, agriculture, *ingenios*)
    legs. 87, 88, 90, 91, 93, 107-110, 136, 153, 154, 173-176, 226, 278, 280,
    288.
    Gracia y Justicia: (information on crime, taxes, property) legs. 816, 825,
    1762, 1780, 1827, 1833, 1927, 1929, 1932.
    Gobierno: (government correspondence on policy issues, appeals of de-
    cisions concerning slaves, data on conditions in Cuba) legs. 3489, 3490,
    3547-3553, 3555, 4438-4440, 4517, 4528[10], 4687, 4709, 4714, 4715, 4721,

4726, 4727, 4740, 4759-4761, 4780, 4786, 4787, 4801, 4802, 4805, 4807, 4809, 4810, 4813-4815, 4818-4820, 4831, 4834, 4881-4885, 4896.

Gobierno. 1899: (miscellaneous government documentation, apparently filed after the loss of Cuba, but generally dated earlier) legs. 4926-4928, 4930-4932, 4939, 4940, 4942, 4943, 4957-4959.

Serie adicional: (contains some information on political prisoners and banditry, as well as indices to various groups of documents) legs. 5531, 5818, 5840, 5844, 5879.

ARCHIVO GENERAL DE INDIAS, SEVILLE
Most of the AGI's holdings on Cuba cover an earlier period. There is important material, however, in the Archivo Polavieja of the Sección de Diversos. Leg. 7 contains information from Camilo Polavieja's period of tenure as governor of the province of Santiago de Cuba and later of the island, and includes documents on banditry and rebellions. Leg. 8 contains a printed volume on an alleged uprising of persons of color in Santiago de Cuba in 1880.

ARCHIVO DEL MINISTERIO DE ASUNTOS EXTERIORES, MADRID
Cuba. Ultramar—Of particular interest for the study of emancipation is the correspondence on the importation of laborers from the colonies of other European powers, located in leg. 2941.

BIBLIOTECA NACIONAL DE ESPAÑA, MADRID
Sección de Manuscritos—On nineteenth-century Cuba see the Papeles Relativos a las Provincias de Ultramar Coleccionados por D. Eugenio Alonso y Sanjurjo, sig. 13228.

REAL ACADEMIA DE HISTORIA, MADRID
Colección Fernández Duro—This rich collection is composed primarily of insurgent documents from the early years of the Ten Years' War. Virtually all of its *legajos* were of use for Chapter II of this study.
Colección Caballero de Rodas—Contains papers of General Caballero de Rodas, briefly captain-general of Cuba during the Ten Years' War.

France

MINISTÈRE DES AFFAIRES ÉTRANGÈRES, PARIS
For scattered information on economic and political conditions, see the dispatches found in Correspondance Commerciale, La Havane, Vol. 22, 1876-June 1885, and Dépêches politiques des Consuls, Espagne, Vol. 92, 1878-1880 and Vol. 96, 1886-1887.

England

PUBLIC RECORD OFFICE, LONDON
A classic source, though not without drawbacks, is the collection of consular reports with particular reference to slavery and the slave trade to be found in Foreign Office 84. See in particular pieces 1542, 1568, 1593, 1641, and 1719.

BRITISH MUSEUM
The Layard Papers in the British Museum Manuscript Collection provide insight into conditions in Cuba and politics in Spain. See in particular Add. mss. 39000-39011, and 39121-39122.

United States

U.S. NATIONAL ARCHIVES
The U.S. National Archives contain a range of materials useful for the study of nineteenth-century Cuba. Those most relevant to this work were the case files and briefs of the Spanish Treaty Claims Commission, found in Record Group 76, Entries 352 and 353.

NINETEENTH-CENTURY CUBAN AND SPANISH PERIODICALS

The Biblioteca del Instituto de Literatura y Lingüística de la Academia de Ciencias and the Colección Cubana de la Biblioteca Nacional José Martí, both in Havana, are major sources for Cuban newspapers of this period. Local periodicals can also be found in provincial archives, such as the Archivo Provincial de Sancti Spíritus, and in the library of the Universidad Central de las Villas in Santa Clara. Single issues of a variety of publications frequently appear with government documents concerning press censorship in the Archivo Histórico Nacional, Madrid, and in the Archivo Nacional de Cuba. The periodicals collection of the Biblioteca Nacional de España in Madrid includes major Cuban and Spanish newspapers and journals.

The periodicals consulted for this study include the following. The researcher should note that frequently only short runs or single issues of the minor papers have survived.

El A.B.C. Periódico independiente de intereses generales. Cienfuegos.
La Antorcha. Trinidad.
Aurora del Yumurí. Matanzas.
Boletín Oficial de la Habana. Havana.
Boletín Oficial de la Hacienda de la Isla de Cuba. Havana.
Boletín Oficial de Hacienda y de Estadística de la Isla de Cuba. Havana.
Boletín Oficial de la Provincia de Santa Clara. Santa Clara.
Boletín Oficial del Ministerio de Ultramar. Madrid.
El Demócrata. Havana.
Diario de la Marina. Havana.
La Discusión. Havana.
El Eco de las Villas. Santa Clara.
El Español. Diario político de la tarde. Havana.
La Fraternidad. Periódico político independiente consagrado a la defensa de los intereses generales de la raza de color. Havana.
La Fraternidad. Semanario de literatura, de intereses generales, y órgano de la Sociedad Artística y Literaria El Progreso. Sancti Spíritus.

Gaceta de la Habana. Havana.

Gaceta de Madrid. Madrid.

El Horizonte. Periódico literario y de intereses generales. Órgano de la clase de color. Esperanza.

La Lucha. Diario republicano. Havana.

Minerva. Revista quincenal dedicada a la mujer de color. Havana.

El Oriente.

El País. Diario Autonomista. Órgano de la Junta Central del Partido Liberal. Havana.

El Parlamento. Havana.

El Popular. Diario Radical. Havana.

El Productor. Havana.

La Propaganda. Periódico Liberal. Sancti Spíritus.

Revista de Agricultura del Círculo de Hacendados de la Isla de Cuba. Havana.

Revista Económica. Havana.

El Sagua. Sagua la Grande.

OTHER PERIODICALS

The Anti-Slavery Reporter. London.

Willett & Gray, *Weekly Statistical Sugar Trade Journal.* New York.

BOOKS, ARTICLES, AND PAMPHLETS

Acosta y Albear, Francisco. *Memoria sobre el estado actual de Cuba.* Havana: A. Pegó, 1874.

Adamson, Alan H. *Sugar Without Slaves: The Political Economy of British Guiana, 1838-1904.* New Haven: Yale University Press, 1972.

Aimes, Hubert H. S. "Coartación: A Spanish Institution for the Advancement of Slaves into Freedmen." *The Yale Review* 17 (February 1909): 412-31.

―――. *A History of Slavery in Cuba, 1511-1868.* New York: G. P. Putnam's Sons, 1907; reprint ed., New York: Octagon Books, 1967.

―――. "The Transition from Slave to Free Labor in Cuba." *The Yale Review* 15 (May 1906): 68-84.

Albert, Bill and Adrian Graves. *Crisis and Change in the International Sugar Economy, 1860-1914.* Norwich: ISC Press, 1984.

Alden, Dauril, ed. *Colonial Roots of Modern Brazil.* Berkeley: University of California Press, 1973.

Anuario de estudios cubanos. Tomo 1. *La república neocolonial.* Havana: Editorial de Ciencias Sociales, 1975.

Aptheker, Herbert. *To Be Free: Studies in American Negro History.* New York: International Publishers, 1948; second edition, 1968.

Armas y Céspedes, Francisco de. *De la esclavitud en Cuba.* Madrid: Establecimiento Tipográfico de T. Fortanet, 1866.

Aufhauser, R. Keith. "Slavery and Technological Change." *The Journal of Economic History* 34 (March 1974): 36-50.

Atkins, Edwin F. *Sixty Years in Cuba: Reminiscences of Edwin F. Atkins.* Cambridge, Massachusetts: Private printing at the Riverside Press, 1926.

Bacardí y Moreau, Emilio. *Crónicas de Santiago de Cuba.* 3 vols. Barcelona: Carbonell y Esteva, 1908-1913; reprint ed., 10 vols. ed. Amalia Bacardí Cape. Madrid: Breogán, 1972-1973.

Ballou, Maturin M. *Due South or Cuba Past and Present.* Boston: Houghton Mifflin, 1885; reprint ed., New York: Young People's Missionary Movement of the United States and Canada, 1910.

Barnet, Miguel. *Biografía de un cimarrón.* Havana: Instituto de Etnología y Folklore, Academia de Ciencias de Cuba, 1966.

Barras y Prado, Antonio de las. *La Habana a mediados del siglo xix.* Madrid: Imprenta de la Ciudad Lineal, 1925.

Bauer, Arnold J. "Rural Workers in Spanish America: Problems of Peonage and Oppression." *Hispanic American Historical Review* 59 (February 1979): 34-63.

Beck, Earl R. "The Martínez Campos Government of 1879: Spain's Last Chance in Cuba." *Hispanic American Historical Review* 56 (May 1976): 268-89.

Berlin, Ira. *Slaves Without Masters.* New York: Random House, 1974.

Berlin, Ira, Joseph P. Reidy, Leslie S. Rowland, eds. *Freedom: A Documentary History of Emancipation, 1861-1867.* Series II: *The Black Military Experience.* Cambridge, England: Cambridge University Press, 1982.

Besada Ramos, Benito. "Antecedentes económicos de la Guerra de los Diez Años." *Economía y desarrollo* 13 (September-October 1972): 155-62.

Bremer, Fredrika. *Cartas desde Cuba.* Havana: Editorial Arte y Literatura, 1980.

Burn, William Laurence. *Emancipation and Apprenticeship in the British West Indies.* London: Jonathan Cape, 1937.

Cano, Bienvenido, and Federico Zalba. *El libro de los Síndicos de Ayuntamiento y de las Juntas Protectoras de Libertos.* Havana: Imprenta del Gobierno, 1875.

Cantero, Justo Germán. *Los ingenios: Colección de vistas de los principales ingenios de azúcar de la isla de Cuba.* Havana: L. Marquier, 1857.

Carr, Raymond. *Spain: 1808-1939.* Oxford: Clarendon Press, 1970.

Centro de Investigaciones Históricas. Instituto de Cultura Puertorriqueña. *El proceso abolicionista en Puerto Rico: Documentos para su estudio.* 2 vols. San Juan, Puerto Rico: 1974, 1978.

Cepero Bonilla, Raúl. *Azúcar y abolición.* Havana: Editorial Cenit, 1948; reprint ed., Barcelona: Editorial Crítica, 1976.

China. Tsung li ko kuo shih wu ya mên. *Report of the Commission sent by China to Ascertain the Condition of Chinese Coolies in Cuba.* Shanghai: Imperial Maritime Customs Press, 1876; reprint ed., Taipei: Ch'eng Wen Publishing Company, 1970.

Clark, William J. *Commercial Cuba.* New York: Charles Scribner's Sons, 1898.

Clark, Victor. "Labor Conditions in Cuba." *Bulletin of the Department of Labor* 41 (July 1902): 663-793.

Código penal vigente en las Islas de Cuba y Puerto Rico mandado observar por Real Decreto de 23 de Mayo de 1879. Madrid: Pedro Núñez, 1886.

Cok Márquez, Patria. "La introducción de los ferrocarriles portátiles en la industria azucarera, 1870-1880." *Santiago* 41 (March 1981): 137-47.

Conrad, Robert. *The Destruction of Brazilian Slavery, 1850-1888.* Berkeley: University of California Press, 1972.

Conspiración de la raza de color descubierta en Santiago de Cuba el 10 de diciembre de 1880 siendo comandante general de la provincia el Exmo. Sr. Teniente General Don Camilo Polavieja y Castillo. Santiago de Cuba: Sección Tipográfica del Estado Mayor, 1880.

Corbitt, Duvon C. "Immigration in Cuba." *Hispanic American Historical Review* 22 (May 1942): 280-308.

————. *A Study of the Chinese in Cuba, 1847-1947.* Wilmore, Ky.: Asbury College, 1971.

Corwin, Arthur F. *Spain and the Abolition of Slavery in Cuba, 1817-1886.* Austin: University of Texas Press, 1967.

Craton, Michael, ed. *Roots and Branches: Current Directions in Slave Studies.* Toronto: Pergamon Press, 1979.

Cuba, Archivo Nacional. *Catálogo de los fondos del Consejo de Administración de la Isla de Cuba.* 3 vols. Havana: Archivo Nacional, 1948-1950.

Cuba, Centro de Estadística. *Noticias estadísticas de la Isla de Cuba, en 1862.* Havana: Imprenta del Gobierno, 1864.

Cuba, Centro de Estudios Demográficos. *La población de Cuba.* Havana: Editorial de Ciencias Sociales, 1976.

Cuba. Comisión de Estadística. *Cuadro estadístico de la siempre fiel Isla de Cuba, correspondiente al año de 1846.* Havana: Imprenta del Gobierno y Capitanía General, 1847.

Dana, Richard Henry, Jr. *To Cuba and Back: A Vacation Voyage.* Boston: Houghton Mifflin, 1859; reprint ed., Carbondale, Illinois: Southern Illinois University Press, 1966.

Davis, David Brion. *Slavery and Human Progress.* New York: Oxford University Press, 1984.

Dean, Warren. *Rio Claro: A Brazilian Plantation System, 1820-1920.* Stanford: Stanford University Press, 1976.

Deerr, Noel. *The History of Sugar.* 2 vols. London: Chapman and Hall, 1949-1950.

Deschamps Chapeaux, Pedro. *El negro en la economía habanera del siglo xix.* Havana: Unión de Escritores y Artistas de Cuba, 1971.

————. *El negro en el periodismo cubano en el siglo xix.* Havana: Ediciones R., 1963.

Diembicz, Andrés. "Poblamiento post-azucarero en Cuba: Perduración y funciones socio-económicas actuales." *Economía y desarrollo* 34 (March-April 1976): 99-115.

Dumont, Henri. "Antropología y patología comparada de los negros esclavos." *Revista Bimestre Cubana* 10, no. 3 (May-June 1915)—11, no. 2 (March-April 1916).

Dumoulin, John. "El primer desarrollo del movimiento obrero y la formación del proletariado en el sector azucarero; Cruces 1886-1902." *Islas* 48 (May-August 1974): 3-66.

Edo y Llop, Enrique. *Memoria histórica de Cienfuegos y su jurisdicción.* 2nd ed. Cienfuegos: J. Andreu, 1888.

Eichner, Alfred E. *The Emergence of Oligopoly: Sugar Refining as a Case Study.* Baltimore: The Johns Hopkins University Press, 1969.

Eisenberg, Peter L. *The Sugar Industry in Pernambuco: Modernization Without Change, 1840-1910.* Berkeley: University of California Press, 1974.

Ely, Roland T. *Comerciantes cubanos del siglo xix.* Bogotá: Aedita Editores, 1961.

———. *Cuando reinaba su majestad el azúcar.* Buenos Aires: Ed. Sudamericana, 1963.

Engerman, Stanley, and Eugene Genovese, eds. *Race and Slavery in the Western Hemisphere: Quantitative Studies.* Princeton: Princeton University Press, 1975.

Entralgo, Elías José. *La liberación étnica cubana.* Havana: Universidad de La Habana, 1953.

Exposición del Exmo. Señor Conde de Vega Mar. Madrid: Establecimiento Tipográfico de T. Fortanet, 1868.

Fernandes, Florestan. *The Negro in Brazilian Society.* Translated by Jacqueline D. Skiles, A. Brunel, and Arthur Rothwell. New York: Columbia University Press, 1969.

Fernández Robaina, Tomás. Unpublished bibliography of Afro-Cuban history.

Fleisig, Heywood. "Comment on Keith Aufhauser, 'Slavery and Technological Change.' " *The Journal of Economic History* 34 (March 1974): 79-83.

Flory, Thomas. "Fugitive Slaves and Free Society: The Case of Brazil." *The Journal of Negro History* 64 (Spring 1979): 116-30.

Fogel, Robert William, and Stanley L. Engerman. "Philanthropy at Bargain Prices: Notes on the Economics of Gradual Emancipation." *The Journal of Legal Studies* 3 (June 1974): 377-401.

Foner, Laura, and Eugene D. Genovese, eds. *Slavery in the New World: A Reader in Comparative History.* New Jersey: Prentice-Hall, 1969.

Foner, Philip S. *A History of Cuba and Its Relations with the United States.* 2 vols. New York: International Publishers, 1962, 1963.

Fox-Genovese, Elizabeth, and Eugene D. Genovese. *Fruits of Merchant Capital: Slavery and Bourgeois Property in the Rise and Expansion of Capitalism.* New York: Oxford University Press, 1983.

Franco, José Luciano. *Los palenques de los negros cimarrones.* Havana: Departamento de Orientación Revolucionaria del Comité Central del Partido Comunista de Cuba, 1973.

Friedländer, Heinrich. *Historia económica de Cuba.* Havana: Jesús Montero, 1944.

Frucht, Richard. "A Caribbean Social Type: Neither 'Peasant' nor 'Proletarian.'" *Social and Economic Studies* 16 (September 1967): 295-300.

Gallenga, A. *The Pearl of the Antilles.* London: Chapman and Hall, 1873.

Genovese, Eugene D. *Roll, Jordan, Roll: The World the Slaves Made.* New York: Random House, 1974.

———. *The World the Slaveholders Made: Two Essays in Interpretation.* New York: Pantheon Books, 1969.

Gerteis, Louis S. *From Contraband to Freedman: Federal Policy toward Southern Blacks, 1861-1865.* Westport, Connecticut: Greenwood Press, 1973.

Gómez, Juan Gualberto. *La cuestión de Cuba en 1884. Historia y soluciones de los partidos cubanos.* Madrid: Imprenta de Aurelio J. Alaria, 1885.

Graham, Richard. "Slavery and Economic Development: Brazil and the United States South in the Nineteenth Century." *Comparative Studies in Society and History* 23 (October 1981): 620-55.

Great Britain. Parliament. *Parliamentary Papers* (Lords), 1875, vol. 23 (Slave Trade No. 2) "Correspondence Respecting Slavery in Cuba and Puerto Rico, and the State of the Slave Population and Chinese Coolies in those Islands."

———. *Parliamentary Papers* (Commons), 1878, vol. 67 (Slave Trade No. 1) "Report on the Labour Question in Cuba."

———. *Parliamentary Papers* (Lords), 1882, vol. 24 (Slave Trade No. 3) "Report by Acting Consul-General Carden on the Number and Condition of the Slaves in Cuba."

Green, William A. *British Slave Emancipation. The Sugar Colonies and the Great Experiment, 1830-1865.* Oxford: The Clarendon Press, 1976.

Guerra y Sánchez, Ramiro. *Azúcar y población en las Antillas.* Havana: Cultural, 1944; reprint ed., Havana: Editorial de Ciencias Sociales, 1976.

———. *La guerra de los diez años, 1868-1878.* 2 vols. Havana: Cultural, 1950-1952; reprint ed., Havana: Editorial de Ciencias Sociales, 1972.

———. *Manual de historia de Cuba.* 2nd ed. Havana: Cultural, 1938; reprint ed., Havana: Consejo Nacional de Cultura, 1962.

———, ed. *Historia de la nación cubana.* 10 vols. Havana: Editorial Historia de la Nación Cubana, 1952.

Gutman, Herbert. *The Black Family in Slavery and Freedom, 1750-1925.* New York: Pantheon Books, 1976.

Hall, Douglas. *Free Jamaica, 1838-1865: An Economic History.* New Haven: Yale University Press, 1959.

Hall, Gwendolyn Midlo. *Social Control in Slave Plantation Societies: A Comparison of St. Domingue and Cuba.* Baltimore: The Johns Hopkins University Press, 1971.

Helly, Denise. *Idéologie et ethnicité: Les Chinois Macao à Cuba: 1847-1886.* Montreal: Les Presses de l'Université de Montréal, 1979.

Higman, B. W. *Slave Population and Economy in Jamaica, 1807-1834.* Cambridge, England: Cambridge University Press, 1976.

Hirschman, Albert O. *Shifting Involvements: Private Interest and Public Action.* Princeton: Princeton University Press, 1982.

―――. *The Strategy of Economic Development.* New Haven: Yale University Press, 1958.

Hoernel, Robert B. "Sugar and Social Change in Oriente, Cuba, 1898-1946." *Journal of Latin American Studies* 8 (November 1976): 215-49.

Holt, Thomas C. "The Problem of Freedom: The Political Economy of Jamaica after Slavery." Forthcoming.

Hyatt, Pulaski F., and John T. *Cuba: Its Resources and Opportunities.* New York: J. S. Ogilvie, 1899.

Ibáñez, Francisco Feliciano. *Observaciones sobre la utilidad y conveniencia del establecimiento en esta isla de grandes ingenios centrales.* Havana: Imprenta y Litografía Obispo 27, 1880.

Ibarra, Jorge. *Ideología Mambisa.* Havana: Instituto Cubano del Libro, 1972.

Iglesias García, Fe. "Algunos aspectos de la distribución de la tierra en 1899." *Santiago* 40 (December 1980): 119-78.

―――. "Características de la población cubana en 1862." *Revista de la Biblioteca Nacional José Martí,* 3rd series, 22 (September-December 1980): 89-110.

―――. "El censo cubano de 1877 y sus diferentes versiones." *Santiago* 34 (June 1979): 167-214.

Izard, Miguel. *Manufactureros, industriales, y revolucionarios.* Barcelona: Editorial Crítica, 1979.

Jenks, Leland Hamilton. *Our Cuban Colony: A Study in Sugar.* New York: Vanguard Press, 1928.

Jiménez, Juan Bautista. *Los esclavos blancos, por un colono de Las Villas.* Havana: A. Álvarez y Comp., 1893.

Jiménez Pastrana, Juan. *Los Chinos en las luchas por la liberación cubana (1847-1930).* Havana: Instituto de Historia, 1963.

Kiple, Kenneth F. *Blacks in Colonial Cuba, 1774-1899.* Gainesville: The University Presses of Florida, 1976.

Klein, Herbert S. "Consideraciones sobre la viabilidad de la esclavitud y las causas de la abolición en la Cuba del siglo diecinueve." *La Torre* 21 (July-December 1973): 307-18.

―――. *Slavery in the Americas.* Chicago: The University of Chicago Press, 1967.

Knight, Franklin W. *The Caribbean: The Genesis of a Fragmented Nationalism.* New York: Oxford University Press, 1978.

―――. *Slave Society in Cuba during the Nineteenth Century.* Madison: University of Wisconsin Press, 1970.

Labra, Rafael María de. *Mi campaña en las Cortes Españolas de 1881 a 1883.* Madrid: Imprenta de Aurelio J. Alaria, 1885.

[―――]. *La raza de color de Cuba.* Madrid: Establecimiento Tipográfico de Fortanet, 1894.

LeRiverend, Julio. *Historia económica de Cuba*. Barcelona: Ediciones Ariel, 1972.

———. "Raices del 24 de Febrero: La economía y la sociedad cubanas de 1878 a 1895." *Cuba Socialista* 5 (February 1965): 1-17.

Litwack, Leon. *Been in the Storm So Long: The Aftermath of Slavery*. New York: Alfred A. Knopf, 1979.

McFeely, William S. *Yankee Stepfather: General O. O. Howard and the Freedmen*. New York: W. W. Norton and Co., 1968.

McPherson, James M. *The Struggle for Equality: Abolitionists and the Negro in the Civil War and Reconstruction*. Princeton: Princeton University Press, 1964.

Maluquer de Motes, Jordi. "La burgesia catalana i l'esclavitud colonial: Modes de producció i pràctica política." *Recerques. Història, Economia, Cultura* 3 (Barcelona: 1974): 83-136.

———. *El socialismo en España, 1833-1868*. Barcelona: Editorial Crítica, 1977.

Marrero, Levi. *Cuba: Economía y sociedad*. Vol. 9. *Azúcar, ilustración y conciencia (1763-1868)* (I) Madrid: Editorial Playor, 1983.

Martínez-Alier, Verena. *Marriage, Class and Colour in Nineteenth-Century Cuba*. Cambridge, England: Cambridge University Press, 1974.

Martínez Cuadrado, Miguel. *La burguesía conservadora (1874-1931)*. Madrid: Alianza Editorial, 1973.

Martínez-Fortún y Foyo, José A. *Anales y efemérides de San Juan de los Remedios y su jurisdicción*. Havana: Pérez Sierra y Comp., 1930-1931.

Martínez Furé, Rogelio. *Diálogos imaginarios*. Havana: Editorial Arte y Literatura, 1979.

Mathieson, William Law. *British Slave Emancipation, 1838-1849*. London: Longmans, Green and Co., 1932; reprint ed., New York: Octagon Books, 1967.

Memorias de la Real Sociedad Económica de Amigos del País de La Habana. 6th series. vol. 1. Havana: Imp. de A. Lagriffoul, 1877.

———. 9th series. vol. 2. Havana: Imp. 'La Antilla' de Cacho-Negrete, 1881.

Mintz, Sidney W. *Caribbean Transformations*. Chicago: Aldine Publishing Co., 1974.

———. "A Note on the Definition of Peasantries." *Journal of Peasant Studies* 1 (October 1973): 91-106.

———. "Reflections on Caribbean Peasantries." *Nieuwe West-Indische Gids/ New West Indian Guide* 57 (1983): 1-17.

———. *Worker in the Cane: A Puerto Rican Life History*. New Haven: Yale University Press, 1960.

Mintz, Sidney W., and Richard Price. *An Anthropological Approach to the Afro-American Past: A Caribbean Perspective*. Philadelphia: Institute for the Study of Human Issues, 1976.

Montalvo, José R. "El problema de la inmigración en Cuba." *Revista Cubana* 8 (December 1888): 524-38.

Moreno Fraginals, Manuel. "¿Abolición o desintegración? Algunas pregun-
tas en torno a un centenario." *Granma*, January 23, 1980.
————. "Azúcar, esclavos y revolución (1790-1868)." *Casa de las Américas*
9 (September-October 1968): 35-45.
————. "Desgarramiento azucarero e integración nacional." *Casa de las
Américas* 11 (September-October 1970): 6-22.
————. "El esclavo y la mecanización de los ingenios." *Bohemia*, June 13,
1969, pp. 98-99.
————. *La historia como arma y otros estudios sobre esclavos, ingenios, y
plantaciones*. Barcelona: Editorial Crítica, 1983.
————. *El ingenio. Complejo económico social cubano del azúcar*. 3 vols.
Havana: Editorial de Ciencias Sociales, 1978.
————. *The Sugarmill: The Socioeconomic Complex of Sugar in Cuba. 1760-
1860*. trans. Cedric Belfrage. New York: Monthly Review Press, 1976.
————. *El token azucarero cubano*. Havana: Museo Numismático de Cuba,
n.d.
————, ed. *África en América Latina*. Paris: UNESCO and Mexico: Siglo
Veintiuno Editores, 1977.
Moreno Fraginals, Manuel, Herbert S. Klein, and Stanley L. Engerman. "The
Level and Structure of Slave Prices on Cuban Plantations in the Mid-
Nineteenth Century: Some Comparative Perspectives." *American His-
torical Review* 88 (December 1983): 1201-18.
Moreno Fraginals, Manuel, Frank Moya Pons, and Stanley L. Engerman.
*Between Slavery and Free Labor: The Spanish-Speaking Caribbean in
the Nineteenth Century*. Baltimore: The Johns Hopkins University Press,
1985.
Mörner, Magnus. *Historia social latinoamericana (Nuevos enfoques)*. Ca-
racas: Universidad Católica Andrés Bello, 1979.
Mullen, Edward J., ed. *The Life and Poems of a Cuban Slave: Juan Francisco
Manzano, 1797-1854*. Hamden, Connecticut: Archon Books, 1981.
Murray, David R. *Odious Commerce: Britain, Spain and the Abolition of
the Cuban Slave Trade*. Cambridge: Cambridge University Press, 1980.
————. "Statistics of the Slave Trade to Cuba, 1790-1867." *Journal of Latin
American Studies* 3 (November 1971): 131-49.
Nadal, Jordi. *El fracaso de la revolución industrial en España, 1814-1913*.
Barcelona: Ariel, 1975.
Nieman, Donald G. *To Set the Law in Motion: The Freedmen's Bureau and
the Legal Rights of Blacks, 1865-1868*. Millwood, New York: KTO Press,
1979.
Nimes, Juan Bautista. *Ingenios centrales, conveniencia o inoportunidad de
su instalación*. Cienfuegos, 1880.
"Noticia de las fincas azucareras en producción que existían en toda la isla
de Cuba al comenzar el presupuesto de 1877-78. . . ." *Revista económica*,
June 7, 1878, pp. 7-24.
O'Kelly, James. *The Mambi-Land or, Adventures of a Herald Correspondent
in Cuba*. Philadelphia: J. B. Lippincott, 1874.

Olivares, José de. *Our Islands and Their People as Seen with Camera and Pencil*. 2 vols. New York: N. D. Thompson, 1899.

Ortiz, Fernando. "Los cabildos afro-cubanos." *Revista Bimestre Cubana* 16 (January-February 1921): 5-39.

———. *Los negros esclavos*. Havana: Revista Bimestre Cubana, 1916; reprint ed., Havana: Editorial de Ciencias Sociales, 1975.

Paquette, Robert Louis. "The Conspiracy of La Escalera: Colonial Society and Politics in Cuba in the Age of Revolution." Ph.D. thesis. The University of Rochester, 1982.

Pepper, Charles M. *To-Morrow in Cuba*. New York: Harper and Bros., 1899; reprint ed., New York: Young People's Missionary Movement of the United States and Canada, 1910.

Pérez, Louis A., Jr. *Cuba between Empires, 1878-1902*. Pittsburgh: University of Pittsburgh Press, 1983.

Pérez de la Riva y Pons, Francisco. *La habitación rural en Cuba*. Havana: Editorial Lex, 1952.

———. *El negro y la tierra, el conuco y el palenque*. Havana: n.p., n.d.

Pérez de la Riva, Juan. *El barracón y otros ensayos*. Havana: Editorial de Ciencias Sociales, 1975.

———. "La contradicción fundamental de la sociedad colonial cubana: trabajo esclavo contra trabajo libre." *Economía y desarrollo* 2 (April-June 1970): 167-78.

———. "Duvergier de Hauranne: Un joven francés visita el ingenio Las Cañas en 1865." *Revista de la Biblioteca Nacional José Martí* 56 (October-December 1965): 85-114.

———. *Para la historia de las gentes sin historia*. Barcelona: Ariel, 1976.

Pérez de la Riva, Juan, and Pedro Deschamps Chapeaux. *Contribución a la historia de la gente sin historia*. Havana: Editorial de Ciencias Sociales, 1974.

Pezuela, Jacobo de la. *Diccionario geográfico, estadístico, histórico de la Isla de Cuba*. Madrid: Mellado, 1863.

Pichardo, Hortensia, ed. *Documentos para la historia de Cuba*. 2 vols. Havana: Editorial de Ciencias Sociales, 1977, 1976.

Polavieja, Camilo. *Relación documentada de mi política en Cuba*. Madrid: Imprenta de Emilio Minuesa, 1898.

Pollitt, Brian H. "Agrarian Reform and the 'Agricultural Proletariat' in Cuba, 1958-66: Some Notes." University of Glasgow, Institute of Latin American Studies, Occasional Paper No. 27, 1979.

———. "Agrarian Reform and the 'Agricultural Proletariat' in Cuba, 1958-66. Further Notes and Some Second Thoughts." University of Glasgow, Institute of Latin American Studies, Occasional Paper No. 30, 1980.

Porter, Robert P. *Appendix to the Report on the Commercial and Industrial Condition of the Island of Cuba*. Washington, D.C.: Government Printing Office, 1899.

———. *Industrial Cuba*. New York: G. P. Putnam's Sons, 1899.

Porter, Robert P. *Report on the Commercial and Industrial Condition of Cuba.* Washington, D.C.: Government Printing Office, 1898.

Poumier, María. *Apuntes sobre la vida cotidiana en Cuba en 1898.* Havana: Editorial de Ciencias Sociales, 1975.

————. "Bandolerismo y colonialismo. Manuel García: ¿Rey de los campos de Cuba?" Unpublished.

Provincia de Matanzas. Exma. Diputación Provincial. *Censo agrícola. Fincas azucareras. Año de 1881.* Matanzas: Imp. Aurora del Yumurí, 1883.

Ramos Mattei, Andrés A., ed. *Azúcar y esclavitud.* San Juan: Universidad de Puerto Rico, 1982.

"Las razas ante las leyes y las costumbres." *Estudios Afrocubanos* 1 (1937): 146-48.

Rebello, Carlos. *Estados relativos a la producción azucarera de la Isla de Cuba, formados competentemente y con autorización de la Intendencia de Ejército y Hacienda.* Havana: n.p., 1860.

Reynoso, Álvaro. *Ensayo sobre el cultivo de la caña de azúcar.* Havana: Imprenta del Tiempo, 1862; Reprint ed., Havana: Josefina Tarafa y Govín, 1954.

Ripley, C. Peter. *Slaves and Freedmen in Civil War Louisiana.* Baton Rouge: Louisiana State University Press, 1976.

Ripley, Eliza McHatton. *From Flag to Flag: A Woman's Adventures and Experiences in the South during the War, in Mexico, and in Cuba.* New York: D. Appleton and Co., 1889.

Roark, James L. *Masters Without Slaves: Southern Planters in the Civil War and Reconstruction.* New York: W. W. Norton and Co., 1977.

Rodney, Walter. *A History of the Guyanese Working People, 1881-1905.* Baltimore: The Johns Hopkins University Press, 1981.

Rosell Planas, Rebeca. *Factores económicos, políticos, y sociales de la Guerra Chiquita.* Havana: Academia de la Historia de Cuba, 1953.

Rosillo y Alquier, Fermín. *Noticia de dos ingenios y datos sobre la producción azucarera de la Isla de Cuba.* Havana: Impr. del Gobierno y Cap. General, 1873.

Rubin, Vera, and Arthur Tuden, eds. *Comparative Perspectives on Slavery in New World Plantation Societies.* New York: New York Academy of Sciences, 1977.

Ruíz, Ramón Eduardo. *Cuba: The Making of a Revolution.* New York: W. W. Norton and Co., 1970.

Sagra, Ramón de la. *Cuba: 1860. Selección de artículos sobre agricultura cubana.* Havana: Comisión Nacional de la UNESCO, 1963.

————. *Historia física, económico-política, intelectual y moral de la Isla de Cuba.* Paris: L. Hachette y ca., 1861.

Schwartz, Stuart B. "Indian Labor and New World Plantations: European Demands and Indian Responses in Northeastern Brazil." *American Historical Review* 83 (February 1978): 43-79.

Scott, Rebecca J. "The Battle over the Child: Child Apprenticeship and the

Freedmen's Bureau in North Carolina." *Prologue: The Journal of the National Archives* 10 (Summer 1978): 100-13.

Sitterson, J. Carlyle. *Sugar Country: The Cane Sugar Industry in the South, 1753-1950.* Lexington: University of Kentucky Press, 1953.

———. "The Transition from Slave to Free Economy on the William J. Minor Plantations." *Agricultural History* 17 (October 1943): 216-24.

Situación política del Departamento Oriental de la Isla de Cuba, desde el 9 de junio de 1878 al 22 de junio de 1879 siendo Comandante General el Excmo. Sr. Mariscal de Campo Don Luis Dabán y Ramírez de Arellano. Santiago de Cuba: Sección Tipográfica del Estado Mayor, 1881.

Sociedad Abolicionista Española, Madrid. *El cepo y el grillete: La esclavitud en Cuba.* Madrid: Sociedad Abolicionista, 1881.

———. *Exposición que al Exmo. Sr. Ministro de Ultramar dirige la Junta Directiva en 1° de Mayo de 1884.* Madrid, 1884.

———. *La violación de las leyes en Cuba. Exposición . . . a las Cortes.* Madrid: A. J. Alaria, 1882.

Spain. Cortes, 1869-1871. *Diario de sesiones de las Cortes Constituyentes.* Madrid: Impr. Nacional, 1870.

Spain. Cortes, 1879-1880. *Diario de las sesiones de las Cortes.* Madrid: Impr. Nacional, 1879, 1880.

Spain. Cortes, 1879-1880. *Discursos de la ley de abolición de la esclavitud en la Isla de Cuba.* Madrid: 1879, 1880.

Spain. Instituto Geográfico y Estadístico. *Censo de la población de España, segun el empadronamiento hecho en 31 de diciembre de 1877.* 2 vols. Madrid: Impr. de la Dirección General del Instituto Geográfico y Estadístico, 1883, 1884.

———. *Censo de la población de España segun el empadronamiento hecho en 31 de diciembre de 1887.* 2 vols. Madrid: Impr. de la Dirección General del Instituto Geográfico y Estadístico, 1891, 1892.

Spain. Ministerio de Ultramar. *Spanish rule in Cuba. Laws governing the Island. Review published by the Colonial Office in Madrid, with data and statistics compiled from official records. (Authorized translation, with additional notes).* New York, 1896.

———. *Cuba desde 1850 a 1873.* Carlos de Sedano y Cruzat, ed. Madrid: Impr. Nacional, 1873.

Starobin, Robert S. *Industrial Slavery in the Old South.* New York: Oxford University Press, 1970.

Steele, James W. *Cuban Sketches.* New York: G. P. Putnam's Sons, 1881.

Stein, Stanley J. *Vassouras. A Brazilian Coffee County, 1850-1900.* Cambridge: Harvard University Press, 1957; reprint ed., New York: Atheneum, 1974.

Steward, Julian H., et al. *The People of Puerto Rico.* Urbana: University of Illinois Press, 1956.

Suárez y Romero, Anselmo. *Colección de artículos.* Havana: Est. Tip. "La Antilla," 1859.

Suzarte, José Quintín. *Estudios sobre la cuestión económica de la Isla de Cuba*. Havana: Miguel de Villa, 1881.

Tannenbaum, Frank. *Slave and Citizen: The Negro in the Americas*. New York: Random House, Vintage Books, 1946.

Thomas, Hugh. *Cuba: The Pursuit of Freedom*. New York: Harper and Row, 1971.

Toplin, Robert Brent. *The Abolition of Slavery in Brazil*. New York: Atheneum, 1975.

————. "The Specter of Crisis: Slaveholder Reactions to Abolitionism in the United States and Brazil." *Civil War History* 18 (June 1972): 129-38.

Townshend, Frederick Trench. *Wild Life in Florida, with a Visit to Cuba*. London: Hurst and Blackett, 1875.

Trelles, Carlos M. *Biblioteca histórica cubana*. 3 vols. Vol. 1: Matanzas: Imprenta de Juan F. Oliver, 1922; Vol. 2: Matanzas: Imprenta de Andrés Estrada, 1924; Vol. 3: Havana: Dorrbecker, 1926.

U.S. Congress. House. *Labor in America, Asia, Africa, Australasia, and Polynesia*. 48th Congress, 2nd Session, 1884-1885. *House Executive Documents* no. 54. Vol. 26.

————. *Reports from the Consuls of the United States April-December, 1886*. 49th Congress, 2nd Session, 1886-1887. *House Miscellaneous Documents*, vol. 4.

U.S. Department of State. *Correspondence between the Department of State and the United States Minister at Madrid, and the Consular Representatives of the United States in the Island of Cuba. . . .* Washington, D.C.: Government Printing Office, 1870.

U.S. War Department. *Report on the Census of Cuba, 1899*. Washington, D.C.: Government Printing Office, 1900.

U.S. War Department. Division of Customs and Insular Affairs. *Translation of the Penal Code in Force in Cuba and Porto Rico*. Washington, D.C.: Government Printing Office, 1900.

Urrutia y Blanco, Carlos de. *Los criminales de Cuba y D. José Trujillo*. Barcelona: Fidel Giró, 1882.

Varona, Enrique José. "El Bandolerismo." *Revista Cubana* 7 (June 1888): 481-501.

Viotti da Costa, Emília. *Da senzala à colônia*. São Paulo: Difusão Européia do Livro, 1966.

Villanova, Manuel. *Estadística de la abolición de la esclavitud*. Havana: 1885.

Ward, J. R. "The Profitability of Sugar Planting in the British West Indies, 1650-1834." *Economic History Review* 2nd Series, 31 (May 1978): 197-213.

Zayas, F. de. "Economía rural." *Revista de Agricultura del Círculo de Hacendados de la Isla de Cuba* 1 (October 31, 1879): 249-53.

————. "Estudios de agricultura. El trabajador, el jornal." (Parts II, III, IV) *Revista de Agricultura del Círculo de Hacendados de la Isla de Cuba* 1 (April 30, 1879): 83-87; (May 31, 1879): 111-15; (June 30, 1879): 135-39.

Index

abolition. *See* emancipation

abolitionism: in Brazil, 284; in Cuba, 136-37, 191, 284; in Spain, 63-64, 111, 122, 284

abolitionists, charges against juntas, 133, 149, 158; denunciations of 1880 law, 174; pressures from, 176, 194; relations with slaves and *patrocinados*, 75n, 184

accommodation, by slaves and *patrocinados*, 169-71

Acosta, Cecilio, 203

administrators: colonial, 7; of estates, 54, 55, 178, 179. *See also* sugar plantations

African languages, 66

Afro-Cuban society, transformation of after emancipation, 264-78

age, disputes concerning, 144. *See also* Moret Law

agricultural census of 1877, 90

Aimes, Hubert, 76

Álava, *ingenio*, 98

Alfonso XII (district), cane farms in, 210

Angelita, *ingenio*, work force on, 69, 103-107

Antolines, Catalina, 79

Arenciba, Gabriela, 167

Argudín, Clementina, 153

Argudín, José Suárez. *See* Suárez Argudín, José

Argudín, Justo, 245

Ariosa, Agustín, 185, 187

Armas, Francisco de, on free labor, 37

Atkins, Edwin, 207, 210, 232; and insurgents, 289

Aufhauser, R. Keith, 27

autonomy: of former slaves and *patrocinados*, 167, 193, 194, 237, 247, 253; of *libertos*, 50-54; of slaves, xii, xiv, 15-19, 77; of workers, 233, 293

ayudantes (assistants), in 1868-1878 insurgency, 48, 59

Azcárate, Nicolás, 267

Badia, José, 286

barracón (slave barracks), 17, 18, 19, 19n

Barrera, José, 103

batey (mill yard), 32, 289

Beal, P. M., 231, 243

Beltrán, José, 182

Bernardino, *patrocinado*, 153

Betancourt, Joaquín, 55

bohío (palm hut), 17, 18, 245

Brazil: abolitionism in, 284; after emancipation, 241; slavery in, 26, 92; sugar in, 208, 284, 285

British West Indies, apprenticeship in, 180, 181. *See also* Jamaica

Brocal, Antonio, 159

caballería (unit of measurement equal to 33.3 acres), 22

cabildos de nación (associations of slave and free persons of African origin), 9, 66, 163, 164; *cabildo* Arriero, 266, 268; *cabildo* Congo, 266; after slavery, 265-68

Calvo and Co., 154

Calvo, Manuel, 67n, 224

Cambaca, Lucas, xi

campesinos (country people): and cane farming, 210; and 1868-1878 insurgency, 45, 46

Canal de Vento, 71

Canary Islands, immigrants from, 215-16

Candelaria, *ingenio*, 32

Candelaria, *potrero*, 53

cane fires, 62, 118, 290, 291

Caracas, *ingenio*, 40n

319

195; use of, by workers, 235, 236
Creole elite, 7
Criolla, Caridad, 156
Criolla, Pánfilo, 154
crops cultivated, by slaves and former slaves, 16, 17, 255-64 passim. *See also conucos*
cuadrilla de Pomares, 203
cuadrillas (work gangs): Chinese laborers in, 99, 101, 120; former slaves in, 229; use of, 203-204
Cuba, geography, 1878 provincial divisions, 4, 21, 21n
Cuban Junta (New York), 62
Cuban Revolutionary Party, 287
Cuevas, Francisco, 252

Dabán, Luis, 115
debt: of Chinese workers, 30; of former slaves, 234; of *patrocinados*, 188; of planters, 35, 35n. *See also* credit
Delicias, *ingenio*, 97n, 101
Demajagua, *ingenio*, 45
Democratic party, 137
depression of 1884, 195
depósitos (depots): of Chinese laborers, 100; of runaway slaves, 124
Desage, Jorge, 103
Deschamps Chapeaux, Pedro, 252n
Desengaño, *ingenio*, 34n
Destino, *ingenio*, 95
Díaz Torriente, Francisco, 101, 102
Dionisio, a *liberto*, 54
discrimination, racial, 8-9, 241, 272, 274
distribution of land. *See* land distribution
domestic service, slaves in, 54, 88
Domínguez, Juana, 163
"Don" (title), use of, 209, 274
dotación (permanent work force), 28, 90n, 110, 112, 203

education, integration of, 272-74, 272n, 275, 278; *See also* children, education of
El Banco, *ingenio*, 103
El Demócrata, 164
El País, 276
El Productor, 230
El Progreso, 273

Eleuterio, a Chinese worker, 151
emancipados (Africans nominally freed from captured slave ships), 223; and the Moret Law, 70, 71
emancipation: character of, xii, xiv, 40, 127, 163, 167-69, 279-82; comparison of Cuba with that elsewhere, 77, 283-85; dynamics of, 6, 168, 189, 193-94; and politics, 39-41, 63-66, 136-37, 283; and regional patterns, 190-92. *See also* Moret Law; *patronato*; slavery; Spain, government of
employers, divisions among, 189. *See also* planters
España, *ingenio*, 98, 173; Chinese workers on, 33
estancias (small farms devoted to food crops), population on, 8, 11
Estrada Palma, Tomás, 114
ethnicity, conflicts over, 59-60, 66
exports of sugar, 84, 207

family strategies, of former slaves, 242-44. *See also* kinship
Felipa, a *liberta*, 53
Fernández de Castro, delegate to Parliament, 124
Fernández, Juan Bautista, 32
Fernandina, *ingenio*, 55
Fernando, *patrocinado*, 154
flight: of *libertos*, 51, 53, 54; of *patrocinados*, 189. *See also cimarrones*
Flor de Cuba, *ingenio*, 33
Florentino, a *liberto*, 60-61
food, issued to workers, 229-30
former slaves, 227-54, 255-93 passim. *See also patrocinados*
Foster-Cánovas treaty, 207, 285
Fox-Genovese, Elizabeth, 109n
free labor, ideology of, 37, 39, 214, 284. *See also* labor
free persons of color: assistance to *patrocinados*, 163, 164, 164n; distribution of, 8; position of, 9
Freedmen's Bureau, 77, 77n, 228, 285
French West Indies, cane farms in, 208

Galicia, immigrants from, 217
Gamboa, Máximo, 222
García, Calixto, 116

García, Manuel, wife of, 223
Genovese, Eugene D., 5n, 28n, 109n, 120n
Gervasia, a slave, 106
godparents. *See compadrazgo*
Gómez, Juan Gualberto, 269, 271
Gómez, Máximo, 114, 287, 288
González, H., 149
Goytisolo, Agustín, 93
gradualism: aims of, 40, 127; character of, xii, xiv, 279-82. *See also* emancipation
Grant, Ulysses S., 47
Great Britain, 217; policy on abolition, 283-84
Guabairo, *colonia*, 243
Guáimaro, Assembly of, 47
Guerra Chiquita, 116-17
Guerra, Ramiro: on Ten Years' War, 41n, 114; on cane farming, 211
guerrilla (irregular Spanish forces), 113
Guiana, immigrants to, 217

Hacienda, intendancy of (Treasury), and vagrancy, 220
Haiti, slave marketing in, 149
Hart, Keith, 28n
Havana (city): population of, 250; and vagrancy, 221, 221n
Havana (province): pattern of emancipation in, 191-92; after slavery, 263
hierarchy, elite concepts of, 237, 237n
Hirschman, Albert O., 27
Hoernel, Robert, 250n
Hormiguero, *ingenio*, 240
hours of work. *See* work rhythms
Hughes, L. F., 232, 290

Ibáñez, Francisco Feliciano, 211; and central mills, 208; and Juntas Protectoras de Libertos, 77-78; lobbying efforts of, 187; and military settlements, 215; and the Moret Law, 73
immigrant labor, in Santa Clara, 260. *See also* immigration
immigration: during and after emancipation, 213-18, 213n, 217; in the 1870s, 101; of families, 216; of fieldworkers, 216
"indemnification of services," under 1880 law, 129, 149, 152, 152n. *See*

also self-purchase
ingenio (complex of fields and sugar mill). *See* sugar plantations
insurgency, 1868-1878, 45-62. *See also* Ten Years' War; insurgents, 1868-1878
insurgency, 1895-1898, 287-93; participation of Afro-Cubans in, 287-89
insurgents, 1868-1878, 45-62 passim; aims of, 46; composition of army, 56-59; policy on *libertos*, 49-52; policy on slavery, 46, 47; weakness of, 113-14
integration, struggle over, 272-78, 274n. *See also* civil rights
interracial marriage, policy concerning, 8, 9, 13, 38

Jamaica, 149, 283; after emancipation, 253
Jiménez, Juan Bautista, 286
Jordan, Thomas, 57, 59
Josefita, *ingenio*, 103
Juan, a *patrocinado*, 146
Junta de Agricultura, 235
Junta for the Repression of Vagrancy, 221-22
Junta of Agriculture, Industry and Commerce, 195, 213
Junta Provincial de Santiago de Cuba, 273
Junta Superior de Instrucción Pública, 273
Juntas de Patronato: behavior of, 133-35, 137-39; composition of, xii, 129; corruption in, 134-35; importance of, 184, 188; and plantation visits, 143, 176, 177, 178; records of, 228; rulings of, 177, 179
Juntas Protectoras de Libertos: character of, 77-79; establishment of, 64; membership and functioning of, 68, 79-81, 79n; on numbers of slaves freed, 71, 72; and slave registration, 122

kinship: after emancipation, 244; importance of, for *patrocinados*, 163; among slaves, 17-19. *See also* compadrazgo

mechanization, of sugar production, 20, 23. *See also* technology

merchants: Catalan, 64; local, 185-86, 210; relations with planters, 7

Mexico, workers from, 102

migration: to Africa, 251-52; to the cities, 250-51; after emancipation, 247-53; out of Matanzas, 263

Minerva: Revista Quincenal Dedicada a la Mujer de Color, 270

Mintz, Sidney: on Caribbean peasantries, 258n; on plantation discipline, 212; on slave marketing, 154-55

mobilization, political, after emancipation, xiv, 288

Mola, Clara, 54

Montalvo, José R., 276

Montalvo, María de la Merced, 76

monte (hills), 56

Monte, *finca*, 249

Montejo, Esteban, 225; on labor, 228, 228n, 233; on plantation stores, 234; on women's work, 243

Morales, Rafael, 51

Moré, Count of Casa: and immigration, 213, 215; lobbying of, 187; on Reglamento governing *patronato*, 173

moreno (black), 269, 270

Moreno Fraginals, Manuel: on abolition, 5n, 15; on Chinese laborers, 28, 28n, 33n; on contradictions within slavery, 26n, 109; on slave family, 17; on slave population, 92, 92n; on sugar, 20, 85, 85n

Moret Law, 63-83; aims of, 65-67; and children, 68, 69, 93; effects of, 68, 71-73, 121; and elderly, 69; evasion of, 93

Moret, Segismundo, 64, 65

Mörner, Magnus, 277n

mortgages. *See* credit; debt

movilizados (released soldiers), on estates, 104

"mutual accord" between *patrono* and *patrocinado*, 147, 169, 187, 188

mutual aid societies, Afro-Cuban, 268-71, 274

ñáñigos (secret societies), 267

Natividad, *ingenio*, 203; plantation store at, 234, 235; wages on, 238

Nicolás, a *patrocinado*, 163

nonregistration of slaves. *See* slaves, registration of

Nueva Teresa, *ingenio*: *colonos* on, 209; self-purchase on, 152-53, 154, 155; work and workers on, 180, 181, 234

O'Kelly: on insurgent communities, 50; on insurgent forces, 56, 57, 58-59; on slave marketing, 16

Ortiz, Ángel, 209

Ortiz, Fernando, on migration to Africa, 252n

Pact of Zanjón, 114, 116

palenques (societies of runaway slaves), 50, 252-53

Panama Canal, workers on, 281n

Pánfilo, a *patrocinado*, 163

pardo (mulatto), 269, 270

partidarios (sharecroppers), on estates, 104. *See also* sharecropping

patrocinados (apprentices): achievement of full freedom, 129, 132-33, 140, 144-45, 147-71; allies of, 161, 163, 163n, 164; appeals by, 131-35, 137, 146-47; behavior of, 141-71 passim, 227; challenges to masters, 157-71; defined, 128. *See also patronato*

patronato (apprenticeship): ambiguity of, 139, 186; character of, 139-41; concept of, 127; early proposals for, 111; establishment of, 123, 124; legacy of, 280, 281; provisions and enforcement, 127-40

patronos (masters), 172-97 passim; defined, 128; during 1868-1878 insurgency, 47; fears of, 165-66, 174; obligations of, 130, 158. *See also* masters

peasantry: development of, 244n, 250; in Santiago de Cuba, 258

Pedro, a *patrocinado*, 163

Pérez, Louis, Jr., 282n

Pérez de la Riva, Juan, 249n

Pérez Ferrer, Adolfo, 79

periodicals, Afro-Cuban, 269

Petra, a *patrocinada*, 147

pigs, raised by *patrocinados*, 144, 150, 159, 160

Pilar, a *liberta*, 49n